Ethics of Global Develo

Poverty, inequality, violence, environmental degradation, and tyranny continue to afflict the world. *Ethics of Global Development* offers moral reflection on the ends and means of local, national, and global efforts to overcome these five scourges. After emphasizing the role of ethics in development studies, policymaking, and practice, David A. Crocker analyzes and evaluates Amartya Sen's philosophy of development in relation to alternative ethical outlooks. He argues that Sen's recent turn to robust ideals of human agency and democracy improves on both Sen's earlier emphasis on "capabilities and functionings" and Martha Nussbaum's version of the capability orientation. This agency-focused capability approach is then extended and strengthened by applying it to the challenges of consumerism and hunger, the development responsibilities of affluent individuals and nations, and the dilemmas of globalization. Throughout the book the author argues for the importance of more inclusive and deliberative democratic institutions.

David A. Crocker is Senior Research Scholar at the Institute for Philosophy and Public Policy and the School of Public Policy at the University of Maryland. He is an officer of the Human Development and Capability Association, and was founder and former president of the International Development Ethics Association (IDEA).

Ethics of Global Development

Agency, Capability, and Deliberative Democracy

David A. Crocker

CAMBRIDGE UNIVERSITY PRESS
Cambridge, New York, Melbourne, Madrid, Cape Town, Singapore, São Paulo, Delhi

Cambridge University Press
The Edinburgh Building, Cambridge CB2 8RU, UK

Published in the United States of America by Cambridge University Press, New York

www.cambridge.org
Information on this title: www.cambridge.org/9780521117388

First published 2008
This digitally printed version 2009

A catalogue record for this publication is available from the British Library

Library of Congress Cataloguing in Publication data
Crocker, David A.
    Ethics of global development: agency, capability, and deliberative
democracy / David A. Crocker.
        p.   cm.
    Includes index.
    1. Economic development – Moral and ethical aspects.   2. Social planning –
Moral and ethical aspects. I. Title.
    HD75.C76 2008
    174–dc22

                                                            2008007230

ISBN 978-0-521-88519-5 hardback
ISBN 978-0-521-11738-8 paperback

To Cathy, Amanda, and Davey
Anna, Julia, and Luke

Philosophy recovers itself when it ceases to be a device for dealing with the problems of philosophers and becomes a method, cultivated by philosophers, for dealing with the problems of men.

John Dewey, "The Need for Recovery of Philosophy," 1917

In terms of the medieval distinction between "the patient" and "the agent," this freedom-centered understanding of economics and of the process of development is very much an agent-oriented view. With adequate social opportunities, individuals can effectively shape their own destiny and help each other. They need not be seen primarily as passive recipients of the benefits of cunning development programs. There is indeed a strong rationale for recognizing the positive role of free and sustainable agency – and even of constructive impatience.

Amartya Sen, *Development as Freedom*, 1999

There are, we have argued, rich lessons here [in the "developmental challenges faced in India"], which cannot be seized without taking interest in the ends and means of development in general and in the intrinsic value, constructive role and instrumental importance of public participation in particular. The basic approach involves an overarching interest in the role of human beings – on their own and in cooperation with each other – in running their own lives and in using and expanding their freedoms.

Jean Drèze and Amartya Sen,
India: Development and Participation, 2nd edn., 2002

Contents

Figures

Acknowledgments

This book is the culmination of thirty years of teaching and writing in development ethics. In the introductory chapter, I recount the stages in the emergence and evolution of development ethics and its relation to my own intellectual journey. In endnotes to each chapter I acknowledge those institutions and individuals who were important in each chapter's origin and improvement. The present occasion enables me to express my deep gratitude to those institutions, groups, and persons who have helped shape the entire project. None of them, of course, is responsible for whatever deficiencies remain.

I benefited enormously from my twenty-five years in the Department of Philosophy at Colorado State University. It was at Colorado State in the late 1970s that I joined colleagues James Boyd (philosophy), Gerald Ward (animal science), and, subsequently, Robert Zimdahl (weed science) in constructing arguably the first university course in international development ethics. Many CSU administrators and faculty, especially Maury Albertson, Ray Chamberlain, Loren Crabtree, David Freeman, Judson Harper, and James Meiman, supported the course and my work in development ethics. I am grateful to the many philosophy and other graduate students, especially Alison Bailey, Les Blomberg, Cynthia Botteron, Rex Welshon, William Slauson, and George Wallace, who contributed so much to my own thinking about ethics and development.

The course would not have been possible without the encouragement of my colleagues in the Department of Philosophy and its chair, Willard O. Eddy, who had a long-term concern with issues of global poverty. Especially important was a vision of applied ethics or practical philosophy that we forged together in departmental dialogue about what philosophy should be at a land grant university. Philosophy, we came to believe, should clarify and seek to resolve public problems, and should do so in a way that is informed by good science and relevant to the ethical assessment of institutional practice. I benefited much from Richard Kitchener's work in philosophy of technology, Dan Lyons and

Jann Benson's study of honor codes and ethical norms in US culture, Bernard Rollin's seminal work in veterinary ethics, and Holmes Rolston's contributions to environmental ethics. Although we often disagreed about the details, we were united by a common commitment that philosophy and public policy belonged together but would have to be changed to realize their potential.

I did much of my early work in development ethics and the capability approach when I was a Fulbright Scholar and Visiting Professor in the School of Philosophy at the University of Costa Rica in 1986–7 and 1992. The great kindness of my Costa Rican colleagues, our many discussions, and their examples as public intellectuals helped me learn about Costa Rica and how development ethics, even done by an outsider, might contribute to better policy and practice. I am particularly indebted to philosophers Victor Breines, Luis Camacho, Guillermo Coronado, Rafael Angel Herra, and E. Roy Ramirez. I also am grateful to sociologist Jorge Rovira Mas, "La Liga" soccer coach Minor Solís, and community organizer and writer Paula Palmer for teaching me much about Costa Rica.

Since 1993, I have had the great good fortune to teach in the University of Maryland's School of Public Policy and to be a senior research scholar in both the School and the Institute for Philosophy and Public Policy, a research unit within the School. The School and Institute have been a perfect venue for my work in development ethics, the capability approach, and democratic theory and practice. The School provides the interdisciplinary context required for my practice of development ethics. I am indebted to the insights and concerns of fifteen years of graduate students in my courses "Moral Dimensions of Public Policy," "Ethics, Development, and Foreign Aid," and "Democracy and Democratization: Theory and Practice." Among the many students who have pushed me to better arguments are Soumya Chattopadhyay, Laura Antkowiak Hussey, Daniel Levine, and Patty Joyce. My thinking on the capability approach and deliberative democracy has also benefited from the PhD proseminars, offered by the Committee on Politics, Philosophy, and Public Policy, that I co-taught at various times with Steve Elkin, Douglas Grob, Judith Lichtenberg, Christopher Morris, Joe Oppenheimer, and Michael Slote. I have especially benefited from the insights of four PhD students who wrote theses under my direction: Peter Balint, Stephen Schwenke, Andrew Selee, and Lori Keleher. Joshua Gillerman, one of my Public Leadership students, ably helped with the page proofs.

The Institute for Philosophy and Public Policy has been a marvelous place to join with other philosophers in the conceptual analysis and normative assessment of public policy. Every part of the book shows the salutary impact on my thinking of Institute colleagues and friends: editors Arthur Evenchik and Verna Gehring, the latter who read and made many improvements at various stages of the entire manuscript; and (past and present) researchers Robert Fullinwider, William Galston, Daniel Levine, Peter Levine, Xiaorong Li, Judith Lichtenberg, David Luban, Mark Sagoff, Jerome M. Segal, Robert Wachbroit, and David Wasserman.

During a fall 2005 visiting professorship in the Faculty of Philosophy at the University of Valencia in Spain, I wrote the first drafts of Chapters 7 and 10. I deeply appreciate the warmth with which my Spanish colleagues welcomed me and the opportunity they provided me to teach and write. I received extremely helpful comments on several chapters from professors Jesús Conill and Adela Cortina and students Daniela Gallegos, Martín Urquijo, and Marta Pedrajas Herrero.

I am deeply grateful to my good friends and colleagues in the International Development Ethics Association (IDEA) for their friendship and contributions to my work. IDEA events, since their beginning in 1984, were the venues in which many of my ideas in this volume were first tried out or refined. My special thanks to Ken Aman, Luis Camacho, Nigel Dower, Jay Drydyk, Des Gasper, Denis Goulet, Christine Koggel, Desmond McNeill, Laura Mues, Christian Parker, Peter Penz, Ramón Romero, Stephen Schwenke, Jerome Segal, and Asunción St. Clair. I also am indebted to the Human Development and Capability Association and its members for providing insightful assessments of my efforts to work out an agency-focused version of the capability approach to development ethics. Among many others, I wish to thank HDCA members Sabina Alkire, Séverine Denoulin, Mozaffar Qizilbash, Henry Richardson, Ingrid Robeyns, and Sakiko Fukuda-Parr for their criticisms and support of my work. I join members of both IDEA and HDCA in expressing sincere appreciation to Amartya Sen and Martha Nussbaum for not only founding the capability orientation but also for the continual encouragement of those of us who assess, extend, and apply it.

I gratefully acknowledge financial support I have received at various stages in the writing of this book: Fulbright (CIES), the Pew Charitable Trusts, the National Endowment for the Humanities, the National Science Foundation, the World Bank, the United States Agency for International Development, and the UNESCO Chair in Development (University of Valencia).

I also wish to thank the exceptionally kind, patient, and professional team at Cambridge University Press: Elizabeth Davey, Philip

G. A. Good, and Chris Harrison, Publishing Director of Social Sciences. Jo Bramwell has been a superb copy-editor.

Finally, I could not have completed this project without the help of many family members. Before an illness toward the end of her life (and death at age ninety-six in August 2007), my mother Geri Crocker corrected earlier versions of many chapters. My philosopher-lawyer brother, Larry, and my philosopher son, Davey, commented on much of the manuscript. Eddie, my dear wife of almost fifty years, helped in innumerable ways, not the least of which was extracting me from the study for a run around Lake Artemesia or a paddle on Lake Kahshe. With the hope of a better future for all the world's children, I dedicate this volume to our wonderful children, Cathy, Amanda, and Davey, and grandchildren, Anna, Julia, and Luke.

1 Introduction

Poverty, degrading inequality, violence, environmental crises, and tyranny continue to afflict the world. In spite of humankind's efforts, these five interrelated scourges are in many places more rather than less pronounced than they were a decade ago. Even in rich countries, poverty and inequality have increased. Efforts to understand and reduce these scourges have taken many forms. Moral reflection on the ends and means of "development," where "development" most generically means beneficial societal change, is one important effort. Such moral reflection, which includes the assessment of the present and the envisioning of better futures, increasingly is called "international development ethics" or the "ethics of global development."[1]

This volume is a work in global development ethics. It explains, justifies, applies, and extends ethical reflection on development goals, policies, projects, and institutions from the local to the global level.[2] The volume is a new statement of my views on development ethics, the capability approach, and deliberative democracy. Throughout, my aim is to move development ethics and the capability approach forward by working out and defending an *agency-focused* version of capability ethics and applying it to the issues of consumption, hunger, governance, and globalization. Although at least portions of seven chapters appeared as earlier versions, I have revised – often radically – each of them to take account of recent literature, reflect changes in my thinking over the last fifteen years, respond to criticism of earlier work, and yield what I hope is a new and harmonious totality.

Central to each of the book's four parts and eleven chapters is my sympathetic and, at times, critical engagement with Amartya Sen's "capability" approach to international development.[3] Since my first encounter with Sen's thought in the mid-1970s, I have increasingly come to recognize, as Hilary Putnam puts it, "the importance of what [Sen] calls the 'capabilities' approach to welfare economics to perhaps the greatest problem facing humanity in our time, the problem of the immense disparities between richer and poorer parts of the globe."[4]

Putnam continues: "At the heart of that [capabilities] approach is the realization that issues of development economics and issues of ethical theory simply cannot be kept apart." The following pages will show that Sen's linking of economics and ethics – and more generally of development studies and ethics – has inspired and stimulated me at each step in my own work in development ethics. My agency-oriented perspective is an effort to build on, make explicit, and strengthen Sen's recent turn to the ideals of public discussion and democratic participation as integral to freedom-enhancing development.

Much of my work since 1990 also has been a response to Martha Nussbaum's articles and books on development and development ethics.[5] Initially more sympathetic to Nussbaum's version of the capability approach than I am now, throughout the present book I will note the increasing differences between Sen's and Nussbaum's versions and develop a perspective that, while closer to Sen's, seeks to do justice to both versions. The most important of these differences, as I shall argue in Parts II and III, concerns Nussbaum's proposal of a list of the ingredients in human flourishing and Sen's qualified rejection of such a list in favor of a stronger role, than Nussbaum permits, for democratic decision. To mark differences between Sen's and Nussbaum's theories and for reasons that will become clear subsequently, I will follow development scholar Des Gasper and refer to Sen's theory as the *capability approach*, Nussbaum's perspective as the *capabilities approach*, and the family of approaches as the *capability orientation*.[6]

To introduce the book as a whole, in this introductory chapter I weave together my own intellectual journey, what I understand to be the evolving stages of development ethics, and the rationale for the volume's four Parts and ten remaining chapters. Other development ethicists, such as Sabina Alkire, Nigel Dower, Jay Drydyk, Des Gasper, Denis Goulet, Martha Nussbaum, Onora O'Neill, and Stephen Schwenke would tell different personal stories and provide somewhat different accounts of the evolution of development ethics. My personal trajectory is only one of the ways development ethics has evolved. For example, some development ethicists have not engaged Sen's capability approach or have done so in ways that differ from my own.

Toward development ethics

In the spring of 1978, two Colorado State University colleagues, an economist and an historian, paid me an office visit that was to redirect my professional life.[7] I had been teaching for twelve years in the Department of Philosophy at Colorado State University, my first position out of graduate school. The two colleagues came with good news and bad news.

The good news was that they had just received a two-year grant from the US Department of Education to establish a MA program in Comparative Rural Development, and that program was to include a graduate seminar in "Ethics and Rural Development." The course was to treat the moral and value issues that emerge in Colorado's impoverished rural and mountain towns as well as in CSU's overseas projects in international rural development.[8]

The bad news was that these colleagues wanted *me* to teach the course. Although flattered by the offer and attracted by the promise of a stipend, I responded incredulously. "You've got the wrong guy." I knew nothing, I said, of rural life and mountain towns (except ski towns like Steamboat Springs). And my experience in the developing world was limited to a year in the early 1960s working with impoverished youth in Cleveland's inner city and to a whirlwind family vacation in the early 1970s to Guaymas, Mexico. Specializing in philosophical ethics, metaethics, and Anglo-American and European social-political philosophy hardly qualified me to teach the course they proposed. My intellectual interests focused on the theories of justice of John Rawls and Robert Nozick, the social theory of the German philosopher Jürgen Habermas, and the Yugoslav Praxis Group's vision of democratic and market socialism.[9] What did such philosophical views have to do with rural development – whatever that was – at home or abroad or with what were then dubbed "Third World" issues? I had my hands full trying to contribute to a dialogue between Anglo-American and European social philosophy.

My two colleagues, however, persisted. "Don't worry (about your qualifications); you will team-teach the course with two other CSU professors – an expert on India, who for several years has lived in India and Iran, and a professor of animal science, who has USAID-funded projects throughout the developing world."[10] And, they continued, the need is great among both graduate students and their professors to address value and ethical questions. Faculty and students learn much about the science of development, such as the causes and effects of poverty, and they acquire the technical skills to install tube wells in Pakistan, set up credit unions in Nicaragua, or generate employment opportunities on Colorado's western slope. But once on the job, a host of questions assail them for which they are ill prepared and have no ready answer: Am I doing more harm than good? What counts as harm and what counts as good? How much truth should I tell my funding agency, especially when they don't want to hear it? Should I challenge my host country's gender inequality or take refuge in "moral relativism?" Is my "development" work contributing to a tyranny's legitimacy or to excessive US influence? How should we define development and how should we try to promote it? Who should answer these questions, what methods should they use, and what should they say?

Still with misgivings, I accepted. The questions *were* important, and I might learn something. I would like to think that I also was disturbed that the world was beset by problems of deprivation and misery that moral reflection might help resolve. During an internship as a youth and community worker in Cleveland's inner city in 1961–2, I had learned that local action coupled with governmental policy could make a difference – for good or ill – in people's lives.

When we three co-teachers met to plan the new course, chaos ensued. The professor of animal science didn't know what ethics had to do with (rural) development and improvement of cattle strains in Bulgaria. The scholar of Indian and Persian culture was worried about Northern and Western ethnocentrism. I couldn't figure out what Rawls's argument from the abstract and hypothetical standpoint of the "original position" had to do with practical ethics or with "development." And what, I asked myself, was "development" anyway? Writings in development economics or development policy scarcely mentioned ethics. The philosophers I admired never talked about development. Given the abstract, otherworldly way in which even applied ethics and sociopolitical philosophy was done in those days, this state of affairs was probably a good thing.

Only when the three of us discovered the work of development scholar and activist Denis Goulet and of sociologist Peter Berger did we begin to get some help on how we might proceed in our course. In different ways, both Goulet and Berger argued that ethics should be put on the development agenda – both for the sake of better development and for the sake of ethics.[11]

Since the early 1960s, Goulet – influenced by French economist Louis-Joseph Lebret and development economists such as Benjamin Higgins, Albert Hirschman, and Gunnar Myrdal – had argued that "development needs to be redefined, demystified, and thrust into the arena of moral debate."[12] Drawing on his training in continental philosophy, political science, and social planning as well as on his extensive grassroots experience in poor countries, Goulet – we discovered – was a pioneer in addressing "the ethical and value questions posed by development theory, planning, and practice."[13] One of the most important lessons we learned from Goulet, in such studies as *The Cruel Choice: A New Concept in the Theory of Development* (1971), is that so-called "development," because of its costs in human suffering and loss of meaning, can amount to "anti-development." Similarly in the book *Pyramids of Sacrifice* (1974), a book that some of our Colorado State "development" colleagues had read, Peter Berger argued that so-called "development" often sacrificed rather than benefited poor people and what was urgently needed was a marriage of political ethics and social change in the "Third World":

> This book deals with two topics that are intertwined throughout. One is Third World Development. The other is political ethics applied to social change. It seems to me that these two topics belong together. No humanly acceptable discussion of the anguishing problems of the world's poverty can avoid ethical considerations. And no political ethics worthy of the name can avoid the centrally important case of the Third World.[14]

With Goulet's and Berger's texts central to our planning and initial syllabus, we had valuable resources for getting ethics onto the agenda of development practitioners and policy analysts. But did philosophical ethics and sociopolitical philosophy have anything to contribute to "ethics and rural development" or – as we soon called it – "ethics and international development" or "development ethics"?

In the 1970s three currents of Anglo-American philosophy appeared promising for our work: John Rawls's theory of justice; Peter Singer's challenging argument that the affluent had a duty to aid famine victims, and the lifeboat ethics debate.

The moral problem of world hunger and the ethics of famine relief were among the first practical issues that philosophers tackled after John Rawls's pivotal 1971 study, *A Theory of Justice*,[15] convinced them that reflection on normative issues should be part of the philosopher's task. Although Rawls himself limited ethical analysis to abstract principles of distributive justice, applied philosophers addressed the ethical and conceptual aspects of a variety of practical problems and policies. In the same year that Rawls's volume appeared, Peter Singer first wrote about famine in East Bengal (now Bangladesh)[16] and, more generally, about "the obligations of the affluent to those in danger of starvation."[17] In his 1974 *New York Times Magazine* article, "Philosophers are Back on the Job,"[18] Singer championed the philosophical turn to applied ethics, employing the ethics of famine relief as a leading example.

Philosophers were back on the job because, as John Dewey had urged fifty years earlier in a statement that functions as one of this volume's epigraphs, "philosophy recovers itself when it ceases to be a device for dealing with the problems of philosophers and becomes a method, cultivated by philosophers, for dealing with the problems of men."[19] One of these human problems in the mid-1970s was whether or not affluent countries and their citizens were in any way morally obligated to send food to famine victims in other countries. Is such aid morally required, admirable but not obligatory, or impermissible? For instance, the editors of a widely used anthology asked, "What moral responsibility do affluent nations (or those people in them) have to the starving masses?"[20] Peter Singer argued that such aid was obligatory and rich people commit moral wrong in refusing or neglecting to aid the starving poor. For, he asserted, "suffering and death from lack of food, shelter, and medical care are bad" and "if it is in our power to prevent something bad from happening, without thereby sacrificing anything of comparable moral importance, we ought, morally, to do it."[21] Finally, claiming that life-saving and suffering-reducing actions are indeed in our power, Singer concluded that famine relief is a moral obligation or duty and not a mere matter of charity. Even though such a duty might be at odds with our moral judgments and complacent consumption practices, we do grievous wrong in not donating to famine relief.

Garrett Hardin, writing in 1974 in *Psychology Today* magazine, likewise argued against charitable aid.[22] While Singer argued that moral duty, rather than charity, should be the basis for aid, Hardin argued that rich nations and individuals (living in lifeboats) have a duty *not* to help the needy (swimming in the sea). Aid would only worsen the problems of hunger, because it would result in more mouths to feed, and would cause other countries to become dependent on handouts rather than solving their own food and population problems.

Throughout the 1970s (and on into the 1980s), often in response to Singer, on the one hand, and Hardin, on the other, many philosophers investigated whether there exists a positive moral obligation to aid distant and hungry people and, if so, what are its nature, justification, and limits.[23]

As we three CSU professors planned and then taught the nation's (and perhaps the world's) first philosophy course in "ethics and development," we took full advantage of the Hardin–Singer debate and the philosophical discussion it had provoked. Something, however, was missing in this literature. Only gradually did we come to recognize that it was important to recast and enlarge this initial moral problematic. Preoccupied as they were with the task of justifying aid to distant people, philosophers paid scant attention to institutional and practical issues. In particular they almost totally ignored what happened to famine relief donations or food aid once they arrived in a stricken country. Did it go to the rich instead of its intended starving recipients? Did food aid glut the national and local markets with the result that food prices fell and local farmers suffered? Was food aid a cause of anti-development in rural areas, perhaps blinding donors to structural injustice that caused the famine in the first place? Were foreign governmental aid agencies, such as USAID, or national programs of poverty alleviation more effective in reducing hunger than private donations to international NGOs? What role might different kinds of food aid have – in contrast to, say, different sorts of population control or agricultural development – in national efforts to reduce chronic deprivation and wrenching inequality? Do outside private and governmental aid sap a poor country's commitment and initiative to confront its problems of hunger and other deprivations?

It is true that Singer in his 1972 essay, and even more in later writings, made clear that what rich countries and individuals were obligated to do was to give that type of aid that was most likely to reduce starvation and death. Although in his initial essay Singer emphasized private donations to international NGOs such as the Bengal Relief Fund, he also stated that effective hunger-reducing action occurred "either through orthodox methods of famine relief or through population control or both."[24] In a 1977 "Postscript" to the initial article, which we used as a text in our CSU class, Singer conceded that if he were to rewrite the initial article, he would have emphasized – as means of reducing hunger – that international donors should require recipient governments to check population growth by such means as dispensing contraceptives and even performing sterilizations. In the same essay, Singer also mentions that a family's economic security might be a factor in reducing the number of children, and this consideration prompts him to reflect further on how he would have rewritten his initial essay:

One other matter that I should now put forward slightly differently is that my argument does, of course, apply to assistance with development, particularly agricultural development, as well as to direct famine relief. Indeed, I think the former is usually the better long-term investment. Although this was my view when I wrote the article, the fact that I started from a famine situation, where the need was for immediate food, has led some readers to suppose that the argument is only about giving food and not about other types of aid. This is quite mistaken, and my view is that the aid should be of whatever type is most effective.[25]

We three CSU professors did miss or at least failed to appreciate Singer's qualifications and his central point that rich nations and people had an obligation to help the global poor in the most effective way or ways possible. Even in my 1996 critique of Singer, I failed to acknowledge that, for Singer, what was most important was rich donor obligation, and that he was open to various ways in which individuals could fulfill that obligation.[26] Claiming no expertise in whether other types of aid are "better or worse than giving to Oxfam,"[27] Singer has more recently insisted, correctly I now believe, that critics are wrong in criticizing him for relying exclusively on private donations: "We should do our best to find out what will produce the best outcome, whether it is giving money, buying fair trade products, voting, joining an organization, or all of those things. Then we should do it."[28]

Singer was right that what was needed – and what philosophers and other ethicists could contribute – was an ethics of aid, and that private donations of money and food could play a role. But my two CSU colleagues and I gradually came to see that such an ethic would be only one part of an ethics of and for national and local development. Singer had framed the issue in an incomplete way and one with potentially negative consequences for international development. We began to see four ways in which we should build on but go beyond Singer.

First, except for a few remarks about how certain kinds of population control might contribute to the relief of hunger and other deprivations, Singer did not – and still does not – investigate the nature and relative effectiveness of actual policies, whether of Oxfam-type famine relief, population control, or development assistance. Practitioners and policy analysts have a variety of approaches to each of these policies, but there is little in Singer to suggest these controversies or to take a position on them. We three professors designed our course to enable our students to understand and assess such diverse ends and means of international development as economic growth, growth with equity, and basic needs.

Second, Singer's focus was almost entirely on rich countries and their citizens and very minimally on what poor nations – their governments and civil societies – were doing or failing to do to solve their own problems. We became increasingly convinced that the question of international aid and responsibilities depended to a large extent on how national development was conceived and what developing nations were already doing (or failing to do) to bring about good or better development. Each country and region has a history of efforts to define and implement good development, and we believed it was important to understand and evaluate these endeavors before we could advocate some form of international assistance. Important examples would be Sen's book on famines[29] and Jean Drèze and Sen's analysis and evaluation of national efforts to combat hunger,[30] volumes that appeared before at least some of Singer's writing on the ethics of combating hunger. Singer, of course, could say that such an investigation of national and local development efforts is permitted and even encouraged by investigating the most effective means to remedy deprivation. The fact that he, as a philosopher, did not investigate various national development efforts did not mean that nonphilosophers could not and should not do so. In contrast, we CSU professors and later development ethicists came to believe that ethicists – whether or not philosophers – should not stand aloof from institutional and policy analysis but should be part of interdisciplinary efforts to understand, assess, and improve national and local development.

Third, Singer's way of framing the ethics of food aid (and, more generally, the ethics of reducing deprivation in poor countries) emphasized that it was affluent countries and individuals who should be the agents in combating hunger and that poor governments and their citizens were but passive recipients. Singer, of course, could say that to the extent that national and local efforts in poor countries successfully relieved suffering, external agents should keep their hands off or find ways to help national agents become more effective. This response, however, converts the moral issue into a strategic one. In addition to the moral importance of the "best outcome" (with respect to preference satisfaction or relief of suffering), it is also crucial, we came to believe, to address the process by which the outcome is attained. Although in the late 1970s we did not have a clear grasp of the language of agency, with the help of thinkers like Denis Goulet and Paolo Freire we were aware that it was important that – where feasible – poor countries develop themselves rather than be the grateful or even deserving recipients of the actions of others. Although failing to recognize the complexity of Singer's argument, Andrew Kuper sees this weakness in Singer's approach: Singer has a "tendency to treat active individuals in developing countries almost wholly as recipients or moral patients. Poor people are neither powerless nor ignorant in respect of important problems and opportunities for action; they need to be addressed as agents, capable of independent action as well as cooperative assistance."[31]

Fourth, related to the last point, that what Goulet called "assistentialism" risked disrespecting and weakening the agency of the poor, we three CSU professors also worried that hunger, as terrible as it was, was not only bad in itself but was a symptom of deeper, more structural problems, such as maldistribution of wealth and power.[32] As important as it was to relieve immediate suffering, it was also crucial for development ethics to criticize current institutional arrangements and to offer better alternatives. Even worse, in fulfilling obligations to alleviate immediate and individual misery, international donors and national agencies might inadvertently and even intentionally maintain a remediable system responsible for great deprivation. This is not to say that no famine relief of individuals is justified, but it is to warn that the good that comes from palliative remedies must be supplemented and sometimes outweighed by the greater good that comes from systemic change.[33] In Chapter 8, I return to these issues and work out in detail an agency-based and systemic capability approach to world hunger and other deprivations.

In summary, taking seriously Singer's challenge that outsiders can and should help the global poor, in planning our course we sought to go beyond Singer and think through the policies and practices by which outsiders could help poor people relieve their own suffering, develop themselves, and improve their own institutions. There would be (and still is) much work to do before development would be part of the philosophical and ethical agenda the way that environment and animal welfare were beginning to be. We were, however, forging a vision about what our course and development ethics might be.[34] We were less concerned than Singer with foundational issues and more committed than Singer to an ethics that was interdisciplinary, institutionally and empirically informed, and policy-relevant.[35]

Still harboring doubts that we could bring development and (philosophical) ethics into fruitful interaction, we launched our new graduate course – jointly listed in the curricular offerings of the Department of Philosophy and of International Education – in the fall of 1978. We put ethics explicitly on the agenda of development policy and practice by inviting CSU professors who had worked with development projects to describe to the class moral dilemmas they had confronted. After doing so, the guest lecturers then challenged the students (and faculty) to try to resolve the quandary, told what in fact they (the visiting professors) actually did, and led a discussion of whether they had done the right thing. An engineering professor recounted his failed efforts to get USAID to change its policy of sending more food aid than a nation could absorb and the related failure of the nation itself to keep food prices sufficiently high to enable local farmers to make a profit. An agricultural economics professor told of his worries, when working on credit unions in Nicaragua in the 1970s, that he was lending credibility to the Somoza dictatorship. Should he continue building credit unions that Nicaragua would need in any regime or should he resign and support the Sandinistas? I would later describe these and other practitioner moral dilemmas in articles in *Revista de Filosofía de la Universidad de Costa Rica* and *World Development* in 1987 and 1991, respectively.[36]

In the same articles, I tried to capture our commitments – strengthened by the course itself – to put ethics on the development agenda. What was called for, I argued, was something more than foundational defenses of doing the right thing or the generation of a professional code of ethics that abstracted from the ambiguities that surround development work. If the urgent problems of development were to be confronted in a morally responsible way, then development agents would have to do more than offer abstract justifications of a duty to aid distant people, restrict their moral judgments to a local watering hole, or enshrine moral norms in an inflexible professional code. Many people working in the development trenches were becoming aware that ethical reflection that was "explicit, contextually sensitive, public, and engaged"[37] might help identify morally relevant features of a practical situation and guide tough choices.

Deepening and broadening development ethics: Costa Rica and the International Development Ethics Association

Despite the CSU course's success during its initial years, it became increasingly clear that something was missing from the class and my work in this field. To make a contribution to this new activity, which we began to call "development ethics," I gradually realized that I needed to live and work in a "developing country." I would have to become less an "outsider" to what was increasingly called "the South," given the pejorative connotations of "Third World." Even as I explored the resources for engaging in development ethics of the European and North American philosophical traditions, I wanted to immerse myself in a culture with a different economic and political history than that of the USA and with intellectual and moral traditions that differed from the ones in which I had worked. To avoid narrowness and bias, I had to see the world with different lenses. Where and how should I do this?

Unexpectedly and fortunately, doors soon opened for a sabbatical year in a developing country perfectly suited to my aims. Attending a 1984 conference in Costa Rica, I discovered at the University of Costa Rica an exciting group of philosophers interested in applied philosophy and development. I had organized an interdisciplinary workshop on "Ethics and Development" within the conference and had presented a paper arguing for a cross-cultural development ethics. The Costa Rican philosophers urged me to return as a visiting professor and help them organize an international conference devoted to development ethics.

Supported by a Fulbright Research Award to study "Ethical Issues in Costa Rican Development," I returned to Costa Rica for twelve months in 1986–7. A recipient of $200 million a year in US aid, Costa Rica was becoming a showcase for Reagan-style democratic capitalism and, unbeknownst to most, a launching pad for US-backed Contras in their effort to undermine the Sandinista Revolution. Costa Rica's long tradition of democratic institutions and pacifism was being strained by the build-up of its Rural and Civil Guards. The press and universities were full of debates about the Costa Rican "path," its differences from the rest of turbulent Central America, and the need to end conflicts in Nicaragua, Honduras, Guatemala, and El Salvador.

During that year in Costa Rica, I learned much about the country and slowly evolved a more nuanced conception of the nature, tasks, methods, and limits of development ethics. From my philosophy and social science colleagues at the University of Costa Rica, I became apprized of Costa Rican and Latin American philosophical and ethical reflection on development. I learned, for example, that in 1974 the Third National Conference of Philosophy in Costa Rica had addressed the theme of "Philosophy and Development." The late Roberto Murillo presented a paper in which he argued for the necessity of "a developed notion of development."[38] Although no one used the concept of "development ethics," some participants took up ethical issues and others discussed the role of philosophy in relation to development. For example, Claudio Gutiérrez treated the need for – but also the risks of – philosophy in Costa Rican development.[39]

In 1980, the Argentine philosopher Mario Bunge published *Ciencia y desarrollo* (Science and Development).[40] In this important book Bunge criticizes one-sided concepts of development and proposes "authentic and sustained development," which he calls "the integral conception of development."[41] In Bunge's normative vision, integral development ought to be simultaneously biological, economic, political, and cultural.

Bunge's work influenced two of my new Costa Rican colleagues: E. Roy Ramírez and Luis Camacho. According to Ramírez, it is important to forge a new concept of development "in order not to confuse it with modernization" and "because it is preferable to decide things for ourselves than to have others decide them for us."[42] For Ramírez, "the great ethical impact" of Bunge's approach is its

constant vigilance not to let forms of oppression pass for liberty, commercial pseudo-culture and the consumption of fantasies for superior culture, diverse manifestations of plunder for progress. Superstition should not pass for rationality, economic inequalities for justice or fear for peace.[43]

Ramírez also offers an explicitly ethical critique of and alternative to what he called "technological determinism," the belief that technology – whether imported or produced nationally – is both necessary and sufficient for development:

In the same way that development cannot be restricted to economic growth, so development cannot be reduced merely to a technological matter. It involves a culture's identity, self-confidence, important degrees of independence, the search for its own answers, the satisfaction of basic needs, an openness to the future, social and mental changes that transform members of a society capable of sustaining, at its own pace and by its own means, more human forms of life.[44]

Camacho also contributed to an ethics of science and technology (especially) in developing countries, evaluated different notions of crisis and development, and proposed relations between advanced countries and Third World countries, including the treatment of the problem of individual development within socioeconomic development."[45] Both Ramírez, with emphasis on individual and national self-determination and his reference to "mental" as well as social changes," and Camacho, when he identifies the problem of "individual development" in the context of socioeconomic development, were intimating that development ethics should take up the issues of moral education and citizen agency and responsibilities.

From my social science as well as philosophy colleagues and the vigorous debate in the press and frequent public conferences, I deepened my understanding of how an ethics of and for development must be closely linked – without either fusion or confusion – to the science, policy, and practice of development.[46] In order to understand different approaches to development and their interweaving of empirical and normative as well as theoretical and practical components, in my 1984 conference paper I had proposed the notion of a "development theory-practice." I now was able to illustrate my schematic framework with many Latin American examples of development "theory-practices." Initially published in Costa Rica as "La naturaleza y la práctica de una ética del desarrollo" (The Nature and Practice of Development Ethics), this essay – considerably expanded and updated – is Chapter 3 of the present volume.

From my academic colleagues as well as my new friends in the various Costa Rican development ministries, and the US and Canadian embassies, field workers with the Inter-American Foundation, and members of the Asociación Talamanqueña para Ecoturismo y Conservación, I learned about the dilemmas and challenges of putting development ideals into practice. From my soccer friends connected to the youth and professional teams of La Liga Deportiva Alajuelense, I experienced at first hand the norms that functioned in – some parts of – everyday Costa Rican life.[47]

During this Fulbright year in Costa Rica, the "Development Ethics Working Group," which we had formed after the 1984 conference, transformed itself into the International Development Ethics Association (IDEA). Although the acronym represents the English word order, we always pronounced "IDEA," which has the same meaning in English and in Spanish, as a word in Spanish (ee-*day*-ah). In June 1987, my Costa Rican colleagues and I mounted IDEA's First International Conference on Ethics and Development. As my conference contribution, I presented some tentative conclusions about Costa Rican development in a paper entitled "Four Models of Costa Rican Development: Analysis and Ethical Evaluation."[48] Finding strengths but also weaknesses in traditional Costa Rican social democracy, the already ascendant free-market liberalism, and attempts to renovate social democracy, I argued for a fourth model that I called "just, participatory, ecodevelopment." This explicitly normative vision, to be discussed in more detail in Chapter 3, was a moral pluralism that argued for the importance of basic human needs, democratic self-determination and participation, respect for the natural world, and equal opportunity for self-development. The emphasis on "democratic self-determination" both emerged from dialogue with Ramírez and Camacho and my work on the Yugoslav Praxis philosophers and foreshadowed my current work on Sen's concept of agency, Adela Cortina's concept of self-mastery (*señorío*), and deliberative democracy.

Unlike many of their fellow Central Americans in the late 1980s, most Costa Ricans were by and large friendly to US visitors. Yet I repeatedly was asked (and asked myself) what business does someone – especially with a name similar to a frontiersman who died at the Alamo – from the United States – especially with its unsavory history of intervening in Latin American affairs – have in evaluating and proposing alternatives to Costa Rica's development model? My answers to that question are reflected in my article "Insiders and Outsiders in International Development Ethics," first published in Spanish in 1990 and in English in 1991. I argue that insiders to a culture – who may or may not be citizens or native born – have obvious advantages in understanding and evaluating their own culture and proposing better development paths. Yet their insider status can also blind them to certain realities and prevent them from facing up to the need for change and advocating a better development vision. In contrast, development ethicists who are cultural outsiders may contribute something to an "alien" society's development dialogue and beneficial change.

These outsider ethicists do have obvious disadvantages, such as ignorance, and temptations, such as arrogance and obsequiousness, compared to their insider counterparts. In the last analysis, it is up to the social insiders to decide on their development path. Yet, I argue, outsiders – or, better, a certain outsider-insider hybrid – may play a valuable role in a group's development. This "insider-outsider mix" may clarify the society's options, reflect the culture back to itself, synthesize disparate ideas or interject novel ones, and say what should be said but what insiders cannot say. I conclude by calling for a global ethic to be progressively fashioned by insider-outsider hybrids from a variety of groups.[49]

My 1986–7 year in Costa Rica was also important for the movement and institutionalization of development ethics as well as for my own work. The first IDEA conference set the model for subsequent IDEA events: development practitioners and activists as well as academics from both North and South participated, and the participants together visited and scrutinized actual development projects or institutions. Moreover, the conference enabled a new group of development ethicists to meet and learn from the pioneer of development ethics, Denis Goulet, whose work had been pivotal ten years earlier in planning the Colorado State development ethics course. And it enabled Goulet, noted for his independent ways, to have an ongoing role in the institutionalization of a "discipline" or "field" that he had helped so much to identify and initiate.

From this modest beginning in Costa Rica, IDEA was to grow steadily in numbers and global reach throughout the late 1980s and early 1990s before leveling off in the mid-1990s. Although its core membership remained in the Americas, IDEA held or co-sponsored conferences and workshops in Mexico (1989), the US (1991), Honduras (1992), Chile (1995), Scotland (1996), India (1997), Honduras (2002), Scotland (2004), and Uganda (2006). Just as my involvement with Costa Rica deepened my work in development ethics and gave me insight into perspectives from the South, so IDEA enabled me to broaden the scope of my work to other societies and dialogue partners.

The current volume's Part I is entitled "Development ethics." The first essay, entitled "Agreements, Controversies, and Challenges," seeks to capture and contribute to the current state of play of development ethics. Many of the questions and answers are the same ones that exercised many of us in the 1980s and became central to IDEA-sponsored events. But there are new dimensions as well; one of them is the importance for development ethics of Amartya Sen and the capability approach.

Engaging the capability approach: ethical foundations

In order to understand and confront development's quandaries, it is not enough to put ethics on the development agenda or to immerse oneself in another culture and intellectual milieu. It is also important to weigh the strengths and weaknesses of various development approaches or "theory-practices," decide which is the most promising, and advance it in both thought and action. A crucial part of that evaluative exercise is what Des Gasper calls the second stage of development ethics. For Gasper, the first stage is what I have called "putting ethics on the development agenda" and what he calls presenting "ethical concerns about development experiences and policies."[50] Gasper's second stage is the examination "of major valuative concepts and theories used to guide, interpret or critique those experiences and actions."[51]

Committed to the philosophical pragmatist notion that human achievement is fallible and the implication that any theory is revisable, I was aware that my tentative proposal of "just, participatory, ecodevelopment" was deficient in several ways: it needed greater specificity and clarity; it lacked decision procedures when its four principles clashed; and it also failed to discuss implementation. What exactly were human needs, what groups should practice democratic self-determination, and what are its limits? What about those who want to use their freedom and reject the good life conceived as *praxis*?[52] In the next five years or so following my return from Costa Rica, I had what I now see as a gradual intellectual conversion. I came to see the importance of Amartya Sen's and Martha Nussbaum's ethically based perspectives – both joint and separate – on international development.

Amartya Sen, since the 1970s, and Martha Nussbaum, since the mid-1980s, have been fashioning a new and important normative approach (Sen) or ethic (Nussbaum) for international development.[53] Global hunger and other severe deprivations, they argue, indicate conceptual and ethical failures as well as scientific, technical, and political ones. Sen, the Indian-born economist, social choice theorist, philosopher, and Nobel laureate, had reflected critically on the moral concepts presupposed in development economics, policymaking, and social action. He also evolved an original normative outlook, articulated in 1999 for the general public in *Development as Freedom*, for the improvement of the theory and practice of international development.[54] Sen's normative perspective owes much not only to Adam Smith and his concept of human freedom but also to the Aristotelian/Marxist tradition and its concept of human existence and well-being. Sen's reworking of this latter ethical tradition had been informed by dialogue with philosopher Martha Nussbaum.[55]

Nussbaum, a leading scholar of Greek thought, political philosopher, and public intellectual, coauthored with Sen an important paper[56] on national and global development ethics and with him edited and introduced a seminal anthology in development ethics, *The Quality of Life*.[57] Moreover, in a series of articles and in several books, Nussbaum compared Sen's ideas with those of Aristotle, advocated what she called "Aristotelian moral inquiry" and "Aristotelian social democracy" as relevant for international development, and set forth her own robust version of the capability orientation. Although, as we shall see, significant theoretical differences increasingly exist between the two, Sen and Nussbaum's collaboration as well as their individual work has contributed much to development ethics.

I first read Sen in the mid-1970s, but it was not until ten years later that I saw his relevance for development ethics. In an article written in 1989 and published in 1991,[58] I recognized Sen as "the most important practitioner of development ethics emerging from within economics in general and development economics in particular."[59] I argued that Sen had increasingly taken up many of the questions of development ethics, and I emphasized that he had judged development economics mistaken when it made economic growth the *end* of development. "At best," as I interpreted Sen, "economic growth is a means – and often not a very efficient means – for the goals of development."[60] Economic development, he had argued, was only instrumentally about economic growth; its ultimate concern is or should be "what people can or cannot do, e.g., whether they can live long, escape avoidable morbidity, be well nourished, be able to read and write and communicate, take part in literary and scientific pursuits, and so forth."[61] I cited approvingly Sen's remarks in which he explicitly linked his conception of development to that of Marx: "[development has to do] in Marx's words, with 'replacing the domination of circumstances and chance over individuals by the domination of individuals over chance and circumstances.'"[62] Sen's underscoring the ideal of human agency in Marx strongly resonated with the interpretation of Marx I had found so attractive in the Yugoslav Praxis Group. In concluding my discussion of Sen, I challenged "the emerging field of development ethics . . . to grasp and assess Sen's proposals."[63]

During the next half-dozen years I took up my own challenge and sought to clarify, compare, and evaluate both Sen's and Nussbaum's perspectives and especially their ethical component. Many in IDEA recognized the fact that since ethics was finally on the development agenda and philosophers were addressing development's normative dimensions, it was time to bring some leading options – those stressing basic needs or human rights or valuable capabilities – in development ethics into critical engagement with each other. In a 1991 conference paper, I focused on Sen's arguments that his capability approach both improved on a needs-based approach and helped justify a rights-based development ethic.[64] In two articles published subsequently, I expanded the original paper and compared Sen with Nussbaum, argued that their perspectives complemented each other, and contended that in fact Nussbaum had explicitly done what Sen had done only implicitly and should do explicitly – defend a definite list of valuable capabilities.[65]

Returning to Costa Rica in 1992, I lectured in Costa Rica, Honduras, and Guatemala on both Sen and Nussbaum. I also rewrote my Sen and Nussbaum articles in Spanish and adapted them to the Costa Rican and Central American political and intellectual context. The result, with a title due more to Nussbaum's influence than to Sen's, appeared in Costa Rica as *Florecimiento humano y desarrollo internacional: La nueva ética de capacidades humanas* (Human Flourishing and International Development: The New Ethic of Human Capabilities).[66]

The first two chapters (4 and 5) of Part II are substantial revisions of my 1991 and 1995 articles and the Costa Rican book. The new chapters, among other things, update the original articles. Not only has a substantial secondary literature emerged in the last decade, but also Sen's and Nussbaum's approaches have both evolved and increasingly diverged. In the early 1990s I stressed what the two had in common and interpreted Sen as implicitly proposing something close to Nussbaum's explicit pluralistic conception of the good or flourishing human life. Now, in spite of ongoing shared commitments and concepts, Sen and Nussbaum, I argue in a completely new Chapter 6, have increasingly different normative outlooks. Sen's rejection of a prescriptive list of valuable capabilities and functionings is part of his participatory and democratic turn. Nussbaum's retention of a list, albeit in a somewhat more flexible form, is part of her view that philosophers (and constitutions) have important prescriptive roles to play. Furthermore, although both have learned from Aristotle, Sen emphasizes Aristotle's critique of material goods as a means to minimally adequate well-being while Nussbaum emphasizes Aristotle's ideal of fully human flourishing. Although both continue to admire the work of John Rawls, in their recent writing they find stimulation in different aspects of Rawls's perspective. Sen develops Rawls's notion of "public reason" in the direction of public discussion and deliberative democracy. Nussbaum argues against many of Rawls's conclusions in *The Law of Peoples* but substitutes

Rawls's notions of an overlapping consensus and political liberalism for her earlier proposal of a universal and comprehensive theory of human flourishing.

Chapters 4–6 also differ from my earlier work in that I have changed my comparative assessments of Sen's and Nussbaum's versions of the capability orientation. Whereas earlier I was attracted to Nussbaum's ideal of the good or flourishing human life and her list of its components, now I argue, especially in Chapter 6, that this approach has limitations. Whereas earlier I thought Nussbaum's notion of capabilities as personal powers was unfortunately missing in Sen, now I argue that his notion of capability as opportunity or freedom does justice to personal traits as well as to environmental constraints and future possibilities. Whereas earlier I merely noted that Nussbaum lacked Sen's notion of agency, I now see that this lacuna is a serious weakness in her approach and one reason for her failing to give sufficient weight to citizen participation and democratic decision-making.

Throughout Part II, I emphasize the evolution of Sen's notion of agency from a theory of motivation, which makes room for altruistic action, to a normative ideal that affirms the importance of the individual and group freedom to deliberate, be architects of their own lives, and act to make a difference in the world. Related to the ideal of agency is that of empowerment, namely, those conditions and processes that enable individuals and groups to strengthen and exercise their agency.

The three chapters in Part II, then, crystallize more than twenty years of my efforts to understand, probe, evaluate, and strengthen the capability orientation as an approach in development ethics. It became clear to me and to others, however, that such engagement with the capability orientation was not enough. To provide the critical confrontation that the perspective deserved, one should also apply and extend the approach as well as critically compare it with other perspectives. And, more generally, development ethics, whether working within a capability theory-practice or not, should assess norms, policies, and institutions at all levels – local, societal, national, and global.

Strengthening and applying the capability approach

In 1993 I accepted the position of Senior Research Scholar at the University of Maryland's Institute for Philosophy and Public Policy and the University's School of Public Policy. In this interdisciplinary context, my academic work increasingly focused on applying development ethics and especially capability norms to various public problems and policies. I was convinced that the development ethicists could help policymakers, development workers, and community leaders understand and remedy pressing human problems. They could do so, however, only if they addressed their work to a variety of academic, professional, and public audiences. My new institutional context afforded ample opportunity for this work.[67]

The present volume's Part III, "Strengthening and Applying the Capability Approach," includes two chapters in which I apply development ethics and the capability approach to the urgent issues of, on the one hand, over-consumption in the North (and the South) and, on the other hand, hunger and under-consumption in the South (and the North). In Chapter 7, I engage the work of Spanish philosopher Adela Cortina and her proposal for an ethic of consumption.[68] Influenced by both Kant's notion of moral autonomy and responsibility and by Habermas's "discourse ethic," Cortina criticizes my earlier attempt to apply the capability approach to consumption and offers an important alternative.

Employing Sen's notion of well-being and a Nussbaum-type list of features of human well-being, in 1998 I had assessed the impact of US consumption choices on the well-being of US consumers.[69] Although I still believe this account has some merit in appealing to the enlightened self-interest of American and other affluent consumers, I now believe this prudential version of the capability approach to be seriously flawed as an *ethic* of consumption. It is especially weak in addressing the consumption choices of consumer-citizens and governments in the light of the effects of these choices not only on one's own well-being but also on the environment, institutions, and especially the capabilities and agency of other people. Most problematic, as Cortina and Des Gasper both noted, was an absence of the consumption responsibilities of rich nations and individuals with respect to the developing world.[70]

In Chapter 7, I aim to develop a more adequate and complete capability approach to consumption by analyzing and evaluating Cortina's ethics of consumption in the context of affluence in the North and deprivation in the South. Appropriately building on Sen's concepts of agency and capability, Cortina skillfully supplements them with a Kantian notion of autonomy, a discourse ethics notion of dialogue, and an ideal of citizen responsibility. Such enrichment enables us to address the moral duties of rich countries and citizens (as well as developing world and global institutions) with respect to consumption choices and their impact, for both good and ill, on the developing world. What results is, I believe, a significantly strengthened capability view of ethical obligation in general and responsible consumption choice in particular. The capability approach, suitably strengthened, enables us to criticize – on moral as well as prudential grounds – over-consumption in the North (and South).

It also enables us to understand and reduce under-consumption in the South (and the North), one effect of which is hunger and food insecurity.

In Chapter 8, I build on and seek to advance my earlier work on a capability approach to world hunger by applying an *agency-oriented* capability lens to understand and combat malnutrition and famine.[71] If the problem in the North (and parts of the South) is often that people consume too much or the wrong things, the problem in the South (and parts of the North) is that the majority of people often lack access to those commodities needed for well-being. Analyzing Sen and Jean Drèze's work on hunger,[72] I argue that development ethicists have several roles to play. They should evaluate the empirical categories employed to describe, explain, and forecast the data about hunger and famine. Moreover, these ethicists should assess and weigh the moral costs and benefits – which include economic and political costs and benefits – of various options for hunger-reducing and famine-eliminating policies and institutions. Most generally, development ethicists should make explicit and evaluate the normative assumptions and implications for nutritional well-being and food security of competing development theory-practices.

Applying the capability approach and strengthening it with an explicit attention to the ideal of agency, I argue that relative emphasis should be shifted (1) from moral foundations to interpretative and strategic concepts, (2) from famine to persistent malnutrition, (3) from remedy to prevention, (4) from food availability to food entitlements, (5) from food and entitlements to capability and agency, and (6) from capability and agency to development as freedom. This last progression, I argue, will take us beyond even the best recent work on world hunger and development aid. Overall, the progression I favor conceives an ethics of food aid as a part of a more basic and inclusive ethics for development.

Returning to Peter Singer's challenge – which had motivated me almost twenty years earlier – that philosophers should address the realities of famine and the ethics of aid, I conclude that since the best long-term cure for hunger is good national and global development, rich and poor nations alike (as well as international actors) should put emergency food aid in a developmental perspective and incorporate an ethics of famine relief into an international development ethics.

Democratizing and extending the capability approach and development ethics

It is important that development ethicists in general and those working within the capability orientation in particular pursue new directions.

Without weakening the shared commitment to the theory and practice of poverty alleviation, development and capability ethicists should take up new topics [73] (as well as revisit old ones), experiment with new methods, seek new theoretical and institutional alliances, and subject their work to both fresh theoretical and practical criticism. There are several reasons why development ethics should undertake new initiatives and take new directions. I argue in Chapter 2 that not only has the world changed in important ways since the origination of development ethics, but the field, in general, and the capability orientation, in particular, confront certain new dangers. Among these are dogmatism, cooptation by mainstream institutions, and a recent modishness concerning both development ethics and the capability approach.

This account of new challenges for development ethics and the capability approach has informed the present book throughout. What Whitehead called the "adventure of ideas" lures us to find better solutions to old problems, avoid sterile scholasticism and false dichotomies, and forge inventive responses to new challenges.

In both Parts II and III I begin charting new directions as I clarify and defend a distinctive agency-focused version of the capability approach and apply it to the challenge of consumerism and world hunger. It is in Part IV's three chapters, however, that I most explicitly explore new directions in development and capability ethics. In Chapter 9, "The Capability Approach and Deliberative Democracy," I contend that democracy as public discussion is an important recent emphasis in Sen's work and holds great promise for development theory, institutions, and practices. I argue that (1) Sen's recent emphasis on citizen voice and public discussion is both important and underappreciated, and (2) the theory and practice of deliberative democracy strengthens Sen's democratic turn and the capability orientation.

In Chapter 10, I apply the agency-focused and deliberative version of the capability approach to decision-making in local or grassroots development. Building on some of Denis Goulet's past work and Jay Drydyk's current work, I analyze and evaluate Sabina Alkire's approach to participation and offer an ideal that I call "deliberative participation." Especially important in my own work is what I hope will be the fruitful interaction between the capability approach and the theory and practice of what Archon Fung and Erik Olin Wright call "Empowered Participatory Governance" (EPG).[74] This approach to robust democracy emphasizes deliberation in all democratic bodies, the vertical integration of local and higher-level bodies, and the integration of, on the one hand, personal/collective agency and, on the other hand, institutional design. EPG and other experiments in local democracy become one basis for responding to criticisms that my marriage of Sen's democratic turn and deliberative democracy fails to protect basic entitlements, undermines autonomy, and is utopian. I also take the criticism that my agency-oriented and democratic version of the capability approach uncritically assumes an unacceptable egalitarianism.

In Chapter 11, the volume's final chapter, I argue that development ethics should take up the new issue of globalization. Development ethicists should ethically assess the various faces of globalization. Eschewing those who either condemn all globalization or uncritically celebrate its achievements, I contend that the new global interconnectedness has been both bad and good for human beings and can be made significantly better. What is called for is that ethically concerned citizens and development ethicists appraise – in relation to what human individuals and communities can do and be – different sorts of global interaction and the institutional responses to these phenomena. Specifically I argue for both the democratization of globalization and the globalizing of democracy. The former would include morally acceptable and effective ways to democratize current global forces and institutions as well as morally acceptable (and unacceptable) ways to promote and deepen democracy on every level. What ties the three chapters of Part IV together is that they extend the capability approach by offering a concept of inclusive, wide-ranging, and deliberative democracy as both a fundamental end and means of local, national, and global development.

The volume as a whole, and especially the chapters in Parts III and IV, emphasizes the ideal and practice of deep and broad democracy, a thread that runs through my career as a teacher and scholar. From Reinhold Niebuhr, I learned (as an undergraduate in the late 1950s at DePauw University) that because people are good, democracy is possible; but because they are evil, democracy is necessary. From William Lee Miller at Yale Divinity School, I grasped the importance of public argument and citizen engagement for a democratic polity. In working with youth in Cleveland's inner city in 1961–2, I tried to put into practice the new ideas of citizen participation that were soon to flower in the New Left. From Richard J. Bernstein, then of Yale's Department of Philosophy, and his hero John Dewey, I grasped that philosophers should deal with human problems and that democracy was a way of life in which people deliberate together to solve common problems.[75] My work with Habermas in the mid-1970s nurtured my commitments to the public sphere and the ideal of dialogue in which the only force was that of the better argument. The Yugoslav vision of democratic socialism led to my belief in the importance of multi-leveled democratic self-management. This volume culminates with a conception of deliberative democracy that

I hope will play an important role in the further evolution of both development ethics and the capability orientation.

To sum up this introductory chapter, the title of the present book – *Ethics of Global Development: Agency, Capability, and Deliberative Democracy* – conveys the book's main and distinctive themes. The four parts of the work represent the stages of development ethics, my professional trajectory in this field, and the organization of the following chapters. First, it was and remains important to get ethics on the development agenda, address the ethical dimension of development "theory-practices," and situate the contribution of development ethicists in relation to that of development academics, policy analysts, practitioners, and activists. Second, development ethics benefits from the clarification and evaluation of the normative foundations of the capability orientation and the strengthening of these foundations by an explicitly ethical ideal of human agency. Third, the volume moves development ethics forward by applying in novel ways the agency-oriented capability approach to the challenges of Northern consumerism and Southern hunger. Finally, the changing world situation offers development ethics and the capability orientation new challenges, among which is that of showing that development on all levels must be democratic as well as poverty-reducing and that democracy should be deliberative as well as electoral.

NOTES

For helpful comments on this chapter, I thank Sabina Alkire, David P. Crocker, Edna D. Crocker, Lawrence Crocker, Des Gasper, Verna Gehring, Xiaorong Li, Ingrid Robeyns, Stephen Schwenke, and Asunción St. Clair. A brief summary appears in David A. Crocker, "Ethics of Global Development: Agency, Capability, and Deliberative Democracy – An Introduction," *Philosophy and Public Policy Quarterly*, 26, 1/2 (2006), 21–7.

1. Des Gasper offers a helpful working definition of "development ethics": "Development ethics looks at meanings given to societal 'development' in the broad sense of progress or desirable change, at the types, distribution and significance of the costs and gains from major socioeconomic change, and at value conscious ways of thinking about and choosing between alternative paths and destinations. It aims to help in identifying, considering, and making ethical choices about societal 'development,' and in identifying and assessing the explicit and implicit ethical theories" (*The Ethics of Development: From Economism to Human Development* [Edinburgh: Edinburgh University Press, 2004], xi).
2. As will become clear in this and the following chapter, one issue in development ethics is whether development ethicists should address beneficial social change in "developed" countries as well as "developing" ones. My own view is that development ethicists should evaluate social structures and seek better alternatives wherever serious unfreedoms – especially poverty and domination – exist.

3. See especially Chapter 4 for Sen's writings on or relevant to development and normative evaluation.

4. Hilary Putnam, *The Collapse of the Fact/Value Dichotomy and Other Essays* (Cambridge, MA, and London: Harvard University Press, 2002), vii–viii. I would amend Putnam's comment, in a way I believe he would accept, so as to say that Sen's perspective also helpfully contributes both to understanding the links between inequality, on the one hand, and deprivation, insecurity, and oppression, on the other, and to combating these interrelated human evils.

5. See especially Chapter 4 for Nussbaum's writings on the capabilities approach to global development.

6. Gasper, *The Ethics of Development*, 183.

7. David Rogers, then Assistant Professor of Economics; and Loren Crabtree, then Assistant Professor of History.

8. The popular wisdom in those days, which I have not be able to confirm, was that Colorado State University received more financial support from the US Agency for International Development (USAID) than did any other university. If true, such involvement in economic development would fit CSU's tradition as a "land grant" university. The Morrill Act and the Land-Grant Colleges Act of 1862 provided funding for institutions of higher learning in each state. The acts mandated that to take advantage of this funding a state would have to endow, support, and maintain "at least one college where the leading object shall be, without excluding other scientific and classical studies, and including military tactics, to teach such branches of learning as are related to agriculture and mechanic arts, in such manner as the legislatures of the State may respectively prescribe, in order to promote the liberal and practical education of the industrial classes in the several pursuits and professions in life" (Morrill Act 1862, sec. 4: <http://usinfo. state.gov/usa/infousa/facts/democrac/27.htm>). Opening its doors in 1879, CSU has continuously contributed to the socially beneficial application of scientific and liberal studies to agricultural and economic development.

9. After completing in 1970 my PhD dissertation on "A Whiteheadian Theory of Intentions and Actions," and influenced by Richard J. Bernstein and his book *Praxis and Action* (Philadelphia: University of Pennsylvania Press, 1971), I had become less interested in a non-normative theory of individual action (What is the difference between my raising my hand and my hand going up?) and more interested in a normative theory for social action, or *praxis*. As a guest professor at the University of Munich in 1973–4, I worked on Habermas's social theory and met with him several times. During that year, I became fascinated with the intellectual work and political dissent (in Tito's Yugoslavia) of the Yugoslav philosophers and sociologists called the Praxis Group. My lecturing and writing about the Group culminated in my 1983 book *Praxis and Democratic Socialism: The Critical Social Theory of Marković and Stojanović* (Atlantic Highlands, NJ: Humanities Press; Brighton: Harvester Press, 1983).

10. James W. Boyd, Professor of Philosophy, and Gerald M. Ward, Professor of Animal Science. In later years I team-taught the course several times with Robert L. Zimdahl, Professor of Plant Pathology and Weed Science.

11. For a more extensive discussion of Goulet and Berger, their role in the emergence of development ethics, and the earlier work that they draw on, see Chapter 2 below and David A. Crocker, "Toward Development Ethics," *World Development*, 19, 5 (1991): 458–61. For recent assessments of Goulet's contributions to development ethics, see Adela Cortina, "Ética del desarrollo: Un camino hacia la paz," *Sistema*, 192 (May 2006): 3–17; and David A. Crocker, "Foreword," in Denis Goulet, *Development Ethics at Work: Explorations 1960–2002* (London and New York: Routledge, 2006), xiv–xxix. See also Gasper, *The Ethics of Development*, 14–18; and Marta Pedrajas Herrero, "El desarrollo humano en la economía ética de Amartya Sen," PhD dissertation, Faculty of Philosophy, University of Valencia, Spain, 2005. Development ethicists around the world were saddened to hear that on December 26, 2006, Goulet lost a long battle with cancer.

12. Denis Goulet, *The Cruel Choice: A New Concept in the Theory of Development* (New York: Anthenaeum, 1971), xix.

13. Denis Goulet, *The Uncertain Promise: Value Conflicts in Technology Transfer* (New York: IDOC / North America, 1977), 5.

14. Peter Berger, *Pyramids of Sacrifice: Political Ethics and Social Change* (New York: Basic Books, 1974), vii.

15. John Rawls, *A Theory of Justice* (Cambridge, MA: Belknap Press of Harvard University Press, 1971). A revised edition appeared in 1999, and a "restatement," edited by Erin Kelly, appeared in 2001: John Rawls, *Justice as Fairness: A Restatement* (Cambridge, MA: Belknap Press of Harvard University Press, 2001).

16. Peter Singer, "Famine, Affluence, and Morality," *Philosophy and Public Affairs*, 1 (1972): 229–43. Singer's initial essay was written in 1971 and first appeared in *Philosophy and Public Affairs* in 1972, the initial year of publication of what was to become the premier philosophical journal in applied ethics.

17. Peter Singer, "Reconsidering the Famine Relief Argument," in *Food Policy: The Responsibility of the United States in the Life and Death Choices*, ed. Peter G. Brown and Henry Shue (New York: Free Press, 1977), 36.

18. *The New York Times Magazine* (July 7, 1974): 17–20.

19. "The Need for Recovery of Philosophy," *John Dewey: On Experience, Nature and Freedom*, ed. Richard J. Bernstein (New York: The Liberal Arts Press, 1960), 67.

20. *World Hunger and Moral Obligation*, ed. William Aiken and Hugh La Follette (Englewood Cliffs, NJ: Prentice-Hall, 1977), 1.

21. Singer, "Famine, Affluence, and Morality," 231.

22. Hardin's most important early essays were "Lifeboat Ethics: The Case Against Helping the Poor," *Psychology Today*, 8 (1974): 38–43, and "Living on a Lifeboat," *Bioscience*, 25 (1974): 561–8.

23. Singer's "Famine, Affluence, and Morality" and Hardin's "Lifeboat Ethics," as well as the first wave of philosophical responses, appeared in *World Hunger and Moral Obligation*, ed. Aiken and La Follette. Two other anthologies of the period, both of which include philosophical essays on ethics and world hunger, are *Lifeboat Ethics: The Moral Dilemmas of World Hunger*,

ed. George R. Lucas, Jr., and Thomas W. Ogletree (New York: Harper & Row, 1976) and *Food Policy: The Responsibility of the United States in the Life and Death Choices*, ed. Peter G. Brown and Henry Shue (New York: Free Press, 1977). For the most important of the early essays as well as more recent work, see *World Hunger and Morality*, 2nd edn., ed. William Aiken and Hugh La Follette (Upper Saddle River, NJ: Prentice-Hall, 1996).

24. Singer, "Famine, Affluence, and Morality," 242.
25. Singer, "Postscript," in *World Hunger and Moral Obligation*, ed. Aiken and La Follette, 35.
26. David A. Crocker, "Hunger, Capability, and Development," in *World Hunger and Morality*, ed. William Aiken and Hugh La Follette, 2nd edn. (Upper Saddle River, NJ: Prentice-Hall, 1996), 211–30.
27. Peter Singer, "Achieving the Best Outcome: Final Rejoinder," *Ethics and International Affairs*, 16, 2 (2002): 127.
28. Ibid., 128.
29. Amartya Sen, *Poverty and Famines: An Essay on Entitlement and Deprivation* (Oxford: Clarendon Press, 1981).
30. Jean Drèze and Amartya Sen, *Hunger and Public Action* (Oxford: Clarendon Press, 1989).
31. Andrew Kuper, "More than Charity: Cosmopolitan Alternatives to the 'Singer Solution,'" *Ethics and International Affairs*, 16, 2 (2002): 116.
32. In "World Hunger: Putting Development Ethics to the Test" (*Christianity and Crisis* [May 26, 1975]: 125–32), an article that I did not read until thirty years later, Denis Goulet (with no indication that he had read Singer's 1972 article on famine relief) argued that world hunger was a symptom of systemic problems of asymmetrical power within and between nations. The "test" for development ethics should be not just to advocate the alleviation of hunger but also to criticize and seek alternatives to its causes. In Chapter 8, I return to Goulet and his contribution to the transition from an ethics of food aid to an ethics of development.
33. In "More than Charity," and in "Facts, Theories, and Hard Choices," *Ethics and International Affairs*, 16, 2 (2002): 125–6, Kuper vitiates his similar criticism of Singer by failing to recognize that Singer explicitly rejects exclusive disjunction between famine relief and systemic change.
34. My evolving conception of development ethics in the 1970s and 1980s owed much to discussions with, and to the work of, two colleagues in CSU's Department of Philosophy: Bernard Rollin and Holmes Rolston. In their respective fields of veterinary ethics and environmental ethics, Rollin and Rolston were pioneers in philosophically rigorous and practically relevant applied ethics. See, for example, Bernard E. Rollin, *Animal Rights and Human Morality* (Buffalo: Prometheus, 1981); and Holmes Rolston, *Environmental Ethics: Duties to and Values in the Natural World* (Philadelphia: Temple University Press, 1988).
35. In Chapters 2 and 3, I explain farther and defend this model of applied ethics or practical philosophy.
36. "Hacia una ética del desarrollo," *Revista de la Filosofía de la Universidad de Costa Rica*, 25, 62 (1987): 20–31; "Toward Development Ethics," *World*

Development, 19, 5 (May 1991): 457–83. See also, "La naturaleza y la práctica de una ética del desarrollo," *Revista de la Universidad de Costa Rica,* 26, 62 (1988): 49–56.

37. "Toward Development Ethics," 463.

38. Roberto Murillo, "Noción desarrollada del desarrollo," *Revista de la Filosofía de la Universidad de Costa Rica,* 12, 35 (1974): 165–9.

39. Claudio Gutiérrez, "Papel del filósofo en una nación en desarrollo," *Revista de la Filosofía de la Universidad de Costa Rica,* 12, 35 (1974): 171.

40. Mario Bunge, *Ciencia y desarrollo* (Buenos Aires: Ediciones Siglo Veinte, 1980).

41. Ibid., 23.

42. E. Roy Ramírez, "Desarrollo y ética," *Revista Comunicación,* 2, 2 (1986): 23. At about the same time, Howard Wiarda made the more general point about "Third World" criticisms of "Western" development models: "Western modernization and development theory is . . . seen as still another imperialist Cold War strategy aimed at tying Third World nations into a Western and liberal (that is, United States) development pattern, of keeping them within our sphere of influence, of denying them the possibilities of alternative development patterns . . . Since that time [the early 1970s] . . . development has been increasingly tarred with the imperialist brush and discredited throughout the Third World, and hence a whole new generation of young Third World leaders and intellectuals no longer accepts Western developmentalist concepts and perspectives and is searching for possible alternatives" (Howard Wiarda, "Toward a Non-ethnocentric Theory of Development: Alternative Conceptions from the Third World," *Journal of Developing Areas,* 17 (1983): 439).

43. Ibid., 25.

44. E. Roy Ramírez, "El 'argumento' tecnológico, la tecnología perniciosa, y la ética," in *Dédalo y su estirpe: La revolución industrial,* ed. Mario Alfaro, Guillermo Coronado, E. Roy Ramírez, and Alvaro Zamora (Cartago: Editorial Tecnológica de Costa Rica, 1988), 48.

45. Luis Camacho, "Ciencia, tecnología, y desarrollo desde el punto de vista de los derechos humanos," in *Ciencia, responsibilidad y valores,* ed. E. Roy Ramírez (Cartago: Editorial Tecnológica de Costa Rica, 1985), 26. See also Luis Camacho, *Ciencia y tecnología en el subdesarrollo* (Cartago: Editorial Tecnológia de Costa Rica, 1993); "Consumption as a Topic for the North–South Dialogue," in *Ethics of Consumption: The Good Life, Justice, and Global Stewardship,* ed. David A. Crocker and Toby Linden (Lanham, MD: Rowman & Littlefield, 1998); *Tecnología para el desarrollo humano* (Cartago: Editorial Tecnológica de Costa Rica, 2005). Ramírez and Camacho both contribute to Edgar Roy Ramírez and Fernando Araya, *Cultura y desarrollo desde América Latina: Tres enfoques* (San José: Editorial de la Universidad de Costa Rica, 1993).

46. Especially helpful were my discussions with sociologist Jorge Rovira Mas, *Estado y política económica en Costa Rica 1948–1970,* 2nd edn. (San José, Costa Rica: 1982); *Costa Rica en los años 80* (San José, Costa Rica: Editorial Porvenir, 1987).

47. See David A. Crocker, "Un intercambio de fútbol: LDA y el Ft. Collins (Colorado) Arsenal," *La Voz de La Liga* 3 (January–February 1987): 21, 28; and "Dos torneos en Colorado," *La Voz de La Liga* 4 (March–April 1987): 28–9.

48. "Cuatro modelos del desarrollo costarricense: Análisis y evaluación ética," *Revista de Filosofía de la Universidad de Costa Rica*, 27, 66 (1989): 317–32. Updated versions in English appeared as "The Hope for Just, Participatory Ecodevelopment in Costa Rica," in *Ethics of Environment and Development: Global Challenge, International Response*, ed. J. Ronald Engel and Joan Gibb Engel (London: Belhaven Press; Tucson, University of Arizona Press, 1990), 130–43; and "Just, Participatory Ecodevelopment in Costa Rica," in *Soziale Arbeit und Internationale Entwicklung*, ed. Gregor Sauerwald, Wigbert Flock, and Reinhold Hemker (Münster: Lit, 1992), 121–34.

49. "Insiders and Outsiders in International Development Ethics," *Ethics and International Affairs*, 5 (1991): 149–73; and "Cross-Cultural Criticism and Development Ethics," *Philosophy and Public Policy Quarterly*, 24, 3 (2004): 2–8.

50. Gasper, *The Ethics of Development*, xii.

51. Ibid.

52. See "Cuatro modelos," 330.

53. For Sen's and Nussbaum's extensive writings on development and development ethics, see the bibliographies in Sabina Alkire, *Valuing Freedoms: Sen's Capability Approach and Poverty Reduction* (Oxford: Oxford University Press, 2002); and Martha C. Nussbaum, *Frontiers of Justice: Disability, Nationality, Species Membership* (Cambridge, MA: Harvard University Press, 2006).

54. Amartya Sen, *Development as Freedom* (New York: Knopf, 1999).

55. For a careful consideration of the relative weight of Smith, Marx, and Aristotle on Sen's thinking and the somewhat different roots of Nussbaum's thought, see Jesús Conill, *Horizontes de economía ética: Aristóteles, Adam Smith, y Amartya Sen* (Madrid: Editorial Tecnos, 2004).

56. Martha C. Nussbaum and Amartya Sen, "Internal Criticism and Indian Rationalist Traditions," in *Relativism, Interpretation and Confrontation*, ed. Michael Krausz (Notre Dame, IN: University of Notre Dame Press, 1989), 219–35.

57. *The Quality of Life*, ed. Martha Nussbaum and Amartya Sen (Oxford: Clarendon, 1993). Much of Sen's and Nussbaum's work in the late 1980s and early 1990s, whether separate or in collaboration, was affiliated with the World Institute for Development Economics Research (WIDER), Helsinki, a branch of the United Nations University.

58. "Toward Development Ethics," 457–83.

59. Ibid., 466.

60. Ibid., 465. In his Presidential Address to the Development Studies Association in 1982, Sen said that although "development economics had not been particularly unsuccessful in identifying the factors that lead to economic growth in developing countries," it "has been less successful in characterizing economic development, which involves expansion of people's capabilities." Sen immediately added: "For this [expansion], economic growth is only a means and often not a very efficient means either": "Development:

Which Way Now?" in *Resources, Values, and Development* (Oxford: Blackwell; Cambridge, MA: Harvard University Press, 1984), 504.

61. Ibid.
62. Ibid.
63. "Toward Development Ethics," 466.
64. "Functioning and Capability: The Foundation of Sen's Development Ethic," in *Ethical Principles for Development: Needs, Capacities or Rights? Proceedings of the IDEA/Montclair Conference*, ed. Kenneth Aman (Upper Montclair, NJ: Institute for Critical Thinking, 1991), 104–72.
65. Part 1 appeared as "Functioning and Capability: The Foundation of Sen's and Nussbaum's Development Ethic," *Political Theory*, 20, 4 (1992): 584–612. Part 2 was published as "Functioning and Capability: The Foundation of Sen's and Nussbaum's Development Ethic, Part 2," in *Women, Culture, and Development*, ed. Martha Nussbaum and Jonathan Glover (Oxford: Clarendon Press; New York: Oxford University Press, 1995), 153–98.
66. *Florecimiento humano y desarrollo internacional: La nueva ética de capacidades humanas* (San José: Costa Rica: Editorial de la Universidad de Costa Rica, 1998).
67. The Washington DC area has offered many venues for applying development ethics in dialogue with development practitioners. Particularly important to me has been my participation in the World Bank's Friday morning "Values for Development Group" and in the reorientation in 2007 of the Inter-American Development Bank's "Initiative on Social Capital, Ethics, and Development." Their respective websites are <www.worldbank.org/fmg> and <www.iadb.org/etica>.
68. See Adela Cortina, *Por una ética del consumo: La ciudanía del consumidor en un mundo global* (Madrid: Taurus, 2002).
69. "Consumption, Well-being, and Capability," in *Ethics of Consumption: The Good Life: Justice, the Good Life, and Global Stewardship*, ed. Crocker and Linden, 366–90.
70. Gasper, *The Ethics of Development*, 180–1; Cortina, *Por una ética del consumo*, 178–9.
71. Crocker, "Hunger, Capability, and Development," in *World Hunger and Morality*, ed. Aiken and La Follette, 211–30.
72. See, for example, Drèze and Sen, *Hunger and Public Action*; and *The Political Economy of Hunger*, 3 vols., I: *Entitlement and Well-being*; II: *Famine and Prevention*; III: *Endemic Hunger*, ed. Jean Drèze and Amartya Sen (Oxford: Clarendon Press, 1990).
73. In a keynote address in an Inter-American Development Bank Conference on "Ethics and Development," Sen challenged development ethicists to take up new issues such as disaster prevention and mitigation, AIDS, and the use of DDT: "Ethics and Development Day at the IDB," Inter-American Initiative on Social Capital, Ethics, and Development, Inter-American Development Bank, January 11, 2005.
74. See *Deepening Democracy: Institutional Innovations in Empowered Participatory Governance*, ed. Archon Fung and Erik Olin Wright (London and New York:

Verso, 2003); Archon Fung, *Empowered Participation: Reinventing Urban Democracy* (Princeton and Oxford: Princeton University Press, 2004).
75. See Richard J. Bernstein, *John Dewey* (New York: Washington Square, 1966, reprinted Atascadero, CA: Ridgeview, 1981); *Praxis and Action* (Philadelphia: University of Pennsylvania Press, 1971); *The Restructuring of Social and Political Theory* (New York and London: Harcourt Brace Jovanovich, 1976); "John Dewey on Democracy: The Task before US," *Philosophical Profiles* (Philadelphia: University of Pennsylvania Press, 1986), 260–72; *Beyond Objectivism and Relativism* (Philadelphia: University of Pennsylvania Press, 1983); *The New Constellation: The Ethical-Political Horizons of Modernity/ Postmodernity* (Cambridge, MA: MIT Press, 1992); *Radical Evil: A Philosophical Interrogation* (Cambridge, UK: Polity Press, 2002); "Can We Justify Universal Moral Norms?," in *Universalism vs. Relativism: Making Moral Judgments in a Changing, Pluralistic, and Threatening World*, ed. Don Browning (Lanham: Rowman & Littlefield, 2006), 3–17; "The Romance of Philosophy," Dewey Lecture, *Proceedings and Addresses of the American Philosophical Association*, 81, 2 (2007), 107–19. See also Hilary Putnam, "A Reconsideration of Deweyan Democracy" and "Afterward," *The Southern California Law Review*, 63 (1990): 1671–97; and "Pragmatism and Moral Objectivity," in *Women, Culture, and Development*, ed. Nussbaum and Glover, 199–224. For Dewey's evolving theory of democracy in the context of his philosophical and professional career, see Robert B. Westbrook's excellent book, *John Dewey and American Democracy* (Ithaca and London: Cornell University Press, 1991).

Part I

Development ethics

2 Agreements, controversies, and challenges

Development ethicists assess the ends and means of local, national, regional, and global development. National policymakers, project managers, grassroots communities, and international aid donors involved in development in poor countries often confront moral questions in their work. Development scholars recognize that social-scientific theories of "development" and "underdevelopment" have ethical as well as empirical and policy components. Development philosophers and other ethicists formulate ethical principles relevant to social change in poor countries, and they analyze and assess the moral dimensions of development theories and seek to resolve the moral quandaries lurking in development policies and practice.[1]

Sources

Several sources exist for the moral assessment of the theory and practice of development. First, activists and social critics, such as Mohandas Gandhi (beginning in the 1890s) in South Africa and India, Raúl Prébisch (beginning in the 1940s) in Latin America, and Frantz Fanon (in the 1960s) in Africa criticized colonialism and orthodox economic development.[2] Second, as discussed in Chapter 1, since the early 1960s, American development scholar, critic, and development practitioner Denis Goulet – drawing inspiration from the work of Louis-Joseph Lebret and Albert Hirschman,[3] Benjamin Higgins, and Gunner Myrdal[4] and American sociologist Peter Berger – pioneered what we now call "development ethics" by arguing that development theory, policy, and practices should be subjected to ethical assessment. Both Goulet and Berger insisted that what was often called development was bad for human beings and that both ethics and development would benefit from interaction.

In Chapter 1, I identified a third source of development ethics: the effort of primarily Anglo-American moral philosophers in the late 1970s and the 1980s to deepen and broaden philosophical debate about famine relief and food aid.[5] Beginning in the early 1970s, often in response to Peter Singer's utilitarian argument for famine relief (1972) and Garrett Hardin's "lifeboat ethics" (1974), many philosophers debated whether affluent nations (or their citizens) have moral obligations to aid starving people in poor countries and, if they do, what are the nature, bases, and extent of those obligations.[6] We saw in Chapter 1 how three Colorado State University professors in the late 1970s devised a course on ethics and development that went beyond Singer's seminal approach and the theoretical debate that it stimulated. By the early 1980s, moral philosophers such as Nigel Dower, Onora O'Neill, and Jerome M. Segal had come to views similar to those of the Colorado State University professors: famine relief and food aid were only one part of the solution to the problems of hunger, poverty, underdevelopment, and international injustice.[7] What is needed, argued these philosophers, is not merely an ethics of aid but a more comprehensive, empirically informed, and policy relevant "ethics of Third World development." The kind of assistance and North/South relations that are called for will depend on how (good) development is understood.

A fourth source of development ethics is the work of Paul Streeten and Amartya Sen. Both economists have addressed the causes of global economic inequality, hunger, and underdevelopment and addressed these problems with, among other things, a conception of development explicitly based on ethical principles. Building on Streeten's "basic human needs" strategy,[8] Sen, as discussed in Chapter 1, argues that development should be understood ultimately not as economic growth, industrialization, or modernization, which are at best means for the expansion of people's "valuable capabilities and functionings":

The valued functionings can vary from such elementary ones as avoiding mortality or preventable morbidity, or being sheltered, clothed, and nourished, to such complex achievements as taking part in the life of the community, having a joyful and stimulating life, or attaining self-respect and the respect of others.[9]

These four sources have been especially influential in the work of Anglo-American development ethicists, such as Sabina Alkire, Nigel Dower, Jay Drydyk, Stephen Esquith, Des Gasper, Denis Goulet, Desmond McNeill, Daniel Little, Onora O'Neill, Thomas Pogge, Stephen Schwenke, and the author.[10] When practiced by Latin Americans, Asians, Africans and non-Anglo Europeans, development ethics also draws on philosophical and moral traditions distinctive of their cultural contexts. See, for example, the work of Osvaldo Guariglia and Bernardo Kliksberg (Argentina); Tarso Genro (Brazil); Cristián Parker and Manfred Max-Neef (Chile); Luis Camacho, Jorge Arturo

Chávez, and E. Roy Ramírez (Costa Rica); Kwame Gyekye (Ghana); Ramón Romero (Honduras); Reiko Gotoh (Japan); Asunción St. Clair (Norway); Adela Cortina, Jesús Conill, Emilio Martínez Navarro, and Marta Pedrajas Herrero (Spain); Wilhelm Verwoerd (South Africa); Godfrey Gunatilleke (Sri Lanka); and Peter John Opio, A. Byaruhanga Rukooko, and Joseph Wamala (Uganda).[11]

Presenting work by these and other thinkers, one anthology and two textbooks in development ethics appeared in the period 2002–4: Bernardo Kliksberg, ed., *Ética y desarrollo: La relación marginada* (2002);[12] Daniel Little, *The Paradox of Wealth and Poverty: Mapping the Ethical Dilemmas of Global Development* (2003);[13] and Des Gasper, *The Ethics of Development* (2004).[14] Three professional organizations have been formed: the International Development Ethics Association (founded 1987); the Human Development and Capability Association (founded 2000); and the Inter-American Initiative on Social Capital, Ethics, and Development (2000), with its network of more than eighty universities.[15] Courses in development ethics have been or are being taught in about twenty universities in at least ten countries.[16] Short courses in development ethics are being considered in international financial institutions.

Such publications, groups, and courses indicate that development ethics has become – like environmental ethics or bioethics before it – a recognized field or multidisciplinary "discipline." I put the last word in inverted commas because development ethics, as I shall argue in this and the next chapter, should not be an exclusively academic inquiry. Rather, it should bridge the gap between theory and practice and does so with interaction in both directions.

Areas of consensus

Questions

Although they differ on a number of matters, development ethicists exhibit a wide consensus about the commitments that inform their practice, the questions they are posing, and the unreasonableness of certain answers. Development ethicists typically ask the following eleven types of questions:

1. What should count as (good) development or development success? What are clear examples of "good" development and "bad" development? How well are various regions, societies, and locales doing in achieving "development?" Development ethics emerged due to

dissatisfaction with conventional wisdom with respect to "development," and it thrives on questioning how good and better development should be conceived.

2. Should we continue using the concept of development instead of, for example, "progress," "economic growth," "transformation," "liberation," "sustainable livelihoods,"[17] or "post-development alternatives to development"?[18] How, if at all, does (good) development differ from "modernization" or "developmentalism," "transformational development" (USAID), or the "Washington Consensus"?

3. If by "development" we mean good socioeconomic change, what fundamental economic, political, and cultural goals and strategies should a society or political community pursue, and what commitments or principles should inform their selection?

4. What moral issues emerge in development policymaking and practice and how should they be resolved?[19] Should gender equality and women's empowerment be promoted in cultures with traditions of male dominance? Should anti-corruption strategies take priority over long-term efforts at poverty reduction and participatory democracy?[20] Should USAID personnel refuse to demote birth control (condoms) to a secondary status compared to policies of abstinence and marital fidelity?[21] Should citizen decision-making in development projects and societal governance be permitted, encouraged, or required?

5. How should the benefits and harms of development be conceived and distributed? Is some composite measure of development success basic, such as economic growth or economic efficiency, or does social justice require equal negative liberty (Nozick), equal political liberty and maximizing the opportunities of the least well off (Rawls), getting all above a minimally adequate threshold (Sen), reducing degrading forms of inequality, or strict economic equality? What category, "currency," or "metric" is relevant for distributive justice? GDP (income), utility, subjective happiness (Graham and Pettinato), social primary goods (Rawls), access to resources (Roemer), basic human needs (Galtung, Max-Neef, Streeten), negative liberty (Bauer and Nozick), free agency or autonomy (Sen, Crocker), capabilities and functionings (Sen, Nussbaum, Crocker), or human rights (Pogge, Vizard)?[22] If human rights are important, should they include positive socioeconomic rights as well as civil and political rights?

6. Who (or what institutions) bears responsibility for bringing about development? A nation's government, civil society, private enterprises, or the market? What role – if any – do or should more affluent states,

international and global institutions, nongovernmental associations, and poor countries themselves have in development of poor nations? What are the obligations of a rich sovereign state for its own citizens and are these duties more demanding than its duties to all human beings, especially the poor in other countries?[23]

7. Regardless of the identity of duty-bearers, how should we understand development responsibilities? Are moral duties based on divine commands, social pacts, general positive duties of charity (which permit donor discretion with respect to specific beneficiaries), specific duties to aid (any needy rights-bearer), negative duties to dismantle unjust structures or halt injurious action, or duties to make reparation for past wrongs? Is the duty of "Do no harm" enough or should citizens and development agents also consider positive duties to aid? And, if the former, how should the duty not to harm be weighed in relation the duty to do good? Is the duty to aid distant peoples a cosmopolitan duty of *justice*, which makes no distinction in duties to compatriots and others, or a humanitarian duty to rescue or assist, which is less demanding than a duty to one's fellow citizens (Nagel)?

8. What should be counted as the virtues and vices of various development agents? How good or obligatory is honesty and how bad or permissible is deception? Should USAID and other donor agencies have a code of ethics or conduct for its personnel? What is the evidence with respect to the role of similar professional codes in improving conduct? Is a code likely to do more harm than good? Would the prohibitions of such a code encourage employees to act in questionable ways just up to the threshold of permissible conduct, thereby encouraging problematic conduct? What would a defensible ethical code look like? Who should decide on such a code and by what process? Should it be imposed from the top or deliberated from the bottom? How should a code be enforced? How does an ethics of professional virtue or conduct relate to an ethics for assessing policy and institutional arrangements?

9. What are the most serious local, national, and international impediments to and opportunities for good development? How should blame for development failures be apportioned among global, national, and local agents? What are the most relevant theories and forms of globalization and how should the promise and risks of globalization be assessed from a moral point of view?

10. To what extent, if any, do psychological egoism, moral skepticism, moral relativism, national sovereignty and political realism, and religious or political fundamentalism pose a challenge to development ethics?

11. Who should decide these questions and by what methods? What are the respective roles of appeal to authority, philosophical reflection, constitutional constraints, public deliberation, donor deliberation, and "learning by doing"? How should development ethicists assess and improve their methods and in relation to what standards?

Answers

In addition to accepting the importance of these questions, most development ethicists share at least ten beliefs or commitments about their field and the general parameters for ethically based development. First, development ethicists typically agree that – in spite of global progress with respect to outlawing or reducing slavery and achieving higher living standards – many experience persistent and grave yet avoidable deprivations in contrast to the few who live in elevated affluence. Development ethicists start from judgments about what Dewey would call a "problematic situation": many people throughout the world undeservedly and needlessly suffer or die. These deaths may be either agonizingly slow, due to poverty of various sorts, or rapid but brutal due to ethnic and military conflict, repressive governments, or fragile states. In our affluent world, these unacceptable sufferings and deprivations need not continue, but should be halted, and people everywhere should have a chance for a good life. Pogge's cool expression of moral outrage is typical of many who share his sentiments:

How well are the weak and vulnerable faring today? Some 2,800 million or 46 percent of humankind live below the World Bank's $2/day poverty line – precisely: in households whose income per person per day has less purchasing power than $2.15 had in the US in 1993. On average, the people living below this line fall 44.4 percent below it. Over 1,200 million of them live on less than half, below the World Bank's better-known $1/day poverty line. People so incredibly poor are extremely vulnerable to even minor changes in natural and social conditions as well as to many forms of exploitation and abuse. Each year, some 18 million of them die prematurely from poverty-related causes. This is one-third of all human deaths – 50,000 every day, including 34,000 children under age five.

Such severe and extensive poverty persists while there is great and rising affluence elsewhere. The average income of the citizens of the affluent countries is about 50 times greater in purchasing power and about 200 times greater in terms of market exchange rates than that of the global poor.[24]

Moreover, development ethicists contend that development practices and theories have ethical dimensions and can benefit from explicit ethical analysis and appraisal. Although important, trying to ascertain what events and conditions exist as well as their likely causes and effects should not take the place of morally assessing what has been, is, and could be. Ethical commitments are lenses that reveal or highlight the moral dimension of human actions, institutions, and their consequences. It is indispensable to understand the causes and consequences of such things as poverty, corruption, repressive governments, and state fragility. It is another thing to evaluate the morally salient features of those phenomena, decide whether alternatives would be morally better, and ascribe responsibilities to various actors. For example, does the economic growth supposedly generated by a given development strategy get translated to expanding important opportunities for a society's most vulnerable citizens? Ethical assessment of past policies and present options enables people who are active in development endeavors to keep their eyes on the ball of reducing remediable and undeserved human death and suffering. Many people work in development in order to make the world better, but the conceptual frameworks that guide them are largely concerned with technical means rather than morally urgent ends. Development ethics is a way of thinking that puts moral questions and answers in the center of thought and action.

In addition, development ethicists tend to see development as a multidisciplinary field that has both theoretical and practical components that intertwine in various ways. Hence, development ethicists aim not merely to understand the nature, causes, and consequences of development – conceived generally as desirable social change – but also to argue for and promote specific conceptions of such change. In backing certain changes, development ethicists assume that choice among alternatives is real and that some choices are better than others.[25]

Furthermore, although they may understand the terms in somewhat different ways, development ethicists are generally committed to understanding and reducing human deprivation and misery in poor countries and regions. Development ethicists persistently remind development agencies that development should be for human beings rather than treating humans merely as tools (or "social capital") for development. Assessment of development policies and projects should emphasize impacts on preventing death as well as relieving suffering and loss of meaning. A consensus increasingly exists that development policymakers and donors should seek strategies in which both human well-being and a healthy environment jointly exist and are mutually reinforcing.

Another matter of agreement is that most ethicists are convinced that what is frequently called "development" – for instance, economic growth – has created as many problems as it has solved. "Development" can be used both descriptively and normatively. In the descriptive sense, "development" is usually identified as a high rate of economic growth, where growth is understood in relation to a society's achievement of high and improving (per capita) gross domestic or national product (GDP, GNP). So conceived, a "developed" society may be either celebrated or criticized. In the normative sense, a developed society – ranging from villages to national and regional communities as well as the global order – is one whose established institutions realize or approximate (what the proponent believes to be) worthwhile goals. These goals include the overcoming of economic and social deprivation. In order to avoid confusion, when a normative sense of "development" is meant, the noun is often preceded by a positive adjective such as "good," "authentic," "humane," "just," or "ethically justified."

Development ethicists also agree that development ethics should be conducted at various levels of generality and specificity. Just as development debates occur at various levels of abstraction, so development ethics should assess (1) basic ethical principles, such as justice, liberty, autonomy, solidarity, and democracy; (2) development goals and models, such as "economic growth," "growth with equity," "a new international economic order," "basic needs," and, most recently, "sustainable development," "structural adjustment," "human development" (United Nations Development Programme),[26] "transformational development" (USAID), and "development as freedom" (Sen); and (3) specific institutions, projects, and strategies.

Most development ethicists also contend that their enterprise should be international or global in the triple sense that the ethicists engaged in this activity come from many societies, including poor ones; that they are seeking to forge a cross-cultural consensus; and that this consensus emphasizes a commitment to alleviating worldwide deprivation.

Although many development ethicists argue that at least some development principles or procedures are relevant for any poor community or polity, most agree that development strategies must be contextually sensitive. What constitutes the best means – for instance, donor aid or withdrawal, state provisioning, market mechanisms, civil society, and their hybrids – will tend to vary in relation to a political community's history and stage of social change as well as to regional and global forces, such as globalization and international institutions.

Finally, this flexibility concerning development models and strategies is compatible with the uniform rejection of certain extremes. Ethically based development is inclusive development: it offers and protects at least a minimally adequate level of development benefits for everyone in a society – regardless of their religion, gender, ethnicity, economic status, sexual preference, or age. Moreover, most development ethicists would repudiate three models: (1) the maximization of economic growth in a society without paying any direct attention to converting greater opulence into better human living conditions for its members, what Amartya Sen and Jean Drèze call "unaimed opulence";[27] (2) a society unconcerned with the (growing) gap between the haves and the have-nots; and (3) an authoritarian egalitarianism in which physical needs are satisfied at the expense of political liberties. That said, development ethicists do and should enter into dialogue with theorists and practitioners who favor societies and projects that are authoritarian, hierarchical, opposed to governmental redistribution, and subordinate individual rights to community stability.

Controversies

In addition to these points of agreement among development ethicists, one also finds several divisions and unsettled issues. One unresolved issue concerns the scope of development ethics. Development ethics originated as the "ethics of Third World Development." There are good reasons to drop – as a Cold War relic – the "First-Second-Third World" trichotomy. However, no consensus exists on whether or how development ethics should extend beyond its central concern of assessing the development ends and means of poor, traditional, or nonindustrial societies. Some argue that development ethicists should criticize human deprivation wherever it exists, including in rich countries and regions, since they too have problems of poverty, powerlessness, and alienation and so properly fall within the scope of development ethics. Some argue that the socioeconomic model that the North has been exporting to the South results in the underdevelopment of both. Moreover, just as the (affluent) North exists in the (geographic) South, so the (poor) South exists in the (geographic) North.

Yet others – let us call them "restrictionists" – restrict development ethics to poor countries by arguing that attention to Northern deprivation, on the one hand, or consumerism, on the other, diverts development ethicists and agents from the world's most serious destitution (in poor countries) and the ways in which rich countries benefit from the current global order.

My own view is that restricting development ethics to "developing" countries is defective in four ways. First, and most obviously, the production processes, consumption, trade, and foreign policy of rich nations often have an enormous impact for good and ill on poor countries and their inhabitants. To be concerned about poor people in poor countries requires both assessment of current policies and practices of rich country inhabitants and governments and ethically based proposals to improve them. Accordingly, in Chapter 7, as part of development ethics, I apply an agency-focused version of the capability approach to assess and improve Northern consumption with respect to the developing world. Moreover, restrictionism falsely assumes that the most severe deprivation occurs in poor countries when in fact, as Sen points out, "the extent of deprivation for particular groups in very rich countries can be comparable to that in the so-called third world."[28] Further, Northern and Southern poverty reduction are linked; migrants from the South making money in the North send valuable remittances to their families back home but may also drain the South of able workers and displace workers in the North. Finally, "best practices" learned from development in the South may be applied to destitution in the North (as well as vice versa). For example, the United States Agency for International Development (USAID) – albeit in a poorly funded and now defunct program called "Lessons without Borders" – attempted to apply lessons learned abroad to destitute US cities. Development agents in different societies often face similar problems – such as unemployment, racism, violence, and powerlessness – and benefit from innovative ways of solving them.

A second unsettled question with respect to the scope of development ethics concerns how wide a net development ethics should cast with respect to the topics it addresses. It is controversial whether development ethicists, concerned with rich country responsibility and global distributive justice, should restrict themselves to official development assistance or whether they also should treat such topics as international trade, capital flows, migration, environmental pacts, terrorism, civil conflict, state fragility, military intervention, humanitarian intervention, and responses to human rights violations committed by prior regimes. The chief argument against extending its boundaries in these ways is that development ethics would thereby become too ambitious and diffuse. If development ethics grew to be identical with all international ethics or even all social ethics, the result might be that insufficient attention would be paid to alleviating *poverty and powerlessness* in various poor communities. Both sides agree that development ethicists should assess various kinds of North–South (and South–South) relations and the numerous global forces, such as globalization, that influence poverty, as well as economic and political inequality in poor countries. What is unresolved, however, is whether development ethics also should address such topics as those listed when – or to the extent that – these topics have no causal relationship to absolute or relative poverty or powerlessness.

In any case, these above listed issues are enormously important, and ethicists, whether or not they put "development" before their title, should be among those to confront them.

Development ethicists also are divided on the *status* of the moral norms that they seek to justify and apply. Three positions have emerged. First, universalists, such as utilitarians and Kantians, argue that development goals and principles are appropriate for all societies. Second, some particularists, especially communitarians and postmodern relativists, reply (sometimes committing a genetic or *ad hominem* fallacy) that universalism masks ethnocentrism and (Northern or Western) cultural imperialism. Pro-development particularists either reject the existence of universal principles or affirm only the *procedural* principle that each nation or society should draw only on its own traditions and decide its own development ethic and path. (Anti-development particularists, rejecting both change brought from the outside and public reasoning about social change, condemn all development discourse and practice.) A third approach – advanced, for example, by Seyla Benhabib, Jesús Conill, Adela Cortina, Nigel Dower, Jonathan Glover, Martha Nussbaum, and Amartya Sen, as well as the author[29] – tries in different ways to avoid the standoff between the first two positions. Proponents of this view insist that development ethics should forge a cross-cultural consensus on general goals relevant for any society, among which is the principle that a society should be free to make its own development choices among a plurality of fundamental norms. Further, these norms are sufficiently general to *require* sensitivity to societal differences.

One should also ask a further question related to the universalism/particularism debate: to what extent, if any, should development ethicists propose visions committed to a certain conception of human well-being or flourishing, and how "thick" or extensive should this vision be? There is a continuum here: at one end of the range, one finds a commitment to individual choice, tolerance of differences, and public deliberation about societal ends and means; at the other end, one finds normative prescriptions and institutional (including constitutional) guarantees with respect to the specifics of a good or flourishing human life but less tolerance for individual and social agency.

As I will argue in later chapters, most plausible is a "threshold" view that identifies an adequate level of agency and well-being that should be open to everyone, regardless of their citizenship. This threshold functions as a "platform" for individuals and communities freely to decide their own conception of the flourishing human life, its elements, and their weightings. One reason for this approach is that it will be easier to get cross-cultural consensus for a "moral minimum" than for a more robust conception of the good life. Another reason is that such an approach both respects the rights of individuals and communities to determine (within limits set by their respect for the like agency and well-being of others) their own conception of the good and enhances the "domain of public reasoning."[30]

Even supposing that development principles have some substantive content (beyond the procedural principle of self-determination that each society or person should decide for itself), there remain disagreements about that content. If one accepts that societal development concerns human development, one still must explore the moral categories crucial to human well-being and development. Candidates for such fundamental moral notions include, as we have seen, utility (preference satisfaction); subjective happiness; social primary goods, such as political liberty, income, wealth, and self-respect; negative liberty; basic human needs; autonomy or agency; valuable capabilities and functioning; human rights; and compassion or care.

Although many think that a development ethic ought to include more than one of these moral concepts, development ethicists differ about which among them ought to have priority. The alternative that I favor, as will become clear in Parts II and III, endorses the development of an understanding of a *minimally adequate or sufficient level of human agency and well-being* (not flourishing) that combines, on the one hand, a neo-Kantian commitment to autonomy and human dignity, critical dialogue and public deliberation with, on the other hand, neo-Aristotelian beliefs in the importance of physical health and social participation. Development duties might then flow from the idea that it is extremely important that all humans have the right to an adequate level of agency and well-being, and persons and groups have the duty to secure and protect these rights as well as to restore them when lost. Donor agencies, such as the World Bank and USAID, should consider the merits of such a rights-based and agency-focused approach to development.

One also finds, as we saw above, an ongoing debate about how development's benefits, burdens, and responsibilities should be distributed within poor (and rich) countries and between rich and poor countries. Utilitarians prescribe simple aggregation and maximization of individual utilities. Rawlsians advocate income and wealth maximization for the least well-off (individuals or nations). Libertarians contend that a society should guarantee no form of equality apart from equal freedom from the interference of government and other people. Pogge broadens the libertarian notion of harm (and rights) and argues that rich elites and nations should refrain from harming the vulnerable and compensate those who have been harmed. Singer continues to challenge development ethicists and citizens everywhere with his argument that if affluent nations and individuals can relieve suffering and death without sacrificing anything of comparable moral worth, they are morally obliged to do so. Capability ethicists defend governmental and civil responsibility to *enable* everyone – even those who are citizens of other countries – to advance to a level of sufficiency (Sen, Crocker) or flourishing (Nussbaum, Little) with respect to either agency or valuable functionings (or both). Nagel distinguishes a stronger duty of justice that governments owe to their own citizens (and that fellow citizens owe to each other) and a less stringent duty of beneficence that such governments and citizens owe to citizens of other countries.

Many development economists and policymakers are personally concerned with distributional and other ethical questions. Such questions, however, are often only implicit in the development economics literature and development policymaking documents. A notable and encouraging exception is the World Bank's *World Development Report 2006: Equity and Development*: "equity considerations must be brought squarely into the center of both diagnosis and policy."[31]

When silence on distributional issues occurs, development ethics should insist not only that policymakers confront the gains and losses that various policies bring to specific individuals and subgroups but also challenge development professionals and citizens to deliberate explicitly about which distributions of burdens and benefits are *most justified morally*. When development professionals do take up the question of distribution, development ethicists should applaud the effort but also argue that it is not enough to offer empirical evidence that "equity" – conceived, for example, as individual's having "equal opportunity to pursue a life of their choosing and be spared from extreme deprivations in outcomes"[32] – is efficacious in promoting efficiency or aggregate growth. Development ethicists should also challenge policymakers and citizens to forge, through fair processes, normatively appropriate ideals of economic and political justice. For "equity" is not only instrumentally valuable but is also good or right in itself. Rather than taking refuge in a doctrine of value neutrality or a narrow construal of their institutions' "mandate" or "comparative advantage," policy professionals should debate with citizens on the merits of substantive concepts of justice as well as procedures for deciding this question.[33]

A controversy also exists in development ethics with respect to whether (good) societal development should have – as an ultimate goal – commitments other than to the present and future human good. Communitarian ethicists ascribe intrinsic value – equal or even superior to the good of individual human beings – to such human communities as family, nation, or cultural group.[34] Others argue that nonhuman individuals and species, as well as ecological communities, have equal and even superior value to human individuals.[35] Those committed to "ecodevelopment" or "sustainable development" often fail to agree on what should be sustained as an *end in itself* and what should be maintained as an indispensable or merely *helpful means*. Nor do they agree on how to surmount conflicts among environmental and other competing values. Economist Joseph Stiglitz clearly recognizes that these and other moral disagreements are sometimes implicit in factual or policy disagreements:

> There are important disagreements about economic and social policy in our democracies. Some of these disagreements are about values – how concerned should we be about our environment (how much environmental degradation should we tolerate, if it allows us to have a higher GDP); how concerned should we be about the poor (how much sacrifice in our total income should we be willing to make, if it allows some of the poor to move out of poverty, or to be slightly better off); or how concerned should we be about democracy (are we willing to compromise on basic rights, such as the rights to association, if we believe that as a result, the economy will grow faster).[36]

Each development ethic and theory of justice offers insights at both the broad policy level and at the level of specific interventions. Although these moral frameworks seldom provide definitive or specific answers, they do call attention to candidates for fundamental ends in the light of which many current strategies and tactics might turn out to be morally questionable or even morally reprehensible. The moral theories provide lenses that enable us to see ourselves, our duties, and others in new and compelling ways. They can reinforce moral motivations and thereby shape both citizen and professional conduct.

An increasingly important disagreement concerns not values directly but the roles in resolving moral conflicts of, on the one hand, various experts, such as judges (and the constitutions they interpret), political leaders, donors and their technical experts, philosophers, or development ethicists, and, on the other hand, popular agency of various kinds. On the one hand, popular participation and democracy are suspect insofar as majorities (or minorities) may dominate others and insofar as people's beliefs and preferences are deformed by tradition, adapted to cope with deprivation, and subject to demagogic manipulation. Moreover, experts often excel at "know how," if not "know why." Finally, in addition to facilitating deliberation by others, ethicists can give advice and take stands without falling into self-righteous moralizing and finger-wagging. On the other hand, rule by experts or guardians can lead to new tyrannies, and many experts fail to facilitate ways in which "recipients" of development can be in charge of making and implementing their own development goals.

As I argue in detail in later chapters, Sen rightly calls for development institutions to reorient their approach from one of providing goods and services to passive recipients to one of enabling countries and their citizens genuine opportunities to be authors of their own lives and development path:

The ends and means of development call for placing the perspective of freedom at the center of the stage. The people have to be seen, in this perspective, as being actively involved – given the opportunity – in shaping their own destiny, and not just as passive recipients of the fruits of cunning development programs.[37]

Such an "agency-centered" development perspective implies, I argue in Part IV, a deepening and broadening of democracy that includes but goes well beyond a universal franchise coupled with free and competitive elections. Crucially important is the engendering of venues – within both government and civil society – in which citizens and their representatives can engage in deliberative give-and-take to solve common problems.

I argue in Part IV that the theory and practice of deliberative democracy, grounded in the ideals of agency, dialogue, reason-giving, and reciprocity, has much to offer development ethics. Rather than focusing exclusively on free and fair elections, as important as they are, the theory and practice of deliberative democracy emphasize social choice through public discussion that aims at solutions – solutions that nearly everyone can accept – to common problems. A political practice as well as a normative theory, deliberative democracy, I argue in Part IV, is informed by and informs promising experiments in democratic governance occurring in Porto Alegre and almost 250 other cities in Brazil, in Kerala (an Indian state of 32 million inhabitants), and in Chicago, Illinois, among other places.

Finally, controversy also exists among development ethicists with respect to which agents and structures are to blame for the present state of global destitution and unequal opportunity and responsible for societal change. Charles Beitz states the empirical aspects of the issue well: "There is a large, complex, and unresolved empirical question about the relative contributions of local and global factors to the wealth and poverty of societies."[38] Some development ethicists, such as Pogge, emphasize that affluent countries dominate if not completely determine the global order, which as a result unjustly tilts against poor countries.[39] This global order and the process of globalization amount, claims Pogge, to a "strong headwind" against which any poor community must struggle and which is largely responsible for development failures: "national policies and institutions are indeed often quite bad; but the fact that they are can be traced to global policies and institutions."[40] Other development ethicists and policymakers ascribe development failure much less to global and foreign sources and much more to national and local causes – such as elite capture of power, widespread corruption, and the lack of democratic institutions.

Let us appropriate and develop Pogge's "headwind" metaphor in a way that captures a view less one-sided and more pluralistic than the "explanatory nationalism" that Pogge usually expresses about the relative weight of external (global structure, rich country role) and internal (developing country role) factors in causing global poverty. Sailors know that the headwind against which they sail is an important but constantly changing and sometimes ambiguous factor and that getting to their destination requires skill and good judgment as well. The headwind is not always steady. Sometimes it gusts and sometimes it lulls (depending on the wind and whether their boat goes behind an island and is temporarily protected from the wind). Likewise, the impact of the global order and rich countries increases and decreases from time to time and place to place.

Moreover, sometimes there are crosswinds, some of which aid the ship and some of which impede progress, and good sailors must take advantage of the former and adjust to the latter. Likewise, the global order opens up opportunities for poverty reduction and democratization as well as impedes them, and wise leaders and peoples discern the difference. Furthermore, the good sailor tacks back and forth in the face of the wind, taking advantage of it for forward progress and not bucking it directly. Likewise, a developing country can find ways to take advantage of and "manage" normally adverse global factors. For instance, a cutback on US aid in Costa Rica enabled Costa Rica to become less dependent on the USA. Additionally, sometimes a headwind changes and becomes a tailwind. Then the global forces and rich country impacts coincide with and supplement internal development efforts. Finally, just as some boats are better than others with respect to resourcefulness, navigability, and stability, so some countries, owing to such things as natural endowments, governance, and human and social "capital," develop further and faster than others.

The moral of this nautical story is clear: just as the national development efforts vary from time to time and place to place, so do the impacts of the global order and the rich countries that dominate this order. Although the wind is always a factor in sailing (sometimes more, sometimes less, sometimes good, sometimes bad, often both), so is the skill of the captain and crew (and their ability to work together). Empirical investigation is important to determine which way and how hard the wind is blowing and how best to use national skills and resources to reach a society's destination. Pogge recognizes the variability of internal factors; in his less careful formulations, however, he fails to recognize the variability and complexity of external factors, the changing balance between external and internal factors, and the always important and sometimes crucial role of internal factors.[41]

This debate over the chief causes of development failure is closely linked to sharp disagreements over the moral appraisal of globalization, which I take up in Chapter 11, and the identification of "agents of justice."[42] Does globalization doom or guarantee good national and local development? Does globalization offer blessings and opportunities as well as miseries and risks? Is it up to developing nation-states and local communities to seize the good and avoid the bad of a globalizing world? Or should the main "agents of justice" be the rich nations, transnational corporations, and global institutions? In Chapter 11, I argue that the challenge is, as economist Joseph Stiglitz says, "to get the balance right . . . between collective action at the local, national, and global levels."[43]

New challenges and directions

The resolution of these controversies within development ethics should be understood in relation to the field's new challenges (and dangers) and the importance of exploring new terrain. Why are new directions in development ethics important?

First, the world itself changes. The end of World War II; the end of colonialism; the rise and fall of the Cold War and the break-up of the Soviet Union; disappearing species, global warming, and natural calamities; the advent of and blowback against neo-liberalism and increased economic integration among states; the end of apartheid; the rapid spread and human toll of HIV-AIDS; the strengthening of a global human rights regime; the accomplishments of national truth and reconciliation commissions and the initiation of the International Criminal Court; the atrocious terrorist attacks on New York, Washington, and elsewhere; the invasion and occupation of Iraq; the difficulties in promoting and sustaining democracy; the incidence of civil conflict and "failed" states – all these events present new challenges to those who reflect morally on the ends and means of national and global development.

Development ethics, I argue throughout this volume, have been and continue to be centrally concerned with understanding and combating human poverty and promoting human well-being throughout the world. Cutting-edge research addresses the issues of ill-being and well-being with respect to those systematically excluded and vulnerable, such as women, the disabled, ethnic and religious minorities, displaced persons and immigrants, and the elderly.[44] Increasingly, however, development ethicists recognize that they should attend not only to the cures of multidimensional poverty but also to poverty's deep causes, such as inequality, and its consequences, such as instability and conflict. Moreover, they realize that often poverty alleviation – because it can conflict with other good goals – should be linked in a complementary way with other morally urgent objectives. In so doing, development ethicists are pushing the frontiers of development and development ethics into new areas. It is not that development ethics should tackle every national and global issue. But it should address those problems that either issue in or stem from increased human poverty. Let me mention just three of them.

First, since the mid-1980s, environmental ethicists and development ethicists, reflecting concerns in the environmental and development communities, have sought ways to balance "conservation" and "development" or, in another formulation, to integrate environmental and development concerns in concepts of "sustainable development," "ecodevelopment," or "sustainable livelihoods."[45] How might conflicts between "nature" (including nonhuman animals) and human well-being be avoided or mitigated? When conflicts cannot be avoided, what should our priorities be, how should they be decided, and who should decide?

A related issue, second, which I address in Chapter 7, is that of consumption and global justice. Peter Singer and Adela Cortina, among others, have insisted on the relationship between environmental damage, mainly due to consumption patterns in affluent societies, and global warming, which then leads to desertification, increased risk of flooding, famines, and destitution in poor countries.[46] Although all industrial and post-industrial societies are guilty of damaging the ecosystem, it is the USA that most consistently refuses to take responsibility for her "collective lifestyle." Hence the topic of "development" and "conservation" is not just that of promoting development and conserving the environment in the South, but also that of underdevelopment in the South being causally linked – through environmental change – to "overdevelopment" or bad development in the North.

A third new direction for development ethics is that of ethical issues in reckoning with a society's past wrongs, such as a government's massively violating human rights and committing genocide against its own citizens or those of other countries. Often a group, nation, or region cannot advance to a better future of genuine development until it reckons ethically and effectively with a terrible past. Failure to hold past rights-abusers accountable for their crimes contributes to a "culture of impunity" and disregard for the rule of law, both obstacles to good development. Reckoning appropriately with past wrongs, in contrast, may contribute to (as well as benefit from) equitable and democratic development.[47]

Even before 9/11, but certainly afterwards, many were convinced that close causal links exist between, on the one hand, insecurity and lack of development, and, on the other hand, security and genuine development. The 1994 *Human Development Report* sought to put security on the development agenda and development on the security agenda.[48] A decade later, the Commission on Human Security, which Amartya Sen and Sadako Ogata co-chaired, proposed that security issues be reframed as less about national security and more about human insecurity in the face of serious and remediable threats.[49] The US-British response to terrorism, however, arguably has continued to emphasize *national* security in the face of terrorism and has done so at the expense of civil liberties as well as of national security. Just as problematic, the "war on terrorism" is distracting attention from other human ills and hijacking resources from efforts to ameliorate them. Among these are the deprivations that rights-based development aims to overcome. As Louise Arbour, the Canadian jurist and the UN's High Commissioner for Human Rights, commented as she departed from Canada's Supreme Court for her new position in Geneva:

The all-consuming nature of the US-led campaign against terrorism is sucking the oxygen out of other initiatives. I think there are other areas of grave concern, one of which I think is the tension between civil and political rights and social, economic and cultural rights, the right to development, which is not recognized by all as being a core human right.[50]

Yet, as many are coming to realize, poverty-reducing and humiliation-reducing development is surely one way of reducing the terrorist threat, for terrorism appeals most to those impoverished and disgraced, and good development decreases deprivations and promotes human dignity.[51]

These examples, in which development is linked with the environment, reckoning with past wrongs, and security, illustrate three ways of extending development ethics to topics traditionally considered outside development. Other such topics include trade,[52] displaced persons, migration,[53] bioethics, global financial structures and flows, and war within or between countries.

Beyond the fact of a changing world, new directions in development ethics are important due to three dangers that must be confronted and avoided: dogmatism, cooptation, and a certain modishness of development ethics in general and the capability orientation in particular. Each of these dangers threatens the critical bite and progressive evolution of ethical reflection on development ends and means.

Dogmatism occurs when an intellectual or practical movement insulates itself from a changing world and external critics. All such movements, including development ethics, the capability approach, and (as we shall see) deliberative democracy, are in danger of absolutizing past achievements instead of subjecting favorite ideas and institutions to continual scrutiny and – where called for – revision. As Richard J. Bernstein has argued and illustrated over the course of his long and fruitful career, it is precisely those ideas to which we are most attached that we should probe for ambiguity, incompleteness, one-sidedness, and downright error.[54] There is certainly something to be said for a movement's seeking unity and coherence so as not to be dissipated and thereby lose its distinctive and critical perspective.[55] Yet, the quest for unity – like the quest for certainty that Dewey persistently excoriated – can become a straitjacket that prevents creative change. Why listen to our critics if we know we've got it right (and are certain that they are wrong)?

Development ethics, especially with the first appearance of textbooks,[56] has become a recognized discipline or field, yet by that very fact may lose its critical soul. One antidote is to build fallibility, revisability, pluralism, and tolerance right into development ethics (and even *that* is no sure-fire solution). Another remedy is to confront and sift through the arguments of those who oppose development ethics; for instance, those who continue to espouse supposedly value-neutral economics, those who object to overly abstract or utopian presentations and insufficient attention to questions of feasibility and implementation, and those who criticize development ethics as a tool of Northern or rich country hegemony.[57]

The capability orientation, likewise, is in danger of calcification as it seeks to establish itself as a distinctive alternative to mainstream (utilitarian) development economics, Rawlsian perspectives, Kantian development ethics, human-rights based approaches, libertarianism, and champions of neo-liberalism. Capability and capabilities ethicists should confront the various critics, whether sympathetic or not, of their perspectives.[58] One of the most important of these criticisms is that the capability approach pays insufficient attention to asymmetries in social power. Some argue that Sen fails to emphasize sufficiently local and household power imbalances, including gender inequalities.[59] Thomas Pogge argues that Sen consistently ignores global power imbalances, puts excessive explanatory weight on national and local factors of poverty, and pays insufficient attention to global causes.[60] Pogge also argues that Sen fails to spell out duties that affluent persons and nations have to change currently unjust global structures and institutions.[61] The three chapters in Part IV, "Deliberative Democracy, Participation, and Globalization," begin to assess these and other criticisms.

One healthy development within the capability orientation is the fact that Sen's and Nussbaum's perspectives exhibit increasing differences in style, intended audience, and substance. The annual conferences of the Human Development and Capability Association include many papers that evaluate the strengths and weaknesses of the human development and capability approaches to development. Yet a danger exists that the capability orientation will be polarized into two dogmatic factions that unproductively argue about a "list" of universal features of a humanly good life. Fans of Nussbaum may dig in their heals and fight for one universal and prescriptive "list" while followers of Sen may just as tenaciously reject universal lists in favor of culturally specific public discussion. It is important not to get seduced into this "Sen or Nussbaum" dichotomy. One way to avoid doing so is to identify strengths and weaknesses in both approaches. Another way is to find ways to mediate between or creatively advance beyond the two.[62] I adopt both strategies throughout the present volume, especially when I argue for (1) a convergence of the capability approach and deliberative democracy (Chapter 9) and (2) the democratic role for lists of valuable capabilities (Chapter 10).[63]

The capability orientation is best characterized not as "Sen plus Nussbaum" or "Sen versus Nussbaum" but as a capacious family of perspectives. Sen was the founder of the orientation while Nussbaum is currently the most prolific family member. Influenced by both of these thinkers, many (often younger) capability friends and relations are applying, extending, and innovatively developing the capability perspective. To do otherwise would be to create a new dogmatism and weaken the approach's intellectual and political voice.[64]

We may also reinforce new directions in development ethics by applauding the way in which development ethics and, in particular, Sen's perspectives on development have begun to penetrate international institutions and popular discourse. Sen gave lectures at the World Bank that eventuated in *Development as Freedom*, the volume that would become the most popular and accessible statement of his ideas. With Bank President James Wolfensohn, Sen coauthored an article printed in the *International Herald Tribune*.[65] Beginning in 2000, Sen keynoted five "Ethics and Development" conferences at the Inter-American

Development Bank (IADB). The Initiative on Social Capital, Ethics, and Development of the IADB sponsored these events while the Government of Norway funded them.[66] The World Bank devoted its *World Development 2006* to the topic of "Equity and Development" and in its Public Sector and Governance unit has begun an initiative, "Ethics and Leadership," to consider ways in which development ethics might be institutionalized within developing countries and the Bank's own operations.[67]

Those of us who have labored in the fields of development ethics are delighted to see such institutions engage in moral (as well as economic) appraisal of development policies. With success in putting ethics on the agenda of these institutions, however, come new dangers. The critical and radical thrust of development ethics and the capability approach may be tamed or sanitized by institutions that talk ethics but keep walking as they did before. To be forewarned is to be forearmed; a great help in this regard are recent studies of the way that international institutions often have taken the sting out of progressive concepts.[68] Another way to reduce the danger of cooptation is for both insiders and outsiders – and hybrid insider-outsiders – in development ethics to apply ethical assessment to the policies and practices as well as to the rhetoric of national development and aid agencies and international financial institutions.[69] Or so I argue in the next chapter.

NOTES

This chapter was adapted from the first section of David A. Crocker, "Development Ethics, Democracy, and Globalization," in *Democracy in a Global World: Human Rights and Political Participation in the 21st Century,* ed. Deen Chatterjee (Lanham, MD: Rowman & Littlefield, 2008). Earlier versions appeared as "Development Ethics," in *Routledge Encyclopedia of Philosophy,* III, ed. Edward Craig (London: Routledge, 1998), 39–44; "Development Ethics and Globalization," *Philosophical Topics,* 30, 2 (2002): 9–28, and in *Ethical Dimensions of Global Development,* ed. Verna V. Gehring (Lanham, MD: Rowman & Littlefield, 2007), 59–63; "Globalization and Human Development: Ethical Approaches," in *Proceedings of the Seventh Plenary Session of the Pontifical Academy of Social Sciences,* ed. Edmond Malinvaud and Louis Sabourin, the Vatican, April 25–8, 2001 (Vatican City: Pontifical Academy of the Social Sciences, 2001), 45–65; and "Globalización y desarrollo humano: Aproximaciones éticas," in *¿Republicanismo y educación cívica: Más allá del liberalismo?* ed. Jesús Conill and David A. Crocker (Granada: Editorial Comares, 2003), 75–98. For helpful comments, I thank Deen Chatterjee, Roger Crisp, David P. Crocker, Edna D. Crocker, Nigel Dower, Jay Drydyk, Arthur Evenchik, Des Gasper, Verna Gehring, Denis Goulet, Xiaorong Li, Toby Linden, Nasim Moalem, Jerome M. Segal, and Roxanne Walters.

1. For fuller sketches of the history of development ethics, see David A. Crocker, "Toward Development Ethics," *World Development*, 19, 5 (May 1991): 457–83; Denis Goulet, *Development Ethics: Theory and Practice* (London: Zed Books, 1995), Preface, Introduction, and Part I; "Development Ethics," in *The Elgar Companion to Development Studies*, ed. David Alexander Clark (Cheltenham: Edward Elgar, 2006), 115–21; Des Gasper, "Development Ethics – an Emergent Field? A Look at Scope and Structure with Special Reference to the Ethics of Aid," in *Ethics and Development: On Making Moral Choices in Development Cooperation*, ed. Cees J. Hamelink (Kampen: Kok, 1997), 25–43; and Marta Pedrajas Herrero, "El desarrollo humano en la economía ética de Amartya Sen," PhD dissertation, University of Valencia, 2005, 29–45.

2. Mohandas K. Gandhi, *An Autobiography: The Story of My Experiments with Truth* (Navajivan Mudranalaya, Ahmedabad: Jitendra T. Desai, 1927); Raúl Prébisch, *The Economic Development of Latin America and Its Principal Problems* (New York: United Nations, E/C.12/R.1, 1950); Edgar J. Dosman, "Raúl Prébisch," in *Elgar Companion*, ed. Clark, 468–73; Frantz Fanon, *The Wretched of the Earth* (1961; reprint, Grove Press, 1986). For the emergence of development economics after World War II, see Gerald L. Meier and Dudley Seers, *Pioneers in Development* (Oxford: Oxford University Press, 1984).

3. See Oswaldo Feinstein, "Hirschman, Albert Otto (b. 1915)," in *Elgar Companion*, ed. Clark, 226–30.

4. See Paul Streeten, "Myrdal, Gunnar (1898–1987)," in *Elgar Companion*, ed. Clark, 399–404.

5. Des Gasper suggests another, more practical, 1960s source of development ethics, namely, those practitioners engaged in moral arguments about famine and emergency relief, human rights activists supporting the covenant on social and economic rights (1966), and religious communities influenced by liberation theology.

6. See *World Hunger and Morality*, 2nd edn., ed. William Aiken and Hugh La Follette (Upper Saddle River, NJ: Prentice Hall, 1996). For Singer's most recent statement of the obligations of rich nations and individuals to poor ones, see Peter Singer, *One World: The Ethics of Globalization* (New Haven, CT: Yale University Press, 2002), esp. ch. 5; "Outsiders: Our Obligations to those Beyond our Borders," in *The Ethics of Assistance: Morality and the Distant Needy*, ed. Deen K. Chatterjee (Cambridge: Cambridge University Press, 2004), 11–32; and "What Should a Billionaire Give – and What Should You?" *New York Times Magazine*, December 17, 2006.

7. See, for example, Onora O'Neill, "The Moral Perplexities of Famine Relief," *Matters of Life and Death: New Introductory Essays in Moral Philosophy*, ed. Tom Regan (New York: Random House, 1980); *Faces of Hunger: An Essay on Poverty, Justice and Development* (London: Allen & Unwin, 1986); "Ending World Hunger," *Matters of Life and Death*, 3rd edn., ed. Tom Regan (New York: McGraw Hill, 1993); Nigel Dower, "What is Development? – A Philosopher's Answer," Centre for Development Studies Occasional Paper Series, 3 (Glasgow: University of Glasgow, 1988); Jerome M. Segal, "What Is Development?," in *Philosophical Dimensions in Public Policy*, ed. Verna

Gehring and William A. Galston (New Brunswick, NJ: Transaction Publications, 2002), originally available as a working paper.

8. Paul Streeten, Shaid Javed Burki, Mahbub ul Haq, Norman Hicks, and Frances Stewart, *First Things First: Meeting Basic Needs in Developing Countries* (London: Oxford University Press, 1981). See also Hugh Stretton, "Streeten, Paul (b. 1917)," in *Elgar Companion*, ed. Clark, 115–21; Johan Galtung, "The New International Order and the Basic Needs Approach," *Alternatives*, 4 (1978/9): 455–76; "The Basic Needs Approach," in *Human Needs*, ed. Karin Lederer (Cambridge, MA: Oelgeschlager, Gunn & Hain, 1980), 55–125; Francis Stewart, *Planning to Meet Basic Needs* (London: Macmillan, 1985); "Basic Needs Approach," in *Elgar Companion*, ed. Clark, 14–18.

9. Amartya Sen, "Development Thinking at the Beginning of the 21st Century," in *Economic and Social Development into the XXI Century*, ed. Louis Emmerji (Washington, DC: Inter-American Development Bank, 1997), 531–51. As noted in Chapter 1, Sen's most systematic and readable statement of his capability approach and development ethic is *Development as Freedom* (New York: Knopf, 1999). See Sabina Alkire, *Valuing Freedoms: Sen's Capability Approach and Poverty Reduction* (Oxford: Oxford University Press, 2002), for the most complete bibliography of Sen's writing on ethics and development through 2001. See also Carl Riskin, "Sen, Amartya Kumar (b. 1933)," in *Elgar Companion*, ed. Clark, 540–5.

10. The following are major writings of these development ethicists: Sabina Alkire, *Valuing Freedoms*; Nigel Dower, *World Ethics: The New Agenda*, 2nd edn. (Edinburgh: Edinburgh University Press, 2007); Jay Drydyk, "Globalization and Human Rights," in *Global Justice, Global Democracy*, ed. Jay Drydyk and Peter Penz (Halifax, NS: Fernwood, 1997), 159–83; "The Development Ethics Framework," in Peter Penz, Jay Drydyk, and Pablo Bose, *Displacement and Development: Ethics and Responsibilities* (unpublished manuscript); Jay Drydyk and Atiya Habeeb Kidwai, "Development-Induced Population Displacement," in *The Economics and Politics of Resettlement in India*, ed. Shobhita Jain and Madhu Bala (New Delhi: Pearson Longman, 2006), 99–114; Stephen L. Esquith, "Complicity in Mass Violence," *Philosophy and Public Policy Quarterly*, 24, 4 (Fall 2004): 28–35; Des Gasper, *The Ethics of Development: From Economism to Human Development* (Edinburgh: Edinburgh University Press, 2004); Denis Goulet, *Development Ethics*; *Development Ethics at Work: Explorations 1960–2002* (London: Routledge, 2006); Daniel Little, *The Paradox of Wealth and Poverty: Mapping the Ethical Dilemmas of Global Development* (Boulder, Co: Westview, 2003); Desmond McNeill, "Equity, Development and the World Bank: Can Ethics Be Put Into Practice?," in *The World Bank Legal Review, II: Law, Equity and Development* (Washington, DC: Martinus Nijhoff and World Bank, 2006), 419–39; Desmond McNeill and Asunción St. Clair, "Development Ethics and Human Rights as the Basis for Poverty Reduction: The Case of the World Bank," in *The World Bank and Governance: A Decade of Reform and Reaction*, ed. Diane Stone and Christopher Wright (New York and London: Routledge, 2006), 29–47; Desmond McNeill and Asunción Lera St. Clair, eds., *Global Poverty, Ethics and Human Rights: The Role of*

Multilateral Organisations (New York and London: Routledge, 2008); Onora O'Neill, *Bounds of Justice* (Cambridge: Cambridge University Press, 2000); Thomas Pogge, *World Poverty and Human Rights: Cosmopolitan Responsibilities and Reforms* (Cambridge: Polity, 2002); David A. Crocker and Stephen Schwenke, "The Relevance of Development Ethics for USAID," a Desk Study for the United States Agency for International Development (April 2005); and David A. Crocker, "Toward Development Ethics," *World Development*, 19, 5 (May 1991): 457–83.

11. Osvaldo Guariglia, *Una ética para el siglo, XXI: Ética y derechos humanos en un tiempo posmetafísico* (Buenos Aires: Fondo de Cultura Económica, 2000); Bernardo Kliksberg, *Más ética, más desarrollo* (Buenos Aires: Temas, 2004); Manfred Max-Neef, *Human Scale Development: Conception, Application, and Further Reflections* (London: Apex Press, 1993); Cristián Parker, "Ética, democracia y desarrollo," in *Ética, democracia y desarrollo humano*, ed. Cristián Parker (Santiago: Lom, 1998), 19–39; Luis Camacho, *Ciencia y tecnología en el subdesarrollo* (Cartago: Editorial Tecnológica de Costa Rica, 1993); *Tecnología para el desarrollo humano* (San José, Costa Rica: Editorial Tecnológica, 2005); "Development Ethics," in *Encyclopedia of Science, Technology, and Ethics*, 4 vols., ed. Carl Mitcham (New York: Macmillan Reference, 2005), I: 513–19; Jorge Arturo Chávez, *De la utopía a la política económica: Para una ética de las políticas económicas* (Salamanca: San Esteban, 1999); E. Roy Ramírez, *La responsabilidad ética en ciencia y tecnología* (Cartago: Editorial Tecnológica de Costa Rica, 1987); Ramón Romero, *Identidad nacional en Honduras: Una reflexión filosófica* (Tegucigalpa: Universidad Nacional Autónoma de Honduras, Editorial Universitaria, 1990); Reiko Gotoh, "Understanding Sen's Idea of a Coherent Goal-Rights System in the Light of Political Liberalism," paper given at the 4th Conference on the Capability Approach: "Enhancing Human Security," University of Pavia, Italy, September 5–7, 2004; Asunción St. Clair, "Development Ethics: Open-Ended and Inclusive Reflections on Global Development," in *Poverty, Politics and Development: Interdisciplinary Perspectives*, ed. Dan Banik (Bergen: Fagbokforlaget, 2006), 324–45; "Global Poverty: Development Ethics Meets Global Justice," *Globalizations*, 3 (2006), 1–18; "A Methodologically Pragmatist Approach to Development Ethics," *Journal of Global Ethics*, 3, 2 (2007): 143–64; Jesús Conill, *Horizontes de economía ética: Aristóteles, Adam Smith, Amartya Sen* (Madrid: Editorial Tecnos, 2004); Adela Cortina, *Por una ética del consumo: La ciudadanía del consumidor en el mundo global* (Madrid: Taurus, 2002); "Ética del desarrollo: Un camino hacia la paz," *Sistema*, 192 (May 2006): 3–17; Emilio Martínez Navarro, *Ética para el desarrollo de los pueblos* (Madrid: Editorial Trotla, 2000); Marta Pedrajas Herrero, "El desarrollo humano en la economía ética de Amartya Sen"; *Ethical Dilemmas of Development in Asia*, ed. Godfrey Gunatilleke, Neelan Tiruchelvam, and Radhika Coomaraswamy (Lexington, MA: Lexington Books, 1988); Peter John Opio, "Towards a New Economic Order: Needs, Functioning and Capabilities in Amartya Sen's Theory," MA thesis, Katholieke Universiteit Leuven, 1993. The "Digital Library" on the web page of the "Initiative on Social Capital, Ethics, and Development" of the Inter-American Development

Bank is a valuable resource of recent work, especially by Latin Americans, in development ethics: <etica@iadb.org>.

12. Bernardo Kliksberg, *Ética y desarrollo: La relación marginada* (Buenos Aires: Editorial El Ateneo, 2002). Earlier anthologies on ethics and development include *Ethics and Development: On Making Moral Choices in Development Cooperation*, ed. Cees J. Hamelink (Kampen: Kok, 1997); *El desarrollo humano: Perspectivas y desafíos*, ed. Aldo Ameigeiras (San Miquel, Argentina: Universidad Nacional de General Sarmiento, 1998); and *Ética, democracia y desarrollo humano*, ed. Parker. An urgent need exists for English-language collections of historically important and recent articles in development ethics.

13. Daniel Little, *The Paradox of Wealth and Poverty*.

14. Des Gaspar, *The Ethics of Development*. See also David Clark, *Visions of Development: A Study of Human Values* (Cheltenham: Edward Elgar, 2002). The Clark volume is a revised PhD thesis and case study rather than a textbook.

15. The groups' respective websites are the International Development Ethics Association, <www.development-ethics.org>; the Inter-American Initiative on Social Capital, Ethics and Development, <www.iadb.org/etica/ingles>; and the Human Development and Capability Association, <www.fas.harvard.edu/~freedoms>. Although not explicitly dedicated to development ethics, other associations – such as the Society for International Development, the United Nations Association, and the World Development Movement – have had serious ethical interests related to development and foreign aid.

16. University of Aberdeen (Scotland), Carleton University (Canada), Colorado State University (USA), Institute of Social Studies (the Netherlands), Michigan State University (USA), Makerere University (Uganda), New School University (USA), Stellenbosch University (South Africa), Uganda Martyrs University (Uganda), University of Bergen (Norway), Universidad de Costa Rica, University of Maryland (USA), Universidad de Múrcia (Spain), Universidad Nacional Autónoma de Honduras, Universidad Nacional Heredia (Costa Rica), University of Notre Dame (USA), University of Oslo (Norway), Universidad de Santiago (Chile), Universidad de of Valencia (Spain).

17. Richard M. Clugston and John A. Hoyt, "Environment, Development and Moral Values," in *Ethics and Development*, ed. Hamelink, 82–103.

18. Arturo Escobar, *Encountering Development: The Making and Unmaking of the Third World* (Princeton, NJ: Princeton University Press, 1995).

19. For a sample of such moral dilemmas in development practice and cooperation, see Crocker, "Toward Development Ethics," 461–4; *Ethics and Development*, ed. Hamelink; and Gasper, *The Ethics of Development*.

20. Although anti-corruption strategies sometimes encompass the objectives of poverty reduction and participatory democracy, a focus on controlling corruption often eclipses these larger development goals and becomes the only end considered. See, for example, Moisés Naím, "Bad Medicine," *Foreign Policy* (March–April 2005): 95–6.

21. See Nicholas D. Kristof, "When Marriage Kills," *New York Times* (March 30, 2005), A 27.

22. Carol Graham and Stefano Pettinato, *Happiness and Hardship: Opportunity and Insecurity in New Market Economies* (Washington, DC: Brookings Institution Press, 2002); John Rawls, *A Theory of Justice* (Cambridge, MA: Belknap Press of Harvard University Press, 1971; rev. edn., 1997); John Roemer, *Theories of Distributive Justice* (Cambridge, MA: Harvard University Press, 1996); Johann Galtung, "The New International Order and the Basic Needs Approach"; Manfred Max-Neef, *Human Scale Development: Conception, Application, and Further Reflections* (London: Apex Press, 1993); Streeten *et al.*, *First Things First*; Len Doyal and Ian Gough, *A Theory of Need* (London: Macmillan, 1991); Des Gasper, *The Ethics of Development*, ch. 6; Peter T. Bauer, *Dissent on Development* (London: Weidenfeld & Nicholson, 1971); Robert Nozick, *Anarchy, State and Utopia* (New York: Basic Books, 1974); Amartya Sen, *Development as Freedom*; Onora O'Neill, *Bounds of Justice*; David Ellerman, *Helping People Help Themselves: From the World Bank to an Alternative Philosophy of Development Assistance* (Ann Arbor: University of Michigan Press, 2005); Martha Nussbaum, *Women and Human Development: The Capabilities Approach* (Cambridge: Cambridge University Press, 2000); Thomas W. Pogge, *World Poverty*; "Can the Capability Approach Be Justified?," *Philosophical Topics*, 30, 2 (fall 2002): 167–228; Amartya Sen, "Elements of a Theory of Human Rights," *Philosophy and Public Affairs*, 32, 4 (2004): 315–56; Polly Vizard, *Poverty and Human Rights: Sen's "Capability Perspective" Explored* (Oxford: Oxford University Press, 2006); Bas de Gaay Fortman, "Human Rights," in *Elgar Companion*, ed. Clark, 260–6.

23. Thomas Nagel argues that duties of socioeconomic justice are the exclusive concern of sovereign states (and their citizens) in relation to their own (fellow) citizens. In relation to citizens of other countries, a sovereign state only has negative duties not to enslave, coerce, or violate civil liberties, as well as the positive duties of humanitarian assistance and rescue. See Thomas Nagel, "The Problem of Global Justice," *Philosophy and Public Affairs*, 33, 2 (2005): 113–47.

24. Pogge, *World Poverty and Human Rights*, 2. Cf. Thomas Nagel, "The Problem of Global Justice," 118. The first paragraph of the United Nations Development Programme's *Human Development Report 2005* drives home a similar point but without Pogge's important reminder of global disparities: "The tsunami was a highly visible, unpredictable and largely unpreventable tragedy. Other tragedies are less visible, monotonously predictable and readily preventable. Every hour more than 1,200 die away from the glare of media attention. This is equivalent to three tsunamis a month, every month, hitting the world's most vulnerable citizens – its children. The causes of death vary, but the overwhelming majority can be traced to a single pathology: poverty. Unlike the tsunami, that pathology is preventable. With today's technology, financial resources and accumulated knowledge, the world has the capacity to overcome extreme deprivation. Yet as an international community we allow poverty to destroy lives on a scale that dwarfs the impact of the tsunami" (United Nations Development Programme, *Human Development Report 2005* [Oxford: Oxford University Press, 2005]), 1.

25. Des Gasper is particularly eloquent in articulating the widely shared assumption that development agents face alternative paths and that development ethics emphasizes "value-conscious ways of thinking about and choosing between alternative paths and destinations" (Gasper, *The Ethics of Development*, xi).

26. United Nations Development Programme, *Human Development Reports* (Oxford: Oxford University Press, 1990–2008). These *Human Development Reports* operationalize the capability approach and address such themes as consumption, globalization, human rights, technology, democracy, the Millennium Development Goals, cultural identity, international cooperation, water, and climate change. See *Readings in Human Development: Concepts, Measures and Policies for a Development Paradigm*, ed. Sakiko Fukuda-Parr and A. K. Shiva (Oxford: Oxford University Press, 2003); Asunción St. Clair, "The Role of Ideas in the United Nations Development Programme," in *Global Institutions and Development: Framing the World?*, ed. Morten Bøås and Desmond McNeill (London: Routledge, 2004), 178–92; Mozaffar Qizilbash, "Human Development," in *Elgar Companion*, ed. Clark, 245–50; Amartya K. Sen, "Human Development Index," in *Elgar Companion*, ed. Clark, 256–60.

27. Amartya Sen and Jean Drèze, *Hunger and Public Action* (Oxford and New York: Oxford University Press, 1989).

28. Sen, *Development as Freedom*, 21.

29. See *Women, Culture and Development: A Study of Human Capabilities*, ed. Martha Nussbaum and Jonathan Glover (Oxford: Clarendon Press; New York: Oxford University Press, 1995).

30. Amartya Sen, "Elements of a Theory of Human Rights," *Philosophy and Public Affairs*, 32, 4 (2004): 333, n. 31.

31. World Bank, *World Development Report 2006: Equity and Development* (New York: World Bank and Oxford University Press, 2005), 3.

32. Ibid., 2.

33. The authors of *World Development Report 2006*, appealing to a narrow construal of the World Bank's mandate and comparative advantage, shy away from arguing for (any concept of) equity as intrinsically good or for any political design as normatively required. See, for example, ibid., 10, 20, and 206.

34. Michael Sandel, *Liberalism and the Limits of Justice* (Cambridge: Cambridge University Press, 1982).

35. Holmes Rolston III, "Feeding People Versus Saving Nature?," in *World Hunger and Morality*, ed. Aiken and La Follette, 248–66.

36. Joseph E. Stiglitz, *Globalization and Its Discontents* (New York: W. W. Norton, 2002), 218–19.

37. Sen, *Development as Freedom*, 53.

38. Charles R. Beitz, "Does Global Inequality Matter?," in *Global Justice*, ed. Thomas W. Pogge (Oxford: Blackwell, 2001), 113. See World Bank, *World Development Report 2006*, 206–7.

39. Pogge, *World Poverty*, 15, 21, 112–6, 141–5.

40. Ibid., 143.

41. In 2006 Pogge formulated a more balanced view of both global and national factors in causing and remedying human rights deprivations ("Severe Poverty: Harm Done Through Social Institutions," keynote address, 7th International Conference on Ethics and Development, International Development Ethics Association, Kampala, Uganda, July 19–22, 2006). He anticipated this more complex view in *World Poverty*, 50.

42. Onora O'Neill, "Agents of Justice," in *Global Justice*, ed. Thomas W. Pogge (Oxford: Blackwell, 2001), 188–203.

43. Joseph E. Stiglitz, *The Roaring Nineties: A New History of the World's Most Prosperous Decade* (New York: W. W. Norton, 2003), xii.

44. See, for example, Nussbaum, *Women and Human Development*; "Capabilities and Disabilities: Justice for Mentally Disabled Citizens," *Philosophical Topics*, 30, 2 (2002): 133–65; *Frontiers of Justice: Disability, Nationality, Species Membership* (Cambridge, MA: Harvard University Press, 2005); David A. Crocker, "Ética del desarrollo y grupos vulnerables," keynote address, Congreso Internacional Sobre Cooperación al Desarrollo, "Cooperacion y Grupos Vulnerables," November 17–19, 2005.

45. In addition to the articles by Rolston and by Clugston and Hoyt cited above, see *Ethics of Environment and Development: Global Challenge and International Response*, ed. J. Ron Engel and Joan Hoff Engel (London: Belhaven Press; Tucson, AZ: University of Arizona Press, 1990); Robin Attfield, *The Ethics of the Global Environment* (Edinburgh: Edinburgh University Press, 1999); *Global Sustainable Development in the 21st Century*, ed. Keekok Lee, A. Holland, and Desmond McNeill (Edinburgh: Edinburgh University Press, 2000); Peter J. Balint, "Balancing Conservation and Development: Two Cases Studies from El Salvador," PhD dissertation, School of Public Affairs, University of Maryland (December 2000); Partha Dasgupta, *Human Well-being and the Natural Environment* (Oxford: Oxford University Press, 2001); Amartya Sen, *Rationality and Freedom* (Cambridge, MA, and London: Belknap Press of Harvard University Press, 2002), ch. 18; Nigel Dower, "The Nature and Scope of Global Ethics and the Relevance of the Earth Charter," *Journal of Global Ethics*, 1, 1 (June 2005): 25–43.

46. Peter Singer, *One World: The Ethics of Globalization*, esp. chs. 2 and 3; Cortina, *Por una ética del consumo*.

47. For my writings and those of other scholars on reckoning with past wrongs, see my "Punishment, Reconciliation, and Democratic Deliberation," *Buffalo Criminal Law Review*, 5, 2 (2002): 509–49, esp. nn. 9 and 87; "Interpretative Ideals and Truth Commissions: Comments on Krausz's 'The Limits of Rightness,'" in *Interpretation and Its Objects: Studies in the Philosophy of Michael Krausz*, ed. Andreea D. Ritivoi and Giridhari L. Pandit (Amsterdam: Rodopi Publishers, 2003), 55–68; "Reckoning with Past Wrongs in East Asia," a paper presented to the workshop "Memory, Reconciliation and Security in the Asia-Pacific Region: Implications for Japan–US Relations," Hyogo, Japan, December 15–17, 2006.

48. United Nations Development Programme, *Human Development Report 1994* (Oxford: Oxford University Press, 1994).

49. Commission on Human Security, *Human Security Now: Protecting and Empowering People* (New York: Communications Development, 2003). See also Nigel Dower, "Development, Violence, and Peace: A Conceptual Exploration," *European Journal of Development Research*, 11, 2 (1999): 44–64; Des Gasper, "Violence and Human Security," in *The Ethics of Development*, ch. 5; "Securing Humanity: Situating 'Human Security' as Concept and Discourse," *Journal of Human Development: Alternative Economics in Action*, 6, 2 (July 2005): 221–45; United Nations Development Programme, *Human Development Report 2005*, ch. 5; Selim Jahan, "Human Security," in *Elgar Companion*, ed. Clark, 266–71.

50. Allan Thompson, "Arbour Ready for UN Role," *Toronto Star* (June 7, 2004), A 20.

51. See Lloyd Dumas, "Is Development an Effective Way to Fight Terrorism?," *Institute for Philosophy and Public Policy Quarterly*, 22, 4 (2002): 7–12. Whether development that reduces poverty also reduces humiliation depends on whether poverty is more than lack of income and whether a distinction is made between well-being (ill-being) and agency or empowerment (lack of agency). I owe this point to Des Gasper.

52. See, for example, Joseph E. Stiglitz and Andrew Charlton, *Free Trade for All: How Trade Can Promote Development* (Oxford: Oxford University Press, 2005); United Nations Development Programme, *Human Development Report 2005*, ch. 4.

53. See Celia W. Dugger, "An Exodus of African Nurses Puts Infants and the Ill in Peril," *New York Times* (July 12, 2004), A1, A8, for a shocking account of hospital conditions in Malawi and the fact that wretchedly poor pay is causing many nurses – seeking a better life for themselves and their families – to emigrate to Great Britain and elsewhere.

54. For Bernstein's writings on Dewey, ethics, and social-political philosophy, see above, ch. 1, n. 64.

55. Sabina Alkire made this point in the training session "The Capability Approach as a Development Paradigm," 3rd Conference on the Capability Approach, Pavia, Italy, September 7–9, 2003.

56. See above, p. 37.

57. For a response to what he calls "economism," see Gasper, *Ethics of Development,* esp. ch. 3. Stephen Schwenke and Ada Pizze of the Inter-American Development Bank's "Initiative for Social Capital, Ethics, and Development" persistently criticize development ethics for failing to deal with the moral issues of practitioners in the development trenches. For arguments that the concept of poverty, the ideal of participation, and the practice of development and development ethics are tools of Western imperialism, see *The Development Dictionary*, ed. Wolfgang Sachs (London: Zed, 1992).

58. Sympathetic and largely constructive critics include Jesús Conill, "Capacidades humanas," *Glosario para una sociedad intercultural*, ed. Jesús Conill (Valencia: Bancaja, 2002), 29–34; *Horizontes de economía ética*; Cortina, *Por una ética del consumo*; and Philip Pettit, "Capability: A Defence of Sen," *Economics and Philosophy*, 17 (2001): 1–20. In Chapter 7 below, not only do

I accept much of Cortina's criticisms of my earlier prudential version of the capability orientation, but I improve my earlier view by modifying it in the light of her Kantian consumption ethic. Sen accepts the thrust of some (but only some) of Pettit's alternatives in "Reply," *Economics and Philosophy*, 17 (2001): 51–6. Other recent critics are less supportive. They include Robert Sugden, "Welfare, Resources and Capabilities: A Review of *Inequality Reexamined* by Amartya Sen," *Journal of Economic Literature*, 31 (1993): 947–62; Richard J. Arneson, "Equality and Equal Opportunity for Welfare," *Philosophical Studies*, 56 (1989): 77–93; "Perfectionism and Politics," *Ethics*, 111, 1 (2000): 37–63; John Roemer, *Theories of Distributive Justice* (Cambridge, MA: Harvard University Press, 1996). For assessments of Nussbaum, see essays by Louise M. Antony, Arneson (referred to above), Hilary Charlesworth, and Richard Mulgan in "Symposium on Martha Nussbaum's Political Philosophy," *Ethics*, 111, 1 (2000). Nussbaum responds to these four assessments in "Aristotle, Politics, and Human Capabilities: A Response to Antony, Arneson, Charelsworth, and Mulgan," *Ethics*, 111, 1 (2000): 102–40. Three collections include important evaluations of both Sen's and Nussbaum's work on the capability orientation: *Women, Culture and Development*, ed. Nussbaum and Glover; *Feminist Economics*, 9, 2–3 (2003); and *Capabilities Equality: Basic Issues and Problems*, ed. Alexander Kaufman (New York: Routledge, 2006).

59. See *Feminist Economics*, 9, 2–3 (2003).
60. See Pogge, "Can the Capability Approach Be Justified?"
61. I thank Ingrid Robeyns for discussions bearing on this paragraph.
62. Several authors utilize one or the other and often both of these strategies. See Séverine Deneulin, "Perfectionism, Paternalism and Liberalism in Sen and Nussbaum's Capability Approach," *Review of Political Economy*, 14, 4 (2002): 497–518; Des Gasper, "Development as Freedom: Moving Economics beyond Commodities: the Cautious Boldness of Amartya Sen," *Journal of International Development*, 12, 7 (2000): 989–1001; "Is Sen's Capability Approach an Adequate Basis for Considering Human Development?," *Review of Political Economy*, 14, 4 (2002): 435–61; "Nussbaum's Capabilities Approach in Perspective – Purposes, Methods and Sources for an Ethics of Human Development," Working Paper (The Hague: Institute of Social Studies, 2003); Mozaffar Quizilbash, "Development, Common Foes, and Shared Values," *Review of Political Economy*, 14, 4 (2002): 463–80. Most of the articles in *Feminist Economics*, 9, 2–3 (2003) freshly assess Sen's work "through the lens of gender" and seek to mediate differences between Sen and Nussbaum. Especially important is Ingrid Robeyns, "Sen's Capability Approach and Gender Inequality: Selecting Relevant Capabilities," *Feminist Economics*, 9, 2–3 (2003): 61–92, in which Robeyns argues against one and only one list and for specific lists for particular purposes and contexts. See also Alkire, *Valuing Freedoms*; and "Public Debate and Value Construction in Sen's Approach," in *Capabilities Equality*, ed. Kaufman. Although closer to Sen than to Nussbaum, Alkire argues for some uses of lists. She also draws creatively on some ideas of John Finnis, a theorist outside the capability orientation.

63. The variety of democratic theory known as "deliberative democracy" also is in danger of becoming a new scholasticism. One way to guard against this threat (a way I will refer to and employ in Chapters 9 and 10) is to bring the theory of deliberative democracy into critical dialogue with other democratic theories and with institutional experiments in deliberative democracy.

64. My views in this paragraph owe much to discussions with Ingrid Robeyns. See Ingrid Robeyns, "The Capability Approach: A Theoretical Survey," *Journal of Human Development: Alternative Economics in Action*, 6, 1 (2005): 93–114. See also Sabina Alkire, "Why the Capability Approach?," *Journal of Human Development: Alternative Economics in Action*, 6, 1 (2005): 115–33.

65. James D. Wolfensohn and Amartya Sen, "Development: A Coin with Two Sides," *International Herald Tribune* (5 May 1999).

66. <www.iadb.org/etica/ingles>.

67. <www1.worldbank.org/publicsector/anticorrupt/LeadershipEthics/bbags.cfm? offset=5>.

68. See, for example, *Global Institutions and Development*, ed. Bøås and McNeill.

69. See Stephen Gould Schwenke, "Morality and Motivation: A Role for a Human Rights Approach in the World Bank's Urban Strategy?" PhD dissertation, School of Public Policy, University of Maryland, 2002; and Crocker and Schwenke, "The Relevance of Development Ethics for USAID."

3   Ethics and development theory-practice

In the first chapter I discussed the aims and trajectory of development ethics and my own participation in this new field. In the last chapter I charted the commitments, areas of consensus, controversies, and challenges facing development ethicists in the early twenty-first century. In the present chapter I clarify further the tasks and methods of development ethics by situating them in the context of what I call "development theory-practice."[1] Before clarifying what I mean by this term and its various ethical and non-ethical components, it will be helpful to provide two examples of moral critique, ethical analysis of policy goals, and ethical norms or principles as they emerge in actual moral dialogue about development. How do development scholars and practitioners – as well as academic ethicists – appeal to ethical norms in evaluating the present, resolving ethical controversies, and envisaging a better future? Sometimes the norms are left unanalyzed; sometimes they are consciously scrutinized. Almost always they are linked to other components, to be analyzed in later sections of this chapter, of a specific development theory-practice. In the examples of ethical assessment and debate that follow, I also take up some of these substantive issues, especially as they apply to Costa Rica, and try to make headway in resolving them.

Development ethics in action

As the first example of the practice of development ethics, consider the following 1987 interview in which a Costa Rican journalist questions the Brazilian development scholar Theotonio Dos Santos: "In accordance with the social, political, and economic conditions of Latin America, what would be the ideal development model in order to be able to surpass this stage of underdevelopment and dependency?"[2]

Not satisfied with a negative critique of Latin American underdevelopment and its dependency on rich nations or the international market, Dos Santos set forth the following vision of positive development:

We would have to develop ourselves [*desarrollarnos*] resolutely toward the satisfaction of the necessities of the population in addition to production for the internal and regional market. We also must increase investments in education, nutrition, health, transportation, that is, those things that attend to the basic needs of the population and that generate employment. Moreover, we should increase investment capability linked to a planned economic process. In the same way, we should disassociate ourselves from the maxim of the world market and the international economy – not totally, but as much as we can . . . An economy turned topsy-turvy [*volcada*] towards exports is, in the conditions in which we live, an economy of debt, the exporting of surpluses, and the accentuation of dependency.[3]

An important aspect of my own work in the late 1980s on Costa Rica had been to evaluate the theoretical assumptions – both normative and non-normative – and practical consequences of a development perspective that stresses, as does that of Dos Santos, basic human needs or basic capabilities.[4] I argued that securing for each Costa Rican the internal ability and external opportunity for a good human life should be "the moral minimum" of Costa Rican development. I adopted US philosopher Henry Shue's account of "moral minimum" as: "The lower limits on tolerable conduct, individual and institutional . . . the least every person can demand and the least that every person, every government, and every corporation must be made to do."[5]

In Chapter 4, I evaluate Amartya Sen's argument that a basic needs approach in development for the 1990s should be updated, reformulated, and deepened by an emphasis on "capabilities." I argue that Sen overstated the differences between the languages of basic needs and basic capabilities and that the idea of basic needs is needed to supplement the idea of basic capabilities.

Regardless of the outcome of this debate, Costa Rica, I argued at the close of the 1980s, should design and implement its development policies and institutions in order to satisfy people's basic needs and capabilities for physical well-being, social well-being, and political participation. I argued, however, that this principle ought to be supplemented and balanced by at least two other principles: respect for nature and democratic self-determination. In the present volume, I return to the norm of democratic self-determination and Dos Santos's notion of "self-development" and – particularly in Chapters 6 and 9 – explain it in relation to my interpretation of Sen's ideal of agency.

Today, we also see development ethics in action in the debate about different ways to clarify the relation between good development and the conserving or preserving natural resources, biodiversity, and wilderness. Compare the rival long-range visions offered by philosopher J. Baird Callicott in 1986 and journalist Nicholas D. Kristof in 2004. Callicott's vision of a development–conservation balance calls for more bears and fewer people:

> Surely we can envision an eminently livable, modern, systemic, civilized techno-logical society well adapted to and at peace and in harmony with its organic environment . . . Is our current mechanical technological civilization the only one imaginable? . . . Isn't it possible to envision, for example, a human civiliza-tion based upon nonpolluting solar energy for domestic use, manufacturing and transportation and small-scale, soil-conserving organic agriculture? There would be fewer things and more services, information, and opportunities for aesthetic and recreational activities; fewer people and more bears; fewer parking lots and more wilderness.[6]

In a lengthy but fascinating passage, Kristof offers an alternative to both Callicott's vision (less "development" and more preservation) and George W. Bush's outlook (more "development" and less conservation) and urges policies for non-wealthy people to enjoy bears in their (the bears', not the people's) own habitat:

> A focus on the American environmental movement has been conservation, and that's why there is such rage at the Bush administration's efforts to log, mine or drill patches of wilderness from the Arctic to Florida. President Bush has done more than any other recent president to shift our environmental balance away from conservation and toward development . . .
>
> Yet the environmental movement is wrong to emphasize preservation for the sake of the wolves and the moose alone. We should preserve wilderness for *our* sake – to remind us of our scale on this planet, to humble us, to soothe us. Nothing so civilizes humans as the wild.
>
> That means that we not only have to preserve wilderness, but we also must get more people into it. It's great that we have managed to save the Artic National Wildlife Refuge. But virtually the only visitors who get to enjoy it are super-wealthy tourists who charter airplanes to fly into remote airstrips.
>
> So how about a hiking trail from Artic Village going north to the Brooks Range, allowing many more people to enjoy the refuge? How about polar bear ecotourism in Kaktovik? Why not democratize the chance to hear wolves howl or be menaced by grizzlies?[7]

It is possible to combine the insights but reject certain aspects of both Callicott's and Kristof's visions. Instead of identifying "development," as does Kristof, with unregulated economic growth ("logging, mining, and drilling"), there is good reason to reconceive it as economic and political processes that expand important human capabilities and free-doms. Like Callicott, one can envisage human institutions in peaceful and mutually beneficial interaction with the natural world. Unlike

Callicott, however, one can emphasize not only that civilized institutions leave a reduced footprint on the natural world but also that these institutions provide opportunities for all to enjoy substantive freedoms. And among those freedoms, which Kristof affirms but Callicott ignores, is that of having real access to wilderness and benefiting from it. Ecotourism is a proven way to provide urban dwellers and other visitors this opportunity while at the same time expanding the capabilities of indigenous forest dwellers themselves. Appropriate ecotourism would exclude enterprises that outsiders own and control and whose profits flow out of the region. The best ecotourist companies are locally owned and operated. Their profits stay local. They emphasize environmental education and sustainable development. They are sensitive to the land's "carrying capacity" and recognize that too many visitors will harm local ecosystems and endanger future ecotourism. Good development means the expansion of valuable opportunities for all, which arguably include income-generating work as well as the enjoyment of wild areas.[8]

I also argued in the late 1980s (and continue to argue now) for a principle of self-determination or agency, a principle absent in the both the Callicott and Kristof passages quoted above. Democratic institutions and citizen participation are crucially important when a society seeks to balance – when they clash – ethical commitments to reduce poverty as well as to protect the environment. More generally, I argue in Part IV, democratic institutions provide a society with a method of weighing, balancing, and prioritizing clashing goods and incommensurable demands.

A conception of Costa Rican development informed by this principle of self-determination requires, I argued in the late 1980s, a network of grassroots communities that practice democratic self-management and scale-up to deepen Costa Rica's representative democracy. Costa Rica, justly famous for its tradition of *representative* democracy, has been described as a test case for democracy in a developing society where "demands tend to outrun resources, achievements to lag behind expectations and promises, and class conflicts to increase."[9] I defended the view, however, that Costa Rica, if it is to pass this test, must evolve toward a more participative as well as representative democracy. This democratic vision that seemed right for tiny Costa Rica in the late 1980s is one that I now believe has global reach. The conception of democracy and deliberative participation, which I work out in more detail in later chapters, is also the basis for my view that a society's democratic bodies should decide on the nature and balance of society's development principles and goals.

The very idea of a development theory-practice

These two examples of development ethics in action illustrate how development ethics, as moral assessment of the ends and means of societal change, has connection with science, policy formation, and institution-building. In the last chapter, I identified the questions that this ethical inquiry seeks to answer, some agreed-upon answers, and some remaining controversies as well as obstacles. My aim now is to show that one should morally evaluate development as an integral aspect of what I call a "development theory-practice."

A development theory-practice is a more or less integrated totality composed of the following components: (A) ethical and other normative assumptions, (B) scientific and philosophical assumptions, (C) development goals, (D) scientific or empirical understanding, (E) policy options and recommendations, (F) critique, and (G) development activities and institutions. As Hegel said, "first distinguish and then unite."[10] The present essay successively analyzes and shows the (ideal) relations among each of these "moments" of "development theory-practice." Figure 3.1 schematizes the components from the most abstract (A and B) at the top of the figure to the most concrete (G) at the bottom. The double horizontal lines indicate the distinction between theory (whether normative or empirical) and practice. The activity of critique is rooted in both theory and practice. The boxes on the left side of the figure express predominately normative considerations, the boxes on the right side indicate largely non-normative or empirical considerations, and the boxes located in the middle embody both the normative and the empirical. The activity of critique, rooted in both theory and practice, is on the figure's left side, for critique evaluates the past and present and prescribes what ought to be.

It must be emphasized that neither Figure 3.1's spatial order nor the sequence of my presentation indicates a temporal or one-way justificatory relation among the elements as they actually occur. Sometimes we think first and then act on the basis of our ideas. Sometimes we revise and correct our abstract ideas on the basis of concrete judgments that are part of or follow from our concrete actions. The more abstract elements are often appealed to in order to justify the more concrete ones. But abstractions can, and I would argue should, also be generated from, tested by, and revised in the light of concrete experiences, exemplars, and practices.[11] Consequently, the solid vertical lines in Figure 3.1 have arrowheads at both ends. Moreover, because I reject sharp and permanent "fact/value" and "empirical/normative" distinctions,[12] the horizontal broken lines signify a reciprocal influence between the normative, on the

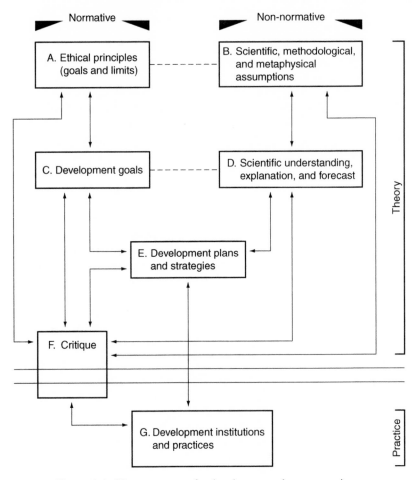

Figure 3.1. The structure of a development theory-practice

left side, and the non-normative, on the right. To say that facts and values, or empirical and ethical claims, are not completely separate is neither to say that they are identical nor to say that it is never worth trying to distinguish them. However, making this distinction is import-ant because it helps us, on the one hand, to uncover value assumptions that masquerade as facts or, on the other hand, to justify beliefs about what actions we *should* take.

The spatial separation of the boxes in Figure 3.1 not only reflects analytic distinctions but also permits or makes concessions to some professional division of labor. Perhaps Mario Bunge is right when he assumes that many people largely work in only one "box."[13] But, in contrast to Bunge, I would argue that many people live and work in various roles or activities at the same time, or change – quickly or gradually – from one to the other.

Figure 3.1's components, then, are distinguishable aspects of a more fundamental reality: the theory-practice of development. When we engage in this activity or field, we do different but related things. When we analyze and assess our own or another development theory-practice, we should expect to find the following components – although some may be implicit, implied, or incomplete and all will be interconnected in a complex but not seamless web. In this chapter, although I sometimes exemplify the general analysis with reference to my own work, I take no stand on which is the *best* development theory-practice. But neither is my analysis of the generic structure of such complexes ethically neutral. My general model will imply that some specific development theory-practices are better than others insofar as they explicitly include and successfully integrate the various components.[14] Let us now consider the nature and relations of each element.

Scientific understanding

Development researchers and investigative reporters seek to understand (in box D) development and underdevelopment as both processes and outcomes. They describe happenings and structures, interpret what these phenomena mean, and try to explain them. Investigators want to understand why nations are "developed," "undeveloped," or "developing." For example, which of the following are (always, sometimes) preconditions for or obstacles to (good) development: capital savings and investment; capitalist (or socialist) ownership of the means of production; class struggle; unions; cooperatives; the (democratic) state; transnational corporations; international lending agencies; and the global economic order?

Scientific understanding is pursued on various levels of generality. There are development studies of economic development as such as well as of developing countries, Latin America, Central America, Costa Rica, and the Talamanca region of Costa Rica. Some investigate the causal mechanisms that led to the failure to realize models popular in the past: for example, the eighteenth-century political model of constitutional democracy or the nineteenth- and twentieth-century economic model of export-led growth and comparative advantage.[15] Some try to explain why the import substitution model of the 1960s and 1970s resulted in a "new dependency."[16] Others identify obstacles that block the realization of new, alternative visions of development. The conservative columnist and Cuban exile Carlos Montaner, repeating what W. W. Rostow had argued twenty-six years earlier, provides a good example of the latter:

The poorest countries of the world are those that trade least and have fewest ties to the economic and financial network of the planet's leading nations. In Haiti, in Bolivia, in Bangladesh or in Ethiopia there is hardly any foreign capital that exploits the citizens of these countries. In the developed world, in contrast, every nation energetically fights to be exploited by foreign investors. We in Latin America cannot give ourselves the luxury of continuing to insist on the intimidating revolutionary language that blames entrepreneurs, industrialists, or financiers for the poverty of a country. It is just the opposite: if our countries are not richer, it is because there are not enough entrepreneurs, industrialists, agriculturists or financiers. What we ought to promote is not reproach but applause for those capable of accumulating wealth; for development is impossible without savings that can be converted into investments.[17]

To decide whether Montaner is right about his claims that savings are a necessary condition for development, one has to understand not only events in the world but also how Montaner is using the term "development." Hence, investigations of the causes of and obstacles to development are conceptual as well as empirical. It is often important to *define and justify* – or at least indicate how one is using – the concepts of development and underdevelopment as well as to gather and interpret phenomena and find their causes.

What we find in development research is not just differences in data sets but also a profusion of perspectives with "development" defined in purely economic terms, such as the rate of economic growth – per capita gross domestic product (GDP), gross national product (GNP), or gross national income (GNI) – or in terms that include a variety of political and social factors, such as "redistribution with growth,"[18] "material well-being with cultural autonomy,"[19] or "the removal of substantive unfreedoms."[20]

To describe (in box D) a region as developed, undeveloped, or underdeveloped often implies an evaluation (in box F) that development is good and underdevelopment bad. The choice of the concepts for understanding development in D (or B) can be linked to normative commitments in C (and A). Hence, the broken lines connecting the empirical (right) and valuational (left) side of Figure 3.1. For example, the use of the concept of class struggle, social conflict, or "ancient tribal animosities" can be informed by a commitment to a society with more social harmony or a more egalitarian distribution of power. The concept of gender is usually used by those who believe that unfortunately it is men who have benefited from development, while women – in spite of or because of their relative "invisibility" in "development theory-practice" – have borne its burdens.[21] Of course, someone who wanted to accentuate conflict could use the concepts of class conflict, and gender distinction could be employed by someone neutral or conservative on gender matters. The point is that often ethical or other normative commitments influence one's choice of descriptive, interpretative, and explanatory categories.[22] Such a "practical intention" is not, as German philosopher Jürgen Habermas argues, part of the *a priori* structure of certain social sciences; for, contrary to Habermas, one *can* pursue scientific knowledge exclusively for its own sake.[23] But such a practical intention is part of one's moral responsibility in the "theory-practice" of social change in general and development in particular.

Ethical as well as scientific values can also motivate inquirers to understand development as objectively and correctly as possible. Development and underdevelopment are phenomena that we should understand, especially if we want to achieve the first and avoid or overcome the second. It is hard to overcome underdevelopment if – as Peter Berger observed in 1974 – we let our hopes or fears distort our understanding of it.[24] And many investigators want to understand the world precisely in order to change it. It is important, and itself a moral obligation, to grasp the facts and their probable causes. Investigators then have the responsibility to use their knowledge to help change for the better the world that they now (more or less) understand.

Scientific and philosophical assumptions

The choices of descriptive and explanatory concepts in D often reflect and presuppose not only normative commitments (in C and A) but also philosophical or meta-scientific assumptions (in B) about reality, nature, human nature, society, social change, and the nature and methods of knowledge and a (good) science of development. For example, various development perspectives can be differentiated on the basis of at least eight sorts of assumptions.

The basic unit of analysis

One finds a number of fundamental units of analysis in theories of development and underdevelopment: utility-maximizing individuals; great personalities; economic classes in conflict (or consensus); the "block in power"; modes of production; ethnic or religious groups; nations; supranational regions; genders; and either an international order (divided into nation-states) or a global order (divided into center and periphery). For example, the dispute that occurred in the 1960s and

1970s between Marxism and dependency theory or world systems, within what Wilber and Jameson call "the political economy development paradigm," was a debate over which category should be more fundamental: national class struggle or the world economic system.[25]

Process or outcomes?

An even more fundamental presuppositional difference is exhibited between conceptions of development that emphasize development as a *process* of beneficial change and those that focus largely or exclusively on development as an *achievement* or desired *outcome*. Of course, some approaches seek to do empirical (and normative) justice to both aspects.

Methodological individualism or atomism versus holism?

As is the case throughout the social sciences, empirical studies of development and underdevelopment differ with respect to the way in which the fundamental units of analysis are combined or divided. Methodological individualists start from externally related atomic units and try to explain larger totalities as the sum or aggregate of such units. For example, neo-classical and neo-Keynesian economics explains economic growth and its absence in relation to individual human beings conceived as utility-maximizing and cost-minimizing agents. Development economics then goes on to explain the unity and diversity of the international economic system in terms of the relative success by which the units – in this case, externally related nation-states – pursue their national interest in development. And development is defined, returning to the microeconomic individual, as per capita GNP. As Geoffrey Hunt explains, methodological atomists view development and underdevelopment as "endogenous," that is, as an achievement or failure due primarily to the nation-state in question: "From the perspective of TDT [traditional development theory] propounded in the West, poverty is 'their problem' and wealth is 'our achievement.'"[26]

In contrast, holists see parts (entities, events, processes, and actions) as internally related to one another and structured by their role in a totality. For instance, Marxists analyze both individual behavior and capitalist underdevelopment as a function of a social formation structured by a "mode of production" that involves both "productive forces" and "productive relations" of unequal power. Uneven development is a function of class exploitation. Dependency and world system theorists, taking their unit of analysis to be the global economic system rather than a particular social formation, conceive underdevelopment to be the product of unequal international power and economic exchange. Underdevelopment of some nations is the structural result either of the development of other nations or of the international order dominated by the developed nations.[27]

The dimensions of analysis

Development can be understood in exclusively economic categories, as is often the case in mainstream development economics, or in social and political categories – for example, modernization theory. Development economics can become the "political economy of development and underdevelopment" when one or more of the following are added to economic concepts: political categories, such as power, the state, property relations, or, most generally, the "rules of the game";[28] social categories, such as caste, class, or stratum; and cultural categories such as ideology, values, religion, or cultural identity. And if an integral or comprehensive concept of development is sought (or presupposed), the various elements can be combined in a variety of ways – for example, as successive stages, reducible variables, or interacting factors.[29]

Synchronic versus diachronic

Some development approaches stress geography and spatial structure. For example, J. P. Dickenson and his colleagues preface their *A Geography of the Third World* by saying: "We feel that there is a need to present a contemporary geography of the Third World, exploring systematic themes in the development process and examining spatial patterns of development and underdevelopment at various scales within the Third World."[30]

Other development theorists give decisive weight to historical, evolutionary, or sequential factors. Keith Griffin exemplifies this "diachronic" perspective:

It was the social and political systems imposed by the colonists, in combination with the demographic changes which followed the Conquest, which were responsible for creating underdevelopment in Spanish America. One cannot explain the poverty of the region today without referring to the region's history.[31]

Inevitability or openness? Structure or agency?

Development perspectives also differ with respect to whether individuals, societies, or other units have freedom of action and, if they do, the nature and extent of that freedom. Is there only one road, predetermined and inevitable, toward development (as outcome)? Or is the future completely open, such that the failure to achieve development is simply a failure of will or the right goals? Do structures determine human action or does individual and collective agency determine structures?

Alternatively, consider Jorge Graciarena's attempt to avoid these extreme answers:

The future, far from being prefixed, is open and takes directions that are difficult to predict but are within certain historical limits that frame what is contextually possible . . . A real, concrete [development] style is always an alternative among various historically possible and potentially viable alternatives. The selection and application of one of these possible alternatives is a political act: the decision of political will formed by a hegemonic coalition of groups that represent social forces with sufficient resources of power to be able to impose the decision in place of other options . . . In a historically concrete and conditioned national situation there is always more than one option possible.[32]

Fundamental suppositions about the nature and reach of freedom are especially prominent when one offers a *general* theory of development. Notice the variety of assumptions involved in Graciarena's definition of "development style":

From a dynamic and integrated perspective, a development style is . . . a dialectical process between relations of power and conflicts, between groups and social classes that derive from dominant forms of capital accumulation, the structure and tendencies of income distribution, and the historical conjuncture and external dependency as well as from values and ideologies. All this occurs in the midst of other structural conditions (technology, natural resources, population) that are present in the analysis as an integrated totality that frames a style's historical possibilities.[33]

Fatalism and extreme determinism are clearly unreasonable and incompatible with efforts to bring about (improved) development. Development agents always confront some choices or alternatives, however constrained. Development "oughts" presuppose genuine development options or alternatives. Development goals presuppose purposive and (more or less) free agents. Economist Branko Milanovic puts the "conditioned freedom" view exactly right:

We can indeed explain past trends, because the history that underlies them (e.g., the Chinese Civil War, the Bolshevik revolution, colonialism, or the industrial revolution) is known to us, and the link between them and the observed outcomes can reasonably be made. But we cannot make sensible projections because we do not know the future political and social, and hence economic, history of the world. It is not because history is random, but because it is created through the interaction between an "objective" reality (institutions, preferences, the past) and actions of people endowed with free will. History is, as Vico wrote, what people make of it. Deterministic theories are incomplete because they cannot take into account that second element, human freedom of action (*le libre arbitre*). Moreover, under the false air of inevitability, they sap all effort to effect social change.[34]

As Milanovic suggests, this view of free will or freedom of choice has relevance for whether the investigator is justified in making (hard and fast) predictions. The anti-determinist assumption also coheres with the view that humans are or should be agents rather than patients and that development is best understood as the removal or reducing of serious unfreedoms. In Part II, I take up the explicitly normative issues when I analyze and strengthen Sen's agency-oriented view of development as freedom.

One road versus many? One science versus many?

Closely related to the considerations of free will and determinism is the question of whether there is *one* development path, whether inevitable or desirable, or *several*, whether determined or chosen. Ruccio and Simon argue, for example, that both mainstream capitalist and orthodox Marxist development theory assume that capitalist development is a normal and necessary stage of development and, more generally, that development is a unilinear process that all countries have undergone or will undergo:

For the neoclassical [theory of development], capitalism was the end of development, while for the Marxist, it was a necessary, if regrettable, stage to be transcended by socialism. But both agreed that any (nonsocialist) country that needed to develop had to do so within the framework of capitalism, and moreover, that the operations of the capitalist system (of course, conceived differently by the two positions) would lead to higher levels of development in the normal course of things.[35]

Furthermore, a unilinear approach assumes that all countries can be arranged on the same (quantitative) scale from least to most developed and that differences merely reflect different starting points and different rates of change.[36] In contrast, a multilineal approach assumes that different countries must, can, or should follow a more or less distinctive development path. For example, in Andre Gunder Frank's development theory, contemporary "Third World" countries, of necessity, develop differently than did those now developed countries precisely because the latter have produced adverse conditions for the former. There has been a "development," caused by colonialism and dependency, of "underdevelopment."[37] Hunt puts the point well in his analysis of "radical" development theories:

For RDT [radical development theory] it is this expansion ["imperialist expansion of capitalism"] that results in, and feeds on, underdevelopment. Underdevelopment is not, then, a universal original condition but an intrinsic dimension of the specifically capitalist mode of production in a late historical phase.[38]

Moreover, many theorists from the South assume that ends and means of their countries can and should be significantly different from Northern precedents. This view is often linked to a methodological historicism or particularism that assumes that general theorizing is either impossible or undesirable because of the important historical and cultural differences among countries (and investigators). Hence, the multilinearists typically differ from the unilinearists on what counts as good (development) science. Unilinearists stress the general and universal and presuppose that science is, in some sense, transhistorical. Multilinearists focus on the local, particular, and indigenous; they charge unilinearists and generalists with (an often unconscious) Western or Northern ethnocentrism, and they advocate such things as a Latin American or African social sciences of development.[39]

Essential versus historical human nature

Development theorists who posit one (deterministic) development path and one transcultural development science typically "ground" their development descriptions, explanations, predictions, and prescriptions on a view that their one principle of change is based on an unchanging human essence. As Hunt says, "neo-Keynesians still appeal to supposed features of human nature (diminishing marginal propensity to consume, preference for liquidity, love of prestige) as transhistorical determinants of economic change."[40] In contrast, other development theorists deny that there is a permanent human nature.[41] Humans can be said to have the "nature" of not having an essential nature or of having the freedom to determine their own nature. What people are is a function of changing relations of specific historical traditions, social production, nature, and – on voluntarist versions – their own choice.

The strategy of the historicist or particularist thinker, says US philosopher Richard Rorty, "has been to insist that socialization, and thus historical circumstance, goes all the way down – that there is nothing 'beneath' socialization or prior to history which is definatory of the human."[42] Historicist development theorists doing development theory in and for their own "social formation" argue that the question "What is it to be a developed human being and society?" should be replaced by questions such as "What is it to be authentic Costa Ricans and have genuine Costa Rican development?" and "How can an inhabitant of our poor 'underdeveloped' society be more than the enactor of a role in a development script written for another place and time?"[43]

Increasingly, economists such as Sen and social scientists such as Jane I. Mansbridge argue that economics has been straitjacketed by egoistic assumption about human motivation.[44] However self-interest is defined – as individual welfare, individual goals, or individual choices – Sen argues that (1) people can have good reasons for acting against their self-interest and that (2) self-interested motivation fails to explain differences in economic productivity among countries.[45]

As I discussed briefly in Chapter 2 and will explain more fully in later chapters, Sen's capability approach, and the use to which I put it in defending deliberative democracy, assume that human beings both are shaped by their group affiliations and have some freedom to shape and transcend their (multiple) identities. Such a view seeks to finesse the essentialist/historicist dichotomy with respect to human "nature."[46]

The above illustrates the way in which development science or development theory in box D can have philosophical or meta-scientific assumptions in box B. The assumptions are not directly part of the scientific investigation of facts, causes, and patterns; rather, they make possible that investigation by supplying its categories. This relationship between B and D is usually non-deductive. B suggests or permits rather than deductively entails D. It is possible that two theory-practices could have the same assumptions in B and yet differ in D (or offer similar descriptions and explanations in D even though their assumptions vary). Moreover, as mentioned earlier, assumptions in B may be modified by anomalies discovered by empirical work in D. Finally, just as the choice of a descriptive vocabulary in D is linked to one's normative commitments in C or A, so scientific and philosophical assumptions include or are related to normative assumptions in A. In both the unilinear and multilinear assumptions discussed above, as well as in essentialist and historicist assumptions about human nature, the line is blurred between what is and what ought – or ought not – to happen in development. The components of a development theory-practice interact within the larger totality.[47]

Critique

We not only want to understand "developed" and "developing" countries, but we also want to determine what is good and bad about a country's being developed or remaining underdeveloped. We want to praise, criticize, and sometimes lay blame; for example, in relation to India's Bhopal disaster in 1983 or Argentina's economic collapse in 2001–2. Hence, (in box F) we make moral judgments the way a clinician would make judgments about her patient's health or illness, improvement or decline. We make these assessments either by reference to (a group's) development goals (in C) or to (its or the evaluator's) more abstract ethical principles (in A). It is also important to evaluate past and present development policies or plans (in E) and actual projects or practices (in G). All these assessments take place in box F.

Sometimes, of course, our evaluations are nonmoral; we judge how efficient or effective the strategies (in E) have been in realizing the goals (in C).[48] In terms of scientific values, such as simplicity and attention to counter-evidence, we evaluate causal explanations. But it is also important explicitly to raise ethical questions about developing societies and other groups and their goals. How important, ethically speaking, *is* the value of efficiency in relation to other goals? We have achieved our development goals, but are they right, just, or best? Moreover, it is not uncommon to find out in practice that we cannot live with our habitual goals or that we need to revise or improve upon them. Good development ethics does not just apply a preformed, *a priori* ethics to practice; through critique linked to practice we can improve our development goals and ethical principles. Consequently, I have placed box F (critique) on the line that divides theory and practice, for critique looks in both directions. Moreover, in the light of other aspects of development theory-practice, development ethicists engage in a critique of critiques: they assess the strengths and weaknesses of their and others' earlier assessments.

It should be underscored that critique is not always negative. It identifies the good as well as the bad. It finds institutional limitations on the good that make it, on balance, bad; but these constraints might be removed so that the good comes to fuller and less compromised realization. The new and better can be conceived and nurtured in the womb of the old and limited.

This conception of "dialectical critique" is meant to include a spectrum of diagnoses and prescriptions – from minor ills to be solved by piecemeal remedies to mortal diseases, such as (bad) development, the latter to be overcome by incremental structural transformation or by revolution. Our speaking of critique, then, leads us to other moments of development theory-practice, namely, conceptions of possible and better futures.

Delineation of options

It is important to understand and evaluate not merely the past and the present. Development scholars and practitioners are also interested in the future. Unless a theory is fatalistic or deterministic, it identifies a developing society's *options* for action, its possibilities for change. I have put such delineation of options in box E because they are policy options, possible courses of action. These options, however, are also related to box D and the scientific understanding of causal mechanisms. More determinist approaches will offer forecasts, projections based on current trends, and even detailed predictions, the latter employed to support or disconfirm causal explanations. Such forecasts of the future are more or less probabilistic, and normally, the longer the range, the less reliable the forecast. Those who call themselves "futurists" explicitly argue that what they offer is more an art of exploring future possibilities than a predictive or even probabilistic science.[49] In any case, development delineation of options vary with respect to whether they are based on present trends or on *changes* in prevalent human action patterns. British philosopher Onora O'Neill puts the point well in relation to predictions of famine:

These predictions are contingent upon certain assumptions about what people will do in the pre-famine period. Famine is said to be inevitable *if* people do not curb their fertility, alter their consumption patterns, and avoid pollution and consequent ecological catastrophes. It is the policies of the present that will produce, defer, or avoid famine.[50]

Another way to put the point is to say that the term "future possibility" is ambiguous. On the one hand, what is possible for a society are those options open to it, given its present structures and patterns of human conduct. On the other hand, what is possible for a society includes, in addition, those options that emerge if and when structures are changed and people act in new ways. A development option that is impossible now may become "feasible" in the future when people act to remove present impediments or establish requisite preconditions. Innovative social theorists can eliminate intellectual obstacles, and creative social agents can "tear up" calcified meanings and surpass what had seemed to be institutional limits.[51] We ought not restrict our analysis of options to what is feasible now or in the short run. In the depths of World War II, the idea of a United Nations or Marshall Plan seemed preposterous to many. It is important to have medium- and long-run perspectives that take into account the results of obstacle-removing human action. As US political theorist Charles Beitz says: "One needs to distinguish two classes of reasons for which it may be impossible to implement an ideal. One class includes impediments to change that are themselves capable of modification over time; the other includes impediments that are unalterable and unavoidable."[52]

Many moral disagreements hinge on conflicting empirical estimates about the possible or probable consequences of various courses of action. For example, the controversy I briefly discussed in Chapters 1 and 2 (and a topic to which I return in Chapter 8), between two utilitarian ethicists, Peter Singer and Garrett Hardin, over the "ethics of famine relief," largely if not entirely reduces to different forecasts over the impact of aid on famine victims and on the larger societal structures.[53] Singer argues that affluent people are morally obligated to send food aid because – or, better, if and when – it prevents, better than available alternative actions, the bad consequences of death and suffering. In contrast, Hardin argues not just that we have no such moral duty, but that we have the duty *not* to send famine relief. His argument is based on the forecast that such aid causes worse long-term consequences than sending no aid at all. Aid recipients, he predicts, will use their added longevity to produce more mouths to feed and, thereby, further transcend the limits of the environment's "carrying capacity." Moreover, for Hardin, a pernicious consequence of aid is that the beneficiary learns to be a passive, dependent recipient of another's charity, rather than an active producer for or prudent investor in the future.

It might seem that this debate between Singer and Hardin could easily be resolved by empirical investigations about the actual short- and long-term consequences of aid. It should be noted, however, that this is not always so simple. For one thing, the data are complex and resist facile generalizations that aid is always or never beneficial.[54] For another, forecasts sometimes express (and conceal) what prognosticators *hope* to see rather than what they *expect* to see (the same thing frequently occurs when someone "predicts" that his or her favorite team will win the World Cup). Sometimes the real difference between two forecasts is due to different moral evaluations of the same phenomena, such as the moral weight given to undoubted present suffering compared to probable future misery. However, since many investigators cling to value or moral neutrality, they bury their moral judgments in what should be a (relatively) value-free part of their inquiry. They let their hopes or fears distort their estimate as to what is possible and likely. Although development theory-practice should make an important place for moral judgment and ethical reflection, it should not confuse judgments about what is possible or likely with judgments about what is good or obligatory. The rejection of the dogma of value neutrality would encourage analysts to make their moral commitments explicit and open to rational scrutiny rather than permit these assumptions to function in a subterranean manner.[55]

Identification of options and likelihoods should avoid both utopian dreaming and "crack-pot" realism. Objective forecasts of feasible options for social change are important for development theory-practice, for they enable us to avoid quixotic goals. The feasible or practically possible is not the same as what is only logically or remotely possible. It is also true, however, that the probable is not the inevitable. We should reject a "hard-headed" realism that baptizes an often unjust status quo when better possibilities are in fact available.

Unfortunately, the future is often hazy, and social projections can be as unreliable as weather forecasting. Moral reflection includes consideration of our moral obligations and ethical principles in situations where we often have only imprecise estimates of probabilities.[56]

Moreover, that I treated forecast before I considered ethical norms should not be taken to imply an invariable sequence. Sometimes what is possible and feasible only becomes apparent from the perspective of a transformative ideal. After committing ourselves to a new and ethically inspiring goal, what had been neutral or even an obstacle with respect to other aims now becomes an opportunity. Furthermore, it is not the case that we always first discover what is possible and then select what is desirable. Sometimes we start with our ends, and then cast about for means. It is to a consideration of the explicitly normative or ethical dimensions of development theory-practice that we now turn.

Development goals and ethical principles

Frequently, moral principles and judgments come into play directly and explicitly when, after analyzing the feasible futures, people choose (in box C) the best of these futures, the basic development goals they intend to pursue. One engages in *relevant* or *realistic* utopianism by selecting a future – from among the available options – that is on balance morally best as well as realizable. One method of doing so is (1) to identify the fragmentary and embryonic advances made in present thought and action, and (2) to affirm the progressive elements while criticizing the aspects that block further flourishing of what is promising. We can improve the good by (partially) liberating it – both theoretically and practically – from its historical limitations.[57]

Sometimes the appropriate critique (in F) of the present and the identification (in C) of the best feasible option for the future are obvious, and immediately we go on to decide (in E) what strategy would be most efficient to reach the desired goal. Sometimes it is not important to appeal to goals or principles. Sometimes we are surer of our concrete judgments than we are of any abstract norms. Sometimes, however, we are justifiably hesitant about our concrete judgments. We worry about biases in our commitments and our past policies or principles, especially when carrying them out has had unintended but negative consequences. We sense an inconsistency among our concrete moral judgments, between them and our development goals, or among our development goals. In these cases, it is appropriate to engage in ethical reflection and dialogue with others. And this reflection includes a consideration of general norms. These norms can be either basic conceptions of (good) development (in C) or, on a more abstract level, ethical principles (in A).[58]

Development ethics consists, then, not only of concrete critique and judgments of moral responsibility, but also reflection on both the general direction in which a society *should* develop and the abstract ethical principles that can guide the choice of these goals. A reasonable development ethic, in the context of development theory-practice, *explicitly* clarifies, defends, applies, and revises development goals and ethical norms that are realizable locally, regionally, nationally, and globally.

Before looking at some examples of such substantive ethical proposals, let us pause to consider some "metaethical" issues concerning the nature of development ethics. The first is the question of whether development ethics should engage in reflection on general abstract ethical principles (in A) or rather should restrict itself to critical reflection on development goals (in C) and critique (in F). In "Tasks and Methods in Development Ethics," Denis Goulet distinguishes four levels of ethical discourse:

Ethical discourse is conducted at four distinct levels: general ends, specific criteria which determine when these ends exist in concrete situations, clusters of interrelated means or systems which constitute strategies congenial or uncongenial to the ends sought, and individual means taken separately.[59]

After discriminating these levels, Goulet argues as follows:

In questions of social change the sharpest ethical disagreements arise in the two middle realms . . . Discussion over general ends rarely engenders debate because such ends are deemed to be universal and are easily disguised behind verbal smokescreens. Even tyrants profess to cherish freedom and warmongers to seek peace. Hence many apparent debates over general ends – ideal conceptions of justice, freedom, reciprocity, equity – are, in truth, controversies over the concrete marks or institutions by which the presence of these ideals can be detected . . . One's ethical stance on ends is dramatically revealed in the means one adopts to pursue them. Consequently, development ethics as "means of the means" requires not that moralists pose ideal goals and pass judgment on the means used by others to pursue these or other goals, but rather that decision-makers, versed in the constraints surrounding vital choices, promote the values for which oppressed and underdeveloped groups struggle: greater justice, a decent sufficiency of goods for all, and equitable access to collective human gains realized in technology, organizations, and research.[60]

Although I agree with much of Goulet's approach, I think this argument is problematic at several points. First, as a matter of fact, there is much evidence to challenge his contention that debate over general ends is rare. It is true that ideals such as liberty, equality, and justice have been and continue to be widely affirmed and that tyrants and many others use noble ideals as camouflage or rationalizations for ignoble acts. But we also find widespread and intense debate about what we should mean or how we should understand these principles. Not just philosophers but also politicians, policymakers, columnists, citizens, and "oppressed and underdeveloped groups" argue about how ideals should be understood and prioritized if we are to think clearly, live with ethical sensitivity, be true to our communities' traditions and hopes, and promote a better world.[61]

Second, not only *do* people deliberate about these norms, they *should* do so both individually and collectively. Such deliberations are often worthwhile for several reasons. They enable critics to unmask the very perversion of moral ideals that Goulet correctly worries about. Debates about fundamental norms are one way of getting clear about alternative social projects and superior social possibilities. Dialogue on abstract themes is one way of "hammering out" new and better conceptions of who a people should be and what they should be committed to. Democratic deliberation about ends as well as means, I shall argue in Chapters 9 and 10, both is a fair way for a group to make collective choices and contributes to individual agency and group empowerment.

Such abstract norms certainly need not and, arguably, should not be viewed as philosophical "foundations" that have to be settled first and from which we deductively derive specific moral judgments and courses of action. For, as I argued earlier, we often do and should revise our more abstract ethical norms on the basis of our concrete experience and judgments about existing practices. Goulet is correct in affirming that one's abstract ethical principles are often revealed through the means one adopts to realize them. But from that point it does not follow that there is no independent role for such principles. Sometimes we are clearer about more abstract principles than we are about more concrete norms or practical judgments; consequently the former sometimes guide us when we decide on the latter. Abstract principles can enable us to perceive in a new way and direct us to challenge accepted practices, especially those constraints that policymakers dogmatically view as given.

This is not to say that development ethics should be done only by "outsiders," let alone by those philosophers who adopt a "God's-eye view." One must concede to Goulet that much social-political philosophy – and not just the Anglo-American varieties – is little more than academic dreaming or intellectual gymnastics with little connection to economic, social, and political realities and even less relevance for public policy dialogue and formation. And certainly I do *not* advocate moralistic finger-wagging. However, if development ethics uncritically accepts what policymakers and citizens perceive as fixed norms and constraints, it most definitely will lose the very opportunity for "creating new possibilities" that Goulet stresses so well. Just as the development ethicists engaged in critique (Figure 3.1's box F) may assess development goals "from below" in the light of concrete experiences and judgments, so they may assess development practices "from above" in the light of innovative but still general versions of abstract ideals.[62]

It is interesting that Rorty, like Goulet, also questions the relevance to actual policy and political debates of "analytic philosophers who specialize in applied ethics."[63] For Rorty, these philosophers err because they claim "that there are special skills associated with analytic philosophy which are useful in resolving policy dilemmas." Similarly, Rorty criticizes "non-analytic" leftist philosophers who try to "relate philosophical doctrines and vocabularies . . . to politics."[64] They fail, says Rorty, because they have "gotten over-theoretical, over-philosophical" and, especially since the late 1960s in the US, have "taken less and less interest in what the rest of the country is worrying about."[65] Rorty does mention one exception to this general indictment:

Habermas, almost alone among the eminent philosophers of the present day, manages to work as Dewey did, on two tracks. He produces both a stream of philosophical treatises and a stream of comment on current events. I doubt that any philosophy professor since Dewey has done more concrete day-to-day work in the political arena, or done more for the goals of US social democrats. Habermas's connection with the German SPD is exactly the sort of eminently useful connection that leftist academics influenced by Dewey used to have with the Democratic Party in the United States.[66]

Unfortunately, Rorty's own highly abstract and meta-theoretical reflections largely fail to put into practice what I would argue is entailed by his own approach – not two separate "tracks" but engaged, revisable, critical assessments of live policy options and of proposals for promising alternatives. Regrettably, Rorty ignores non-analytic thinkers, such as Adela Cortina and Denis Goulet, and "post-analytic" philosophers, such as Robert K. Fullinwider, William A. Galston, Judith Lichtenberg, Jonathan Moreno, Martha Nussbaum, Thomas Pogge, Mark Sagoff, Peter Singer, and David Wasserman, who do ethically oriented public policy but do not believe they have unsharable "analytic skills." Although Rorty might not consider these thinkers to be "eminent philosophers of the present day," they are making contributions to a variety of "theory-practices." And one way they are making this contribution is in arguing for and promoting – in their teaching, writing, lecturing, and consulting – the shareable skills of ethical critique and reflection.[67] Ethical reflection will come to grips with "the day-to-day" debates about international development only if applied philosophers as well as other ethicists do development ethics – however abstractly or concretely – in the context of the scientific and practical components of development theory-practice.

Development plans and strategies

Much philosophical ethics hitherto has failed to attend to questions of *achieving* or *institutionalizing* moral norms – as if correct moral thinking were all that was needed and then the world would automatically "right itself." Once again I reject both sharp fact/value as well as conceptual/empirical distinctions. Challenging the notion of philosophy and ethics as exclusively expert knowledge, I advocate a culture in which conceptual, ethical, and political questions are debated by many citizens, whether or not they are professional philosophers or ethicists. Indeed, just as it is important for those who call themselves philosophers to be more knowledgable about empirical and political matters, so social scientists, politicians, development practitioners, and citizens should be more capable of applying moral intelligence to development matters. In my experience it is interdisciplinary people who can be expected to do the best interdisciplinary work.

Taking into consideration – but also contributing to – science, ethics, and evaluation of past practice, development planners formulate policies, design projects, and recommend actions. The questions now are: What ought to be done? Who ought to do it? When and how ought they to do it? Who should make these social decisions and how? What are the social mechanisms or institutional designs and devices available to realize and maintain the chosen model of authentic development?

Practical, nontheoretical questions now dominate attention because development agents plan and recommend in order to transform the world and achieve (their concept of) development as beneficial change. Ethics is not forgotten, for we must still consider various strategies from an ethical as well as an economic or political point of view. We want an ethics of means as well as an ethics of principle and vision. We want an ethics of social change in an unjust world, where we want to avoid being either moral fools or amoral operators.[68] We want good outcomes but we want to achieve them by just and fair means. We need to ask not only which means efficiently and effectively will obtain our ends, but also which means are ethically intolerable, acceptable, or obligatory. Moreover, we should question the relative importance of standard notions of economic efficiency when they collide with other goals or constraints such as cultural identity or human rights. We should clarify and evaluate the implicit ethical assumptions, content, and consequences of various development strategies and tactics.

Collective agency, an important theme throughout this book, means that citizens acting in concert with and through their elected representatives are responsible for the development of their own community, region, and country. If countries are to progress towards the goal of authentic development, it will be largely because of critical discussion among and collective participation by citizens themselves, especially those worst off. More generally, in ethically justified development, a people – sometimes with assistance from outsiders – defines and develops *itself* and is not coerced or developed *by* someone else. The implication for national or international development professionals is clear. The help they give to others should enhance autonomy rather than produce dependency.

More than ninety years before Sen's concern to rehabilitate the notion of agency and its implications for outside assistance and democracy promotion, John Dewey and James H. Tufts criticized what Robert B. Westbrook calls the "paternalistic benevolence" of social leaders or reformers:

The vice of the social leader, of the reformer, of the philanthropist and the specialist in every worthy cause of science, or art, or politics, is to seek ends which promote the social welfare in ways which fail to engage the active interest and cooperation of others. The conception of conferring the good upon others, or a least attaining it for them, which is our inheritance from the aristocratic civilization of the past, is so deeply embodied in religious, political, and charitable institutions and in moral teachings, that it dies hard. Many a man, feeling himself justified by the social character of his ultimate aim (it may be economic, or educational, or political), is genuinely confused or exasperated by the increasing antagonism and resentment which he evokes, because he has not enlisted in his pursuit of the "common" end the freely cooperative activities of others. This cooperation must be the root principle of the morals of democracy.[69]

Concrete and detailed recommendations, of course, are appropriate in development planning. These practical proposals may range from large-scale, regional, or national hydroelectric projects, to small, neighborhood credit unions for single mothers. Like the clinician, the development planner is intent on improving these particular people or, better, enabling them to improve themselves. It is important that general theories be supplemented and corrected by the idiosyncrasies of a unique country or supranational or subnational region in a particular phase of its history.

A further – sometimes neglected – point is that moral principles and goals can enter into development policymaking in two different ways.

As norms (in either boxes A and C of Figure 3.1) for what is good or right, development planners themselves make planning decisions inspired, guided, or constrained by ethical principles and development goals. However, the planner may also recommend that certain values be promoted, scrutinized, or weakened in a population as a *means* to achieve some other development goal such as economic growth or democratic decision-making. The presence (or absence) of certain operative values explains the presence (or absence) of development success or failure (variously conceived). Then, on the basis of this alleged causal link, the development theorist recommends, on the basis of what she considers to be the most reasonable principles, the promotion, strengthening, or weakening of certain (perhaps different) values that function in the society being investigated. For example, some mainstream economists assume and/or recommend "rationality," conceived as self-interested behavior, as the explanatory and causal key to development. Mitchell A. Seligson describes a version of this approach to explaining and removing the widening international and domestic gaps between rich and poor:

The widening gap between rich and poor nations is viewed as being principally a cultural problem. Specifically, the cultural values associated with industrialization are seen as foreign to many developing nations, which are deeply attached to more traditional values. Yet the values of punctuality, hard work, achievement, and other "industrial" values are keys to unlocking the economic potential of poor countries, according to these scholars. Most adherents of this perspective believe that such values can be "inculcated" in a population through deliberate effort. Others argue that the values will emerge naturally as the result of a worldwide process of diffusion of values functional for development. This perspective has been incorporated into a more general school of thought focusing on the process called "modernization." Development occurs and the international gap is narrowed when a broad set of modern values *and* institutions are present.[70]

On this first account, development scholars treat values scientifically and instrumentally rather than normatively or critically. Development social scientists, such as anthropologists, describe values or moral norms operative in the lives of people and ask whether these moral commitments help explain and forecast development and underdevelopment. Policymakers often want to know what moral commitments, if any, are aids or obstacles for bringing about development.

Critical or reflective ethics, on the other hand, does not only value moral commitments instrumentally, it also asks what principles (ends and constraints) would be intrinsically good or reasonable to have, and how they should be promoted (consistent with human agency and other values). Development ethics asks what *should be* the ends and morally acceptable means of development rather than merely how societies mobilize values to reach some *given* conception of development. Planners and other development agents *do* ethics when they reflect ethically on development ends and means. They *use* moral values instrumentally when trying to instill them as factors to bring about some model of development. Even if it is scientifically correct that "industrial" values explain and are causal factors in (some view of) development, it follows neither that these values are justified, nor that it is ethically permissible to "inculcate" them, nor that the development model in question is ethically justified.

These remarks can be summarized in relation to Figure 3.1. What one development theory-practice proposes (in A) as an ethical principle, or (in C) as a development goal, a contending theory-practice may advocate (in E) as a means, based on scientific understanding (in D) of the value or moral belief as a causal factor. Moreover, it is also possible that the same value can be viewed as both a reasonable end and an efficient (and morally acceptable) means. Basic need satisfaction or capacity-building, for instance, can be viewed as ends of development, the means to economic growth, or both ends and a means. Economic growth can be viewed as the goal of development or as the means to basic need satisfaction or capability expansion, or both. In Sen's capability approach, "expansion of freedom is viewed as both (1) the *primary end* and (2) the *principal means* of development."[71]

This view that the same variable can be both an end and a means provides a basis for a criticism of some positions taken on so-called "social capital" or "human capital." These approaches are flawed when they view human beings, their education, skills, and trusting relationships, as *only* "means of production" and not also as "the end of the exercise":[72]

While economic prosperity helps people to have wider options and to lead more fulfilling lives, so do more education, better health care, finer medical attention, and other factors that causally influence the effective freedoms that people actually enjoy. These "social developments" must directly count as "developmental," since they help us to lead longer, freer and more fruitful lives; *in addition* to the role they have in promoting productivity or economic growth or individual incomes.[73]

Three additional points are relevant to the relations of different levels of Figure 3.1. First, boxes C and D together rarely deductively entail E. Practical reasoning is an art, which the Greeks termed *phronēsis*, wherein more abstract beliefs can help one arrive at practical diagnoses, prognoses, or recommendations but do not logically entail them.[74] One implication, which I spell out in my analysis of deliberative democracy, is that two individuals (or subgroups of a group) may reach the same policy from different normative and empirical starting points. Even people at odds over ultimate goals and basic beliefs may agree on courses of action. Second, two individuals (or subgroups) can have the same development commitments and beliefs and derive (without inferential error) diverse proposals for practice. Third, although the idea of a development-theory practice implies that the integration (without fusing) of a theory-practice's components is a good thing, a certain looseness among the components is also desirable. If a development theory-practice were a seamless web or a prison, deliberation among proponents of *different* theory-practices would be extremely difficult. When theory-practices share some components and when a theory-practice's components do not all stand or fall together, deliberation among persons representing rival perspectives may yield innovative agreements and solve practical problems.

Practice

Norms and policies are more or less realized in many sorts of development actions and practices. Practice, both good and bad kinds, occasions theorizing. Theory generally guides agents who act to bring about (their conception of) development. People theorize, normally, with the intention of changing as well as understanding the world. As Aristotle realized, people engage in reflective ethics not just better to understand the good, but ultimately to do good, "to act on our knowledge."[75] Likewise, theorists and practitioners engage in development theory-practice not just to understand good and better development, but to bring it about.

The practice and the theory of development are, ideally, dialectically related within a development theory-practice. Neither has permanent priority. It is important to revise our policy and institutions on the basis of theoretical successes and failures. Likewise, we should revise our normative and non-normative theories on the basis of our practical achievements and failures. An unsettling gap frequently exists between the ideal and the real, between Figure 3.1's boxes A, C, and E, on the one hand, and box G, on the other. Critique in box F can be unflinchingly honest about this gap between theory and practice. Critique helps us tailor ethical principles and development goals to real world challenges. Critique also enables us to learn the lessons of cases of failure as well as success. As Sen remarks in words with Deweyan echoes: "While . . . success stories have to be supplemented by accounts of failures and deflections, lessons can be learned from what went wrong, in order to do things better next time. Learning by doing is a great ally of the rationalist reformer."[76]

The closing of the gap between theory and practice, however, is more than a discursive cliché or a theory. It also depends on individual and collective development agents putting their ethical commitments into practice to improve basic institutions – be they local, national, or global. Australian Anna Malavisi, the former Field Director in Bolivia for International Service, puts it exactly right:

There is a risk that ethics becomes just another "buzzword" in the development debate, being understood in a superficial way, diluting its true significance. Including an ethical dimension in development should allow for a more profound analysis and reflection on the failings of development and guide policymakers, practitioners, activists and other members of the civil society in ways to tackle the moral questions faced in development and provide effective solutions to decrease human suffering, inequalities and enhance freedom.[77]

Elaborating Sen's point about the role of successful (and unsuccessful) cases, I add one final ingredient to a development theory-practice. Each development theory-practice partially defines itself by taking actual projects, societies, or regions as "exemplars"[78] of good and bad development. People often judge Norway or Costa Rica, for instance, as concrete examples of a social democratic model of good development. Others offer Hong Kong, South Korea, Singapore, and Taiwan ("The Gang of Four") as paradigm cases – now somewhat tarnished – of the so-called "East Asian development model." Porto Alegre, Brazil, and Kerala, India, have become iconic of deliberative and democratic development. South Africa exemplifies a transition from racist and conflictual authoritarianism to a rights-respecting and pacific democracy. Hugo Chávez's Venezuela exemplifies what one analyst calls "competitive autocracy."[79]

If we tried to add a "theory-practice's" exemplar to our Figure 3.1, it would be most accurate to depict it within box G but with waves radiating out to all other boxes. For a concrete development exemplar tends to function as a dominant image that informs and integrates all aspects of the "theory-practice." Yet, exemplars are not bedrock; they can be changed or, more likely, redescribed on the basis of other elements of the theory-practice. When theory and practice fail to fit together, there is no algorithm to tell us which element or elements should be altered. Our final appeal is to ongoing, critical dialogue about the ends and means of development.

Concluding remarks

It is best, at least in our present age of disciplinary and practical divisions, that development theory-practice in general and any specific theory-practice include the work of many hands so that its various components, discussed in this chapter, can make their appropriate contribution. The ongoing dialogue should include many voices. It ought to be at least multidisciplinary and perhaps a new integrated field to ensure the presence of various theoretical elements – economics, but also sociology, political science, history, ecology, agronomy, law, theology, and philosophy. It ought to transcend the distinction between the pure and applied sciences and therefore include such fields as agricultural economics, education, engineering, health, nutrition, and social work. The moral dialogue ought to include theological ethics, so as not to neglect the resources of the religious communities, as well as secular ethics, in order to forge an improved global and public moral consensus.

Development ethics ought to go beyond theoreticians and include development policymakers, politicians, activists, journalists, and citizens. It ought to involve rural as well as urban participants if urban bias (for instance, preference for low food prices) is to be corrected without neglecting either rural needs (for example, good prices for agricultural products) or crucial rural/urban linkages, such as good roads. Public discussion should involve both women and men in order to eliminate sexism. Members of various groups should participate in order to weaken if not altogether extinguish racism, classism, and an academic bias against traditional practices and popular wisdom. The participants should come from the South as well as the North to avoid ethnocentric imperialism. It is crucial to have participants from the Middle East as well as the West and the East so that the issues of anti-terrorism, development, tolerance, and peace can be intimately linked. What has been called "hubristic imperialism" must be challenged and transformed into ethically based global leadership. Deliberative dialogue and democratic decision-making, as I argue in detail in Part IV, should be institutionalized on various levels and in diverse venues. It must involve citizens as well as governmental experts and private consultants if citizens are to have a real opportunity to participate effectively.

In sum, when done well, international development ethics requires global dialogue and democratic deliberation in a variety of venues – from small villages, through development-planning ministries, to the World Bank. Perhaps what is most important for this dialogue is that it occurs in a context in which the big, strong, and rich do not coerce the small, weak, and poor. Our notion of good development itself should include as well as contribute to unrestricted and unforced moral dialogue and democratic deliberation. As Sen observes, "political participation and dissent are *constitutive parts of development itself.*"[80] If these persons and groups are integrated in public discussion and democratic deliberation, we will be moving toward the right kind of development ethics and, we hope, toward genuine development and a better world.

NOTES

The present chapter draws on but enlarges and updates "La naturaleza y la práctica de una ética del desarrollo," *La Revista de Filosofía de la Universidad de Costa Rica*, 26 (1988): 49–56; and "Development Ethics and Development Theory-Practice," Discussion Paper CBPE 93–2, Center for Biotechnology Policy and Ethics, Texas A&M University, 1993. Both papers benefited greatly from suggestions made by Alison Bailey, Cynthia Botteron, Rafael Angel Herra, Christopher Johnson, Jorge Rovira Mas, Bernard Rollin, and Holmes Rolston. I am grateful to my Costa Rican colleagues for their friendship and insightful criticism of my work during my 1986–7 and 1992 Fulbright Visiting Professorships at the School of Philosophy of the University of Costa Rica.

1. I first employed the concept of a "development theory-practice" in "Toward Development Ethics," *World Development*, 19, 5 (1991): 457–83. Sources for this idea were William Frankena, *Three Historical Philosophies of Education* (Chicago: Scott Foresman, 1965) and *Philosophy of Education* (New York: Macmillan, 1965); Alison Jaggar, *Feminist Politics and Human Nature* (Totowa, NJ: Rowman & Allanheld; Brighton: Harvester Press, 1983); Orlando Fals-Borda, "The Challenge of Action Research," in *The Political Economy of Development and Underdevelopment*, 3rd edn., ed. Charles K. Wilber (New York: Random House, 1983), 65–73; Alasdair MacIntyre, *After Virtue*, 2nd edn. (Notre Dame: University of Notre Dame Press, 1984); and Catherine Z. Elgin (see below, n. 14). MacIntyre defines a practice as "any coherent and complex form of socially established cooperative activity through which goods internal to that form of activity are realized in the course of trying to achieve those standards of excellence which are appropriate to, and partially definitive of, that form of activity, with the result that human powers to achieve excellence, and human conceptions of ends and good involved, are systematically extended" (MacIntyre, *After Virtue*, 18). My view of a development theory-practice enlarges MacIntyre's definition to include both theory and conduct as elements. Moreover, each development theory-practice has its own conception of the "human powers to achieve excellence" and of the "ends and the goods involved." Clearer to me now than in the 1980s – when I first employed the notion of "development theory-practice" – is the Deweyan character of the idea of a development theory-practice. For Dewey's conception of the dialectical relation of theory and (political) practice, see below, n. 47.
2. Theotonio Dos Santos, "El modelo de desarrollo de Costa Rica está agotado," *Seminario Universidad*, 757 (January 9–15, 1987): 14.

3. Ibid.
4. David A. Crocker, "Cuatro modelos del desarrollo costarricense: un análisis y evaluación ética," *Revista de Filosofía de la Universidad de Costa Rica*, 27 (1989): 317–32; "The Hope for Just, Participatory Ecodevelopment in Costa Rica," in *Soziale Arbeit und Internationale Entwicklung*, ed. Gregor Sauerwald, Wigbert Flock, and Reinhold Hemker (Münster: Lit, 1992), 121–34.
5. Henry Shue, *Basic Rights: Subsistence, Affluence and US Foreign Policy*, 2nd edn. (Princeton, NJ: Princeton University Press, 1996), xi.
6. J. Baird Callicott, "The Search for an Environmental Ethic," in *Matters of Life and Death: New Introductory Essays in Moral Philosophy*, 2nd edn., ed. Tom Regan (New York: Random House, 1986), 415.
7. Nicholas D. Kristof, "Lost in Space," *New York Times* (July 24, 2004), A 27.
8. David A. Crocker, "Cuatro modelos del desarrollo costarricense"; and "The Hope for Just, Participatory Ecodevelopment in Costa Rica."
9. Richard Biesanz, Karen Zubris Biesanz, and Mavis Hiltunen Biesanz, *The Costa Ricans* (Englewood Cliffs, NJ: Prentice-Hall, 1982), 178. For an argument for a basic right to effective citizen participation, see Shue, *Basic Rights*, 65–87. For an argument that the empirical evidence shows that both income-poor and rich democracies generally outperform – with respect to both economic growth and human development —autocracies at comparable levels of GDP, see Morton H. Halperin, Joseph T. Siegle, and Michael Weinstein, *The Democracy Advantage: How Democracies Promote Prosperity and Peace* (New York and London: Routledge, 2005).
10. In graduate seminars in the early 1960s at Yale University, US philosopher John E. Smith often cited this Hegelian maxim, but I have been unable to find it in Hegel's works.
11. See David A. Crocker, *Praxis and Democratic Socialism: The Critical Social Theory of Marković and Stojanović* (Brighton: Harvester Press, 1983), chs. 2 and 6.
12. See Hilary Putnam, *The Collapse of the Fact/Value Dichotomy and Other Essays* (Cambridge, MA, and London: Harvard University Press, 2002).
13. Mario Bunge, *Ciencia y desarrollo* (Buenos Aires: Ediciones XX, 1982), 27–38.
14. Catherine Z. Elgin's general characterization of "a system of thought" comes very close to my concept of a "theory-practice," which I apply to the "domain" of international development. I would only make more explicit than Elgin does in the following passage the dialectical links between thought and action: "A category scheme provides the resources for stating various truths and falsehoods, for exhibiting particular patterns and discrepancies, for drawing specific distinctions, for demarcating conceptual boundaries. Purposes, values, and priorities are integral to the design. They constitute the basis for organizing the domain in one way rather than another. And the acceptability of any particular scheme depends on the truths it enables us to state, the methods it permits us to employ, the projects it furthers, and the values it promotes. Together these constitute a system of thought. A failure of the components to mesh undermines the system, preventing it from doing what it ought to do." Catherine Z. Elgin,

"The Relativity of Fact and the Objectivity of Value," in *Relativism: Interpretation and Confrontation*, ed. Michael Krausz (Notre Dame: University of Notre Dame Press, 1989), 89.

15. See Victor Bulmer-Thomas, *The Political Economy of Central America since 1920* (Cambridge: Cambridge University Press, 1987).

16. "El modelo de desarrollo de Costa Rica está agotado," 15; *Socialismo o fascismo: El nuevo carácter de la dependencia y el dilema latinoamericano* (Mexico: Editorial Educol, 1978).

17. Carlos Montaner, "Indagaciones sobre la libertad y la prosperidad," *La Nación* (October 26, 1986): 15A–16A. Cf. W. W. Rostow, *The Stages of Economic Growth: A Non-Communist Manifesto* (New York: Oxford University Press, 1960). For a very different analysis that (1) stresses mass poverty, powerlessness, and hopelessness as the factors that block authentic development and (2) defines (authentic) development quite differently, see Denis Goulet, "Obstacles to World Development: An Ethical Reflection," *World Development*, 11 (1983): 609–24; and *Development Ethics*, ch. 14.

18. Hollis Chenery, *Redistribution with Growth: Policies to Improve Income Distribution in Developing Countries in the Context of Economic Growth* (Oxford: Oxford University Press, 1974).

19. Ariel Dorfman, "Bread and Burnt Rice: Culture and Economic Survival in Latin America," *Grassroots Development: Journal of the Inter-American Foundation*, 8 (1984): 25.

20. Amartya Sen, *Development as Freedom* (New York: Alfred A. Knopf, 1999), xii. For a useful review of thirty major concepts of development that have emerged (many to be discarded) since World War II, see David Alexander Clark, *Visions of Development: A Study of Human Values* (Cheltenham, and Northampton, MA: Edward Elgar, 2002), ch. 1. See also Diana Hunt, *Economic Theories of Development: An Analysis of Competing Paradigms* (New York and London: Harvester Wheatsheaf, 1989); and Marta Pedrajas Herrero, "El desarrollo humano en la economía ética de Amartya Sen," PhD dissertation, Faculty of Philosophy, University of Valencia, Spain, 2005, 46–172.

21. See Gita Sen and Caren Grown, *Development, Crises, and Alternative Visions: Third World Women's Perspectives* (New York: Monthly Review Press, 1987); *Women, Culture and Development: A Study of Human Capabilities*, ed. Martha Nussbaum and Jonathan Glover (Oxford: Clarendon Press; New York: Oxford University Press, 1995); Martha Nussbaum, *Women and Human Development: The Capabilities Approach* (Cambridge: Cambridge University Press, 2000); and the journal *Feminist Economics*, esp. 9, 2–3 (2003).

22. I suggested in Chapter 2 that "development" is ambiguous, being used in both descriptive ways and normative (positive or negative) ways. See also Amartya Sen, "Description as Choice," in *Choice, Welfare, and Measurement* (Oxford: Blackwell; Cambridge, MA: MIT Press, 1982) 432–9; "Economic Methodology: Heterogeneity and Relevance," *Social Research*, 56 (1989): 313–16; *Development as Freedom*, 54–60, 92–4, 97–8, 250–2. For a useful discussion of the way in which normative commitments can provide focus for description and explanation in "positive" development studies, see Des

Gasper, *The Ethics of Development: From Economism to Human Development* (Edinburgh: Edinburgh University Press, 2004), ch. 2.

23. See Jürgen Habermas, *Knowledge and Human Interests* (Boston, MA: Beacon Press, 1971); E. Roy Ramírez, *La responsibilidad ética en ciencia y tecnología* (Cartago: Editorial Tecnológica de Costa Rica, 1987).

24. Peter L. Berger, *Pyramids of Sacrifice* (London: Penguin, 1974), 24.

25. See "Paradigms of Economic Development and Beyond," *Directions in Economic Development*, ed. Charles K. Wilber and Kenneth P. Jameson (Notre Dame: University of Notre Dame Press, 1982), 1–41; David F. Ruccio and Lawrence H. Simon, "Radical Theories of Development: Frank, the Modes of Production School, and Amin," in *The Political Economy of Development and Underdevelopment*, 4th edn., ed. Charles K. Wilber (New York: Random House, 1988), 121–73; Edward Weisband, *Poverty Amidst Plenty: World Political Economy and Distributive Justice* (Boulder, CO: Westview Press, 1989). In *Economic Theories of Development*, chs. 6–8, Diana Hunt critically compares the neo-Marxist paradigm, dependency analyses, and the Maoist paradigm of development. In his recent writings Thomas W. Pogge explicitly embraces Immanuel Wallerstein's "world systems" approach that explains (and condemns) national political and economic failures by reference to "a global order maintained by the rich democracies and their foreign policies": *World Poverty and Human Rights Cosmopolitan Responsibilities and Reforms* (Cambridge: Polity Press, 2002), 147. See Immanuel Wallerstein, *The Essential Wallerstein* (New York: New Press, 2000).

26. Geoffrey Hunt, "Two Methodological Paradigms in Development Economics," *Philosophical Forum*, 18 (1986): 55. For a brief but clear discussion of the differences between (1) an explanatory individualism that *explains* events by reference to (human) individual motivation or action ("motivational" or "ontological individualism") and (2) a "justificatory or moral individualism" in which "it is only individuals ultimately that matter morally speaking and hence justifications for moral principles, actions, and policies must ultimately refer to the well-being and freedom of individuals," see Allen Buchanan, *Justice, Legitimacy, and Self-Determination: Moral Foundations for International Law* (Oxford: Oxford University Press, 2004), 158.

27. For a fuller consideration of the individualism/holism distinction in development economics, see Geoffrey Hunt, "Two Methodological Paradigms."

28. For "rules of the game," or institutional constraints that shape human interaction, including economic performance, see Douglass C. North, *Institutions, Institutional Change and Economic Performance* (Cambridge: Cambridge University Press, 1990).

29. For an example of the latter sort of integrative theory, see Bunge, *Ciencia y desarrollo*, 19–24.

30. J. P. Dickenson, C. G. Clarke, W. T. S. Gould, *et al.*, *Geography of the Third World* (London: Methuen, 1983), xv.

31. Keith Griffin, *Underdevelopment in Spanish America* (London: George Allen & Unwin, 1969), 48; reprinted as "Underdevelopment in History,"

in *The Political Economy of Development and Underdevelopment*, 2nd edn., ed. Charles K. Wilber (New York: Random House, 1979), 88.

32. Jorge Graciarena, "Poder y estilos de desarrolo: Una perspectiva hetero-doxa," *Revista de la Cepal*, 1 (1976): 187. For an interesting and important use of Graciarena's thesis in an interpretation of Costa Rica, see Jorge Rovira Mas, *Estado y política económica en Costa Rica 1948–1970*, 2nd edn. (San José: Editorial Porvenir, 1983). For a clarification of the history of the "structure versus agency" debate in the social sciences, a discussion of the recent turn in development studies to "agency," and the view that structure is increasingly conceptualized as a set of parameters that actors use to order their practices, see Jan Douwe van der Ploeg, "Structure and Agency," in *The Elgar Companion to Development Studies*, ed. David Alexander Clark (Cheltenham: Edward Elgar, 2006), 607–12.

33. Graciarena, "Poder y estilos," 184.

34. Branko Milanovic, *Worlds Apart: Measuring International and Global Inequality* (Princeton: Princeton University Press, 2005), 148.

35. Ruccio and Simon, "Radical Theories," 124.

36. Ibid. Cf. Thomas Carothers' argument that "the transition paradigm" of democracy promotion assumes that all nations moving away from authoritarianism are on a single and inexorable path – with no u-turns or dead-ends – to full democracy: Thomas Carothers, *Critical Mission: Essays on Democracy Promotion* (Washington, DC: Carnegie Endowment for International Peace, 2004), 167–83.

37. Ibid., 125–6.

38. Geoffrey Hunt, "Two Methodological Paradigms," 62.

39. See Howard J. Wiarda, "Toward a Nonethnocentric Theory of Development: Alternative Conceptions from the Third World," in *The Political Economy of Development and Underdevelopment*, 4th edn., 59–82, esp. 75–7. For a recent discussion of what he calls "universalist" and "relativist" conceptions of development, see Gasper, *The Ethics of Development*, ch. 2.

40. Geoffrey Hunt, "Two Methodological Paradigms," 59.

41. Although they cast themselves as opponents of all "development" theories, policies, and practices, the essayists in *The Development Dictionary*, ed. Wolfgang Sachs, (London: Zed, 1992), arguably are anti-essentialists in the sense that they reject a fixed human nature.

42. Richard Rorty, *Contingency, Irony, and Solidarity* (Cambridge: Cambridge University Press, 1989), xiii.

43. The text is an application to development theory of a point that Rorty makes with respect to the "Western Democracies" in ibid.

44. Amartya Sen, "Rational Fools: A Critique of the Behavioral Foundations of Economic Theory," *Philosophy and Public Affairs*, 6 (1977): 317–44; "Economic Methodology: Heterogeneity and Relevance," *Social Research*, 56 (1989): 319–29; Denis Goulet, *Incentives for Development: The Key to Equity* (New York: New Horizons Press, 1989); and *Beyond Self-Interest*, ed. Jane J. Mansbridge (Chicago: University of Chicago Press, 1990).

45. Sen, *Development as Freedom*, ch. 11.

46. See Amartya Sen, "Reason Before Identity," Romanes Lecture, given in Oxford, November 17, 1998; "Beyond Identity: Other People," *The New Republic*, 223, 25 (2000): 23–30; *Identity and Violence: The Illusion of Destiny* (New York and London: W. W. Norton, 2006); and Sabina Alkire, *Valuing Freedoms: Sen's Capability Approach and Poverty Reduction* (Oxford: Oxford University Press, 2002), 140–1.

47. Some development theory-practices have the ambition of deductively deriving ethical principles and goals (in A and C) as well as development goals and strategies (in D) from metaphysical assumptions in B. In contrast, some Marxists and Richard Rorty contend that metaphysical assumptions provide no "back-up" or justification for practice but merely rationalize or articulate it. My own approach, which I can only suggest here, would be to emphasize the way in which metaphysical assumptions can both influence and be influenced by other elements of a development theory-practice. We both tailor development practice to (metaphysical) theory and tailor theory to practice. See Robert B. Westbrook, *John Dewey and American Democracy* (Ithaca, NY: Cornell University Press, 1991), 366–7, n. 37. For Rorty's sympathetic critique of Dewey, see Richard Rorty, *The Consequences of Pragmatism* (Minneapolis, MN: University of Minnesota Press, 1982), 74; and "The Priority of Democracy to Philosophy," in *The Virginia Statute for Religious Freedom*, eds. Merrill D. Peterson and Robert C. Vaughn (New York: Cambridge University Press, 1988), 257–82.

48. See Gasper, *The Ethics of Development*, ch. 3, for a helpful discussion of diverse conceptions of the values of both efficiency and effectiveness.

49. See Eleanora Barbieri Masini, "Philosophical and Ethical Foundations for Future Studies," *World Future Studies*, 17 (1981): 1–14. See also Joseph E. Stiglitz's important point that development advisors have a duty to make clear the *degree* of probability of their forecasts as well as the cognitive quality of the evidence on which the forecasts are based: "On Liberty, the Right to Know, and Public Discourse: The Role of Transparency in Public Life," in *Globalizing Rights: The Oxford Amnesty Lectures 1999*, ed. Matthew J. Gibney (Oxford: Oxford University Press, 2003), 115–56.

50. Onora O'Neill, "Lifeboat Earth," in *World Hunger and Moral Obligation*, ed. William Aiken and Hugh La Follette (Englewood Cliffs, NJ: Prentice-Hall, 1977), 160.

51. Rorty argues that it is innovative political action in the "Third World" that is likely to open up new institutional possibilities in the rigidified, worn-out, and apathetic ("Alexandrian") First and Second Worlds: "To say, as I have been saying here, that if there is hope it lies in the imagination of the Third World, is to say that the best any of us here in Alexandria can hope for is that somebody out there will do something to tear up the present system of imaginary significations within which politics in (and between) the First and Second Worlds is conducted. It need not be equalization of incomes, but it has to be something *like* that – something so preposterously romantic as to be no longer discussed by us Alexandrians. Only some actual event (rather than some hopeful book), the actual success of some political move made in some actual country, is likely to help." Richard Rorty,

"Unger, Castoriadis, and the Romance of a National Future," *Northwestern University Law Review*, 82, 2 (1987–8): 351. Arguably Brazil in the early twenty-first century can lay claim to two such "preposterously romantic" events, both of which seem to be bearing normative fruit – the election to the Brazilian presidency of Luiz Inácio Lula da Silva and the city of Porto Alegre's fifteen years of experience with a participatory budgeting process. For the latter, see Gianpaolo Biaocchi, "Participation, Activism, and Politics: The Porto Alegre Experiment," in *Deepening Democracy*, ed. Archon Fung and Erik Olin Wright (London and New York: Verso, 2003), 45–76.

52. Charles R. Beitz, *Political Theory and International Relations* (Princeton: Princeton University Press, 1979), 156. See also my critique of what I call "realistic anti-utopianism," *Praxis and Democratic Socialism*, 168–73.

53. See Onora O'Neill's treatment of Singer's and Hardin's contrary forecasts and moral evaluations in "Ending World Hunger," in *Matters of Life and Death: New Introductory Essays in Moral Philosophy*, 3rd edn., ed. Tom Regan (New York: McGraw-Hill, 1993), 235–79.

54. In the mid-1980s Roger C. Riddell helpfully (1) examined the mixed record of foreign aid and (2) criticized the hasty generalizations of those who find aid always good or always bad. See Roger C. Riddell, *Foreign Aid Reconsidered* (Baltimore: Johns Hopkins University Press, 1987). For more recent assessments, see World Bank, *Assessing Aid: What Works, What Doesn't, and Why* (New York: Oxford University Press, 1998); William Easterly, *The Elusive Quest for Growth: Economists' Adventures and Misadventures in the Tropics* (Cambridge, MA: MIT Press, 2002); William Easterly, *The White Man's Burden: Why the West's Efforts to Aid Have Done So Much Ill and So Little Good* (New York: Penguin, 2006); Roger C. Riddell, *Does Foreign Aid Really Work?* (Oxford: Oxford University Press, 2007). For critical assessments of Easterly's most recent book, see Amartya Sen, "The Man Without a Plan: Can Foreign Aid Work?," *Foreign Affairs* (March/April 2006): 171–7; and Nicholas Kristoff, "Aid: Can It Work?" *New York Review of Books*, LIII, 15 (October 5, 2006): 41–4. In Chapter 8, I take up the issue of food aid and what we know of its variable impact on people's lives.

55. See Gasper, *The Ethics of Development*, esp. chs. 3 and 4, for helpful unmasking of value assumptions lurking in apparently value-neutral economics.

56. Onora O'Neill argues against utilitarianism as a moral theory precisely because it requires an impossible predictive "science of society." O'Neill tries to make a virtue of the necessary absence of a social science crystal ball by working out a version of Kantian ethics that is "far less sensitive than is utilitarian reasoning to gaps in our causal knowledge" and does not require "impossible calculations" of the future: O'Neill, "Ending World Hunger," 266, 255.

57. For this notion of the positive dimension of critique, see Crocker, *Praxis and Democratic Socialism*, esp. 23–32. For a similar view of the way in which "thought" reflects upon and seeks to improve practice, see Jane Mansbridge, "Practice-Thought-Practice," in *Deepening Democracy*, ed. Fung and Wright, 175–99.

58. Jorge G. Castañeda argues that the goals of the Latin American left – that "there must be a fundamental shift in resources and policy emphasis from

the rich to the poor in order to solve the region's problems" – can and should "constitute the aims and aspirations of all Latin Americans": *Utopia Unarmed: The Latin American Left After the Cold War* (New York: Vintage, 1993): 429, 475. For Castañeda's more recent reflections on two lefts in Latin America – a "wrong" (populist) left and a "right" (social democratic) left, see his "Latin America's Left Turn," *Foreign Affairs*, 85, 3 (May/June 2006): 45–59.

59. Denis Goulet, *Development Ethics: A Guide to Theory and Practice* (New York: Apex Press, 1995), 11.

60. Ibid., 11–12. I analyze and evaluate Goulet's own rather abstract principles in my "Foreword" to Goulet, *Development Ethics at Work: Explorations 1960–2002* (London: Routledge, 2006), xiv–xxxiii.

61. In a review of James M. McPherson's history of the US Civil War, *The Battle Cry for Freedom: The Civil War Era* (New York: Oxford University Press, 1988), Jean Baker comments on the appropriateness of the volume's title: "According to McPherson, the Civil War was a revolution, on both sides. Both the North and South were fighting for alternative views of freedom, an ideal inherited from their shared revolutionary past." For the South, but not for the North, continues Baker, freedom included "the right to own slaves and to take them anywhere as private property, including the territories such as Kansas, and the right to be free from the interfering North": Jean Baker, "Our Other Revolution," *New Republic* (September 5, 1988): 39.

62. For a conception of a social, cross-cultural version of John Rawls's method of "reflective equilibrium," see David A. Crocker, *Praxis and Democratic Socialism*, ch. 6. One-sided positions emphasize abstract principles at the expense of concrete judgments or vice versa. For the latter, see Richard J. Bernstein, "One Step Forward, Two Steps Backward: Richard Rorty on Liberal Democracy and Philosophy," *Political Theory*, 15, 4 (1987): 538–63, esp. 549. For the former, see Richard Rorty, "Thugs and Theorists: A Reply to Bernstein," *Political Theory*, 15, 4 (1987): 564–80, esp. 577, n. 20. David Alexander Clark, impatient with abstract normative theorizing, goes to the other extreme of uncritically appealing to the values of the poor: "a new approach, which draws on the perceptions of development among the poor, is required to provide potentially sterile debates about the nature of human well-being and development with new impetus": *Visions of Development*, 6. In Chapters 9 and 10 below, I offer an ideal of deliberative and democratic participation as a way of avoiding the dangers of both top-down theorizing and unscrutinized popular preferences.

63. Richard Rorty, "Philosophy as Science, as Metaphor, and as Politics," in *The Institution of Philosophy*, ed. Avner Cohen and Marcelo Dascal (La Salle, IL: Open Court, 1989), 32–3, n. 37.

64. Rorty, "Thugs and Theorists," 569–70.

65. Ibid.

66. Ibid., 580, n. 31. See also Rorty, "Philosophy as Science, as Metaphor, and as Politics," 33, n. 38.

67. For a discussion of the "practical turn" in Anglo-American philosophy, see Stephen Toulmin, "The Recovery of Practical Philosophy," *American*

Scholar, 57, 3 (1988): 337–52; and Crocker, "Toward Development Ethics," 471–3. For recent examples of philosophers making contributions to multi-disciplinary and public issues, see *Disability, Difference, Discrimination*, ed. Anita Silvers, Mary B. Mahowald, and David Wasserman (Lanham, MD: Rowman & Littlefield, 1998); *Philosophical Dimensions of Public Policy, Policy Studies Review Annual*, 13, ed. Verna V. Gehring and William A. Galston (New Brunswick, NJ, and London: Transaction, 2002); Pogge, *World Poverty and Human Rights*; Peter Singer, *One World: The Ethics of Globalization*, 2nd edn. (New Haven, CT, and London: Yale University Press, 2004); *Philosophy and Public Policy Quarterly*; Robert K. Fullinwider and Judith Lichtenberg, *Leveling the Playing Field: Justice, Politics, and College Admissions* (Lanham, MD: Rowman & Littlefield, 2004); *Animal Rights: Current Debates and New Directions*, ed. Cass R. Sunstein and Martha C. Nussbaum (New York: Oxford University Press, 2004); and Jonathan Moreno, *Is There an Ethicist in the House? On the Cutting Edge of Bioethics* (Bloomington, IN: Indiana University Press, 2005); Mark Sagoff, *The Economy of the Earth: Philosophy, Law, and the Environment*, 2nd edn. (Cambridge: Cambridge University Press, 2007). For representative Spanish work in engaged policy-oriented applied ethics, see Adela Cortina, *Ética aplicada y democracia radical* (Madrid: Tecnos, 1993); *Ciudadanos del mundo: Hacia una teoría de la ciudadanía* (Madrid: Alianza Editorial, 1997); *Los ciudadanos como protagonistas* (Barcelona: Galaxia Gutemberg, Círculo de Lectores, 1999); Adela Cortina *et al.*, *Construir confianza: Ética de la empresa en la sociedad de la información y las comunicaciones* (Madrid: Trotta, 2003); Adela Cortina and Domingo García-Marzá, eds., *Razón pública y éticas aplicadas: Los caminos de la razón práctica en una sociedad pluralista* (Madrid: Tecnos, 2003).

68. See Archon Fung, "Deliberation before the Revolution: Toward an Ethics of Deliberative Democracy," *Political Theory*, 32, 2 (2005): 401.

69. John Dewey and James H. Tufts, *Ethics* [1908], *The Middle Works of John Dewey, 1899–1924*, V, ed. Jo Ann Boydston (Carbondale, IL: Southern Illinois University Press, 1983), 276; cited in Westbrook, *John Dewey*, 185. Westbrook's perceptive gloss on this passage is as relevant for twenty-first-century *development* professionals as it was for early twentieth-century social reformers: "As Dewey perceived, the language of middle-class benevolence often betrayed a view of the masses as inert material on which reformers might work their will, and he called instead for a reconstructed conception of helping others which enlisted their full and willing participation in the provision of social welfare": Westbrook, *John Dewey*, 185; see also 40–2.

70. Mitchell A. Seligson, "The Dual Gaps: An Overview of Theory and Research," in *The Gap Between Rich and Poor: Contending Perspectives on the Political Economy of Development*, ed. Mitchell A. Seligson (Boulder, CO: Westview Press, 1984), 5.

71. Sen, *Development as Freedom*, 36.

72. Ibid., 296.

73. Ibid., 295.

74. What Stephen Toulmin says about the clinician can be generalized to the practical reasoner and then applied to the development planner, community member, or other development agent. See Toulmin, "The Recovery of Practical Philosophy," 345–7. On *phronēsis*, see Richard J. Bernstein, *Beyond Objectivism and Relativism: Science, Hermeneutics, and Praxis* (Philadelphia: University of Pennsylvania Press, 1983); and "Can We Justify Universal Moral Norms?," in *Universalism vs. Relativism: Making Moral Judgments in a Changing, Pluralistic, and Threatening World*, ed. Don Browning (Lanham, MD: Rowman & Littlefield, 2006), 3–17.

75. Aristotle, *Nicomachean Ethics*, trans. Terence Irwin (Indianapolis: Hackett, 1985), 1179b.

76. Sen, *Development as Freedom*, 255.

77. Anna Malavisi, "The Application of Ethics in Development Practice," abstract, conference paper "Global Ethics, Development, Environment and the Earth Charter," April 14–17, 2004, Aberdeen, Scotland.

78. I use "exemplar" in Thomas Kuhn's sense of a "community's standard examples," as "concrete problem solutions, accepted by the group, as in a quite usual sense, paradigmatic." See Thomas S. Kuhn, *The Essential Tension: Selected Studies in Scientific Tradition and Change* (Chicago: University of Chicago Press, 1977), 298, 306.

79. Javier Corrales, "Hugo Boss," *Foreign Policy* (January/February 2006): 32–40.

80. Sen, *Development as Freedom*, 36; see also 291.

Part II

The capability approach: ethical foundations

4   Critique of alternatives

In the three chapters of Part II, I analyze, evaluate, and begin to strengthen the ethical dimensions of the capability orientation to international development. The two leading practitioners of this orientation – Amartya Sen, its originator, and Martha Nussbaum, an important proponent – have made novel and influential contributions to the several dimensions of a development theory-practice, which I distinguished in Chapter 3.[1] Their development ethics are situated, as such ethics should be, in the context of dialectical interaction with other elements of a development theory-practice. These include the conceptual definition and empirical investigation of development as well as policy recommendations for achieving development and overcoming underdevelopment. What we view as worth promoting, as intrinsically valuable, will make a difference in both causal analysis and policy recommendations. One reason for the importance of these two versions of the capability orientation is that they fruitfully link, without confusion or fusion, those elements in development theory and practice that have been unfortunately and even disastrously separated.

My concern in this and the next two chapters, however, is with the way in which Sen and Nussbaum answer many of the fundamental ethical questions related to development, questions that I identified and discussed in Chapter 2. In the present chapter I analyze, compare, and evaluate how Sen and Nussbaum criticize alternative ethical perspectives: commodity approaches, utilitarianism, and basic needs. In the next two chapters, Chapters 5 and 6, I analyze where Sen and Nussbaum agree and where they differ with respect to the orientation's fundamental ethical concepts of functioning, capability, and agency. Moreover, I evaluate the merits and weaknesses of these two versions of the capability orientation and begin to work out a version that retains the virtues of each without their respective shortcomings. Taken together, the three chapters of Part II will be a useful setting for Parts III and IV, in which I further strengthen, apply, and extend the capability orientation.

Methodology: digging for foundations

What, Sen asks, is "the right approach to development"?[2] More specifically, what should be our most fundamental *ethical* category or categories by which developmental "rightness" might be determined? To answer this question, says Sen, is to establish the "foundation" for an ethic in contrast to that ethic's principles or their application.

We must be careful about the precise sense in which Sen and Nussbaum are "foundationalists." The foundation that both are seeking is not "a knockdown proof of something from some fixed area of external fact."[3] That is, they are not trying to ground or deductively derive an ethic from some metaphysics of nature or from what they call an "externalist"[4] account of a transhistorical human essence. Such a foundationalism would depend on a metaphysical or scientific realism that purports to give a "God's eye view" of the way things, including human beings, essentially are or should be. It would seek to transcend human discourse and to be "radically independent of our actual choices, our self-understandings, our hopes and loves and fears."[5] Rather, what is needed is an "internalist"[6] foundationalism that aims to surmount the dichotomy of absolutism or objectivism and relativism. The former aspires to nonhistorical Truth, and the latter settles for prevailing local or provincial truths.[7] We start "digging"[8] from *within* human experience and discourse and engage in an evaluative inquiry about what things we do and should count as intrinsically worthwhile in our human lives. We stop searching when we find, through "cooperative critical discourse"[9] (Nussbaum) or "public discussion" (Sen), what sorts of ethical concepts best interpret these objects of intrinsic value: "Any moral theory would have to begin with some primitive diagnosis of value . . . I accept fully that one has to dig for foundations, but there is a substantial issue involved in deciding where to stop digging."[10]

Sen's and Nussbaum's "foundationalism," then, returns to the questions (and some of the answers) of classical Greek *eudaimonia*. How should human beings live their lives?[11] What should we mean by human and communal well-being? What *sorts* of things are intrinsically good for human beings and not just instrumentally valuable, such as economic growth or efficiency? Is happiness the ultimate goal or is it a by-product of, some evidence for, or at odds with intrinsic value? Are commodities such as food or income intrinsically good, or are they good only because they lead to something else? What is this something else? What are the bearers of intrinsic values? In what ethical space or spaces should we operate? Have we come to the end of the line when we talk of economic growth in income, meeting certain needs, or respecting certain rights? Or can one find more fundamental ethical categories?

This ethical inquiry proceeds by a cross-cultural extension of Rawlsian "reflective equilibrium." In this pursuit, we seek to balance considered judgments and ethical principles through reciprocal, dialogic scrutiny of proposals.[12] We strive, individually and communally, for consistency and harmony among our ethical beliefs and desires: "What the individual comes to see more clearly is a conception of the good that he receives from society and according to which he intends to live in a society; the communal agreement is arrived at as a result of the reciprocal scrutiny and clarification of different individual proposals."[13]

Important for Nussbaum in this shared inquiry is critical reflection on "stories of communal self-definition and self-clarification."[14] These narratives, originating from various communities, address and help us reflect on the ethical (rather than metaphysical) boundaries between humans and gods, on one hand, and between humans and beasts, on the other. Sen differs from Nussbaum in at least two respects. Although on occasion he draws critically on traditional narratives, such as the Bhagavagita, Sen is more apt to enter into dialogue with and scrutinize earlier thinkers, such as Adam Smith, popular wisdom, and personal anecdotes in order to arrive at the foundational ethical concepts that both are internally consistent and match his (and other people's) most confident and considered judgments. Second, as I shall argue later, especially in Part IV, Sen, unlike Nussbaum, ascribes a robust role to each group (local, national, global) publicly deliberating and democratically deciding which freedoms and other goals are important, how they should be prioritized in relation to each other, and how they should inform policy formation.

This difference between Sen and Nussbaum is not insignificant, but for the present it is more important to see that both thinkers reject not only ethical "proofs" from metaphysical or self-evident starting points but also uncritical appeals to popular wisdom or the values of common people. Both Sen and Nussbaum would reject those investigators, such as David Clark, who seek "scientifically" to ground an ethic by an uncritical appeal to ordinary people's values.[15] One problem, of course, is that no agreement exists on many value issues, and even if there were consensus, Hume was right in arguing that moral philosophers cannot derive an "ought" (what is good or right) from an "is" (what people believe is good or right). Nussbaum, following Aristotle, seeks the most reasonable view of human flourishing through comparing, sifting, and *critically assessing* both popular and philosophical views. She offers an ideal of the humanly good life both as following from her engagement with past and present views and as a proposal for further cross-cultural debate.[16] Sen contends that prevailing beliefs and values are often the result of unscrutinized tradition, indoctrination (by which dominators make allies of their victims), or the adaptation of preferences in order not to expect too much from a threatening and miserly world. Sen avoids these risks – without appealing to a "pre-set" list of valuable capabilities – by arguing on moral grounds that groups should democratically deliberate and decide matters of values and public policy.

In one essay in the late 1980s, Nussbaum embraced a second method of ethical inquiry, which, she asserted, applies to some but not all ethical principles. The ethical investigator can advance general norms by showing that they are presupposed in the very practice of shared critical inquiry. To engage in this sort of inquiry is to "self-validate"[17] certain norms – such as mutuality and practical rationality – that define the activity. One cannot deductively demonstrate these norms without begging the question and presupposing them in the procedure. But any attempt to disprove these norms, by means of argument and critical dialogue, shows that the critic respects the norms informing the dialogue. This "self-validating argument"[18] does not provide a knockdown proof, for, as Aristotle saw, the critic is always free to walk away from (or change) the communal inquiry and the form of life in which it is embedded. Instead, the strategy is to appeal to beliefs and practices to which most of us are already committed. The practice, then, of communal ethical inquiry is supposed to have a "self-validating structure," and this structure "commends" what issues from inquiry as "a good basis for further ethical investigation."[19] However, if the supposedly "self-validating" exercise ultimately depends on what people already believe, it would seem to have the same defects as Clark's uncritical appeal to ordinary views, or, if the appeal were to critically scrutinized judgments in reflective equilibrium, then it would be but another form of the method of reflective equilibrium. That Nussbaum has not employed this argument again is probably wise.

Ethical approaches: analysis and assessment

Sen and Nussbaum propose, based on the method of critical and cross-cultural dialogue and reflective equilibrium, that the best general category for human well-being is the ethical "space" or "metric" of human functionings and capabilities. It is important to note, in anticipation of Chapters 5 and 6, that Sen differs from Nussbaum in distinguishing human agency from human well-being, whether well-being achievement (functioning) or well-being freedom to achieve (capability). Sen stresses that humans are authors of their own lives as well as creatures whose lives can go well or badly (by virtue of luck or agency, their own or that of others). For Sen, then, the best normative foundation is that of human achievement, of which human well-being and human agency are two kinds, and the freedom to achieve, of which well-being freedom and agency freedom are the two kinds. Once we get to these two kinds of achievement and freedom, we are at the level of intrinsic value. That which is intrinsically valuable for human beings provides the basis for inquiry into instrumentally valuable means. For Nussbaum, these human achievements are valuable functionings and capabilities to function, which include a capacity for practical reason and control, and, she believes, can and should be put into a fixed list. Let us see how Sen's and Nussbaum's agreements and disagreements about normative foundations emerge from their assessments of leading alternative answers.

The commodity approach: the crude version

One way to define fundamental ethical categories is to identify certain market commodities, or, more generally, material goods or resources as intrinsically good or ethically basic in some other way. Income, (per capita) gross national or domestic product (GNP or GDP), and economic growth (in goods and services or living standards) were early favorites of postwar development economists and development practitioners. Despite a chorus of critics, economic growth continues to dominate development theory and policy formation. Let us call this version the "crude" commodity approach. This perspective has, argues Sen, both strengths and weaknesses. It correctly understands that development does not occur without material prosperity. People cannot *be* at all, let alone have well-being or a good life, without having certain goods in certain amounts. Moreover, commodities can be evidence for as well as causes (and consequences) of valuable human functionings. The commodity approach's good idea goes bad, however, insofar as it transforms mere means into ends. The result is what Sen, following Marx, calls, "commodity fetishism." Instead of focusing on what goods "can do for people, or rather, what people can do with these goods and services,"[20] the commodity approach often collapses into a valuation of goods *themselves* as intrinsically good. So what? Sen and Nussbaum offer four criticisms.

First, Sen and Nussbaum appeal to our considered judgments that commodities are good not in and of themselves but only by virtue of their relationship to – what they do *for* – human beings or what human beings can do *with* them:

> A person's well being is not really a matter of how *rich* he or she is . . . Commodity command is a *means* to the end of well being, but can scarcely be the end itself.[21]

> Commodities are no more than means to other ends. Ultimately, the focus has to be on what life we lead and what we can or cannot do, can or cannot be.[22]

> The basic idea used by the Aristotelian conception to argue against this [commodity or resource approach] is the idea that wealth, income, and possessions simply are not good in themselves. However much people may actually be obsessed with heaping them up . . . what they have really, when they have them, is just a heap of stuff. A useful heap, but a heap nonetheless, a heap that is nothing at all unless it is put to use in the doings and beings of human lives.[23]

Except for misers who seem to prize their money for its own sake, most people have reason to value even their prized possessions because of what their treasures do for them – for instance, afford enjoyment – or for what they can do with their treasures.

A second criticism is what I call the "interpersonal variability" or "one-many" argument.[24] Due to variations among individuals, the same commodity either may help some and harm others or may promote the well-being of some a lot and of others only a little. Although food intake normally will enhance human functioning, it will kill the person choking on a fish bone. To function well, Milo the wrestler needs, on the one hand, more food than the infant and the disabled and, on the other hand, less food than a wrestler of similar size but stricken with parasites.[25] Pregnant or lactating women have different nutritional requirements than they did before the conception or birth of their children. The usefulness of one and the same commodity varies among persons or for the same person at different times. A concept of human well-being that focuses on goods rather than persons inevitably neglects the "variable conversion" of goods into valuable human functionings and capabilities:

> In getting an idea of the well-being of the person, we clearly have to move on [from commodities and characteristics of commodities] to "functionings," to wit, what the person succeeds in *doing* with the commodities and characteristics at his or her command. For example, we must take note that a disabled person may not be able to do many things an able-bodied individual can, with the same bundle of commodities.[26]

What explains this variable convertability? Sen distinguishes many factors, both personal characteristics and environmental features, which result in one commodity (for example, a kind of meat or medicine) having such different impacts on individuals' "beings and doings": "(1) metabolic rates, (2) body size, (3) age, (4) sex (and, if a woman, whether pregnant or lactating), (5) activity levels, (6) climatic conditions, (7) presence of parasitic diseases, (8) access to medical services, (8) nutritional knowledge."[27]

A third criticism makes the last point in societal rather than individual terms. An exclusive focus on commodities or resources easily leads to a kind of cultural relativity or conventionality. For example, the clothing that promotes basic functioning of being protected from the elements differs in the rainforests of Costa Rica and the tundra of Alaska. Sen makes the same point with respect to the valuable capability of appearing in public without shame.[28] He frequently cites Adam Smith's remark about the indispensability of a linen shirt for such public appearances in eighteenth-century England.[29] One would be hard pressed even to find a linen shirt in 21st-century Costa Rica, let alone be publicly shamed for appearing in public without one. The important point is that the capability orientation can retain the notion of a culturally invariant (absolute) core to both well-being and deprivation while at the same time construing any *specific* means of provisioning as relative to historical and cultural contexts.[30] But also the same human functioning can be promoted, even in the same society, by various goods or differing packages of goods. Sen calls this phenomenon "a *many-one* correspond-ence"[31] between commodities bundles and given functions or capabili-ties. Being adequately nourished can result from radically different diets. Being in good health can be promoted by different proportions of good food and preventive or curative medical care. This simple but profound idea, following from the means/end distinction, is one basis for resolving the impasse – referred to in Chapters 2 and 3 – between universalists and relativists or particularists.

Nussbaum, drawing on Aristotle, states a fourth criticism of the com-modity approach. Not only are goods neither ultimate ends nor invariant means to such ends; they also can be bad when we get too much of them. More or bigger is not always better. Too much of a good thing can be bad.[32] Goods and the hunger for them often make people excessively competitive, domineering, and arrogant, and engender "a mercenary attitude toward other kinds of good things."[33] This attitude can go so far as to result in what Nussbaum calls "a commodification of parts of the self,"[34] in which market transactions and legal proceedings concern-ing rape treat women's bodies as commodities. In this connection, one might also mention body-building and beauty contests as well as the increasing use of steroids and cosmetic surgery. It is clear that a crude commodities approach gives us no basis for deciding – as individuals, families, communities, or polities – what is enough, what is too much, and what is just right. In Chapter 7, I return to this issue and argue that the capability ethic can be useful in guiding individuals in making consumption choices and communities in establishing consumption policies.

The commodity approach: the Rawlsian version

A much more sophisticated version of the commodity perspective is that which John Rawls developed until his death in 2003.[35] Seeking to measure personal advantage or enlightened self-interest and to make interpersonal comparisons, Rawls proposes a theory of what he calls "social primary goods," among which income and wealth have a certain centrality. Rawls's theory of primary goods, however, differs in important ways from the crude commodity view. Neither in *A Theory of Justice* nor in his subsequent writings does Rawls hold that his primary goods are *intrinsically* good. In fact, an essential part of Rawls's liberalism and what he calls "anti-perfectionism" is the claim that questions of ultimate or inherent goodness are, within limits specified by his theory, to be viewed as matters of individual choice rather than governmental concern. Yet Rawls does offer a list of primary goods as playing an important role in his theory of "justice as fairness." This role, at least at first blush, seems to rule out consideration of those human capabilities and functionings that Sen and Nussbaum judge to be *the* – or, at least, *one* – appropriate "space" for a social ethic. Let us look briefly at Rawls's complex theory of primary goods and the points of difference that have emerged not only between Rawls on the one hand, and Sen and Nussbaum on the other, but also between Sen and Nussbaum.

A Theory of Justice lists "social primary goods" as "rights and liberties, powers and opportunities, income and wealth," and "self-respect."[36] These goods are supposedly what all rational individuals want regardless of their ultimate goals in life: "Other things equal, they prefer a wider to a narrower liberty and opportunity, and a greater rather than a smaller share of wealth and income."[37] Rawls offers this list of goods not as what people should desire and governments should promote as ultimate. Instead, he proposes the list as "a thin theory of the good" that can be employed in his justificatory device of the "original position" to motivate his rational contractors as they choose principles of justice. The primary goods tell us what these parties desire and count as their rational advantage. The list also provides Rawls with criteria for a person's "legitimate claims" and thereby enables him to make interpersonal comparisons with respect to how "well off" people are. In Rawls's approach, the concept of the right is prior to the good in the sense that a conception of justice, allegedly chosen by the parties in the original position, provides a fair framework within which people choose and pursue their *own* conception of the good. Unlike what he calls a "perfectionist" theory of justice, Rawls's own theory does not propose a "thick concept of the good," an ultimate concept of human excellence, which a government should promote and to which people should aspire.[38]

In his more recent writings, Rawls sought to dispel the notion that in *A Theory of Justice* he was attempting to deduce his principles of justice from some morally neutral concept of rationality coupled with an empirical theory about what people everywhere in fact want. Rawls's later writings stress that the primary goods, still to be used to derive the principles of justice, are themselves to be justified as required by our conceptions of citizens as free and equal "moral persons" capable of taking part in social cooperation:

These goods, we say, are things that citizens need as free and equal persons, and claims to these goods are counted as appropriate claims.[39]

Primary goods are singled out by asking which things are generally necessary as social conditions and all-purpose means to enable human beings to realize and exercise their moral powers and to pursue their final ends (assumed to lie within certain limits).[40]

What, precisely, is Rawls's concept of socially cooperating moral persons and his revised list of the primary goods allegedly needed by such persons? For Rawls, moral persons are "characterized by two moral powers and by two corresponding highest-order interests in realizing and exercising these powers."[41] First, moral persons have the capacity for and interest in a "sense of justice," that is, understanding and acting from principles of justice. Second, moral persons have the capacity and desire to form, revise, and rationally pursue a conception of the good. Citizens in a "well-ordered society" view themselves and others as moral persons. They also cooperate with one another insofar as they comply with the shared conception of justice and, within its constraints, decide on and pursue their own good. These constraints rule out authoritarian societies and conceptions of the good based on domination and servility. To be free and equal, citizens must have (minimal levels of) certain primary goods. Rawls's earlier list is now slightly expanded to include the following: "basic rights and liberties," such as freedom of conscience and political liberties; "freedom of movement and free choice of occupation against a background of diverse opportunities"; "powers and prerogatives of offices and positions of responsibility"; "income and wealth"; and "the social bases of self-respect."[42]

In this "thin theory of the good," Rawls calls income and wealth "all-purpose means" and designates the remaining items as "features of institutions."[43] We democrats, says Rawls, assume that these items are instrumentally good as means required for democratic citizenship. That is, within the fair limits set by justice, we assume that free and equal moral persons will need each of these goods to advance their final ends. It is up to citizens – not the state or philosophers – to decide on their own ultimate goals.

Rawls calls his later theory, with its stress on the ideal of moral personhood and democratic citizenship, a "political conception" of justice. Assuming the fact of irreducible diversity – with respect to conceptions of the good – in a democratic society, Rawls rejects as utopian any "comprehensive" and "general" moral doctrine. A doctrine is comprehensive when it includes a conception "of what is of ultimate value in human life";[44] it is general when it applies not only to the public sphere but to other areas of life as well. By contrast, a political conception of justice, of which "justice as fairness" is the favored example, is an "overlapping consensus" of and for free and equal citizens. The consensus concerns instrumental goods and distributive principles that are relevant solely for the political realm. The right is prior to the good in that "the principles of 'political' justice set limits to permissible ways of life"[45] and personal conceptions of intrinsic good. Given the fact of ideological diversity, a government that made the good prior to the right would have to promote one and only one conception of the good and make distributions on that basis. But, for Rawls, this "promotion" unacceptably would necessitate a coercive use of state power and thereby violate people's freedom to decide on their own final ends.

Hence, in Rawls's version of the commodity approach, the moral space of commodities is affirmed not as the "site" of final ends but rather as a "platform" of means indispensable for realizing certain democratic ideals, including the ideals of social cooperation and autonomous choice. Assuming these ends and means, Rawls proposes public principles of justice – for and only for the political domain – as a fair framework that constrains each citizen in her decision of her final ends (which may or may not include the values of political participation and autonomous choice).

How do Sen and Nussbaum assess this subtle and complex Rawlsian perspective? On one hand, Sen applauds Rawls's "far-reaching theory of justice" for having "contributed greatly to a radical regeneration of modern political philosophy and ethics."[46] He expresses an "enormous" personal debt to Rawls and even says that his own view is but "one possible extension of the Rawlsian perspective."[47] In particular, Sen agrees with Rawls's arguments that utilitarianism (1) reduces the person to "the place in which that valuable thing called happiness takes place,"[48] and thereby fails to do justice to human agency, and (2) implies that to maximize utility, those with gourmet tastes should receive more income than those with "cheap" tastes.[49] By contrast, Rawls's democratic citizens have responsibility for choosing personal ends consistent with the justly available primary goods. Finally, Rawls's "'principles of justice' safeguard the 'priority' of individual liberty, subject to similar liberty for all."[50] (Rawlsian liberty is negative in the sense of freedom *from interference* by others or the state.) Hence, Sen concludes, "the Rawlsian theory of justice has, in fact, done much to draw attention to the political and ethical implications of individual freedom."[51]

Despite his admiration for Rawls's intention and achievement, Sen finds serious shortcomings in Rawls's theory of justice, especially in his concept of social primary goods. First, Sen, followed by Nussbaum, applies to Rawls's theory a variant of his (Sen's) "individual variation argument":

> Making comparisons of the primary goods different people have is not quite the same as comparing the freedoms actually enjoyed by different persons, even though the two can be closely related. Primary goods are *means* to freedom, but they cannot represent the *extent* of freedom, given the diversity of human beings in converting primary goods into the freedom to pursue their respective objectives.[52]

Rawls's theory of primary goods, argues Sen, would be a good way to judge people's "advantage" and make interpersonal comparisons if people were quite similar. However, in fact "we *are* diverse in *different* ways."[53] Rawls, however, fails to do justice to "*interindividual* variation" in the relation between primary goods and "the freedom to pursue ends":[54] "Variations related to sex, age, genetic endowments, and many other features give us unequal powers to build freedom in our lives even when we have the same bundle of goods."[55] Hence, equality in holding Rawlsian primary goods "can go hand in hand with serious inequalities in actual freedoms enjoyed by different persons."[56] For someone who cannot walk, the freedom to move about and, more generally, the ability "to lead the life that he or she would choose"[57] will require more income or resources than will the same freedom for a "normal" person. Freedom in the comprehensive, positive sense is not merely – as in negative freedom – "the absence of restraints that one person may exercise over another (or the state or other institutions may exercise over individuals)."[58] Positive freedom includes the absence of other kinds of restraints, such as poverty and ignorance, and the presence of options that people have reason to value. Rawls's focus on primary goods, coupled with his negative concept of liberty, neglects the positive freedoms people "actually enjoy to choose between different ways of living that they can have reason to value."[59] Justice must concern not just primary goods and negative freedoms; it must also concern the *extent* of positive freedom to achieve. Justice includes a concern for "the *overall* freedom to achieve" that includes both negative freedom and an "equality of effective freedoms."[60]

Rawls, Sen concedes, is not completely "ignoring"[61] the special needs of the disabled, old, and ill but is unfortunately "postponing"[62] their treatment. If the reason for such postponement is that these problems are uncommon, both Sen and Nussbaum insist that such defects and accidents are widespread.[63] If, argues Nussbaum, the reason is that the physically handicapped are not fully cooperating members of society, this would seem inconsistent with Rawls's stress on citizens as *moral* persons.[64] Rawls appears to believe that the problem of individual variation can be handled after the basic contract and during the legislative or judicial stages of his "four-stage sequence."[65] But if so, then the fact that different people might have greater and lesser abilities to influence the later stages implies that these differences would be more appropriately considered in the original contract.[66] Finally, Sen and Nussbaum stress that one finds many morally significant variations among people beyond differences due to defect or accident. These differences include such things as unequal social power or entitlement, which Rawls's analysis largely overlooks.[67] Such injustices can be uncovered and sometimes removed if we focus not merely on commodities but on what impedes or promotes their equal conversion into capabilities. Both resources and access to them are necessary as means. But because people are diverse, and diverse in different ways, the moral space in which justice is discussed must focus on the freely chosen conversion of accessed resources into valued ways of doing and being.

Second, both Sen and Nussbaum argue that Rawls moved into the "space" of capabilities but did so in an incomplete, vacillating, and misleading way. Recall that in his more recent writings Rawls explicitly defends his primary goods by arguing that they are necessary for moral personhood and social cooperation. In turn, moral personhood involves the capacity for autonomous choice of one's basic goals. Rawls, then, argues Sen, "is really after something like capabilities," for "he motivates the focus on primary goods by discussing what the primary goods enable people to do."[68] More specifically, Rawls's critique of utilitarianism appears to presuppose something like Nussbaum's notion, which she employed in the 1990s and subsequently dropped, of the "separateness of persons."[69] Similarly, Rawls in effect is endorsing at least one human capacity, that of capability to choose, albeit as an ideal presupposed in democratic practice rather than as a "final end." Furthermore, Rawls often lists "the social sources of self-respect" as one of his primary goods, and this description suggests that self-respect, if not a commodity itself, has an institutional source. However, Sen argues, Rawls also says that the primary good in question is "self-respect" as such, "an ability to achieve"[70] a certain sort of personal functioning. Finally, Rawls includes such noncommodity goods as liberties, rights, opportunities, and (most recently) "absence of physical pain" on his list of primary goods. Although Rawls is inclined to speak of these items – except for the last one – as "features of institutions" rather than of persons, Nussbaum suggests that Rawls's expansion of the list beyond income and wealth showed that he is groping toward a notion of human capabilities.[71]

Rawls replies only to Sen's first criticism, but his response is relevant to both objections. The "individual variability" argument is vitiated, says Rawls, because it presupposes the very thing that Rawls's *political* conception is intended to avoid, namely, a comprehensive and general moral doctrine. Sen and Nussbaum respond to Rawls's counter-argument in two interestingly different ways, and this difference, I believe, is based on a significant difference in their versions of the capability ethic.

Sen accepts Rawls's premise that we need a *political* conception of justice, that is, one that people can agree to regardless of substantive differences with respect to their concepts of the good life. Even so, Sen defends "actual freedom" or "capability for choice" by arguing that it is *not* part of a "comprehensive" moral conception, that is, one proposing an ultimate and universally valid conception of the good and responsible life. Sen contends that Rawls misunderstands Sen's objection and Sen's own view of "the *actual freedoms* enjoyed by different persons – persons with possibly divergent objectives – to lead different lives that they can have reason to value."[72] Sen insists that his employment of actual freedoms rather than commodities does *not* presuppose a particular comprehensive doctrine: "Capability reflects a person's freedom to choose between alternative lives (functioning combinations), and its valuation need not presuppose unanimity regarding one specific set of objectives (or, as Rawls calls it, 'a particular comprehensive doctrine')."[73] One reason why Sen sometimes stresses capability rather than actual functionings is precisely that we often value highly the freedom for a particular achievement or way of living without valuing very highly (or at all) that functioning or way of life. One may believe that religious liberty is important without valuing this particular religious way of life or indeed any such life.

Sen's point is that Rawls's primary goods, including the good of negative freedom, should be viewed as *means* to a positive freedom that makes possible the choice of various ways of living and diverse conceptions of ultimate ends. Whatever conception of the good life is offered, it is better – due to individual variability – to operate in the space of positive freedom or capability than in that in primary goods (or of exclusively functionings).

Moreover, Rawls's objection still fails to address adequately the problem of disabilities. For an unacceptable implication of Rawls's doctrine of social primary goods is that, due to convertability deficits mentioned earlier, "a disadvantaged person may get less from primary goods than others *no matter what comprehensive doctrine* he or she has."[74]

Furthermore, with respect to persons with disabilities, Sen can say that Rawls draws the line between liberty and non-liberty at an arbitrary point because he excludes from his concept of basic liberties the freedom of movement of the person who cannot walk. Such a person's freedom is enhanced not only when people refrain from preventing her from walking but also when she is provided with wheelchairs, curb easements, and elevators. Once we expand the notion of liberty to include positive as well as negative liberties, we are still far from a comprehensive or general moral view. Sen is not prescribing how to weigh specific negative and positive liberties, nor, within the latter, is he elevating walking, let alone trekking and being "on the road again," as essential elements in the humanly good life.

This is not to say that Sen's view is morally neutral, for, as I will discuss later, both pure utilitarianism and pure libertarianism are excluded by Sen's "capability space." But neither, for that matter, is Rawls's theory completely doctrine-neutral, for authoritarianism and Nietzschean perfectionism are inconsistent with Rawls's assumption that the parties in the original position are forging a conception of fair terms of cooperation for free and equal moral subjects or citizens. Sen's "capability-based assessment of justice" is more determinate than Rawls's theory because, if Sen is correct, his own perspective also rules out nonauthoritarian views, such as Rawls's, that fail to endorse positive liberty and make adequate room for the ideal of agency. Such exclusions, however, still would leave room for a vast range of different combinations of goods and functionings that different individuals and communities might choose or have reason to value:[75]

Even within the overall perspective of social commitment to individual freedom, there can, of course, be distinct views of the relative weights to be attached to different aspects of freedom, e.g., negative and positive freedoms respectively. An acceptance of that general perspective must not be seen as closing the door to differences of views on the relative weights.[76]

It is not that Sen is rejecting the possibility or desirability of citizens or theorists going further, within capability space, and working out a more determinate conception of "the" good life. Increasingly, however, Sen recognizes that there are two approaches to the problem of selecting, ranking, weighing, and trading off various ways of living: (1) social choice and (2) philosophical prescription. In social choice, members of a group engage in a social choice exercise and, even though they still disagree on many basics, forge an agreement on what to do. One social choice exercise is that of democracy, and in Part IV, especially in Chapter 9, I argue that the ideal and practice of deliberative democracy fits with and enriches Sen's normative commitments and is compelling in its own right. In philosophical prescription, the philosopher assumes or seeks to discover or construct *the* conception of the good human life. Sen correctly recognizes that Nussbaum is doing just that: "People do, of course, have different aims. Whether at a deep and sophisticated level a shared set of general objectives can be fruitfully assumed is an important question that has been addressed in the Aristotelian perspective by Martha Nussbaum."[77]

Regardless of whether Nussbaum's project or similar projects are ultimately successful, however, "it is important to recognize that interpersonal comparison of capabilities are not rendered impossible by the absence of an agreed 'comprehensive doctrine.'"[78] We can make some headway in social ethics by finding the right moral space and thereby excluding not only authoritarian views but such incomplete and one-sided views as welfarism (with its exclusive stress on utility), libertarianism (with its sole focus on negative liberty),[79] and Rawlsian theory (with its failure to acknowledge positive freedom).

Nussbaum responds to Rawls's counterargument in two ways, both of which are different from Sen's argumentation. Nussbaum's strategy has taken two very different forms. In her work before *Women and Human Development*, Nussbaum interpreted Rawls's moral theory as – contrary to his intentions – a comprehensive and ultimate conception of the good but one that Nussbaum contended was significantly incomplete. In *Women and Human Development*, by contrast, Nussbaum accepts that Rawls has offered a *political* conception of justice and a noncomprehensive or non-ultimate conception of the human good. Nussbaum then argues that Rawls's conception can be improved upon by her own equally "political" (non-metaphysical, non-ultimate) but more adequate view. I now examine each of Nussbaum's strategies.

In her earlier strategy, rather than following Sen and defending "actual freedom" or "choice" as *relatively* doctrine neutral, Nussbaum bit the bullet and argued that Rawls's ideals of autonomous choice and sociality were *themselves* part of his (liberal) conception of the human good. Rawls, argued Nussbaum, cannot defend his own theory of primary goods without himself assuming a comprehensive and superior conception of good human functionings and capabilities. Rawls cannot evaluate his primary goods as having worth without himself presupposing a thick theory of good living, without taking "some stand about what functions are constitutive of human good living."[80] If income and wealth are needed to be a moral person and citizen, then the capacity for personal and political choice and the ideal of cooperative living are being urged as part of the good life, at least in the *political* domain. Once this point is accepted, then, in Nussbaum's initial view, we can debate whether *other* sorts of capabilities, as powers of the person, should also be part of our conception of human flourishing – not only in the political domain but also in nonpolitical domains, such as in families and religious communities. The philosopher's job, then, is (1) to describe what it really means to live a fully human or flourishing life; and (2) in the light of this ultimate conception of the good, to prescribe the responsibility of every political (and nonpolitical) community. In what does that responsibility consist? In guaranteeing that every one who so chooses be able to achieve *the* flourishing human life.

In this first strategy Nussbaum offered her complex norm of human flourishing as a "thick, vague" conception of the good. She described it as a thick conception because her goal was to propose a universally valid concept of good, essential, or flourishing humanity. She described her norm, however, as "vague" for its general outlines permitted and even required that each group specify the norm in its own way.

In her subsequent and current strategy, Nussbaum abandons the project of coming up with an ultimate, nonpolitical (in Rawls's sense) conception of the good life and instead embraces Rawls's project of a *political* conception that citizens in fact do or could accept in spite of their different commitments on ultimate values. However, she still differs from the later Rawls on two key points. First, she offers her now *political* vision of the good life as relevant for members of *any* community, whether democratic or not. Second, whereas Rawls argues that the content and justification for the *political* conception should come from "public reason" – that is, from the conceptions accepted by or acceptable to the (majority of) members of the community – Nussbaum gives to the philosopher the job of formulating and defending the political conception of the good human life, which then should be embodied in every political community's constitution.

If we depart from Rawls's views, should we choose Sen's or Nussbaum's (or some other) strategy in criticizing Rawls's sophisticated "commodities" perspective? Originally I argued that both Sen's criticism and Nussbaum's first strategy have their place, but they must be seen as operating on different levels.[81] Sen, I argued, is "carving out," to trade in shovels for knives, "capability space." Nussbaum, I contended, is arguing that we should fill in or elaborate that space with a definite list of "capabilities" that include but go well beyond Rawls's two moral powers and his ideal of social cooperation. On my original interpretation, the responses of Sen and Nussbaum to Rawls, then, presuppose two sorts of moral inquiry that take place on distinct levels of ethical determinateness. On this reading, Sen identifies the general moral space of functioning and capability; and then Nussbaum fills in the picture by identifying those "central functional capabilities" that are (allegedly) necessary and sufficient for the good human life.

Perhaps because Sen and Nussbaum have sharpened their views since my original essay in 1992, I now see an important difference between the ways Sen and Nussbaum (on either of her two strategies) respond to Rawls and identify and rank capabilities and functionings. Sen, as we shall see in more detail in the next chapter, is not opposed to all listing of valuable functionings. What he sometimes expresses as "reluctance"[82] in searching for, and at other times forthrightly rejects, is "one predetermined canonical list of capabilities, chosen by theorists without any general social discussion or public reasoning."[83] Why? Because Sen contends that such a list would take away from individuals and communities the freedom and responsibility to decide for themselves, to be authors of their own lives: "To have such a fixed list, emanating entirely from pure theory, is to deny the possibility of fruitful public participation on what should be included and why."[84] Nussbaum, in contrast, fears that a political community, whether democratic or not, may fail to guarantee for all citizens what she takes to be the optimal capabilities. To establish this guarantee philosophically, she argues for her list; to secure the guarantees institutionally, she argues that the list should be embodied in a society's constitution. In later chapters I evaluate and try to resolve this controversy.

The welfare (utilitarian) approach

The commodities approach, whether crude or Rawlsian, overemphasizes goods and neglects people. The welfare approach, of which utilitarianism is a prime example, overemphasizes people's mental states and neglects other aspects of their well-being. The welfare approach does advance beyond the commodity approach by interpreting human well-being and good development as a feature of persons themselves.[85]

It goes astray, however, by paying exclusive attention to but one aspect of human well-being, namely, welfare interpreted as utility. Utility, however interpreted, is an incomplete conception of individual well-being and fails to yield an appropriate concept of human equality.

In objecting to welfarism, Sen focuses his criticism on two of the three components of the utilitarian moral theory that undergirds much of neo-classical economics and development economics and that continues to function as a dominant outlook in philosophical ethics. Sen distinguishes these three features of utilitarianism as follows:

(1) *Consequentialism*: The rightness of actions – and (more generally) of the choice of all control variables [e.g., acts, rules, motives] – must be judged entirely by the goodness of the consequent state of affairs.
(2) *Welfarism*: The goodness of states of affairs must be judged entirely by the goodness of the set of individual utilities in the respective states of affairs.
(3) *Sum-ranking*: The goodness of any set of individual utilities must be judged entirely by their sum total.[86]

Sen is sympathetic to a broadly conceived consequentialism, especially if it is able to accommodate rights-respecting *actions* in the states of affairs to be evaluated.[87] What he finds morally problematic in utilitarianism is its welfarism and its method of sum-ranking. I now consider what Sen finds deficient in the former, and later take up his criticism of the latter.

Sen recognizes that welfarism[88] comes in different forms depending on whether individual utility is interpreted as pleasure or happiness (a mental state), desire fulfillment (a person getting what she wants), or (informed) choice between options. For our purposes, it will suffice to concentrate on Sen's evaluation of the happiness and the desire fulfillment interpretations.[89]

Sen identifies two fundamental shortcomings in welfarism. First, welfare, in any of the three interpretations, is not the only thing that is valuable.[90] Welfarism conceives of humans as no more than loci or "sites"[91] of certain mental states or the gratification of desires. This angle of vision unfortunately abstracts from what Sen calls the "agency aspect"[92] of the person. Humans are not only experiencers or preference-satisfiers; they are also judges, evaluators, and doers. They decide on and revise their conceptions of the good as well as satisfy desires based on those conceptions. They form intentions and act on them, sometimes alone and sometimes in concert, and thereby sometimes change the world and themselves. And these basic aims, as I discuss in detail in Chapter 5, often go well beyond the agent's pursuit of utility and are even at odds with utility or any other conception of well-being or "personal advantage."[93]

With Sen's concept of agency, unfortunately neglected or de-emphasized by many interpreters, Sen is trying to do justice to a Kantian emphasis on autonomy.[94] Agency and well-being are, for Sen, two fundamental and irreducible normative dimensions of being human. Sometimes the two coincide, as when I decide and act to protect or advance my own well-being or when I make my own self-interest or passivity the only thing that matters. But agency and well-being can also diverge: a hunger striker or soldier risks his well-being (a component of which is his happiness) when what he chooses as a higher cause may result in a lessening or destruction of his well-being. It should be noted, and I return to this point in subsequent chapters, that Nussbaum, although she recently has employed some agency rhetoric, has no *concept* of agency in her normative arsenal because she believes she captures all that is important in Sen's concept with her own concepts of practical reason and control. In later chapters I criticize her arguments and argue that the absence of a concept of agency helps account for her reservations about democracy and democratic deliberation.

Second, Sen has powerful arguments that "utility does not adequately represent well-being."[95] Even if we restrict ourselves to the well-being aspect of human existence, a "metric of utility" is often a markedly poor reflection of personal well-being or deprivation. Sen does allow that being happy can be evidence for and even a component of well-being[96] and that (being capable of) happiness is one part of well-being.[97] Everything else being equal, it is better to be happy than miserable. Sen even goes so far as to call the mental state of being happy a "momentous functioning"[98] and "momentous achievement."[99] But happiness or desire fulfillment certainly is not sufficient for well-being and is woefully inaccurate as a complete measure of well-being.

To make his case, Sen offers what I called in 1992 his "small mercies argument."[100] People, contends Sen, may be seriously deprived and yet be quite cheerful. If they do not expect much from life, they may take great joy in whatever "small mercies" happen to come their way. Such a "small mercies" outlook occurs in Ralph Waldo Emerson's essay "Experience," in a passage apparently unknown to Sen:

I am grown by sympathy a little eager and sentimental, but leave me alone and I should relish every hour and what it brought me, the potluck of the day, as heartily as the oldest gossip in the bar-room. I am thankful for small mercies. I compared notes with one of my friends who expects everything of the universe and is disappointed when anything is less than the best, and I found that I begin at the other extreme, expecting nothing, and am always full of thanks for moderate goods . . . If we will take the good we find, asking no questions, we shall have heaping measures.[101]

It must be admitted that Emerson is trying to get his readers to recognize that it is the everyday and ordinary ("on the highway"), rather than academic "analysis," that is the source of life's good things.[102] Sen is worried, however, that it is precisely philosophical, political, or religious ideas that often mentally condition those who are objectively deprived – deprived of even Emerson's "moderate goods" – to accept and find justification for one's deprivation.[103] Given the influence of such "notions of legitimacy and correctness,"[104] very poor people adjust their aspirations and desires to the little that is feasible;[105] "induced by hopelessness," they make "defeatist compromises with harsh reality."[106] Given a sufficiently low level of aspiration and high level of accustomed misfortune, a person not surprisingly is overjoyed by "small mercies" and "his heart leaps up whenever he sees a rainbow in the sky."[107] Sen observes: "In some lives small mercies have to count big."[108] Instead of one's subjective mental state reflecting objective deprivations, those "deprivations are gagged and muffled."[109]

> The hopeless beggar, the precarious landless labourer, the dominated housewife, the hardened unemployed or the over-exhausted coolie may all take pleasures in small mercies, and manage to suppress intense suffering for the necessity of continuing survival, but it would be ethically deeply mistaken to attach a correspondingly small value to the loss of their well-being because of their survival strategy.[110]

> "He that desires but little has no need of much" may well be good advice for contentment and for coming to terms with a harsh reality. But it is not a formula for judging well-being. Nor is it a recipe for social justice.[111]

One result of this "false consciousness" is that "acute inequalities often survive precisely by making allies out of the deprived." Sen continues: "The underdog comes to accept the legitimacy of the unequal order and becomes an implicit accomplice."[112] Another consequence of the pervasiveness of what Jon Elster calls "adaptive preferences"[113] is that social ethicists should be wary of uncritically appealing to the values of poor and deprived people. Clark makes precisely this mistake, even though he accurately explains Sen's "small mercies" argument.[114] I argue in Chapter 9 that deliberative democracy offers a way that both takes seriously people's judgments and subjects them to collective rational scrutiny.

One can be happy or satisfied, then, yet lack wellness of being. The other side of this dialectical coin is that people may have well-being and even opulence (be "well off") and yet be unhappy and frustrated;[115]

their unfulfilled desires may be for rare Rioja wines and a top-of-the-line Mercedes. I return to this issue in Chapter 7, when I examine whether the capability approach can generate a reasonable ethics of consumption.

Finally, although discontent does not necessarily reflect well-being, it sometimes should be evaluated positively; grievances about an unjust social arrangement may be an important ingredient in individual self-assertion, collective action, and social progress.[116]

Together these considerations show the moral deficiencies of welfarist and utilitarian methods of moral "accounting" and interpretations of individual well-being. Human well-being cannot be identified with utility; and, for Sen, the human good cannot be identified with well-being. To make these identifications is to baptize deprivation as well as international and national injustice. What we need is a perspective that is concerned with what people are able to do and be – where being happy and getting satisfaction is only an aspect of well-being, and being able to be happy or to get what one desires is only *one* valuable capability among others.[117] Nussbaum puts it well:

The Aristotelian takes desire seriously as *one* thing we should ask about, in asking how well an arrangement enables people to live. But she insists that we also, and more insistently, ask what the people involved are actually able to do and to be – and, indeed, to desire. We consider not only whether they are asking for education, but how they are being educated; not only whether they perceive themselves as reasonably healthy, but how long they live, how many of their children die; how, in short, their health *is*.[118]

Basic needs

The basic needs approach (BNA) to international development, as worked out in the 1970s and 1980s by development economists and policymakers such as Paul Streeten, Frances Stewart, and Mahbub ul Haq, draws "attention, in an immediate and powerful way, to the importance of the type of life that people are able to lead."[119] It is, argues Sen, both an important breakthrough and a perspective in need of a deeper and more secure "foundation."[120] Sen offers his capability approach as just such an improved needs approach.

What does Sen find attractive about the BNA? The BNA criticizes those approaches that define development in relation to the economic growth – even the *equitable* economic growth – of commodities or utilities. Economic and societal development, says the BNA, is a matter of human well-being, which in turn is a function of meeting certain basic or human needs. We cannot really say that a society is developed unless it provides the opportunity for all its citizens to meet their basic needs. Streeten and his colleagues put it eloquently in 1981: "A basic needs approach to development attempts to provide the opportunities for the full physical, mental, and social development of the human personality and then derives the ways of achieving this objective."[121]

Sen also defends the BNA against the objection that economic growth and meeting needs are mutually exclusive, that a basic needs perspective inevitably reduces a country's economic growth and material prosperity. Sen's response is threefold. First, economic growth is an important means and not an end in itself. Second, although necessary or at least helpful, economic growth is not enough. Economic growth can take place without the basic needs of the majority being satisfied, as for instance in Brazil in the 1980s or Saudi Arabia in the 1990s; and a country, such as Costa Rica, can have modest economic growth and do well in meeting the needs of its citizens. Third, the "needs versus growth" controversy, properly understood, is not one of meeting needs versus economic prosperity but one of satisfying needs now versus meeting them in the future – *both* of which require economic goods as a means.[122]

Although strongly sympathetic, Sen also makes five criticisms of the BNA, which I term as follows: (1) the foundations criticism, (2) the individual variability criticism, (3) the social interdependence criticism, (4) the minimality criticism, and (5) the passivity criticism. I analyze and evaluate each.

The foundations criticism

Sen's first criticism of the BNA is that it lacks an adequate foundation. Again, this does not mean that the BNA has failed to produce a conclusive or transcendental justification for itself; for, as argued above, Sen is rightly satisfied with the fallibilistic justification provided by wide reflective equilibrium. To lack a foundation, rather, means that the BNA has left needs hanging, intuitively plausible but both conceptually ambiguous and argumentatively unsupported (as a nonreducible moral category). The BNA has failed to resolve the "unsettled question" of what, among conflicting interpretations, should be meant by the appeal to needs. Is need satisfaction important because of the mental state of *satisfaction*? This answer would fall back into welfarism. Is meeting needs reducible to providing people with certain amounts of commodities? If so, then the BNA becomes a new version of commodity fetishism, with the attendant defects discussed above. The BNA has often failed to consider whether the category of needs is morally ultimate. What Sen is trying to get at, I believe, is that the BNA has failed to clarify the nature and variety of needs and to justify (basic) needs as a moral category more fundamental than commodities, utilities, human flourishing, or rights.[123]

Sen argues that the BNA can advance by explicitly raising the question of foundations and answering it by interpreting needs as capabilities. The focus must be on certain intrinsically valuable human achievements and capabilities such as "being healthy, being well-nourished, being literate . . . [and] being able to freely choose to lead a particular life."[124] If we interpret basic needs as intrinsically valuable functionings (and capabilities to function), we will have a concept of human well-being that is morally appropriate, conceptually fundamental, and operationally practical. We will be able to accomplish the original aim of the BNA without falling back into either commodity fetishism or utility subjectivism.

In response to Sen's 1983 paper,[125] Paul Streeten, one of the key architects of the BNA, explicitly raised the "foundational" question for the BNA: "Do basic needs refer to the conditions for a full, long and healthy life, or to a specified bundle of goods and services that are deemed to provide the opportunity for these conditions?"[126] Indicating a difficulty in answering his question, Streeten continues: "Very little is known about the causal links between the provision of specific items, the capacity to meet certain needs, and the achievement of a full life."[127] In contrast, Sen's capability ethic, interpreting basic needs precisely *as* actual freedoms or capabilities, conceives these freedoms as part of the *content of human well-being* rather than the *conditions for* or *means to*, a full or flourishing life.[128] Sen would approve of Streeten's willingness to question commodities as bedrock. Sen, however, would urge Streeten to penetrate more deeply and construe meeting one's needs as having freedoms to pursue functionings that one has reason to value.

The individual variability criticism
In fact, according to Sen, the BNA has often collapsed into a commodities approach and hence is subject to the criticisms of "commodity fetishism," that is, an exaggerated or exclusive stress on commodities. The human *need* for food has tended to be replaced by a focus on the *food* needed. Although the BNA recognized in principle that different amounts of the same commodity were needed by different individuals, it tended operationally to define "basic needs" in terms of (certain amounts of) food, water, shelter, and hospital beds. Sen especially underscores what I called earlier his "interpersonal variability argument": "My main difficulty has been with the way basic needs are typically defined in terms of needs for *commodities*, and *that* I think

is a mistake . . . because of the enormity of interpersonal variations in converting commodities into capabilities."[129] Moreover, according to Sen, the BNA largely neglected what he called the "many-one correspondence" between commodities and capabilities: even in the same individual, the same functioning often can be achieved by more than one bundle of goods and services. The BNA, then, has not been able to exorcise fully the ghost of commodity fetishism. This failure, Sen appears to imply, is traceable to the *theoretical* failure of the BNA to carve out a distinctive space for the concept of needs. It may be, however, that a nuanced needs approach can meet Sen's criticism by carefully distinguishing need-satisfiers from the needs met.[130]

The social interdependence criticism

Sen's third criticism of the BNA, the "social interdependence argument," is rather tentative and undeveloped. A BNA will stress human needs for certain commodities. Even with respect to the need for food, it will be difficult to specify a bundle or amount of foodstuff *absolutely* or in a culturally and individually invariant way. The problem is only compounded when we move to such important social capabilities as being able to appear in public without shame or take part in community life. These sorts of achievements and capabilities make essential reference to the actions or judgments of *other* people. The commodity requirements for certain capabilities are not just a matter of matching a certain (amount of the) commodity with an isolated individual but must take into account "social interdependence."[131] A particular person's capability to appear in public without shame will make essential and substantial reference to the culturally relative judgments or evaluations of other social members concerning what counts as acceptable apparel. For example, Sen correctly sees that one "needs" more (and different) consumer goods in an affluent society than in an impoverished one.

In this criticism, Sen impales the BNA on the horns of a dilemma. Either the BNA collapses into a commodities approach (with respect to certain capabilities) or it does not. If it does, then it will not be able to specify the commodities in a culturally invariant way. The linen shirt required to avoid public shame in eighteenth-century England will not do the job in twenty-first-century Los Angeles. If the BNA takes the other horn, however, then "the needs of commodities may not be absolutely specifiable at all."[132] By contrast, Sen claims, we can specify absolute or culturally invariant deprivation and achievement in terms of functionings or capabilities. Unfortunately, Sen provides no argument for this contention, and it may be that needs and capabilities would be in the same boat with respect to either quantitative measurement or qualitative conception. How, for example, would we describe, let alone measure, invariant physical functioning with respect to body weight and "nonstunted" stature of Pygmies and Watusi? It seems optional whether we say that Pygmies and Watusi need adequate body weight and stature (or the relation between the two) or we say that one of their valuable functions is having adequate body weight and stature (or the relation between the two). We may be able to say with equal justification that all people have a universal need for X or that all people have a universal capability for X, where X in either case is sufficiently general as to permit different concrete specifications in different cultural contexts. If there is a distinction that makes a difference between needs talk and capabilities talk and one that favors the latter, that difference would appear to lie elsewhere.

The minimality criticism

Sen's fourth objection to the BNA goes like this. Because people have all sorts of needs from trivial ones to urgent ones, the BNA makes a distinction between basic and nonbasic needs and then interprets *basic* needs in terms of quantitative *minima* of the commodities – such as food, water, shelter – required to meet those needs. The focus is on meeting "minimum needs and no more."[133] Apart from the problem just discussed of falling back on commodities, Sen finds – depending on how the phrase is interpreted – two additional defects in this focus on "minimum needs and no more."

One meaning of BNA's concept of "minimal needs and no more" is that only *physical* needs are what count. Here physical needs would be those needs which food, health care, and shelter meet. One difficulty here, in addition to the overly narrow conception of well-being, is that the "haves," whether individuals or nations, easily can get the mistaken notion that their moral responsibilities end when minimal levels of physical needs are satisfied regardless of whether or not there are such things as opportunities for other valuable functionings, such as social and political participation, avoiding humiliation, and having self-respect. Humans do not live by bread alone; nor do they have reason to value merely good physical functioning. A focus on "basic needs and nothing more" lends itself to an excessive contraction of the concept of well-being and of moral responsibility. If the focus is on "*equality* of capabilities,"[134] then we go well beyond the norm of physical survival to that of being able to live a long, adequately nourished and adequately healthy life. The problem here, of course, is that many BNAs affirm the equal or even superior importance of nonphysical needs.[135] Just as Sen correctly wants to include more than physical capabilities in his concept of a life that goes well, so BNA advocates often embrace a good deal more than meeting physical needs.

Second, even if a robust notion of basic needs is employed, Sen argues that there is a second problematic meaning of "basic needs and no more." On this rendering, there is a sharp distinction between *basic and nonbasic* needs. Alternatively put, a *threshold* exists for need satisfaction, and getting people in poor countries to or over this line is the exclusive concern of development agents. The targets of development action are only those individuals who fall below the line, and those *poor* countries some percentage of whose citizens fall below the line.

Sen judges this view of BNA as a "familiar" but "unfair" caricature of the BNA, one that insists on one application of the approach to the unfortunate exclusion of other applications. Sen seeks to rescue the BNA from this caricature and limited application. First, the BNA is incomplete in failing to offer a way to distinguish the minimum level. Second, regardless of how many individuals fall below some poverty line, it is most urgent to seek improvement in the lives of those who are *most below* the threshold and more urgent to help those who are more below than those who are less so.[136] Otherwise, development agents may count as unqualified success those efforts that enable those just below the line to move just above it. But such success may do little to alleviate the *depth* of a group's deprivation. Third, sometimes it may be impossible to meet even the minimal needs of the neediest people, but that fact does not end social responsibility. It may be more urgent to reduce the shortfall of the neediest in relation to the – for them – unreachable threshold than getting the less needy (closer) to the threshold. Those most needy might receive proportionately more assistance so as to better close the gap between their level of need satisfaction and the threshold. Fourth, even if the proportions or absolute numbers on either side of the threshold stayed the same, an emphasis on meeting minimal needs may deflect development agents from reducing gaps within the top sector, within the bottom sector, or between the top and the bottom (both *within* and *between* nations), especially when such inequalities make the most needy even needier. Hence, a basic needs approach (BNA) caricature "may lead to a softening of the opposition to inequality in general."

Given these deficiencies in the idea of "minimum needs and no more," Sen calls not for rejecting the BNA approach altogether but for seeing it as "just one application of a more capability approach," an approach that can also be employed to address such questions as the depth of poverty, those unable to reach the threshold, and inequalities within and between rich and poor countries. In any case, it would be a mistake to construe Sen's minimality criticism as Sen's rejection of the very idea of a threshold (or the related distinction between the basic and the nonbasic, whether needs or capabilities). What Sen rejects, as we have seen, is a "concentration on just the minimum requirements." I committed this error in my 1992 article "Functioning and Capability" when I claimed that Sen rejected and had good reason to reject the idea of a threshold (and the related idea of a distinction between basic and nonbasic needs) and correctly replaced it with the ideas of *degrees* of advantage or well-being construed as degrees of valuable capabilities in individuals or (on average) in countries and other groups.[137] I now believe that I was wrong both in interpreting Sen and on the substantive issue.

It is true that, to my knowledge, Sen does not use the term "threshold" (until a 2004 discussion of "threshold conditions" that freedoms/capabilities must have "to qualify as the basis for human rights"[138]). This fact has led Martha Nussbaum mistakenly to assert that Sen does not employ the *concept* of threshold.[139] In "Equality of What?," however, Sen answers the question raised in the article's title with the answer "equality of 'basic capabilities': a person being able to do certain basic things."[140] Twelve years later he defines a "basic capability" as "the ability to satisfy certain elementary and crucially important functionings up to certain levels."[141] Two components are involved in this conception. First, the basic capabilities include both "elementary" ones, those that are (largely) physical and not substantially dependent on socially variable conventions, and those more complex (socially interdependent) freedoms that are also "crucially important ones":

The substantive freedoms include elementary capabilities like being able to avoid such deprivations as starvation, undernourishment, escapable morbidity and premature mortality, as well as the freedoms that are associated with being literate and numerate, enjoying political participation and uncensored speech and so on. In this constitutive perspective, development involves expansion of these and other basic freedoms.[142]

Second, a basic capability is the ability to realize *a certain amount or level* of an elementary or "crucially important" functioning. Hence, this aspect of the conception of basic capability clearly yields a *threshold*, even a quantitative threshold.

An important reason for Sen's affirming the idea of *basic* capability or a certain amount of an especially "important" freedom is that such ideas map nicely onto and arguably helps justify the ideal of human or basic moral rights:

Some of the relevant freedoms can also yield straightforward notions of rights. For example, minimal demands of well-being (in the form of basic functionings, e.g., not to be hungry) and of well-being freedom (in the form of minimal capabilities, e.g., having the means of avoiding hunger), can well be seen as rights that command attention and call for support.[143]

The importance of human rights relates to the significance of the freedoms that form the subject matter of these rights. Both the opportunity aspect and the process aspect of freedoms can figure in human rights. To qualify as the basis of human rights, the freedoms to be defended or advanced must satisfy some "threshold conditions" of (i) special importance and (ii) social influenceability.[144]

Part of what Sen appropriates from the BNA approach, then, is the notion of a threshold. A responsible government protects and promotes everyone's human or moral rights in the sense of ensuring, among other things, that those social members who *can* cross the line with respect to valuable functioning and choose to do so will be so empowered. It is wise, I believe, to retain BNA's use of threshold and a basic/nonbasic distinction as long as we do not neglect the fact that there are good reasons not to pay *exclusive* attention to the threshold and merely getting people to or over it. But, whether we emphasize basic needs or basic capabilities, we should be concerned not just with people's being empowered to cross a threshold of well-being but also with the *depth* of deprivation and the *gaps* between those at various levels of capability achievement or need satisfaction.

What Sen has not shown in his minimality criticism, however, is that the BHN approach must be viewed as but one application of the capability approach rather than as a free-standing normative perspective. It is unclear why Sen does not leave open the possibility that proponents of the BNA might both reject the *caricature* of BNA and still retain the language of need satisfaction rather than capability or capability achievement. Perhaps Sen is ultimately worried that needs language invariably connotes passivity.

The passivity criticism

Sen's fifth and final reason for transforming a needs-based ethic into a capability ethic concerns what I call "the passivity criticism":

"Needs" is a more passive concept than "capability," and it is arguable that the perspective of positive freedom links naturally with capabilities (what can the person *do*?) rather than with the fulfillment of their needs (what can be *done for* the person?).[145]

Sen concedes that the needs perspective is rhetorically appropriate for development aid to dependants such as children, the ill, and the severely disabled. The very old should also be added to this list. Development workers must do certain things to meet the needs of beneficiaries who, unfortunately, are – at least temporarily – unable to help themselves. Increasingly Sen expresses his point not in relation to the concept of capability but by appeal to his equally fundamental norm of agency (and empowerment).

It is good that individuals and communities are authors of their own lives, that they make their own decisions and have an impact on the world rather than be chess pieces moved by others or by natural events. Because we live in a world that frequently threatens autonomy, an adequate ethic should distinguish between this norm of *agency*, in which individuals decide for themselves and make a difference in the world, and *well-being* (both capabilities and functionings), which may be the result of luck or of the action of others. Good public action respects, promotes, and restores people's agency as well as expanding opportunities for well-being. Most adults, right now, and children, in the future, are assumed to be moral agents, and genuine social development aims to provide the conditions in which they *themselves* can select and acquire valuable capabilities, including that of substantial choice. As I have anticipated and shall argue in detail, Sen's emphasis on agent-centered development, with its emphasis on democracy and human rights, becomes even more pronounced in his latest writings, especially *Development as Freedom*.[146]

It is clear that Sen's norm of agency implies the limitations of any need-based development orientation in which poor people and nations are viewed as helpless beneficiaries of donor assistance. Something is amiss when development schemes impose valuable capabilities and functionings on passive recipients rather than empowering beneficiaries to acquire and exercise those capabilities themselves. This is one reason why Sen's capability approach supplements well-being (capability and functioning) with agency and balances the opportunity and process aspects of freedom.

However, just as Sen increasingly recognizes that capabilities and functionings without agency are insufficient, so a BNA can include on its list of basic needs such things as a need for self-help and autonomous choice. To meet or fulfill other basic needs can then be interpreted as "empowering" the recipients – with various sorts of aid – to meet their meta-need of autonomous, self-reliant action and thereby develop themselves and their societies. With the right sort of rhetorical recasting, the "passive" connotations of the BNA can be replaced with expressions that suggest "recipient" agency, without denying the liberating role that external help may play. Such recasting, however, requires that the BNA explicitly expands its list of "basic" needs well beyond its favorites – "material," "biological," or "subsistence" needs – and that it includes and perhaps emphasizes a *need* for autonomy or self-determination. Philosophers Gillian Brock and Soran Reader do exactly that:

Someone might worry that needs-centered ethicists are likely to be paternalistic, since if we focus on meeting the needs of others, we may be inattentive to their own capacities, desires, and preferences. Sophisticated beings, like persons, have complex needs like a need for autonomy, a need to be enabled to meet their own needs, and a need to have at least some of their non needs-based preferences recognized. Moral agents who fail to take account of such needs when they are crucial, would fail to give people what they need.[147]

If either a need-based approach or capability approach can yield a useful notion of (but not fixation on) a threshold as well as a conception of the self as agent, we must still ask whether a concept of needs has any role that cannot be played (or played as well) by Sen's notions of concepts of capability, functioning, and agency. Here we receive some help from Nussbaum.

Nussbaum argues that there are two nonreducible roles that the concept of need plays in a capability ethic. First, humans *need* to develop their nascent valuable capabilities into mature ones. Their "undeveloped," implicit, or embryonic capabilities are "*needs* for functioning":[148]

The Aristotelian conception . . . begins from the intuitive idea of a being who is neither a beast nor a god. This being comes into the world (the single world there is, the world of nature) characterized both by certain basic powers and by amazing neediness – by rich neediness, we might say, borrowing a phrase from Marx, in the sense that the very powers of this being exist as needs for fulfillment and claim, for their fully human development, rich support from the human and natural world.[149]

A need is satisfied when these implicit or potential capabilities become explicit or actual capabilities:

On this account, B-capabilities [Nussbaum's term for undeveloped or potential internal capabilities] are *needs* for functioning: they give rise to a claim because they are there and in a state of incomplete realization. They are conditions that reach towards, demand fulfillment in, a certain mode of activity. If that activity never arrives, they are cut off, fruitless, incomplete. As Aristotle insists, their very being makes reference to functioning; so without the possibility of functioning, they are only in a shadowy way even themselves.[150]

As she makes clear, Nussbaum's appeal to needs here is not to subjective desires or preferences or to some inner drive or tendency to "self-actualization." By "needs for functioning" she seems to mean that we *should* value and promote the development of our own and others' good potential capabilities and then realize them in functioning. Talk of our human *need* for *actual* capabilities and *actual* functionings is a way of saying that actuality is prior to possibility in the ethical sense that (1) actual capabilities are more valuable than merely latent ones and (2) actual valuable capabilities refer forward to functioning and, hence, "have a claim to be assisted in developing, and exert that claim on others, and especially, as Aristotle saw, on government."[151] This is not to say that valuable capabilities or freedoms are not also valuable in themselves, or that government should force its citizens to function in certain ways. It is to say, however, that "if functioning never arrives on the scene they [valuable capabilities] are hardly even what they are."[152]

It is not that the concept of need formulates some value-neutral fact about our being that biologically drives toward functioning or entails a personal or social duty. Rather, our cross-cultural human self-interpretations are such that we deem ourselves obliged to promote the acquisition and realization of certain capabilities or freedoms (in ourselves and others). And we view it as especially tragic when a young person, full of promise, dies before having the chance to develop and realize her excellent powers and seize her opportunities. To say that people have a need to develop themselves is to say that it is good, choice-worthy, and even obligatory that people acquire actual (and not just potential) capabilities and have the opportunity to realize them in functionings. Sen, I believe, can and should accept this point as one ingredient in a concept of personal and social responsibility. Where Sen and Nussbaum will differ, however, and here I side with Sen, is over whether the philosopher or the community itself should decide on the good potentials or valuable opportunities.[153] I return to this issue in the next and later chapters.

Nussbaum gives the concept of need a second role; she argues that valuable human capabilities are acquired and displayed precisely in relation to certain human needs in the sense of lacks and limits. A good athlete presses against her human limitations and makes them recede. But to extinguish deficiencies and limitations altogether – for instance, by gaining infinite speed by divine steroids – would eliminate both competition and the competitor. The same is true of virtue and responsibility. Without various vulnerabilities like death, we would not have the capability or freedom to be courageous in the face of our eventual demise. Without various deficiencies in ourselves and others, we would not have responsibilities to aid others and improve ourselves.

Sen has not really taken up these questions, but it seems clear that his intent is to push freedoms and capabilities as opportunities as far as he can without resorting to other concepts like the concept of need.[154] Sen's theory of actual freedom would be more comprehensive and humanly nuanced, however, if he followed Nussbaum and viewed humans not only as capable of valuable functions but also in *need* of certain powers and opportunities in a context of human limits, vulnerabilities, and standard threats. The agent's decisions of how to grow and function – of how to develop, do, and be – are to be made not just in relation to resources and opportunities but in relation to certain human deficiencies, disabilities, vulnerabilities, and expected threats that we must struggle against in humanly appropriate ways. Nussbaum is on the right track when she realizes that – as important as the concepts of capabilities and basic capabilities prove to be – important uses still exist for the language of needs. Because humans are needy in certain ways, it makes sense to say that – given our human limitations– without certain capabilities or freedoms our lives are likely to go very badly. And given our human vulnerabilities, certain powers and freedoms give us the chance for – as well as being components of – our lives going well.

Taking up Nussbaum's two suggestions for a nonreducible role for needs within a capability orientation we arrive at a twofold conclusion. First, the idea of "*rich* neediness" points to our responsibilities to realize those potential and actual freedoms that are valuable. Second, a concept of human *neediness* formulates those human limitations and vulnerabilities in relation to which certain powers and freedoms enable us to press against our limits, often avoid serious harm, and have a chance to live well.[155]

Concluding remarks

To summarize, Sen and Nussbaum identify – sometimes in similar ways and sometimes in different ways – both strengths and weaknesses of fundamental ethical categories employed in four ethical perspectives for assessing national and international development. Commodities, both crude commodities (income, goods, services) and Rawlsian social primary goods, are necessary but insufficient either for positive freedom or for adequate functioning. Utility at best captures part of a life going well but at worst justifies severe deprivation and inequality. A basic human needs approach is concerned that development benefits human beings in ways that go beyond their subjective preferences and satisfy certain fundamental needs. This perspective, however, sometimes falls back on commodities or utilities, fails to clarify and defend its basic assumptions, and may employ language excessively susceptible to various kinds of misuse. On the other hand, as Nussbaum sees, there may be roles for the concept of needs within a capabilities approach, and Sen's agency and capability approach may not advance clearly over improved versions of the basic needs approach. Implicit in Sen's and Nussbaum's assessments of commodities, utilities, and needs are their own normative concepts of capability (Sen and Nussbaum) and agency (Sen), to which we now turn.

NOTES

This chapter is a thorough revision of the second section of "Functioning and Capability: The Foundation of Sen's and Nussbaum's Development Ethic," *Political Theory*, 20, 4 (1992): 584–612, and *Florecimiento humano y desarrollo internacional: La nueva ética de capacidades humanas* (San José: Editorial de la Universidad de Costa Rica, 1998), 9–59. I gave papers from which the published essays were derived at the International Development Ethics Association Workshop "Ethical Principles for Development: Needs, Capacities or Rights?," Montclair State University (1991), the World Conference of Philosophy, Nairobi, Kenya (1991), and the University of Costa Rica, the National Autonomous University, and the University of San Carlos (Guatemala). I received helpful comments from Des Gasper and Verna Gehring.

1. For a discussion of the way in which Sen and Nussbaum – sometimes together but more often separately – contributed prior to 1992 to each of the seven components of the capability theory-practice of development, see Crocker, "Functioning and Capability," 584–8.
2. Amartya Sen, "The Concept of Development," in *Handbook of Development Economics*, I, ed. Hollis Chenery and T. N. Srinivasan (Amsterdam: North-Holland, 1988), 19.
3. Martha Nussbaum, "Aristotle on Human Nature and the Foundations of Ethics," in *World Mind and Ethics: Essays on the Ethical Philosophy of Bernard Williams*, ed. J. E. J. Altham and Ross Harrison (Cambridge: Cambridge University Press, 1995), 25.
4. Martha Nussbaum and Amartya Sen, "Internal Criticism and Indian Rationalist Traditions," in *Relativism, Interpretation and Confrontation*, ed. Michael Krausz (Notre Dame, IN: University of Notre Dame Press, 1989), 299–325; and Martha Nussbaum, "Human Functioning and Social Justice: In Defense of Aristotelian Essentialism," *Political Theory*, 20, 2 (1992): 202–47.
5. Nussbaum, "Human Functioning."
6. Nussbaum and Sen, "Internal Criticism and Indian Rationalist Traditions"; and Nussbaum, "Human Functioning."
7. This "internalist" conception of ethical inquiry, truth, and objectivity draws on Nussbaum's critique of Plato and interpretation of Aristotle in Martha Nussbaum, *The Fragility of Goodness: Luck and Ethics in Greek Tragedy and Philosophy* (Cambridge: Cambridge University Press, 1986), as well as on Hilary Putnam's distinction between externalist and internalist realism. See Hilary Putnam, *Realism with a Human Face* (Cambridge, MA: Harvard University Press, 1990); "Pragmatism and Moral Objectivity," in *Women, Culture, and Development*, ed. Martha Nussbaum and Jonathan Glover (Oxford: Clarendon Press; New York: Oxford University Press, 1995),

199–224; and *The Collapse of the Fact/Value Dichotomy* (Cambridge, MA: Harvard University Press, 2002).

8. Amartya Sen, *Resources, Values and Development* (Oxford: Blackwell, 1984), 310.

9. Martha Nussbaum, "Therapeutic Arguments: Epicuras and Aristotle," in *The Norms of Nature: Studies in Hellenistic Ethics*, ed. Malcolm Schofield and Gisela Striker (Cambridge: Cambridge University Press, 1986), 62.

10. Sen, *Resources, Values and Development*, 310. The metaphor of digging leaves something to be desired. On the one hand, the image suggests a builder getting down to bedrock in order to erect a building on a firm foundation. Such an independent and preexisting grounding unfortunately suggests the very externalism that Sen and Nussbaum wish to avoid. On the other hand, the activity of digging suggests an archaeologist excavating ancient ruins of which only the foundations remain. As such, the metaphor hardly conveys the idea of the basic concepts of a living moral outlook. I owe this point to discussions with Les Blomberg.

11. Amartya Sen, *On Ethics and Economics* (Oxford: Blackwell, 1987), 2–4; Nussbaum, *Love's Knowledge: Essays on Philosophy and Literature* (Oxford and New York: Oxford University Press, 1990), 23–9, 172–6; and "Human Capabilities, Female Human Beings," in *Women, Culture and Development*, ed. Nussbaum and Glover, 61–104, 180.

12. See my *Praxis and Democratic Socialism: The Critical Social Theory of Marković and Stojanović* (Atlantic Highlands, NJ: Humanities Press; Brighton: Harvester Press, 1983), ch. 6; John Rawls, *A Theory of Justice*, rev. edn. (Cambridge, MA: Belknap Press of Harvard University Press), 18–19, 42–45; and *Justice as Fairness: A Restatement*, ed. Erin Kelly (Cambridge, MA: Belknap Press of Harvard University Press, 2001), 29–32.

13. Nussbaum, "Therapeutic Arguments: Epicuras and Aristotle," 61.

14. Nussbaum, "Aristotle on Human Nature and the Foundations of Ethics," 13.

15. David Alexander Clark, *Visions of Development: A Study of Human Values* (Cheltenham: Edward Elgar, 2002), 33.

16. Nussbaum, "Aristotelian Social Democracy," in *Liberalism and the Good*, ed. R. Bruce Douglass, Gerald R. Mara, and Henry S. Richardson (London and New York: Routledge, 1990), 203–52, 219; "Human Capabilities, Female Human Beings," 80; and *Women and Human Development* (Cambridge: Cambridge University Press, 2000), esp. ch. 2.

17. Nussbaum, "Aristotle on Human Nature and the Foundations of Ethics," 17.

18. Ibid.

19. Ibid., 21–2.

20. Sen, *Resources, Values and Development*, 510.

21. Amartya Sen, *Commodities and Capabilities* (Amsterdam: North-Holland, 1985), 28.

22. Nussbaum, "Aristotelian Social Democracy," 210.

23. Ibid.

24. Sen, *Resources, Values and Development*, 511; *Commodities and Capabilities*, 26; "Well-being, Agency and Freedom: The Dewey Lectures, 1984,"

Journal of Philosophy, 82, 4 (1985): 199; "Freedom of Choice: Concept and Content," *European Economic Review*, 32 (1988): 277; "The Standard of Living," in *The Standard of Living: The Tanner Lectures on Human Values*, ed. Amartya Sen, J. Muellbauer, Ravi Kanbur, K. Hart, and Bernard Williams (Cambridge: Cambridge University Press, 2000), 16; *Inequality Reexamined* (Cambridge, MA: Harvard University Press, 2002), 8, 36–8, 109–12; *Development as Freedom* (New York: Knopf, 1999), 67–74, 90–4; Martha Nussbaum, "Aristotelian Social Democracy," 211; *Women and Human Development*, 60–1.

25. Milo the wrestler, rather than a newcomer in the World Wrestling Federation, was an Athenian athlete made – perhaps unduly – famous by being featured in Aristotle's *Nicomachean Ethics*, 1106b3, and Nussbaum, "Aristotelian Social Democracy," 211.

26. Nussbaum, "Aristotelian Social Democracy," 211; Sen, *Commodities and Capabilities*, 10.

27. Sen, "Well-being, Agency, and Freedom," 199; see also *Development as Freedom*, 70–1.

28. Sen, *Resources, Values and Development*, 27, 332–8. See also *Inequality Reexamined*, 115–16; and *Development as Freedom*, 71–4.

29. Sen, *Resources, Values and Development*, 335.

30. Sen, "The Standard of Living," 18; *Resources, Values and Development*, 333 and essay 14. See also *Inequality Reexamined*, 115–16; *Development as Freedom*, 89; Nussbaum, "Non-relative Virtues: An Aristotelian Approach," *Midwest Studies in Philosophy*, 13 (1993): 32–53; *Women and Human Development*, 105.

31. Sen, *Resources, Values and Development*, 512.

32. Nussbaum, "Aristotelian Social Democracy," 210.

33. Ibid., 256, n. 20.

34. Nussbaum, "Human Functioning," 42.

35. See Rawls, *Theory*, 54–5, 78–81; "Kantian Constructivism in Moral Theory: The Dewey Lectures 1980," *Journal of Philosophy*, 77, 9 (1980): 515–72; "Social Unity and Primary Goods," in *Utilitarianism and Beyond*, ed. Amartya Sen and Bernard Williams (Cambridge: Cambridge University Press, 1982), 159–85; "Justice as Fairness: Political not Metaphysical," *Philosophy and Public Affairs*, 14 (1985): 223–51; "The Idea of an Overlapping Consensus," *Oxford Journal of Legal Studies*, 7 (1987): 1–25; "The Priority of Right and Ideas of the Good," *Philosophy and Public Affairs*, 17 (1988): 251–76; "The Domain of the Political and Overlapping Consensus," *New York University Law Review*, 64, 2 (1989): 233–55; *Political Liberalism*, 2nd edn. (New York: Columbia University Press, 1996), 178–90; *Justice as Fairness*, 168–76.

36. Rawls, *Theory*, 54. In the initial edition of *Theory* (1971), Rawls's list includes "powers": *Theory*, 1st edn., 62.

37. *Theory*, 2nd edn., 348.

38. Ibid., 22, 230–1, 285–92, 347–8.

39. Rawls, "The Priority of Right," 257.

40. Rawls, "Kantian Constructivism," 526.

41. Ibid., 535.
42. Rawls, *Political Liberalism*, 181.
43. Ibid.
44. Rawls, "The Priority of Right," 252.
45. Ibid., 251.
46. Amartya Sen, "Individual Freedom as a Social Commitment," *New York Review of Books*, 37 (June 14, 1990): 49–54.
47. Sen, *Resources, Values and Development*, 339. See Sen, "Equality of What?," in *The Tanner Lectures on Human Values*, I, ed. Sterling M. McMurrin (Salt Lake City: University of Utah Press, 1980), 218; *Inequality Reexamined*, 75–9; *Development as Freedom*, 63–5.
48. Sen, *Resources, Values and Development*, 308.
49. Ibid., 279–80.
50. Sen, "Individual Freedom," 52.
51. Ibid.
52. Ibid. See Sen, *Inequality Reexamined*, 81–7; *Development as Freedom*, 72–6; Nussbaum, *Women and Human Development*, 65–70, 88–9.
53. Amartya Sen, "Justice: Means Versus Freedoms," *Philosophy and Public Affairs*, 19, 2 (1990): 121. See also *Inequality Reexamined*, 85–7.
54. Ibid., 120; Sen, *Inequality Reexamined*, 85.
55. Ibid., 121; Sen, "Equality of What?," 215–16; and "Individual Freedom," 52.
56. Sen, "Justice: Means Versus Freedoms," 115; *Inequality Reexamined*, 85–6.
57. Sen, "Individual Freedom," 49.
58. Ibid.
59. Sen, "Justice: Means Versus Freedoms," 115.
60. *Inequality Reexamined*, 86.
61. Sen, "Equality of What?," 216.
62. Amartya Sen, *Choice, Welfare and Measurement* (Oxford: Blackwell; Cambridge, MA: MIT Press, 1982), 30.
63. Sen, "Justice: Means Versus Freedoms," 116; Nussbaum, "Aristotelian Social Democracy," 211; and "Human Functioning," 46.
64. Nussbaum, "Aristotelian Social Democracy," 211.
65. Rawls, *Theory*, 171–6.
66. Sen, "Justice: Means Versus Freedoms," 117, n. 18.
67. For Sen on economic and social inequality, see his *On Economic Inequality*, enlarged edition, with a substantial annexe "*On Economic Inequality* after a Quarter Century" by James E. Foster and Amartya Sen (Oxford: Clarendon Press, 1997); and Jean Drèze and Amartya Sen, *India: Development and Participation*, 2nd edn. (Oxford: Oxford University Press), esp. xiv–xv, 1–5, 54–6, 69–71, 343–5, and 352–8. In fairness to Rawls, it should be noted that a strain exists in *Theory* in which Rawls recognizes and seeks to mitigate the fact that unequal power and advantage result in the unequal *value* of primary goods such as liberty; see *Theory*, 244–6; and Alan Gilbert, "Equality and Social Theory in Rawls: A Theory of Justice," *Occasional Review*, 8/9 (1978): 92–117. Norman Daniels tries to strengthen the Rawlsian approach's ability to deal with both physical disability and unequal social power by emphasizing, more than does Rawls himself, Rawls's principle of "fair equality

of opportunity." See Norman Daniels, "Equality of What: Welfare, Resources, or Capabilities?" *Philosophy and Phenomenological Research*, 50, Supplement (Fall 1990): 273–96.

68. Sen, *Resources, Values and Development*, 320.
69. Nussbaum, "Human Functioning," 45.
70. Sen, *Resources, Values and Development*, 32.
71. Nussbaum, "Aristotelian Social Democracy," 249, n. 73. See *Women and Development*, 65–70.
72. Sen, "Justice: Means Versus Freedoms," 112.
73. Sen, *Inequality Reexamined*, 83. Cf. "Justice: Means Versus Freedoms," 117.
74. Sen, *Inequality Reexamined*, 83.
75. See Sen, "Justice: Means Versus Freedoms," 114. Discussions with Lawrence Crocker helped me clarify Sen's notion of positive freedom and his critique of Rawls.
76. Sen, "Individual Freedom," 54.
77. Amartya Sen, "Gender Inequality and Theories of Justice," in *Women, Culture and Development*, ed. Nussbaum and Glover, 269.
78. Ibid.
79. Sen, "Individual Freedom," 54.
80. Martha Nussbaum, "Nature, Function, and Capability: Aristotle on Political Distribution," in *Oxford Studies in Ancient Philosophy*, supp. vol. (Oxford: Clarendon Press, 1988), 152; and "Aristotelian Social Democracy," 214, 227, 248, n. 73.
81. Crocker, "Functioning and Capability," 599.
82. Amartya Sen, "Human Rights and Capabilities," *Journal of Human Development*, 6, 2 (2005): 157.
83. Ibid., 158.
84. Ibid.
85. Sen, *Commodities and Capabilities*, 23.
86. Sen, *Resources, Values and Development*, 278. See also *Inequality Reexamined*, 73–5; and *Development as Freedom*, 58–60.
87. See Amartya Sen, "Consequent Evaluation and Practical Evaluation," *Journal of Philosophy*, 97, 9 (2000): 477–502.
88. Conceptual confusion often results not only because economists have at least three different interpretations of "welfare" but also because economists and others often use the terms "welfare" and "well-being" interchangeably. As we shall see, Sen sharply distinguishes his concept of well-being from the concepts of welfare and utility. This confusion is compounded in Spanish because one term, *bienestar*, is used to translate both the English "welfare" and "well-being." Hence, Spanish readers are understandably confused when Sen offers a non-welfarist concept of well-being.
89. Both Sen and Nussbaum appreciate that certain forms of philosophical utilitarianism – for instance, those emphasizing informed or enlightened preferences – have departed significantly from the pure preference theory of economic utilitarianism and are approaching the "capability perspective." See Sen, *Commodities and Capabilities*, 24; *Inequalities Reexamined*, 43, n. 15;

Nussbaum, *Love's Knowledge*, chs. 2 and 3; and "Human Functioning," 41. See R. B. Brandt, *Theory of the Good and the Right* (Oxford: Clarendon Press, 1979); James Griffin, *Well-being: Its Meaning, Measurement and Moral Importance* (Oxford: Clarendon Press, 1986). It is beyond the scope of the present study to analyze and evaluate whatever gaps remain between philosophical utilitarianism and the capability ethic.

90. Sen, *On Ethics and Economics*, 4.
91. Amartya Sen and Bernard Williams, "Introduction," *Utilitarianism and Beyond*, ed. Amartya Sen and Bernard Williams (Cambridge: Cambridge University Press, 1982), 4.
92. Sen, "Well-being, Agency and Freedom," 169.
93. Sen, *On Ethics and Economics*, 58–9.
94. In my 1992 article "Functioning and Capability," 600, I noted Sen's agency-based criticism of utilitarianism, but I failed to recognize sufficiently the importance that Sen gave – as early as the 1980s and early 1990s – the concept of agency.
95. Ibid., 47.
96. Sen, *Commodities and Capabilities*, xi.
97. Sen, "Well-being, Agency and Freedom," 195–6.
98. Ibid., 200.
99. Sen, *On Ethics and Economics*, 60. Following Aristotle, Nussbaum conceives of pleasure as supervening on activity rather than, as Sen is inclined to, as a separate and special functioning. See Nussbaum, *Love's Knowledge*, 56–8, 108–13. After citing Sen's endorsement of happiness as a "momentous functioning," David Clark surprisingly and mistakenly, I believe, faults Sen for not affirming the importance in ordinary lives of the pleasures that may derive from such activities as playing and watching sports, watching television, hanging out with friends, and wearing fashionable clothes (Clark, *Visions of Development*, 39–48). Sen acknowledges the importance in most people's lives of various kinds of mental states, such as happiness and pleasure. However, as the "small mercies argument," to be discussed next, makes clear, the experience and search for pleasure can hide ways in which pleasure either camouflages or causes ill-being.
100. Crocker, "Functioning and Capability," 601.
101. Ralph Waldo Emerson, *The Complete Essays and Other Writings of Ralph Waldo Emerson*, ed. Brooks Atkinson (New York: Modern Library, 1940), 351.
102. In his comments on a draft of my original *Political Theory* article, Tracy Strong urged this interpretation of Emerson.
103. Sen, "Well-being, Agency and Freedom," 188.
104. Sen, "Gender Inequality and Theories of Justice," 2.
105. Sen, *Resources, Values and Development*, 309.
106. Ibid., 512.
107. Sen, "Equality of What?," 217.
108. Ibid.
109. Sen, "Well-being, Agency and Freedom," 191.
110. Sen, *On Economics and Ethics*, 45–6.

111. Sen, *Resources, Values, and Development*, 34. See also "Well-being, Agency, and Freedom," 191; *Inequality Reexamined*, 6–7, 55; *Development as Freedom*, 62–3; "Elements of a Theory of Human Rights," *Philosophy and Public Affairs*, 32, 4 (2004): 328–9.
112. Sen, "Gender and Cooperative Conflicts," in *Persistent Inequalities*, ed. Irene Tinker (New York: Oxford University Press, 1990), 126.
113. Jon Elster, *Ulysses and the Sirens* (Cambridge: Cambridge University Press, 1979).
114. Clark, *Visions of Development*, 33.
115. Sen, "Well-being, Agency and Freedom," 196; and Nussbaum, "Aristotelian Social Democracy," 213.
116. Sen, *Resources, Values, and Development*, 512.
117. Sen, "Equality of What?," 211; see Sen, *Resources, Values and Development*, 318; *Inequalities Reexamined*, 53–5; and *Development as Freedom*, 58–62; and Nussbaum, *Women and Human Development*, ch. 2.
118. Nussbaum, "Aristotelian Social Democracy," 213.
119. Sen, "The Standard of Living," 24. See Paul Streeten, with Shavid Javed Burki, Mahbub ul Haq, Norman Hicks, and Frances Stewart, *First Things First: Meeting Basic Needs in Developing Countries* (New York: Oxford University Press, 1981); Frances Stewart, *Planning to Meet Basic Needs* (London: Macmillan, 1985); and "Basic Needs Strategies, Human Rights and the Right to Development," *Human Rights Quarterly*, 11 (1989): 347–74; Jerome M. Segal, "What Is Development?" Working Paper DN-1 (College Park, MD: Institute for Philosophy and Public Policy, 1986), and in *Philosophical Dimensions of Public Policy, Policy Studies Review Annual*, 13, ed. Verna V. Gehring and William A. Galston (New Brunswick, NJ, and London: Transaction, 2002), 211–19; Peter Penz, "The Priority of Basic Needs: Towards a Consensus in Development Ethics for Political Engagement," in *Ethical Principles for Development: Needs, Capacities or Rights?* ed. Ken Aman (Upper Montclair, NJ: Institute for Critical Thinking, Montclair State University, 1991), 35–73; Manfred Max-Neef, "Development and Human Needs," in *Real-Life Economics: Understanding Wealth Creation*, ed. Paul Elkins and Manfred Max-Neef (London: Routledge, 1992), 197–213; Sabina Alkire, *Valuing Freedoms: Sen's Capability Approach and Poverty Reduction* (Oxford: Oxford University Press, 2002), 11–15, 157–63; Des Gasper, *The Ethics of Development: From Economism to Human Development* (Edinburgh: Edinburgh University Press, 2004), ch. 6. Important accounts of needs-centered ethical or political theory include David Wiggins, "Claims of Need," in *Morality and Objectivity*, ed. Ted Honderich (London: Routledge, 1985); David Braybrooke, *Meeting Needs* (Princeton: Princeton University Press, 1987); Nancy Fraser, *Unruly Practices* (Cambridge: Polity Press, 1989); Len Doyal Ian Gough, *A Theory of Need* (London: Macmillan, 1991); Gillian Brock, "Braybrooke on Needs," *Ethics*, 104 (1994): 811–23; *Our Responsibilities to Meet Others' Needs*, ed. Gillian Brock (Lanham, MD: Rowman & Littlefield, 1998); Gillian Brock and Soran Reader, "Needs-Centered Ethical Theory," *Journal of Value Inquiry*, 36 (2002): 425–34.

120. As early as 1973, Sen himself had argued for the superiority of a needs framework over other currently available options: "In this book my emphasis has been primarily on needs, and the analytical framework presented here is biased in that direction": *On Economic Inequality*, 104. As late as 1981, Sen describes his own emerging view as "a version of a needs-based approach": *Resources, Values and Development*, 301.

121. Streeten *et al.*, *First Things First*, 33.

122. Sen, *Resources, Values and Development*, 515. Cf. Penz, "The Priority of Basic Needs."

123. Perhaps the failure to "ground" needs and the tendency to define them in terms either of commodities or utilities are due to the referential structure or "relational formula" of our concept of needs: person A needs X in order to Y. It is easy to slide from the need for X either to X itself (what is needed) or to Y (the purpose for which it is needed). See David Braybrooke's canvassing of the "charges against the concept of needs" in *Meeting Needs*, ch. 1.

124. Sen, "The Concept of Development," 16–17.

125. Sen, *Resources, Values and Development*, essay 20.

126. Paul Streeten, "Basic Needs: Some Unsettled Questions," *World Development*, 12, 9 (1984): 974.

127. Ibid.

128. Later I distinguish between Sen's norm of well-being and Nussbaum's "thicker" norm of the full life or human flourishing. In "Needs-Centered Ethical Theory," *Journal of Value Inquiry*, 36 (2002): 430, Gillian Brock and Soran Reader say that "a need is basic if satisfying it is necessary for flourishing to be possible."

129. Personal correspondence from Amartya Sen, February 3, 1991.

130. See Alkire, *Valuing Freedoms*, 157–63; and Manfred Max-Neef, "Development and Human Needs," in *Real-Life Economics*, ed. Max-Neef, 197–213; Gasper, *The Ethics of Development*, ch. 6.

131. Sen, *Resources, Values and Development*, 514.

132. Ibid.

133. Ibid., 515.

134. Ibid.

135. Max-Neef, "Development and Human Needs"; and Abraham Maslow, *Motivation and Human Personality*, 2nd edn. (New York: Harper & Row, 1970).

136. Sen, *Inequality Reexamined*, ch. 7; James Foster and Amartya Sen, " '*On Economic Inequality*' after a Quarter Century," annexed to Amartya Sen, *On Economic Inequality*, 168–70.

137. Crocker, "Functioning and Capability," 605–606.

138. Sen, "Elements of a Theory of Human Rights," 319.

139. Nussbaum, *Women and Human Development*, 12.

140. Sen, "Equality of What?," 218. See also Sen, *Resources, Values and Development*, 297; "Well-being, Agency and Freedom," 217.

141. *Inequality Reexamined*, 45, n. 19.

142. Sen, *Development as Freedom*, 36.

143. Sen, "Well-being, Agency and Freedom," 217. Cf. Brian Orend's conception of human rights in relation to a complex normative and threshold notion of "having vital interests in a minimally good life": Brian Orend, *Human Rights: Concept and Context* (Peterborough, ON: Broadview, 2002), 62–5.
144. Sen, "Elements of a Theory of Human Rights," 319; see also 318–30.
145. Sen, *Resources, Values and Development*, 514.
146. Sen, *Development as Freedom*, 11.
147. Brock and Reader, "Needs-Centered Ethical Theory," 431–32. See also n. 119 above for the writings of Doyal and Gough, Max-Neef, and Gasper.
148. Nussbaum, "Nature, Function, and Capability," 169. See also Nussbaum, "Human Capabilities, Female Human Beings," 88.
149. Nussbaum, "Aristotelian Social Democracy," 243 (Footnote in quotation omitted).
150. Nussbaum, "Nature, Function, and Capability," 169. See also Nussbaum, "Human Capabilities, Female Human Beings," 88.
151. Nussbaum, "Human Capabilities, Female Human Beings," 88.
152. Ibid.
153. At this juncture, I leave open whether the question, which I address in the next chapter, of whether capabilities are best understood as (potential) inner powers (Nussbaum) or substantive opportunities (Sen).
154. See Bernard Williams' probing of whether there is some concept more basic than capability: "The Standard of Living," 101.
155. See Brock and Reader, "Needs-Centered Ethical Theory," 430–3.

5 Agency, functioning, and capability

Having examined Sen's and Nussbaum's assessments of alternative ethical approaches to development, we are in a position in the present chapter to analyze and evaluate the fundamental concepts in their respective ethical outlooks. A fundamental and often underemphasized or completely neglected distinction in Sen's ethic is that between agency, which includes both agency freedom and agency achievement, and well-being, which includes both capability and functioning. In the first section I explain the distinction between agency and well-being and the cross-cutting distinction of achievement and freedom. After analyzing and evaluating the evolution of Sen's concept of agency from an empirical concept of human motivation to an ethical ideal of autonomy and action, I argue that Nussbaum's concepts of practical reason and control are both less robust and less defensible than Sen's ideal of agency. In the second section I analyze, compare, and evaluate Sen's and Nussbaum's concepts of functioning and capability and the different roles these concepts play in their respective normative outlooks. In the next chapter I analyze and evaluate differences that have emerged with respect to Sen's and Nussbaum's favored ways of *evaluating* capabilities and functionings.

Agency and well-being, freedom and achievement

Central to the normative "foundation" of Sen's development ethic are two cross-cutting distinctions: (1) agency and well-being, and (2) achievement and freedom. With the help of Figure 5.1, I explain the basic ideas.

Sen conceives of *agency* and *well-being* as two distinguishable but linked aspects of human life, each of which calls for respect (aid, protection) on the part of individuals and institutions.[1] The centrality of these two concepts in Sen's development ethic is suggested by the title of a 1995 essay, "Agency and Well-being: The Development Agenda."[2] In his initial account, one Sen set forth in articles and books through 1993,

150

	Agency	Well-being
Achievement	Agency Achievement	Well-being Achievements (Functionings)
Freedom	Agency Freedom	Well-being Freedoms (capabilities)

Figure 5.1. Agency and well-being; achievement and freedom

Sen describes agency achievement in the following way: "a person's agency achievement refers to the realization of goals and values she has reasons to pursue, whether or not they are connected with her own well-being."[3] A person's well-being, in contrast, concerns not "the totality of her considered goals and objectives" but rather only her "wellness," "personal advantage," or "personal welfare." This state of a person, her beings and doings, may be the outcome of her own or other people's decisions or the result of causes internal or external to the agent. Well-being or its contrary, ill-being, concerns "the state of a person – in particular the various things he or she manages to do or be in leading a life":[4]

The well-being of a person can be seen in terms of the quality (the "well-ness," as it were) of the person's being. Living may be seen as consisting of a set of interrelated "functionings," consisting of beings and doings. A person's achievement in this respect can be seen as the vector of his or her functionings. The relevant functionings can vary from such elementary things as being adequately nourished, being in good health, avoiding escapable morbidity and premature mortality, etc., to more complex achievements such as being happy, having self-respect, taking part in the life of the community, and so on. The claim is that functionings are constitutive of a person's well-being, and an evaluation of well-being has to take the form of an assessment of these constituent elements.[5]

Both agency and well-being have two dimensions, namely, actual *achievements* and the *freedom* for those achievements. As agents, persons achieve their goals in the world. Although "the freedom of agency that we individually have is inescapably qualified and constrained by the social, political, and economic opportunities available to us,"[6] social arrangements can also extend the reach of agency freedom. Likewise, a person's well-being consists not only of her current states and activities (functionings), which may include the *activity* of choosing, but also in her freedom or opportunities (capabilities) to function in ways alternative to her current functioning. A person's own well-being, whether functionings or capabilities, is often part – but need not be all – of a person's objectives; for a person may also pursue goals that reduce her well-being and even end her life.

What is the point of Sen's initial distinction? It provides conceptual space for a Kantian conception of moral freedom and breaks decisively with any deterministic psychological egoism that claims that humans are no more than, and are bound to be, "strict maximizers of a narrowly defined self-interest."[7] Some people most of the time and many people some of the time *do* strive to increase their own well-being. However, insofar as humans can and do devote themselves to people and causes beyond and even against their own welfare, Sen can answer a skeptical realist's concern about any normative theory that proposes a just treatment of conflicting interests or freedoms:

> If conflicts of interest are very sharp and extensive, the practical feasibility and actual emergency of just social arrangements may pose deep problems. There are reasons for skepticism here, but the extent and force of that skepticism must depend on the view we take of human beings as social persons. If individuals do, in fact, incessantly and uncompromisingly advance only their narrow self-interests, then the pursuit of justice will be hampered at every step by the opposition of everyone who has something to lose from any proposed change. If, on the other hand, individuals as social persons have broader values and objectives, including sympathy for others and commitment to ethical norms, then the promotion of social justice need not face unremitting opposition at every move.[8]

Moreover, Sen might have added, as he did in a 2006 address, that effective implementation of development policies can and should build on people's sense of fairness and concern that they and others be treated fairly.[9] That people are often committed to general norms about fairness is anecdotally illustrated by the way people at the front of a queue respond to someone who butts in front of those to the rear. Sen himself provides empirical filling for this sort of altruistic conceptual space by referring to his own empirical work[10] and that of many other social scientists, such as Albert Hirschman.[11] Also relevant are experiments that show that participants in controlled games often choose not to maximize their own self-interest.[12] Sen also marshals evidence from momentous events suggested by the names "Prague or Paris or Warsaw or Beijing or Little Rock or Johannesburg" as evidence that "among the things that seem to move people . . . are concern for others and regard for their ideas."[13]

I suggest a second and, I believe, equally convincing reason for the distinction between well-being and agency, one to which I return in comparing Sen and Nussbaum. This distinction provides normative space for the commonplace that an agent in pursuit of a worthy goal may sacrifice her health, friends, and even life itself.

Sen's ideal of agency

Increasingly after 1993, Sen supplements his initial *empirical* account of agency, one that makes room for both self-regarding and other-regarding human motivation, with a very different and explicitly *normative* account that proposes human agency as something we have reason to value. Already in 1992, Sen edged towards this normative account of agency when he ramified his initial distinction between well-being and agency and distinguished two kinds of agency achievement or success: (1) "*realized* agency success," a generic concept of agency, and (2) "*instrumental* agency success,"[14] a more specific and "participatory" concept of agency.

In "realized agency success," my objectives – whether self-regarding or other-regarding – are realized, but someone or something else may be the cause or the "lever" of the achievement. Only in "instrumental agency success" – the specific and "more *participatory*"[15] variety of agency – does agency require that the person herself either brings things about by her *own* efforts or plays an "active part" in some collective action. Perhaps responding to G. A. Cohen's criticism that Sen's normative outlook is guilty of "athleticism," Sen's generic concept of agency permits some other individual or group – other than the person or group whose aims are realized – to exercise or "control" the "levers" of change.[16] My agency freedom is enhanced, not only when I actually do something, but when something I value occurs even when I had nothing to do with its occurrence but would have chosen it had I *had* the chance and the means:

If my agency objectives include the independence of my country, or the elimination of famines, the first view of agency achievement would be well met if the country *does* become independent, or if famines *are* in fact eliminated, irrespective of the part I personally manage to play in bringing about that achievement.[17]

This generic concept of agency freedom and achievement does have some advantages. It does permit us to say that institutions and *other* people can bring about or contribute to the realization of our goals: "a person's ability to achieve various valuable functionings may be greatly enhanced by public action and policy."[18] Moreover, infants and very old people are capable of healthy functioning even though they make few if any decisions and are dependent on the care of others. Many good (and bad) things happen to people because of what other agents do for (or to) them. Sen wisely does not make an absolute of "self-help" or "athleticism." It is not the case that my evening meal is drained of worth unless I freely cook it myself or that my colleagues do not have a role to play in realizing my goal that my university be better.

It does not follow, however, that we should follow Sen and say that the actions of others that realize my goals, which I would have realized for myself if I could have done so, are cases of *my* agency.[19] Someone else's preparation of my lunch should not count as my agency or action merely because I wanted this meal and would have prepared it myself if I had had the opportunity and means.[20] Here we must distinguish a variety of cases, only some of which qualify as agency achievement. Then, within agency achievement we should distinguish indeed between two kinds of agency, but draw it in a different way and for a different purpose than does Sen. I propose that we distinguish not between the generic "realized agency" and the more specific "instrumental" agency but rather between (1) the agency of others, (2) my indirect agency, and (3) my direct agency.

Suppose the restaurant chef at Rudy's Cafe, without knowledge of me or my desires, prepares a dish that I desire, order, eat, and would have prepared myself if I were home. I exercise agency in the ordering, eating, and nourishing myself but not in preparing the food. Although past preferences and consumer choices like mine may have played a role in Rudy's Cafe offering today's chile, my preference today for this meal had no causal role in the cook's action. In contrast, if the chef knows what I always order, expects me today, and prepares the meal before my accustomed arrival, my (assumed) desire for this meal is indeed a causal factor in the cook's decision of what to prepare. Still, however, I have had no agency in *preparing* the meal because I had no intention to prepare the meal and performed no intentional action in the preparation. Even though the counterfactual related to Rudy's Cafe – I would have prepared the same meal had I had the chance – is true, this hypothetical agency is not actual agency.

Let us consider a related and more complicated non-agency case. We might be tempted to say that I have *indirect* agency in the preparation of the meal if the chef (say, my wife) cooks my favorite meal because she knows that I will cook the meal if she does not, and she (a gourmet cook) wants to avoid a botched supper, which she believes will occur if she leaves the cooking to me (a lousy cook). Here I seem to have agency because my conditional cooking the meal (should my wife not cook the meal) seems to be a causal factor in her deciding to cook. But, even in this case, my wife's act of cooking would not be agency on my part. For my intention would have been that *I* cook the meal and not that *she* cook it. Indeed, my wife anticipates my (conditional) agency, and this anticipation does play a role in her action. But I have not exercised my agency unless I both intended that my wife cook the meal, which I did not, and I intentionally did something to bring it about, which I did not, or intentionally refrained from doing something that would have prevented her action, which I did not. Her anticipation of my agency is an indirect cause for her action, but this anticipation is not an exercise of my agency.

Let us consider now cases of both direct and indirect agency. I would exercise direct agency if I myself decided to cook the meal and did so alone. I exercise my agency indirectly if I intend that this sort of meal be prepared and if I play some role in its preparation. That role may be more or less important; for instance, the onion I slice may be optional rather than essential seasoning.

My role also may be more or less direct depending on whether I am in charge and on my place in the causal chain that results in the intended meal. If, because I have a deadline, I ask my wife to cook the meal without my help, my request plays only an initiating role in the causal chain that issues in the meal. If I replace the fuse, when the kitchen current shorts out, I contribute to the meal preparation but only remotely. If I refrain from distracting my wife's concentration on her cooking by choosing not to read to her an op-ed piece from today's paper, my action of omission plays a role in her successful realizing of our joint intention. In these cases, I am an agent in the action but only in an indirect or fairly remote way.

Rather than extending, as does the notion of "realized agency success," the notion of agency to include whatever event happens to realize my preferences (and would be chosen by me if I had the chance), the notion of indirect agency enables us to make the important point that tyrants are restrained not only by the direct doing of their so-called "subjects" (for example, mass agitation) but also by the tyrant's knowledge that his subjects intend to blockade the city should the tyrant fail to accede to certain popular demands.[21] My indirect agency, with both backward and anticipatory reference, also occurs when my senator casts a vote to disconfirm the President's nomination for Attorney General. She casts the vote, and I do not. But I have exercised indirect agency if I have influenced her decision, perhaps because she expects that I will hold her accountable if she votes against my expressed will. If the senator knows what I and other constituents have elected her to do and stand for, and if she knows that she will lose our support if she votes for the nominee, then my agency has been indirectly exercised through my representative.

This last example leads us to see the merit but also a limitation in what I have called indirect agency. In modern society's complex organizations, such as representative democracy, Sen correctly recognizes that "it is often very hard, if not impossible, to have a system that gives each person all the levers of control over her own life."[22] Yet, it does not follow that even in complex societies no further issue exists as to who makes decisions, who is in charge, or "how controls are, in fact, exercised."[23] One challenge of movements to deepen democracy is to find ways to strengthen and extend direct agency, make indirect agency less indirect, and link direct and indirect agency, for instance by establishing venues for representatives and constituents to deliberate together between elections for, or votes in, representative bodies.[24]

In 1992, Sen happily recognized that what he called "active" or participatory" agency is "closely related to the nature of our values" in the sense that we place a high value on bringing about our goals through our *own* efforts. After 1992 Sen drops or at least downplays the generic meaning of agency, refrains from discussing nonparticipatory agency, and emphasizes only what in 1992 he called "instrumental agency success." It is important that we recognize that others can realize our goals on our behalf even though we have had no role – direct or indirect – in the process. But rather than including this sort of case under the category of my "realized agency," it is more perspicuous, I have argued, to classify it as an example of "realized goals." Another agent has performed an action that achieved for me what I had intended to do for myself.

The abandonment of the generic category of "realized agency" is, I believe, no loss. What is important is that people individually and collectively conduct their own lives, sometimes realizing their own self-regarding goals, sometimes realizing (or helping realize) other's goals, and sometimes by forming joint intentions and exercising collective agency. We exercise agency or control not when our goals are merely realized but when, in addition, we *intentionally* realize or contribute directly or indirectly to the realization of our goals.[25]

How does Sen understand the ideal of agency and why is such agency important? Especially in his 1999 *Development as Freedom*, but also in other writings after 1993, Sen proposes and applies a complex ideal of agency (and a related ideal of empowerment as the acquisition of this kind of agency). Although he has not yet subjected the ideal to the careful analysis that we have come to expect of him, I draw on his scattered remarks and offer the following interpretation or "rational construction" of his current view. A person is an agent with respect to action X just in case she (1) decides for herself (rather than someone or something else forcing the decision) to do X; (2) bases her decisions on reasons, such as the pursuit of goals; (3) performs or has a role in performing X; and (4) thereby brings about (or contributes to the bringing about of) change in the world.[26]

Rather than make each one of these conditions necessary and together sufficient for agency, let us say that the more fully an agent's action fulfills each condition the more fully is that act one of agency. The agent decides for herself rather than being forced by someone else or by impersonal forces. The person is autonomous in the sense that "the person herself decides the issue at hand"[27] rather than someone else deciding for her.

Full agency is "reasoned agency."[28] Decision is not for *no* reason, based on a whim or impulse, but is for *some* reason or to achieve a goal, regardless whether that goal is self-regarding or other-regarding. The agent does more than form an intention or make a resolve, however; she freely performs, either alone or with others, acts of commission or omission. Even though the agent gets what she intends – for instance, the elimination of the famine – if she did not get it, at least partially, because of her own (direct or indirect) action (individually or with others), she is not an agent. A person may have many effects on the world, but effects express agency only when they are done consciously, on purpose, and for a purpose. Because of this act, the agent alters the world – sometimes in ways intended or foreseen and sometimes in unintended or unexpected ways. When the agent intentionally achieves her goal, she is in this instance an agent, the author of her own life. This self-determining and efficacious aspect of Sen's ideal of agency is nicely anticipated by Isaiah Berlin's concept of positive liberty:

I wish to be the instrument of my own, not other men's, acts of will. I wish to be a subject, not an object . . . I wish to be a somebody, not nobody; a doer – deciding, not being decided for, self-directed and not acted on by external nature or by other men as if I were a thing, or an animal, or a slave incapable of playing a human role, that is, of conceiving goals and policies of my own and realizing them.[29]

A person's agency contrasts with cases in which a person is passive in the face of others' actions or a mere conduit through which other agents work their will or impersonal forces unleash effects. In the former case, someone else either makes a decision for the person, acts for her, or acts on her. In the latter case, a person's apparent "decision" is nothing but the effect of internal or external forces:

In terms of the medieval distinction between "the patient" and "the agent," this freedom-centered understanding of economics and of the process of development is very much an agent-oriented view. With adequate social opportunities, individuals can effectively shape their own destiny and help each other. They need not be seen primarily as passive recipients of the benefits of cunning development programs. There is indeed a strong rationale for recognizing the positive role of free and sustainable agency – and even of constructive impatience.[30]

The term "agency," like the term "capability," confuses many people. Not only does one think of travel agencies, rather than individual or collective actors (in Spanish, *protagonistas*), but, as Sen makes clear early in *Development as Freedom*, what institutional economics means by "agent" is contrary to Sen's meaning:

The use of the term "agency" calls for a little clarification. The expression "agent" is sometimes employed in the literature of economics and game theory to denote a person who is acting on someone else's behalf (perhaps being led on by a "principal"), and whose achievements are to be assessed in the light of someone else's (the principal's) goals. I am using the term "agent" not in this sense but in its older – and "grander" – sense as someone who acts and brings about change, and whose achievements can be judged in terms of her own values and objectives, whether or not we assess them in terms of some external criteria as well. This work is particularly concerned with the agency role of the individual as a member of the public and as a participant in economic, social and political actions (varying from taking part in the market to being involved, directly or indirectly, in individual or joint activities in political and other spheres).[31]

It is also clear from this passage's last sentence that Sen considers the "agency role" of individuals, acting alone or in groups, as of fundamental importance in his vision of *Development as Freedom*. Rather than stressing, as he did in 1992, the difficulty of citizens purposefully operating the "levers" of change, in his recent work as part of his democratic turn he emphasizes the importance of direct as well as indirect citizen involvement in democratic governance, and he seeks ways to close the gap between the two. In Parts III and IV, I consider further why agency is important and address the implications of this ideal of (active) agency for a deepening of democracy and citizen participation in local development. One reason why development, conceived as good social change, is important for Sen is that it provides a variety of social arrangements in which human beings express their agency or become free to do so. The ethically sensitive analyst evaluates development policies and practices in the light, among other things, of the extent to which they enhance, guarantee, and restore the agency of individuals and various groups:

Societal arrangements, involving many institutions (the state, the market, the legal system, political parties, the media, public interest groups, and public discussion forums, among others) are investigated in terms of their contribut-ion to enhancing and guaranteeing the substantive freedoms of individuals, seen as active agents of change, rather than passive recipients of dispensed benefits.[32]

As we shall see in Chapter 9, one challenge for Sen and for deliberative democratic theorists is to give an account of how public deliberation provides devices for *collective* agency, a process for combining the deci-sions and agency freedoms of many agents. For Sen, groups as well as individual persons can and should be authors of their own lives.

Although the concept of capability is undeniably important in Sen's development ethic, regrettably his approach has become widely known as the "capability approach." This designation is multiply misleading. I shall argue that in some contexts functionings are, for Sen, more important than capabilities. Moreover, since agency freedom as well as well-being freedom is normatively fundamental, Sen is right to refer to his overall approach as "the freedom-centered perspective on the ends and the means of development,"[33] and I suggest that an equally appropriate label would be "the agency-focused capability approach." Finally, since agency achievement and agency freedom are not only morally important, but often neglected in both political thought and the interpretation of Sen, there is sometimes good reason to call this outlook "an agent-oriented view"[34] or "an agent-oriented approach."[35] In Chapter 7, I consider whether Sen's ideal of agency is or should be *more* important than his normative notions of well-being (functioning and capability). For now, however, it is sufficient to stress that Sen's commitment to public participation in social change "involves an over-arching interest in the role of human beings – on their own and in cooperation with each other – in running their own lives and in using and expanding their freedoms."[36]

Nussbaum and agency

Nussbaum, who agrees with Sen about the complexities of human motivation, softens, or better, recasts his distinction between well-being (capabilities and functionings) and agency (freedom and achievements):

One set of distinctions prominently used by Sen is absent in my own version of the capabilities approach. This is the distinction between well-being and agency, which, together with the distinction between freedom and achievement, struc-tures much of his recent writing about capabilities. I agree with Sen that the concepts introduced by these distinctions are important: but I believe that all the important distinctions can be captured as aspects of the capability/functioning distinction.[37]

By "agency" Nussbaum generally means choice as a part of what she calls "practical reason." She conceives practical reason as "being able to form a conception of the good and to engage in critical reflection about the planning of one's life," and she puts it on her list of ten "central human functional capabilities."[38] Moreover, it is clear that her conception of the equal worth of persons has much to do with the human ability to plan, act, and make a difference in the world: "We see the person as having activity, goals, and projects – as somehow awe-inspiringly above the mechanical workings of nature, and yet in need of support for the fulfillment of many central projects."[39] Furthermore, the tenth and last valuable capability on Nussbaum's post-1998 lists is "control" over one's political and material environment,[40] and in these writings she sometimes refers to human beings as "centers of agency and freedom"[41] or "sources of agency and worth."[42] At least once she puts agency and well-being on an equal normative footing when she says that her brand of liberalism opposes political organizations "that seek a good for the group as a whole without focusing above all on the well-being and agency of individual group members."[43] Yet she does not match these locutions with Sen's careful and systematic distinction between agency and that well-being. Why not? I believe there are at least two reasons.

First, Nussbaum contends that Sen's contrast between agency and well-being may cause some readers accustomed to utilitarianism to think that agency is exclusively where the action is and that well-being is a totally passive affair. What she is getting at is that utilitarians often use the terms "welfare" and "well-being" interchangeably, and what they mean by both is the (passive) enjoyment experienced when one's preferences are satisfied. To focus normatively on objective functionings and capabilities, such as actual healthy functioning, rather than on subjective satisfactions, Nussbaum argues, is to break decisively with utilitarian passivity. Sen's distinction between agency and well-being, she contends, drains (at least for economists and other utilitarians) the concept of well-being – and hence those of capability and functioning – of activity. Hence, she rejects Sen's distinction.

It is true that it is often difficult for audiences, especially but not exclusively in the Spanish-speaking world, to grasp Sen's rejection of the identification of "welfare" and "well-being" and a conception of "well-being" whose components include a plurality of capabilities and functionings, rather than mental reactions such as satisfactions. And these functionings do include not only "beings" or states of a person but also "doings" or activities (whether or not intentional actions). However, Nussbaum's argument overstresses the "athletic" character

of Sen's view of functionings and capabilities. Contrary to the interpretation of G. A. Cohen, Sen insists that "there is no underlying presumption that we have the capability to lead a malaria-free life only if
we have ourselves gone around exterminating the malaria-causing
insects."[44] Similarly, one of the functionings that people sometimes
value and choose – especially during vacations or at the end of a hard
day – is that of repose and cessation of striving.[45] Moreover, a utilitarian
or neo-classical economist view could be expansive enough to include
preferences for strenuous activities.

It is precisely Sen's concept of agency that enables him to distinguish
his view most decisively from mainstream economics and philosophical
utilitarianism. Sen's empirical concept of agency enables him to claim
that people *can* and often *do* act to realize other-regarding goals, even
when to do so is disadvantageous to themselves. His normative ideal of
agency is the basis for contending that individuals and groups can and
often *should* run their own lives, rather than have them controlled by
others or impersonal forces. Nussbaum is right to affirm the active
character of (many) functionings and the importance of well-being
freedom (capabilities) as well as functionings. Without a separate ideal
of agency, however, she is unable to do full justice to people's actual
freedom to shape their own lives, including their *own* decisions with
respect to which freedoms to make most important in their lives.

Second, and more fundamentally, the very structure of Nussbaum's
capabilities approach requires that she reject Sen's normative duality of
agency and well-being in favor of an integrated and complex norm
of human well-being composed of both functionings and capabilities.
Sen holds that – both individually and collectively – persons as agents
should decide on their own values, prioritize their freedoms, and perform their own actions. The contrast is not between activity and passivity
as such but between a person deciding for herself (or a group deciding
for itself) and being the "recipient" of someone else's decision (even
if that decision coincides with what the person herself would decide).
Whether or not to emphasize individual advantage or some non-
self-regarding cause, and how to understand and weigh the plural
components of well-being – for Sen these options are to be decided by
the agents involved. As we shall see in later chapters, the ideal of agency
ranges even over the decision not to value agency. This choice should
be *my* or *our* choice and not that of someone else.

In contrast, Nussbaum gives prescriptive priority to her own vision of
truly human functioning and capabilities – of which practical reason is
only one component. This vision, the result of philosophical argument,
is to be enshrined in a nation's constitution and should function to

protect but also constrain individual and collective exercise of practical reason in the making of public policy. Nussbaum restricts the scope of practical agency to that of specifying the norms the philosopher sets forth and the constitution entrenches. Nussbaum, more Aristotelian and less Kantian, understands the philosopher's role as that of providing "the philosophical underpinning for an account of basic constitutional principles that should be respected and implemented by the governments of all nations, as a bare minimum of what respect for human dignity requires."[46] The basic choice that Nussbaum leaves to individuals and communities is how to *specify* and *implement* the ideal of human flourishing that she – the philosopher – offers as the moral basis for constitutional principles.

Furthermore, unlike Sen, Nussbaum does not restrict human well-being to personal advantage or self-regarding goals and, hence, she has no need to open conceptual space for the human agent to be able to choose between her own well-being and altruistic actions or impersonal causes. Instead, Nussbaum includes "affiliation" as one of her ten valuable capabilities. Affiliation, she says, is "being able to live with and toward others, to recognize and show concern for other human beings, to engage in various forms of social interaction; to be able to imagine the situation of another and have compassion for that situation; to have the capability for both justice and friendship."[47]

Nussbaum even goes so far as to designate affiliation, along with practical reason (including the capacity for choice), as one of the two especially important capabilities or "architectonic functionings"[48] that pervade ("organize and suffuse") all capabilities in the sense that these super-capabilities make "truly human" the pursuit of the other central capabilities. In contrast, Sen conceives well-being freedoms and achievements as a (self-interested) subclass within agency achievement. Sen finds it valuable that individuals and communities have the freedom to choose not only how to conceive their personal advantage, that is, the nature and weights of their well-being freedoms, but also what weight they should give their own well-being in relation to the well-being of others and their impersonal causes, such as social justice.

With his empirical concept of agency, Sen gives an account in which people can advance their central goals, their causes, in ways that reduce their well-being as personal advantage. When Nussbaum builds affiliation and friendship into her expansive notion of human flourishing, she obscures the personal sacrifices sometimes required to pursue or obtain a worthy goal. Sometimes we must make a difficult choice because the goods of healthy and affiliative functioning do not go together with the process or outcome of political functioning.

With his concept of agency, Sen does not himself prescribe moral or constitutional choices but underscores that individuals and collectives have the freedom to make choices *for themselves* (or at least decide to give the choice to someone else). Among these choices is that between – or the balance between – well-being and our central goals and values (including that of agency itself).[49]

Hence, although dualities exist in both Sen's and Nussbaum's perspectives, they are drawn along different lines and serve different purposes. Sen, addressing economists, development policy analysts, and self-interested citizens, starts with a conception of humans as pursuing their own *well-being*, but emphasizes – without formulating a conception of human flourishing – that individuals and communities are *agents* that can and should decide on the nature and importance of their own advantage in relation to other goals and values. Nussbaum, more at home with the world of Greek thought, finds it difficult to draw the sharp distinction between individual and communal good and prescribes an ideal of partial human flourishing that includes both affiliation (altruism) and practical reason.[50] The norm of human flourishing, in Nussbaum's most recent writings, is only *partial* because she now offers her list "not [as it was in her earlier formulations] as a complete account of the good or of human flourishing," but as a "political account" of "the basic social minimum" that human dignity requires.[51]

Accepting Rawls's distinction between a comprehensive and a political conception of the good, Nussbaum's social minimum consists, she says, of the "capacities, liberties, and opportunities that have value in any plan of life that citizens may otherwise choose."[52] While Sen claims that people and societies should use their agency individually and collectively to determine the nature and importance of that social minimum, Nussbaum assigns that job to philosophical reflection (albeit in and through critical dialogue with many people).

Well-being achievement and freedom

In addition to the norm of agency – both agency achievement and agency freedom – Sen proposes, as I sketched above, that institutional arrangements and development policies and practices be evaluated and constructed in relation to the norm of human well-being. In turn, as I discussed above in a preliminary way, Sen understands human well-being or personal advantage not as preference satisfaction in the economist's sense but in relation to the concepts of functioning and capability. Nussbaum also employs these concepts, but – as

I anticipated earlier and will return to subsequently – she does so not in relation to a concept of well-being, which contrasts with the concept of agency, but rather in relation to a robust normative and political notion of (partial) "human flourishing" that includes altruistic elements. With this difference in their uses of the concepts of functioning and capability as a backdrop, I turn now to a more detailed interpretation of what each thinker means by functioning and capability.

Functioning

Sen frequently explains his concept of human functioning by the example of riding a bicycle.[53] Important differences exist between the bicycle, the activity of riding, any mental state or utility that accompanies the riding, and any subsequent effects of the riding. The bicycle itself is a mere object, a commodity that may be bought or sold. I may own the bike, be near it, and be sitting on it (even when it is moving), and yet not be *riding* it. To be riding the bike is to be engaged in a purposive human activity with or by means of the bike. The bike is necessary but not sufficient for the cycling. The cycling, as both process and result, is an "achievement" of the rider – as any parent knows when their child first begins to peddle the new bike. While riding, the cyclist may or may not be enjoying the activity or satisfying some desire.

The bicycle example is somewhat misleading if it suggests that intentionality, purposiveness, or voluntariness are necessary conditions, in Sen's account, for all human functionings. A cyclist usually chooses to ride and has an aim in riding, but may also cycle against her will – as when a parent plops the recalcitrant youngster on the bike and shoves it down the driveway. Sen also extends the concept of functioning beyond intentional action to include *any* "state of existence of a person."[54] Included as functionings, then, would be not only the choosing that initiates the riding but also the mental state – whether one of joy, boredom, or fear – that happens to accompany the activity. Moreover, also included under the concept are states or processes of a person such as an accelerated heartbeat (a physiological functioning *during* the riding) or being physically or psychologically fit (functionings *caused by* the riding).

Consider another example I have found useful in teaching. A student may "illustrate" many functionings during a class period: (1) *choosing* to pay attention or think of something else; (2) *intentionally* paying attention or taking notes; (3) enjoying or being bored by the lecture; (4) unintentionally daydreaming, nonvoluntarily digesting lunch;

(5) being enlightened or misinformed; (6) subsequently, engaging in professional activity informed by the course. Sen defines a person's "achieved living"[55] as the person's combined "doings and beings,"[56] "the set of functions a person actually achieves."[57]

In his choice of the term "functioning," Sen might be accused here of hijacking a term from Aristotelian biology (something's function as its natural, characteristic, or proper activity), mathematics, or symbolic logic, and obscurely using "functioning" when perfectly good everyday words such as "activity" would do better. Yet, "activity" and even more so "action" often suggest free, intentional, or purposive behavior; and Sen wants a word that designates both voluntary "activity," such as reading, and involuntary activity, such as beating hearts and digestive processes. Moreover, we often say things like "I'm not functioning very well today" or "He is functioning at a very high level."

In relation to Sen's concept of functioning, Nussbaum's concept is somewhat narrower. Although Sen conceives of choosing (category 1, above) as a distinguishable (intentional, mental, inner) functioning, Nussbaum understands choosings as nothing more than the voluntary or chosen dimension of an intentional human functioning. For Nussbaum, choosings as distinguishable functionings would be more transcendental than human: the acts of will of disembodied angels, demigods, or Cartesian egos. Likewise, processes without choosings (category 4) would be less than human; for example, "the sleeper's life of non-guided digestive functioning,"[58] the lives of pigs,[59] and presumably the movements of robots. One reason for Nussbaum's divergence from Sen is that she seems uneasy about a model in which choosings are inner acts of will. It is beyond the scope of this chapter to assess the implication, merits, and problems in each position. Suffice it to say, however, that Sen's view of deciding as a distinguishable functioning fits well with his view that agents have sufficient transcendence over both external conditions and internal dispositions to be able to exercise at least some control over their conduct, including the decision to sacrifice their own well-being. By contrast, Nussbaum's conception of choosing not as a distinguishable event but as an *aspect* of intentional functioning fits with her failure to give prominence to agency in the sense of self-determination or self-rule.[60]

A second difference in their respective concepts of human functioning concerns mental states (category 3, above) of happiness or pleasure (or their opposites). Sen conceives such mental states as distinguishable functionings as well as ones that people often have reason to value. Nussbaum, on the other hand, takes what she believes to be a less utilitarian and more Aristotelian position. Although she counts "being able to have pleasurable experiences, and to avoid non-necessary pain,"[61] as one of the valuable human functional capabilities, she refuses to make the experience of pleasure a *separate* functioning. Pleasure or satisfaction, argues Nussbaum, is supervenient on (or a dimension of) functioning rather than itself a functioning.[62]

What is the general normative significance of Sen's notion of functioning? The concept of functioning coupled with the (about to be discussed) notion of capability for functioning provides Sen, as introduced above, with a conceptual framework, "space," or "currency" for interpreting human well-being and deprivation: the "primary feature of a person's well-being is the functioning vector that he or she achieves."[63] Moreover, this interpretation "builds on the straightforward fact that how well a person is must be a matter of what kind of life he or she is living, and what the person is succeeding in 'doing' or 'being.'"[64]

By contrast, rival normative approaches are restricted to other, less urgent or less complete sorts of information. The commodities that the crude and Rawlsian perspective value are, at best, only *means* to human well-being and not its *end* or content. Given interpersonal variability, different amounts and kinds of goods can result in the same sort and level of functioning (and freedom to function). And the same kinds and amounts of goods can result in wildly different levels of achievement (and freedom to achieve) in different people or in the same person at different times. A focus on functioning enables us to keep very clear about the comprehensive and constant ends and the variable means of social progress. The welfarist perspective, concerned only with the goal of utilities, neglects or "muffles" all other sorts of human functioning. Happiness or preference satisfaction may be coupled with malfunctioning, and discontent may accompany or spur the most important of activities. Sometimes, even the discipline of *development* economics has been one-sided, for not infrequently it has emphasized rate of economic growth or, better, quantity of life (longevity), and neglected the quality of the lives people lead, for example *being* healthy and *being* educated. At this point, we have not treated the views of Sen and Nussbaum concerning which achievements are important or valuable. We do know, however, that development is *for* people and the lives they lead rather than *merely* a matter of whether they possess certain goods, satisfy certain preferences, or contribute to economic growth.

Before analyzing their related notion of capability for functioning in the next section and Sen's and Nussbaum's different approaches to evaluating particular functionings and capabilities, it is important to stress the normative role of functioning and valued functionings (whatever they turn out to be). G. A. Cohen, although correctly seeing how important capabilities are in Sen's ethics, fails to recognize that Sen (and Nussbaum) also gives independent and intrinsic value to certain functionings.[65] It is true that with respect to responsible adults, Sen (and Nussbaum agrees) gives more normative emphasis to "freedom to achieve valuable ways of functioning"[66] than he does to the valuable functionings themselves.[67] But, with respect to those who are not able to choose – the very young, very old, and extremely disabled – we rightly value their healthy functioning as more important than their *capability for* and *choice of* various functionings.[68]

For Sen, there are additional reasons for the importance of functionings. Functionings in a conceptual sense are the primitives by which capabilities are defined. If I have the capability of being healthy, the capability is defined in relation to the functioning of being healthy (and not vice versa). The capability for good health is valuable because *inter alia* healthy bodily functioning is valuable. "Freedom for what?," we might say, is a question that cannot be replaced by "Is there freedom?" Praise for freedom as such, especially in political discourse, does not get us very far. Sen is very clear, for example, that it is good to be free from having to make a bunch of distracting or trivial choices.[69]

Moreover, both Sen and Nussbaum recognize that some functionings (for instance, being healthy) may "function" as a platform – may be instrumentally valuable – for having and choosing capabilities for other functions, for instance being able to run. Public action often should be concerned that human beings *actually* function at certain minimal levels in order that they be free to choose to advance beyond or retreat from that level. A very sick person may not even be in a position to decide whether to strive for a level of healthy functioning. Only if a young person can read at some level is she sufficiently informed to be able to decide to improve or abandon her reading.

Furthermore, one reason why it is bad to reduce someone's freedom is that it decreases her opportunities for achieving valued or valuable functionings. Moreover, in certain contexts functionings may be more important than capabilities because the former may be easier than the latter to identify and measure.[70] Finally, although the capabilities for healthy and nutritional well-being normally trump, for adults at least, being healthy and adequately nourished, a good government may correctly decide, as a way of protecting agency, to ensure that everyone is inoculated from a deadly virus even if they choose not to be. At least in this context, healthy functioning (being inoculated) trumps the capability to be inoculated. Let us now focus on Sen's and Nussbaum's concepts of capability, a term that contrasts with but is defined in relation to their concepts of functioning.

Capability

It is not enough, argue both thinkers, to single out certain functionings as *the* content of human well-being (Sen) or of human flourishing (Nussbaum). As Aristotle says, a distinction should be made between actuality and potentiality. An important difference exists, for example, between a stone and a sleeping human, with respect to some activity like cycling. Neither the stone nor the sleeping cyclist is engaged in riding. Only the cyclist, however, *can* ride, is free to ride, or is *capable* of cycling.[71] For Sen and Nussbaum, economic and, more generally, social development is, among other things, the protection, promotion, and expansion of valued or valuable capabilities.

We must ask several questions, not all of which Sen and Nussbaum themselves explicitly pose or answer. What, precisely, is meant by "capability"? How do capabilities relate to functionings, on the one hand, and to freedoms, on the other? Given the high evaluation, just analyzed, of actual functionings, why posit capabilities and insist on their intrinsic importance? In later chapters I analyze and evaluate Sen's and Nussbaum's very different ways of identifying, ranking, and trading off valuable capabilities. Now, however, my concern is with the very idea of a capability.

What *sorts* of things are the capabilities that Sen proposes? A person's "being and doing" is her combination of actual functionings, her "functioning vector," the particular life she actually leads. The person leads *this* life of "beings and doings" but *could* lead alternative lives. The person's "capability set"[72] is the total set of functionings that are "feasible," that are within her reach, that the person could choose.[73] As I discuss later in this chapter, Sen ramifies this conception to include that possibilities come in sets of "compossibilities." Being able to sit, read, and sip a glass of Rioja are compossible, but given certain facts about me and the world, are incompatible with the realization at the same time of other compossibles, such as jogging and greeting passing neighbors. Our capability set is a "set of capability sets."[74]

Sen introduced the notion of "capability" to refer to the extent of freedom that people have in pursuing valuable activities or functionings:[75] "A person's 'capability' refers to the alternative combinations of functionings that are feasible for her to achieve. Capability is thus a kind of freedom: the substantive freedom to achieve alternative functioning combinations (or, less formally put, the freedom to achieve various lifestyles)."[76]

On this view, two people could have the same capability set and choose different bundles of actual functionings. Conversely, they could have different capability sets and have the same (sorts of) functionings.[77] One of Sen's favorite examples of the latter also amounts to a compelling argument for adding capability to the moral space of functioning. It is this argument that in the mid-1980s initially attracted me to Sen's ideas. Both a person starving and a person fasting – for example, a North Korean infant and a hunger striker in Burma – exemplify the functioning of being severely undernourished. But, it is clear, the two do not enjoy "the same level of well-being."[78] The difference lies in the absence of certain options for the one and the presence of these options for the other. The former is neither free not to be severely undernourished nor free to function in many other desirable ways. The latter, in contrast, has the significant capability or freedom not to starve: "B [the faster] *could have* in a straightforward sense, chosen an alternative life style which A [the non-faster] could not have chosen."[79]

Sen gives us several reasons, in interpreting human well-being, to add the category of "capability to function" to the category of functioning. One reason why valuable functionings are valuable is that they realize valuable capabilities. Moreover, valuable functionings gain some of their value from the fact that they are chosen (Sen) or "done in accordance with practical reason"[80] (Nussbaum) rather than determined by someone else or necessitated by circumstances. Further, even though I am not now functioning in a valuable way, it is good that I have an array of options, and even better when this array includes valued alternative functionings. Capabilities, as well as the activity of choosing, add something intrinsically and not merely instrumentally valuable to a human life, namely, positive freedom in the sense of available and worthwhile options: "Choosing may itself be a valuable part of living, and a life of genuine choice with serious options may be seen to be – for that reason – richer."[81] Using deontological (right-based) as well as teleological (good-based) language, Sen also says: "it may be simply taken to be 'right' that individuals should have substantial well-being freedom."[82]

Finally, capabilities as well as functionings are important in grasping the aim and limits of good government. For both Sen and Nussbaum, responsible lawmakers and development policymakers aim at getting people, if they so choose, up to or over a threshold of minimal valuable or valued functionings in order that they may be able, if they so choose, to have more "well-being" (Sen) or to function in more fully human ways (Nussbaum). The purpose is not, as Rawls fears, to impose a certain conception of the good life on human beings, but to enable them to cross a threshold so that they have certain choices. Drawing out the implication of capability or well-being freedom for "ethical and political analysis," Sen observes that "in forming a view of the goodness of the social state, importance may be attached to the freedoms that different people respectively enjoy to achieve well-being . . . A good society, in this view, is also a society of freedom."[83]

Nussbaum puts it well:

The conception [Aristotelian social democracy] does not aim directly at producing people who function in certain ways. It aims, instead, at producing people who are *capable* of functioning in these ways; who have both the training and the resources to so function, should they choose. The choice itself is left to them. And one of the capabilities Aristotelian government most centrally promotes is the capability of choosing; of doing all these functions in accordance with one's own practical reason . . . The government aims at capabilities, and leaves the rest to the citizens.[84]

Both Sen and Nussbaum want to avoid a paternalistic, let alone dictatorial, government that makes decisions for (adult) people. In Nussbaum's formulation, it is not the task of government to "dragoon"[85] people or even "nudge or push"[86] them – she is thinking of responsible adults – into functioning in certain ways but to provide them with the capabilities to so function if they choose to do so. The goal of political planning would not be to require such functionings as "political participation, religious functioning, and play," or even "to promote actual health as a social goal."[87] Rather, with respect to those who can choose, the goal is to promote the *capability* of choosing good functionings rather than promote actual functionings.

Although I cannot pursue the point here, where Sen and Nussbaum differ is that for Sen a "society of freedom" includes a variety of ways in which citizens participate in making the policies that affect them. For Nussbaum, in contrast, citizen participation in governance is restricted to electing representatives who in turn pass laws either constrained by or that specify the philosophically defended norms enshrined in national constitutions.

Let us probe further Sen's and Nussbaum's conceptions of capability. Not only is the notion of capability susceptible to different interpretations, but a close reading reveals some important differences between the two thinkers. Let us begin with Sen's conception and ask two questions. First, what *sorts* of things are the capabilities that Sen describes? Second, what factors explain the varieties and range of a person's capabilities?

With respect to what Sen and Nussbaum mean, in general, by capabilities, at least five interpretations are possible. Capabilities might be construed as one or some combination of the following: (1) inclinations or desires, (2) needs, (3) concrete or specific skills, (4) general character traits, or (5) opportunities. Let us look at each candidate in turn.

Desires?

It is clear that Sen does not identify capabilities with either inclinations, preferences, or desires. The faster, who is capable (in Sen's sense) of being well nourished, does not want, all things considered, to be well nourished. He or his body may need nourishment to survive, but the faster does not want or prefer to be nourished.

Needs?

Likewise, capabilities are not needs. Someone could have the capability of fasting but no need to fast because her body does not require it (for example, for purgative purposes) and her political situation is not desperate; other actions might have the same or better results at less cost to the actor. Someone might have a biological need to be nourished (in order to survive); but, if she had decided to fast, Sen would say she was capable of being well nourished in addition to her biological need for nourishment.

Specific skills?

The relation of capabilities to abilities, powers (of a person), or skills is more complicated. We need to be cautious here, because one ordinary use of "capability" is that of "ability," whether natural or acquired. A good midfielder in soccer must have good endurance and be capable of accurate passing, playmaking, and dribbling. And Sen sometimes explicitly defines capabilities as abilities: "A functioning is an achievement, whereas a capability is the ability to achieve."[88] This definition, however, does not help much because Sen is using "ability" in this context in a way that is similar in breadth to his expanded use of the everyday term "capability."

It is true that if A has the capability for X, then the having of that capability may be partially due to the fact that A has some ability or skill. If I have the capability of walking, I have the ability to stand, move my legs, keep my balance, and so forth. If I have the capability of voting, I have the ability of getting to the polls (or mailing my absentee ballot), reading the ballot options, and pulling the lever or clicking on the computer option. However, among the personal traits necessary for either voting or walking are characteristics *other than* abilities or skills. In spite of having the requisite abilities or skills, I lack the capability of voting if I am under age, a felon in prison, or a foreigner. In spite of having the needed learned abilities, I may lack the capability of walking here and now because I am immobilized by a momentary blackout.

Moreover, my capabilities depend not only on personal traits – whether abilities or other traits – but also on features of the natural and institutional environment. My capability of walking across the road-way depends on the policewoman's signal to walk and the absence of oncoming cars or class 5 hurricanes. I do not have the (full) capability of voting if I live in an authoritarian state that has abolished voting, or one, as was the case in Saddam Hussein's Iraq, that permits "voting" for only one candidate. Hence, A's capability for doing X may have reference to personal traits other than abilities or skills as well as to "enabling" features of the environment. A's lack of capability for Y may have reference to more or something other than A's inabilities, for the lack may be due to A's features which are not abilities or to specific environmental barriers or constraints. Could I have a given capability without having some abilities? I certainly have the capability of playing cricket even though I have never played it and have never acquired specific cricket skills (although baseball skills might come in handy).

What we can conclude, then, is that A's having a capability for X may – but need not – depend on having a related ability, and if certain abilities are involved much more may be involved as well. Hence, David Clark correctly argues against my earlier interpretation of Sen's concept of capability when I said: "For Sen, to say that someone has the capability or ability to move about freely is to speak not of powers, skills, or other traits *possessed by* the person but rather of possibilities or options *facing* the person."[89] I now believe that I was right in what I affirmed but not in what I denied. A person's capability (for a particular functioning) is a possibility, option, freedom, or opportunity "facing" the person. But this freedom may be due to a variety of *internal* factors, including abilities and other personal traits, as well as *external* factors.

General powers?

A fourth interpretation of Sen's concept of capability and its relation to that of functioning would be, like Nussbaum, to conceive capabilities not as abilities or specific skills, such as a surgeon's ability to use a scalpel, but as more general personal powers, capacities, or potentialities, such as a healthy newborn's power of (unaided) breathing or the power of a person to move about, imagine, or reason. So understood, capabilities would exhibit what Nussbaum calls different "levels."[90] Capabilities would be formed from an "undeveloped" or latent state (what Nussbaum calls "basic capabilities" and what we might think of as "a capacity for a capacity"), maintained, exercised, neglected, or thwarted in one's maturity, and diminished or lost in old age. Nussbaum calls the infant's powers "basic capabilities: the innate equipment of individuals that is the necessary basis for developing the more advanced capabilities, and a ground of moral concern."[91] The developed capabilities – or what I call "actual" in contrast to potential capabilities – Nussbaum designates as "internal capabilities": that is, "developed states of the person herself that are, so far as the person herself is concerned, sufficient conditions for the exercise of the requisite functions."[92]

Internal capability, "mature conditions of readiness"[93] to choose particular functionings, would be based on – or rather *be* – general powers that can be nurtured, acquired, developed, maintained, exercised, impeded, diminished, lost, and (sometimes) restored. These personal powers are (or fail to be) realized, embodied, or expressed in correlative functionings, which for Nussbaum are, as we saw, intentional activities. Good actions, which for Nussbaum (following Aristotle) compose "flourishing living" (*eudaimonia*),[94] would embody the best of these internal potentials.

Nussbaum, recognizing Sen's point that *external* conditions often figure in what counts as a capability, contends that external factors may either thwart or facilitate the exercise of internal capabilities. She expresses this point by proposing yet a third level of capabilities, "combined capabilities," which she says "may be defined as internal capabilities *combined with* suitable external conditions for the exercise of the function."[95]

One might quibble that "combined capabilities" suggests the combination of two or more capabilities, which Nussbaum does not mean, rather than the "combining" of an internal power with favorable external circumstances. Yet Nussbaum's central point is clear and a good one. Having internal powers is necessary but not sufficient for (good) functioning, for one must also have available certain "external and social conditions."

Suppose, contrary to fact, that the skill of riding a bicycle were one of the valuable *general* capabilities, as proposed by Nussbaum. To perform the function of riding requires that one have (or immediately acquire) the internal ability to ride, access to a bike, and no environmental conditions, such as icy streets, that hinder bike-riding. Instead of saying that combined capabilities are internal capabilities plus suitable external conditions, it would be more perspicuous if Nussbaum had said that actual or developed capabilities refer both to *internal* capacities and to *external* opportunities or enabling conditions. Whether or not a functioning is a real option, whether or not one is able to achieve it, would depend not only on one's various internal states but also on access to resources, the presence of enabling conditions (such as legal rights), and the absence of preventing conditions (such as legal prohibitions or threatening bayonets).

Nussbaum views one task of government as helping its citizens acquire the philosophically prescribed actual or developed capabilities (as internal powers):

> The list is a list of capabilities, and not actual functionings, precisely because the conception is designed to leave room for choice. Government is not directed to push citizens into acting in certain valued ways; instead, it is directed to make sure that all human beings have the necessary resources and conditions for acting in those ways. It leaves the choice up to them.[96]

Nussbaum's account appropriately emphasizes that good societies and good development policies promote, through various institutions and practices, good human development. Responsible institutions promote the formation, exercise, maintenance, strengthening, and restoration of certain good human powers.[97]

Opportunities?

The best interpretation of what Sen means by "capability," however, is not capability as internal power but capability as a certain sort of real *possibility, genuine opportunity, or substantive freedom*. As I have noted, in an earlier article I mistakenly argued that Sen sees capabilities as *no more than* opportunities, in contrast to Nussbaum, who more adequately conceives capabilities as human powers or capacities. I now believe that for Sen capabilities are like three-place predicates. If I have a capability to or for X, (1) I face the option or have the real possibility of X, and this possibility both refers to or is partially dependent on (2) my powers and other internal traits, and (3) external enabling and non-preventing conditions. For Sen, capabilities are options or choices open to the person, possible functionings from which a person may choose.

What sort of possibility? Obviously not logical possibility, for it is not a logical contradiction that precludes the starving person from eating. Nor is it merely a logical possibility than gives the affluent hunger striker the capability of being nourished. Moreover, a possibility as option for choice is not to be identified with the concept of formal or legal opportunity, in which a person has an opportunity for X if and only if there are no laws that prohibit her being or having X. If both of us are US citizens and nonfelons over the age of thirty-five, we both have the legal opportunity to become President of the United States. But, unless you are (in 2008) Hillary Rodham Clinton or Barack Obama, this legal sense of opportunity is not a real or substantive opportunity. For you and I have neither the internal capabilities nor the external enabling conditions to be President.

Here an interchange between Bernard Williams and Sen is instructive.[98] Sen would say that someone living in smog-filled Los Angeles lacks the capability of breathing unpolluted air. Williams, on the other hand, thinks Sen should say that this inhabitant lacks the "ability"[99] of breathing unpolluted air "here and now,"[100] but has the general capability to breathe unpolluted air and could realize the capability by migrating to another location.

Sen's response is brief but revealing. First he agrees with another point that Williams makes, namely, that we must not think of capabilities singly but rather as "sets of co-realizable capabilities."[101] Sen's way of putting this point is that capabilities are members of sets of capabilities, "sets of n-tuple functionings from which the person can choose any one n-tuple."[102]

Sen means that we cannot simply ask whether a Los Angeles inhabitant has the capability of breathing fresh air. For the question would have to address the Angelino's set of co-realizable possibilities, and these possibilities would refer or be due to both personal powers and environmental features, including access to resources. Supposing the resident to have lungs able to function without mechanical assistance, one of the resident's "n-tuples" might include staying in Los Angeles, due to irremediable lack of means, in an area that remains permanently beset with pollution. Another set would include the resident's possibility, due to (present or potential) wealth or (reckless) desperation, of migrating to a locale with clean air. About the resident so conceived, Sen says that we can say that prior to migration she had the requisite capability to breathe unpolluted air because "that alternative must be seen in terms of the post-migration n-tuple of *all* functionings"[103] – obviously including the living in a place with unpolluted air. Depending on her external constraints and real options, however, there will be some point at which we can say that the Los Angeles resident has no (or little) capability for breathing fresh air because her lack of substantive options makes it practically impossible for her to leave Los Angeles (or only with extreme risk or cost). On Sen's view, the issue for this Angelino, again assuming the internal power to breathe without a respirator, is not whether to migrate from Los Angeles or clean it up so that she can *exercise* some *internal* ability to breathe *clean air*. Rather, the issue is: given that the person can breath at all and *something* can be done to enable the person to breath *clean air*, is it *worth* – or, to what extent is it worth – giving up other options and achieving the real but costly option of breathing clean air by, for example, working to reduce the pollution in Los Angeles or moving somewhere with clean air?[104]

One interesting implication of this analysis is that capability, understood as a real opportunity, is a *matter of degree*. Degree of capability has to do not only with the agent's external natural and social environment and the agent's internal abilities or powers but also with the agent's assessment of costs (including risks) and benefits of options. The affluent Hollywood agent to the stars might be relatively unable to breathe unpolluted air, not because he lacks the money to move elsewhere, but because he judges relocation would be too risky to maintain his clients and connections.[105]

Hence, for Sen, I would still claim that – rightly understood – "capabilities are not powers of the person that might or might not be realized in different situations," but I would underscore and make more central in my interpretation that for Sen capabilities are "options [that] may refer to but are not identical with traits of a person."[106] What we are free to do, what our real possibilities are, has essential reference to what we are, including our powers, as well as to the means we can muster, and what our environment permits or withholds.

This "opportunity" or "freedom" interpretation of Sen's concept of capability is confirmed by Sen's recent employment of the distinction between the process aspect and the opportunity aspect of freedom and his explicit identification of the latter with capability:

> Freedom, in the form of capability, concentrates on the *opportunity* to achieve combinations of functionings (including, inter alia, the opportunity to be well-nourished or in good health . . .): the person is free to use this opportunity or not. A capability reflects the alternative combinations of functionings over which the person has the freedom of effective choice.[107]

Sen's construal of capability as real opportunity or effective freedom enables him to make clear both the contribution and the limits of capabilities in theories of justice. Capabilities as (valuable) opportunities contribute to a theory of justice because they make it clear that an exclusive focus on incomes, primary goods, (access to) resources, and even functionings do not provide all we need to know about a person's life going well or badly.[108] Capabilities as "actual opportunities" or "substantive freedoms" tell us what people, given their personal traits and (social or natural) environment, are free to do and be:

> The capability approach can capture the fact that two persons can have very different substantial opportunities even when they have exactly the same set of means: for example, a disabled person can do far less than an able-bodied person can, with exactly the same income and other "primary goods" . . . The capability

perspective concentrates on what actual opportunities a person has, not the means over which she has command.[109]

These "actual opportunities" or real options, we have seen, make reference not to means or command over means but to one's personal traits as well as natural and social environmental features. Included in the latter would be resources and access to them.[110]

Sen also makes it clear that capabilities as "substantive opportunities" are only one part of an approach to justice or normative collective choice. As discussed earlier in this chapter, Sen is equally concerned with agency or "the process aspect of freedom": "Capabilities and the opportunity aspect of freedom, important as they are, have to be supplemented by considerations of fair processes and the lack of violation of the individual's right to invoke and utilize them."[111]

Types of functionings and capabilities

Sen and Nussbaum sketch several distinct types of functionings and types of capabilities. We have already seen Nussbaum's distinction between "levels" of capability. In Nussbaum's typology, a basic capability is an undeveloped or potential capacity. When this potential is actualized, through nurture and maturation, the result is an "internal" capability, which can be exercised or realized in the correlative functioning. An agent's internal capability becomes a "combined" capability when external enabling conditions exist and no external circumstances block or prevent the realization in action of the internal capability.

Although Sen construes capabilities as "substantive opportunities" rather than personal powers plus external enabling conditions, he does make a distinction analogous to Nussbaum's levels. As we have seen, he distinguishes between those opportunities that are more or less proximate and more or less feasible. Luke both lacks and has the capability to ride the bike he just got for his sixth birthday. Due to his current lack of balance and the time it would take to acquire that balance, he is not yet capable of riding the bike. But, in a longer-term sense, Luke has the capability to ride the bike because he will soon acquire better balance, or his parents, at some cost, will make the time to work with him more (or both). Here feasibility concerns not only empirical likelihood but also normative costs and benefits.

Sen identifies several additional types of functionings and capabilities. First, functionings and capabilities may be referred to either positively or negatively. For instance, not being diseased would be part of the positive functioning of being healthy. Second, actual and possible functionings can be described more or less generally. The general capability of being free from avoidable morbidity is further specified by being capable of being free from malaria. Being able to ride a bicycle presupposes and specifies being able to move about. The most inclusive or general normatively positive capability would be the "capability to function well" (Sen),[112] or, more robustly, the "capability to live a rich and fully human life, up to the limit permitted by natural possibilities" (Nussbaum).[113] Third, functionings and capabilities can differ with reference to the judgments and other activities of others. We have seen that the capability to appear in public without shame has a reference to the *judgments* of others in a way that is not true of the capability to be able to move freely. Moreover, some functionings and capabilities are more or less universal, shared or shareable by (almost) all human beings. Some, like the capability to play wide receiver, and not just the culturally relative goods that contribute to them, are specific to particular times, places, and physical abilities. Finally, and for our purposes most importantly, well-being capabilities and functionings, like agency freedoms and achievements, can be evaluated and ranked in various ways. I address this topic, so central to an ethics of and for development, in the next chapter.

Concluding remarks

Sen makes it clear that the concept of capabilities as "substantive opportunities" is an important but not the only normative concept in development ethics, a theory of justice, or a theory of collective choice. Unlike Nussbaum, Sen embeds his concept of capability as substantive freedom within a complex concept of human well-being or personal advantage in which functionings as well as capabilities are normatively important. Moreover, unlike Nussbaum, Sen is equally concerned with individual and collective *agency* as well as with individual and communal *well-being*. An important part of the "fair process" of decision-making is that individuals and groups run their own lives. As agents – rather than pawns of fate, servile tools, or passive recipients – people often can and, where possible, should make their own decisions, realize their goals through their own efforts, and make a difference in the world. Individual agency comes into play when individuals decide which of their freedoms and functionings to value and which to rank highly. Collective agency takes place when individuals engage in a collective process that results in a joint decision and action. When this process expresses the agency of all affected and respects individual rights, we have collective agency that is democratic. The clarification and defense of that claim, however, must wait until Part IV.[114]

NOTES

This chapter includes a substantial revision and modification of sections 1.1–1.3 of "Functioning and Capability: The Foundation of Sen's and Nussbaum's Development Ethic, Part 2," in *Women, Culture and Development*, ed. Martha Nussbaum and Jonathan Glover (Oxford: Clarendon Press; New York: Oxford University Press, 1995); and ch. 3 of *Florecimiento humano y desarrollo internacional: La nueva ética de capacidades humanas* (San José: Editorial de la Universidad de Costa Rica, 1998). Figure 5.1 is adapted from my "Sen and Deliberative Democracy," in *Capabilities Equality: Basic Issues and Problems*, ed. Alexander Kaufman (New York: Routledge, 2006), 156. I gave lectures or papers from which the published essays were derived at Montclair State University, the University of Costa Rica, the National Autonomous University of Honduras, and the University of San Carlos (Guatemala). Thanks to the following people for their suggestions to improve earlier drafts: Cynthia Botteron, Teresa Chandler, Eddie Crocker, Geri Crocker, Lawrence Crocker, Jay Drydyk, Verna Gehring, Patty Joyce, Lori Keleher, Daniel Levine, Michael Lozonky, Peter Penz, William Slauson, and David Wasserman. I benefited from conference commentators Joan Whitman Hoff and Jerome M. Segal. I am especially grateful to Amartya Sen and Martha Nussbaum for their encouragement and enormously helpful comments on the first draft of the initially published essay.

1. Amartya Sen, "Well-being, Agency and Freedom: The Dewey Lectures 1984," *Journal of Philosophy*, 82, 4 (1984): 169–221; *Inequality Reexamined* (Cambridge, MA: Harvard University Press), 39–42, 56–72; and *Development as Freedom* (New York: Knopf, 1999), 189–91.

2. In *A Commitment to the World's Women: Perspectives on Development for Beijing and Beyond*, ed. Noeleen Heyzer, S. Kapoor, and J. Sandler (New York: UNIFEM, 1995).

3. Sen, *Inequality Reexamined*, 56; Amartya Sen, "Capability and Well-being," in *The Quality of Life*, ed. Martha Nussbaum and Amartya Sen (Oxford: Oxford University Press, 1993), 36.

4. Sen, "Capability and Well-being," 31.

5. Sen, *Inequality Reexamined*, 39 (two footnotes omitted).

6. Sen, *Development as Freedom*, xi–xii.

7. Amartya Sen, "Individual Freedom as a Social Commitment," *New York Review of Books*, 37 (June 14, 1990): 54.

8. Ibid.

9. Amartya Sen, "The Importance of Ethics for the Efficient Design and Implementation of Development Policies and Projects," Inter-American Initiative on Social Capital, Ethics, and Development, "Ethic and Development Day at the IDB," Inter-American Development Bank, February 24, 2006.

10. Amartya Sen, *Choice, Welfare, and Measurement* (Oxford: Blackwell; Cambridge, MA: MIT Press, 1982).

11. See Sen, "Individual Freedom as a Social Commitment," 54; *On Ethics and Economics* (Oxford: Blackwell, 1987), 16–28; *Development as Freedom*,

362–5. In the latter, Sen cites, for example, Albert O. Hirschman, *The Passions and the Interests* (Princeton: Princeton University Press, 1977).

12. See Norman Frohlich and Joe E. Oppenheimer, *Choosing Justice: An Experimental Approach to Ethical Theory* (Berkeley: University of California Press, 1992).

13. Sen, "Individual Freedom as a Social Commitment," 54.

14. *Inequality Reexamined*, 56–7.

15. Ibid., 57.

16. G. A. Cohen fails to see this possibility when he charges Sen with "athleticism" with respect to the concepts of both agency and capability. See "Equality of What? On Welfare, Goods, and Capabilities," in *The Quality of Life*, ed. Nussbaum and Sen, 25–6.

17. Sen, *Inequality Reexamined*, 57–8.

18. Sen, "Capability and Well-being," 44 (note omitted).

19. My criticism of Sen's generic concept of "realized agency" and my proposal that he replace it with a distinction between direct and indirect agency owes much to discussions with David Wasserman.

20. My arguments against Sen's generic ideal of agency have benefited from discussions with Jay Drydyk, Patty Joyce, Lori Keleher, Daniel Levine, and David Wasserman.

21. See Philip Pettit, *Republicanism* (New York: Oxford University Press, 1997).

22. Sen, *Inequality Reexamined*, 65.

23. Ibid.

24. Cf. Iris Marion Young, *Inclusion and Democracy* (Oxford: Oxford University Press, 2000), ch. 4.

25. Sen's concept of agency is narrower than that of the World Bank's *World Development Report 2006: Equity and Development* (Washington, DC: World Bank and Oxford University Press, 2005), 5, 48–50, and 205. The *Report* defines agency as "the socioeconomically, culturally, and politically determined ability to shape the world around oneself" (ibid., 5). Not only does this definition, with its notion of a "determined" ability, undermine the agent's *self*-determination or "free agency," but it also unacceptably includes under the concept of action *any* impact that people have on the world, no matter how unthinking or unconscious: "Some of [agency] is unconscious – for example when people engage in land transactions without questioning them, they reproduce the institutions of land tenure and the markets in land" (ibid., 48–9). I leave open the question of whether unintended but foreseen or reasonably foreseeable consequences are themselves expressions of agency – either because there is some higher-order intention or for some other reason.

26. Although I put the point in a way that suggests that actions are only positive doings, I also mean to include as actions decisions to omit or refrain from positive action when such decisions or (negative) refrainings or omissions are intentional and make a difference in the world. When a handshake is customary, (the decision) not to shake an offered hand is, at least in Western culture, an act that rebuffs.

27. Amartya Sen, *Rationality and Freedom* (Cambridge, MA: Harvard University Press, 2002), 619.

28. Jean Drèze and Amartya Sen, *India: Development and Participation*, 2nd edn. (Oxford: Oxford University Press, 2002), 19. Cf. Sen, *Inequality Reexamined*, 56, n. 1.
29. Isaiah Berlin, *Four Essays on Liberty* (Oxford: Oxford University Press, 131; cited in Rob Reich, *Bridging Liberalism and Multiculturalism in American Education* (Chicago: University of Chicago Press, 2002), 100. See Reich's excellent discussion of "minimalist autonomy" in *Bridging Liberalism*, ch. 4.
30. Ibid., 11.
31. Sen, *Development as Freedom*, 18–19.
32. Ibid., xii–xiii. See also ibid., 11.
33. Sen, *Development as Freedom*, 53.
34. Ibid., 11.
35. Ibid., 191.
36. Drèze and Sen, *India*, 33.
37. Nussbaum, *Women and Development*, 14.
38. Ibid., 79.
39. Ibid., 73.
40. Ibid., 80.
41. Martha Nussbaum, *Sex and Social Justice* (Oxford: Oxford University Press, 1999), 20.
42. Ibid., 63; and Nussbaum, *Women and Human Development*, 58, 69.
43. Nussbaum, *Sex and Social Justice*, 8.
44. Sen, "Capability and Well-Being," 45–6.
45. David A. Crocker, *Praxis and Democratic Socialism: The Critical Social Theory of Marković and Stojanović* (Atlantic Highlands, NJ: Humanities Press; Brighton: Harvester Press, 1983), 106–9.
46. Nussbaum, *Women and Human Development*, 5; cf. 51, 116.
47. *Sex and Social Justice*, 41; *Women and Human Development*, 79.
48. Nussbaum, "Aristotelian Social Democracy," in *Liberalism and the Good*, ed. Bruce Douglass, Gerald Mara, and Henry Richardson (London and New York: Routledge, 1990), 226.
49. I am indebted to David Wasserman for comments and discussion that helped me grasp these reasons for favoring Sen over Nussbaum with respect to the concept of agency.
50. Sen, of course, believes that a person's well-being or advantage and her altruistic achievement can coincide and even reinforce each other. In contrast to Nussbaum, however, he does not advocate an ideal of human flourishing with both self-regarding and other-regarding dimensions. I owe this point to Jay Drydyk.
51. Nussbaum, *Women and Human Development*, 5, 59, 204.
52. Ibid., 148.
53. Amartya Sen, *Resources, Values, and Development* (Oxford: Blackwell; Cambridge, MA: Harvard University Press, 1984), 334; and *Commodities and Capabilities* (Amsterdam: North-Holland, 1985), 10.
54. Sen, *Commodities and Capabilities*, 10.
55. Amartya Sen, "Justice: Means Versus Freedoms," *Philosophy and Public Affairs*, 19 (1990): 113.

56. Ibid.
57. Amartya Sen, "Well-being, Agency and Freedom," 198. See also *Inequality Reexamined*, 4–5, 39–42, 49–54, 76–84, 108–12; *Development as Freedom*, 75–6, 131–4.
58. Martha Nussbaum, "Aristotle on Human Nature and the Foundations of Ethics," in *World, Mind and Ethics: Essays on the Ethical Philosophy of Bernard Williams*, ed. J. E. J. Altham and Ross Harrison (Cambridge: Cambridge University Press, 1995).
59. Martha Nussbaum, *Love's Knowledge: Essays on Philosophy and Literature* (New York and Oxford: Oxford University Press, 1990), 211.
60. For an argument that Nussbaum's refusal to view choosings as functionings enables her to avoid an infinite regress of choosings or acts of will, see Crocker, "Functioning and Capability," 154, n. 1.
61. Nussbaum, *Women and Human Development*, 79.
62. Ibid., and Martha Nussbaum, *The Fragility of Goodness: Luck and Ethics in Greek Tragedy and Philosophy* (Cambridge: Cambridge University Press, 1986), 294–5.
63. Sen, "Well-being, Agency and Freedom," 198. Here Sen employs the term "functioning vector" for a person's set of functioning achievements. At least once, however, he uses "vector" to indicate that the elements of each of a person's sets "are measured in terms of real numbers": see "Justice: Means Versus Freedoms," 114, n. 7.
64. Sen, *Commodities and Capabilities*, 46.
65. See G. A. Cohen, "On the Currency of Egalitarian Justice," *Ethics*, 99 (1989): 941–4; and "Equality of What?," 9–29.
66. Amartya Sen, "Individual Freedom as a Social Commitment," 52.
67. Sen, *Inequality Reexamined*, 49–53, 148; "Capability and Well-Being," 38–40; *Development as Freedom*, 74–6.
68. At least since 1998, Nussbaum has recognized the importance of functioning rather than capability in relation to children and adults "who do not have full mental and moral power" (Nussbaum, *Women and Human Development*, 89–90). See also Nussbaum, "The Good as Discipline, the Good as Freedom," in *Ethics of Consumption: The Good Life, Ethics, and Global Stewardship*, ed. David A. Crocker and Toby Linden (Lanham, MD: Rowman & Littlefield, 1998), 332; "Disabled Lives: Who Cares?" *New York Review of Books*, 48 (2001): 34–7; *Frontiers of Justice: Disability, Nationality, Species Membership* (Cambridge, MA: Harvard University Press, 2006), 171–2. In the last volume, Nussbaum argues that, with respect to "self-respect and dignity itself," "actual functioning is the appropriate aim of public policy" (ibid.).
69. Sen, *Inequality Reexamined*, 59–64.
70. See ibid., 52–3.
71. As we shall see, Nussbaum takes the concept of capability one step further than Sen when she distinguishes between a person's "developed" and "undeveloped" capabilities. Like the stone, the cyclist's infant offspring is incapable of cycling, but, unlike the stone, the infant has an undeveloped capability for riding that can become a developed capability. We might say

that the infant – unlike the stone – has a capability for (acquiring) a (riding) capability.

72. Sen, "Well-being, Agency and Freedom," 201; and Amartya Sen, "Freedom of Choice: Concept and Content," *European Economic Review*, 32 (1988): 289.
73. Sen, "Well-being, Agency and Freedom," 200–1. See *Inequality Reexamined*, 39–40.
74. I owe the phrase to Jay Drydyk.
75. Jean Drèze and Amartya Sen, *Hunger and Public Action* (Oxford: Clarendon Press, 1989), 42; and Sen, "Justice: Means Versus Freedoms," 114.
76. Sen, *Development as Freedom*, 75; *Inequality Reexamined*, 40; "Elements of a Theory of Human Rights," *Philosophy and Public Affairs*, 32, 4 (2004): 332–8.
77. Sen, "Justice: Means Versus Freedoms," 116.
78. Amartya Sen, "The Concept of Development," in *Handbook of Development Economics*, I., ed. Hollis Chenery and T. N. Srinivasan (Amsterdam: North-Holland, 1988), 17.
79. Sen, "Well-being, Agency and Freedom," 201; emphasis in text. For a more recent statement, see "Elements," 334–5.
80. Nussbaum, "Aristotelian Social Democracy," 214.
81. Sen, *Inequality Reexamined*, 41.
82. Ibid., 40.
83. Ibid.
84. Nussbaum, "Aristotelian Social Democracy," 214. Cf. Nussbaum, *Women and Human Development*, 6, 33, 88, 101.
85. Nussbaum, *Women and Human Development*, 59, 160; *Frontiers of Justice*, 171.
86. Nussbaum, *Women and Human Development*, 87.
87. Nussbaum, *Frontiers of Justice*, 171.
88. Sen, "The Standard of Living," in *The Standard of Living: The Tanner Lectures on Human Values*, ed. Amartya Sen, J. Muellbauer, Ravi Kanbur, K. Hart, and Bernard Williams (Cambridge: Cambridge University Press, 2000), 36.
89. Crocker, "Functioning and Capability," 165. See David Alexander Clark, *Visions of Development: A Study of Human Values* (Cheltenham, and North-ampton, MA: Edward Elgar, 2002), 63.
90. Nussbaum, *Women and Human Development*, 84–6; *Sex and Social Justice*, 44–5. Cf. Nussbaum's earlier formulation of the trichotomy in "Nature, Function, and Capability: Aristotle on Political Distribution," in *Oxford Studies in Ancient Philosophy*, supp. vol. (Oxford: Clarendon Press, 1988), 160–72.
91. Nussbaum, *Women and Human Development*, 84.
92. Ibid.
93. Ibid.
94. Nussbaum, *The Fragility of Goodness*, 6.
95. Nussbaum, *Women and Human Development*, 85.
96. Martha Nussbaum, "Human Functioning and Social Justice: In Defense of Aristotelian Essentialism," *Political Theory* 20, 2 (1992): 225.
97. *Human Development Report 1990*, which Sen helped write, does speak of the "formation" and "use" of human capabilities; see United Nations

Development Programme, *Human Development Report 1990* (Oxford: Oxford University Press, 1990), 18, 26. But these locutions do not fit well with the "capability as freedom" approach that Sen takes in his own writings.

98. Sen, "The Standard of Living," 99–100, 109.
99. Ibid., 99.
100. Ibid.
101. Ibid., 100.
102. Sen, "Justice: Means Versus Freedoms," 114; and "The Standard of Living," 109.
103. Sen, "The Standard of Living," 109.
104. For an argument that Los Angeles's smog problem is due to "unplanned, sprawling, privatized growth" that features private cars and clogged highways and the lack of public transportation and parks, see Harold Meyerson, "In L. A., Visibility and a Vision," *Washington Post* (January 11, 2006), A 21.
105. I thank David Wasserman for helping me develop this point.
106. Crocker, "Functioning and Capability," 163.
107. Sen, "Elements," 335.
108. Ibid., 332.
109. Ibid.
110. See ibid., 332–3, n. 29. This focus on capabilities as real opportunities (which refer to personal and environmental features) enables Sen to distinguish his view from sophisticated "resourcist" theories that emphasize "access to resources" rather than merely resources as such. It may be, however, that when "access to resources" is included in features of the social environmental (as seems to be the case with government provisioning such as "public health care"), then Sen's view and that of sophisticated resourcists converge.
111. Ibid., 338.
112. Sen, "Well-being, Agency and Freedom," 200.
113. Nussbaum, "Aristotelian Social Democracy," 217.
114. See Crocker, "Sen and Deliberative Democracy."

6 Evaluating capabilities and functionings

Sen and Nussbaum both conceive good social and economic development as, *inter alia*, social change that promotes *valuable* capabilities and functionings, but the two development ethicists have importantly different conceptions of the evaluative exercise and the status of its results. In this chapter I ask and seek to answer several questions about Sen's and Nussbaum's respective views concerning the evaluation of human capabilities and functionings.

First, what is the result of Sen's and Nussbaum's evaluative exercises? Sen defends the "evaluative space" of capability and functioning; but, while he provides examples of capabilities and functionings that people have reason to value, he himself does not offer a "predetermined, canonical list"[1] of (universally valid) capabilities or functionings. In contrast, Nussbaum offers just such a list. What is the content of Nussbaum's list? How and how well does she defend it? Why does Sen argue against such a list? Finally, *who* do Sen and Nussbaum claim should evaluate functionings and capabilities and what methods should they employ? Here one finds a sharp and growing disagreement between Sen and Nussbaum. Nussbaum emphasizes philosophical theorizing in determining valuable capabilities while Sen stresses agency-manifesting processes of public discussion and democratic choice. How should we understand and assess this dispute? Finally, what view does each thinker hold with respect to the *range* of evaluations? For Sen, with his focus an individual's personal advantage or "wellness," functionings/capabilities range in value from the trivial to the most valuable. For Nussbaum, human capabilities and functionings are to be "evaluated as valuable from an ethical view point," with the result that "some human abilities exert a moral claim" as components in "human flourishing" and some, like the "capacity for cruelty,"[2] do not. Which view is most reasonable?

Valuable functionings and capabilities: what are they?

It is not enough to carve out the space of functionings and capabilities; for these actual and possible functionings may differ in value or be valued in different ways. What international and national development should do is to expand capabilities, especially *valuable* or *valued* ones, and promote valuable or valued functionings. What are Sen's and Nussbaum's conceptions of good functionings and capabilities and the "evaluative exercises" that select and rank capabilities? What is the basis for and nature of a list, if there is to be one, and of the rankings? Sen clearly recognizes the importance of the task of developing his capabilities approach to include "different evaluation exercises":[3] "It is valuation with which we are ultimately concerned in the functionings approach."[4] However, in 1985 in *Commodities and Capabilities,* he recognized the difficulties in approaches to evaluation: it is hard to put the right questions, let alone get the right answers. In that same volume he confessed that he had "no magic solution to offer in dealing with these complex questions."[5]

Sen gradually came to hold the view that it is groups themselves – rather than philosophers or other theorists – who should conduct the "evaluative exercises" that yield the selection and weighting of valuable capabilities and functionings. To some extent, Sen arrived at this view on evaluation in and through his dialogue with Nussbaum and her philosophical proposal of a universally valid list of fully human capabilities. Because of the pivotal role that Nussbaum's "list" played in the evolution of Sen's own ideas, as well as her view's intrinsic interest, I now discuss the nature and status of Nussbaum's list and Sen's reasons for rejecting such a normative vision.

Nussbaum's philosophical list of valuable capabilities

Since the late 1980s, Nussbaum has been evolving for development ethics a prescriptive list of what she now calls "central human functional capabilities." Recent versions[6] of her list, an example of which is below, differ from earlier versions. The items on recent lists are more general than was the case earlier, with the advantage that, for example, lacking a specific sensory capability would no longer make someone less than fully human or incapable of full flourishing.[7] Moreover, her lists since 1995 or so make more room for human and legal rights.

Nussbaum intends her list to provide a universally valid conception of (partial) human flourishing and one that each government should embody in its constitution and implement in its laws and policies.[8]

Before assessing the status and merits of such a list and why Sen refuses to propose a list – at least one understood as "predetermined" and "canonical" – it will be helpful to have Nussbaum's current version before us.

Nussbaum's post-1995 list of "central human functional capabilities"

(1) *Life.* Being able to live to the end of a human life of normal length; not dying prematurely, or before one's life is so reduced as to be not worth living.

(2) *Bodily health.* Being able to have good health, including reproductive health; to be adequately nourished; to have adequate shelter.

(3) *Bodily integrity.* Being able to move freely from place to place; having one's bodily boundaries treated as sovereign, i.e., being able to be secure against assault, including sexual assault, sexual abuse, and domestic violence; having opportunities for sexual satisfaction and for choice in matters of reproduction.

(4) *Senses, imagination, and thought.* Being able to use the senses, to imagine, think, and reason – and to do these things in a "truly human" way, a way informed and cultivated by an adequate education . . . Being able to use imagination and thought in connection with experiencing and producing self-expressive works and events of one's own choice . . . Being able to search for the ultimate meaning of life in one's own way. Being able to have pleasurable experiences, and to avoid non-necessary pain.

(5) *Emotions.* Being able to have attachments to things and people outside ourselves; to love those who love and care for us, to grieve at their absence; in general, to love, to grieve, to experience longing, gratitude, and justified anger. Not having one's emotional development blighted by fear and anxiety, or by traumatic events of abuse or neglect.

(6) *Practical reason.* Being able to form a conception of the good and to engage in critical reflection about the planning of one's life.

(7) *Affiliation*
   (a) Being able to live with and toward others, to recognize and show concern for other human beings, to engage in various forms of social interaction; to be able to imagine the situation of another and to have compassion for that situation; to have the capability for both justice and friendship.
   (b) Having the social bases of self-respect and non-humiliation; being able to be treated as a dignified being whose worth is

equal to that of others. This entails, at a minimum, provisions against discrimination on the basis of race, sex, sexual orientation, religion, caste, ethnicity, or national origin. In work, being able to work as a human being, exercising practical reason and entering into meaningful relationships of mutual recognition with other workers.

(8) *Other species*. Being able to live with concern for and in relation to animals, plants, and the world of nature.

(9) *Play*. Being able to laugh, to play, and to enjoy recreational activities.

(10) *Control over one's environment*

    (a) *Political*. Being able to participate effectively in political choice that governs one's life; having the right of political participation, protections of free speech and association.

    (b) *Material*. Being able to hold property (both land and movable goods), not just formally but in terms of real opportunity; having property rights on an equal basis with others; having the right to seek employment on an equal basis with others; having the freedom from unwarranted search and seizure.

In writings before 1999, Nussbaum tended to view each of these items as necessary and together sufficient for the good human life. She now relaxes her claim and calls her list "open-ended and subject to ongoing revision and rethinking,"[9] but still insists that the "ten" capabilities "all are part of a minimum account of social justice: a society that does not guarantee these to all its citizens, at some appropriate threshold level, falls short of being a fully just society, whatever its level of opulence."[10]

Commentators have assessed Nussbaum's lists in various ways.[11] One way is to ask whether any item on the list, for instance "play" or altruistic acts, should be removed because it is too culture- or individual-specific or even ethnocentric. In the last chapter, I analyzed how Sen's concept of human "well-being" was concerned with personal advantage and only brought in aid to others if such aid increased the individual's wellness. Another way to evaluate Nussbaum's list is to ask whether it leaves out some component of human flourishing, for instance raising children, being religious, or engaging in meaningful work. These assessments are worth doing, but I shall not engage in this evaluation here. Instead, I evaluate Nussbaum's (1) strategy of trying to derive her list from a Kantian idea of human dignity and (2) conception of the normative status of her list.

In her most recent writings Nussbaum embeds her list of central capabilities in a moral theory with one ultimate principle and two "orienting principles." Nussbaum's highest-level principle is "a principle of each person as end"[12] in the sense that each and every human being has a dignity based on her threshold ability to choose her own conception of the good life. In a telling passage, in which she uses the terms "awe," "awe-inspiring," and "awe-inspiringly" in relation to the notion of human dignity (and its basis in practical reason and social cooperation), Nussbaum observes:

> The core idea [in Marx] is that of the human being as a dignified free being who shapes his or her own life in cooperation and reciprocity with others, rather than being passively shaped or pushed around by the world in the manner of a "flock" or "herd" animal. A life that is really human is one that is shaped throughout by these human powers of practical reason and sociability.
> This idea of dignity has broad cross-cultural resonance and intuitive power . . . We see a human being as having worth as an end, a kind of awe-inspiring something that makes it horrible to see this person beaten down by the currents of chance – and wonderful, at the same time, to witness the way in which chance has not completely eclipsed the humanity of the person. As Aristotle puts it, "the noble shines through." Such responses provide us with strong incentives for protecting that in persons that fills us with awe. We see the person as having activity, goals, and projects – as somehow awe-inspiringly above the mechanical workings of nature, and yet in need of support for the fulfillment of many central projects.[13]

In the light of this ultimate principle, Nussbaum offers her list of central capabilities. The list, she says, formulates "an intuitive idea of a life that is worthy of the dignity of the human being,"[14] or, put another way, "an intuitive conception of truly human functioning and what is entailed by it."[15] Specifying or "rephrasing" the principle of each person as end, Nussbaum offers the "orienting" "principle of each person's capability."[16] Nussbaum explains this principle as "the threshold levels of capabilities" that "can provide a basis for central constitutional principles that citizens have a right to demand from their governments."[17] Nussbaum's prescription, which all states ought to embody in their constitutions, follows: "the capabilities in question should be pursued for each and every person, treating each as an end and none as a mere tool of the ends of others."[18] Because a person's action (or the state's action) to realize her own valuable capabilities might harm the valuable capabilities of other persons, Nussbaum adds a second "orienting" principle: "the principle of moral constraint."[19] A capabilities version of Mill's no-harm principle, this principle states that the state should intervene in order to protect a human being's central capabilities when and only when they are threatened by the actions of others or of the state itself.[20] On the basis of these principles Nussbaum argues, for example, against female genital mutilation, sati, and the caste system – even though the victims of these practices might consent to them.

Before continuing, let us assess this effort to justify her list not just by reference to widespread considered judgments but by appeal to a Kantian idea of human dignity. According to this idea, humans equally are ends in themselves and not merely means for others to use. Moreover, this intrinsic worth refers to something about all or at least most human beings: their ability, individually and jointly with others, to shape their own lives. My problem with her argument is not with this conception of human dignity or its grounding in human autonomy, for a very similar if not identical assumption is involved in Sen's ideal of human agency. My problem is that Nussbaum's reference to Kantian dignity does no work with respect to any of the specific items on her list. She does not show, for example, that because humans have inherent dignity they should be permitted, encouraged, or enabled to have bodily integrity, use their senses, play, or control their political environment. It is hard to see how the dignity of someone with advanced dementia hinges in any way on her capability to play or control her environment. One suspects that this Kantian commitment to equal dignity is less a basis for Nussbaum's list and more a graft onto an Aristotelianism whose logic seems to justify *unequal* moral and political worth of those with human parents.[21] However, even the Kantian doctrine of dignity, based as it is on the idea of equal moral autonomy, will exclude some human beings. Not only do some humans have more actual and potential autonomy than others, but as philosopher David Wasserman recognizes and Nussbaum seems to concede, "individuals with the most severe cognitive impairments simply cannot fashion their own conception of the good life, no matter how intensive the support they receive from society."[22]

Apart from this problem of justifying her list, what role does the list play in Nussbaum's capabilities approach and what role does she intend it to play in society? As mentioned above, she intends that this list of "good human functioning" should precede, and be the basis for consideration of, the responsibilities, constitutional principles, and structures of a "fully just" political arrangement. It would seem that Nussbaum should then say that she is offering what Rawls would call a nonpolitical or metaphysical conception of justice, one that is grounded in an ultimate moral conception (human autonomy) that is at odds with other moral outlooks, for instance ones that stress obedience to authority.

In Rawls's liberal (and "political") theory, the right is prior to the good. Rawls proposes what he takes to be a fair framework – albeit informed by ideals of moral personality and social cooperation – in which people, within limits, are free to pursue their *own* conception of the ultimate good. How does Nussbaum stand with respect to Rawls's political liberalism?

As I discussed in Chapter 4, in her late 1980s and early 1990s essays Nussbaum sharply distinguished her normative view from that of Rawls. Taking issue with Rawls, Nussbaum argued that the good – in the sense of a vision of the good or flourishing human life – is prior to the right and that the aim of government goes beyond fairly distributing Rawls's primary goods and Sen's positive freedoms, as important as both these tasks are. The more determinate and guiding aim of just legislators should be that of promoting "the capability to live a rich and fully human life."[23] Nussbaum, taking the space of capability and functioning as settled, initially proposed her list of the ten irreducible components of good human functioning. People in every place and time have inner powers – if not external opportunities – to live life (as an end or good in itself) in this way.

Nussbaum offered her initial list as a "thick, vague conception of the good." It was thick because it proposed not, as did Rawls's social primary goods, the *means* for any good life, but the *content* of *the* good life. A good and just society would promote and protect a flourishing life for everyone. But did this view not mean that the government in a just society would be paternalistic, making decisions for individuals and communities about how they should live rather than allowing them to make those decisions for themselves?

To meet this charge, Nussbaum stressed that the list was not only "thick" but also "vague," in the sense that the items were general and required that individuals and communities can and should specify them in their own way. Moreover, holding governments responsible to promote *capabilities* rather than functionings, Nussbaum contended that people were not forced by the government to flourish but could choose a non-flourishing way of life. A third anti-paternalist aspect of her earlier position was that one of the valuable capabilities was precisely the ability to reflect critically and to decide autonomously one's concept of the good.

Despite these liberal or non-paternalist qualifications, Nussbaum still described her position as endorsing a universalist conception of a fully human life and the related government responsibilities to promote it. I was not the only one in the late 1980s and early 1990s to applaud – in a climate of postmodern and other relativisms – Nussbaum's effort to defend, in political philosophy in general and development ethics in particular, a universal conception of the good or flourishing human life. At last, I believed, we could appeal to a universal standard to assess developing (and developed) societies and propose universally valid principles to construct a better future.[24]

In her most recent version of the capabilities approach, however, Nussbaum has altered her course and adopted a liberal view akin to that of Rawls.[25] She still sees the task of any just government as that of promoting her list of capabilities and argues that these capabilities are intrinsically valuable components of – and not merely means to – any fully human life. Now, however, she likens these capabilities to Rawlsian primary goods in the sense that the list identifies those capabilities and opportunities people should have *regardless* of their conception of the good:

> Although this list of central capabilities is somewhat different in both structure and substance from Rawls's list of primary goods, it is offered in a similar political-liberal spirit: as a list that can be endorsed for political purposes, as the moral basis of central constitutional guarantees, by people who otherwise have very different views of what a complete good life for a human being would be.[26]

The idea seems to be that the list can and should function as a moral-political charter for all peoples. It is not clear, however, whether she means that the idea of human dignity and the list derived from this idea are trans-political conceptions that can function politically because all accept them or, less robustly, that these norms are compatible with any ultimate moral outlook. However we interpret Nussbaum's present position, it is important to understand Sen's assessment of Nussbaum's project in its various versions.

Sen and the evaluation of capabilities and functionings

In a 1995 essay, I took Sen's many examples and informal enumerations of capabilities or functionings that people had reason to value, and I displayed the great extent to which they "mapped on" to Nussbaum's systematic 1995 list[27] of ten "central functional human capabilities," some with many sub-items. Although sometimes it is difficult to decide whether Sen and Nussbaum proposed at that time different formulations of the same item, or different items, I tallied twelve agreements, thirteen items unique to Nussbaum, and only one item unique to Sen. Consulting the writings with the addition of Sen's 1992 *Inequality Reexamined*, David Clark did the same sort of mapping and discovered one additional item unique to Nussbaum and eight additional items unique to Sen.[28]

I have come to believe that this mapping exercise is misleading, for it suggests that Sen and Nussbaum are up to the same thing. Although it is true that Sen and Nussbaum "discuss" the same or similar items as valuable capabilities, not only do they have – as we saw in chapter 5 – somewhat different concepts of capability (and functioning), but they understand the status and justification of these capabilities in different ways. I say "discuss" because, whereas Nussbaum *prescribes* her list as universally valid, Sen merely *illustrates* the capabilities that people – both individually and collectively – have reason to value in and through various evaluative exercises, including that of public discussion and democratic deliberation.

What does Sen himself say about Nussbaum's list, both its content and the procedure by which she generates it? In his 1993 essay "Capability and Well-Being," Sen discusses her 1988 account of Aristotle's view that "that there is just one list of functionings (at least at a certain level of generality) that do in fact constitute human good living."[29] Sen assesses this proposal in two very different ways. First, he claims that Aristotle's view, which Nussbaum at least partially endorses, "would not be inconsistent with the capability approach presented here, but *not*, by any means, *required* by it."[30] On this assessment, Sen represents the capability approach as a general and "incomplete" approach that might consistently and fruitfully yield several different "evaluation exercises," each of which – in its own way – would select and weigh functionings and capabilities, propose evaluative procedures, and take a position on such foundational questions as "the metaphysics of value." Seen from this angle, Nussbaum's version of the capabilities approach would be one (but only one) possible specification.[31] Moreover, it would be a mistake to identify Nussbaum's specific theory with the generic capability approach, let alone reject other specifications.

In line with this account of Sen's assessment of Nussbaum's "list," Sen himself puts forward the United Nations Development Programme's Human Development Index (HDI), a much shorter list of functionings or capabilities (purchasing power, longevity, and education). The purpose of this "list" is to provide simple, easily communicable, and quantitative criteria to assess how a nation is doing in comparison with its own past or the current achievements of other nations.[32]

Second, Sen makes other remarks in the same essay, however, that suggest a different and less irenic response to Nussbaum's list. He says, for example, that he has "no great objection" to a "route" that offers "a unique list of functionings for a good human life."[33] This judgment suggests, however, that he does have *some* objection. The objections are twofold. In the 1993 essay he worried that Nussbaum's list "may be tremendously over specified."[34] It might be wished that Sen had identified the items on Nussbaum's list that particularly seem guilty of overspecification. In 2005, he again expresses concern about the fixity and finality – or dangers thereof – of some lists, Nussbaum's included:

> To insist on a "fixed forever" list of capabilities would deny the possibility of progress in social understanding, and also go against the productive role of public discussion, social agitation, and open debates. I have nothing against the listing of capabilities (and take part in that activity often enough), but I have to stand up against any proposal of a grand mausoleum to one fixed and final list of capabilities.[35]

A third interpretation, which Nussbaum herself offered in 2000, of Sen's evaluation of her list was clearly incorrect (even in 2000), namely, that he takes no stand with respect to the project of a list or Nussbaum's particular list:

> Most importantly, Sen has never made a list of the central capabilities. He gives lots of examples, and the *Human Development Reports* organize things in ways that correspond to at least some of the items on my list. But the idea of actually making the list and describing its use in generating political principles is not his, and he should not be taken as endorsing either the project or its specific contents.[36]

Nussbaum is certainly right that Sen has never sought a fixed, universally correct, and all-purpose list. But if I am right in my analysis above, Nussbaum fails to capture Sen's stance on lists. Sen is willing to accept some lists, for example the HDI, as one among many specific evaluative routes. No list, however, should be "fixed forever," too specific, or beyond the reach of rational scrutiny and public discussion.

Apart from his assessment of Nussbaum's particular list, does Sen suggest or argue for any other specific evaluation procedures, assumptions, and results? In "Capability and Well-Being," he leaves his approach "incomplete" and offers no specific evaluative exercise. Moreover, in that essay and again in *Inequality Reexamined,* he argues that, in describing and defending the moral space or "objects of value" of agency, capability, and functioning, he has already engaged in an evaluation that has "substantial cutting power."[37] For, as we saw in Chapters 4 and 5, on the basis of the moral space of agency, capability, and functioning, Sen compellingly rejects as either instrumental or partial the proposed moral spaces of per capita GNP, Rawlsian primary goods, happiness, preference satisfaction, or basic needs. By ruling out some candidate objects of value and defending his proposed moral space, Sen contends that he has shown that "the perspective of capabilities provides a fuller recognition of the variety of ways in which lives can be enriched or impoverished."[38] If Sen justifies evaluation on these *general* "objects of value," why does he not go further and both select and weigh specific valuable capabilities, argue for their meta-ethical or metaphysical status, and defend a particular evaluative procedure? There are two related reasons.

First, assuming that "reasoned agreement" is "an important fundamental foundational quality central to political and social ethics" and that it may be easier to get agreement on "objects of value" than on general meta-ethical issues or a specific evaluative method, Sen thinks it better first to work for agreement "on the choice of an evaluative space."[39] Hence, he calls his stopping short of offering a specific evaluative route not a permanent and principled end of a journey but a "pause."[40] This term suggests that with sufficient agreement about his proposed evaluative space, it might be reasonable – at least for certain purposes – to advance a more specific evaluative method by which valuable achievements and freedoms might be selected and weighed.

A second reason for his refraining – at least through the early 1990s – from entering the evaluative "lists" is that Sen assumes that any evaluation exercise should be chosen and shaped in the light of the individual's or group's purposes and context and that these purposes and contexts may vary widely. Sen himself frequently gives the same or very similar examples of capabilities or functionings that, he claims, people have reason to value and that "can" be good candidates for assessing standards of living, poverty, and (gender) inequality in different countries or in the same country at different times.[41] It is clear that Sen's own purpose in his World Bank lectures, which were the basis for his 1999 *Development as Freedom*, is that of redefining development in relation to the expansion of several freedoms (as both ends and means) and in relation to the ideal of agency, the basis for deciding on and weighing valuable capabilities and functionings:

This book [*Development as Freedom*], however, is not intended primarily for people working at or for the [World] Bank, or other international organizations. Nor it is just for policy makers and planners of national governments. Rather, it is a general work on development and the practical reasons underlying it, aimed particularly at public discussion . . .

In line with the importance I attach to the role of public discussion as a vehicle of social change and economic progress (as the text will make clear), this work is presented mainly for open deliberation and critical scrutiny.[42]

Furthermore, Sen argues, it is not exclusively theorists who make proposals for public and professional discussion with respect to "substantive freedoms." Members of a group or community of whatever scope (neighborhood, local, regional, national, continental, global) may face a concrete problem, such as how much of globalization to accept, but disagree about what should be done. Their adoption of democratic deliberation and decision-making may enable them to "feed" their individual assessments "directly into social assessment"[43] that, among other things, will select and weigh agency achievements as well as valuable capabilities and functionings.

Given his view of this plurality of evaluative problems related to different practical and normative purposes, it is not surprising that Sen refrains from celebrating *any* approach as the royal road to evaluation. However, neither of these reasons permanently blocks Sen or those influenced by his work from specific evaluation procedures and revisable lists for particular evaluative contexts. With respect to the first reason (lack of agreement about values and evaluative procedures), a sea change has in fact occurred in international development theory and practice since the 1980s and early 1990s. In that period, Sen's capability approach was only one among many contending approaches to international poverty and inequality. Now, however, many development theorists, policy analysts, field workers, and community leaders routinely invoke Sen's name and, more importantly, his view that development should expand and protect valuable human capabilities. Given this growing consensus, many now ask, "Which capabilities/functionings are most valuable?," "Who should decide?," and "How should the decisions be made?" Increasingly, Sen himself has answered not only by giving examples or making proposals of "substantive freedoms" that people have reason to value but by increasingly and explicitly identifying public discussion and democratic decision-making as among the evaluative procedures appropriate for certain purposes. Or so I shall argue later in this chapter and in Part IV.

In summary, I have examined the nature of Nussbaum's list and the two ways that Sen assesses it. The first way, the irenic response, is to view Nussbaum's list as one among several possible specifications of the general capability approach. The second and more critical path is to raise serious questions about Nussbaum's list. In spite of her disclaimers to the contrary and her ongoing revisions, Nussbaum's offering of a fixed or preset list, Sen correctly worries, is incompatible with ongoing, context-sensitive, and revisable public discussion. Either way, Sen's general capability theory and his own proposal for appropriate evaluative exercises differ from Nussbaum's with respect to who should select valuable capabilities and how they should do so. I now consider in more detail this methodological difference between Sen and Nussbaum.

Valuable functionings and capabilities: who decides and how?

Who should select which capabilities and functionings are (most) valuable, and how should they do it? Nussbaum emphasizes the role of philosophers but leaves some room for the methods of global dialogue and Rawlsian reflective equilibrium. Sen, who employs reflective equilibrium to argue philosophically for the evaluative space of freedom and achievement (both agency and well-being varieties), argues (at least since the mid-1990s) that groups as well as individuals themselves should select and weigh various freedoms and achievements (including capabilities and functionings) and that groups should do so by expressing their agency through rational scrutiny, public discussion, and democratic deliberation. The "evaluative exercises" and moral authority that, with some qualifications, Nussbaum gives to philosophers, Sen gives to democratic publics.

I examine now both Nussbaum's and Sen's evaluations of the roles of philosophers, constitutions and judges, democratic bodies, and individuals in evaluating capabilities and functionings. Often in response to the charge of paternalism, Nussbaum does assign a role, albeit limited, to philosophical dialogue, public discussion, democratic decision-making, and individual freedom or autonomy. However, these concessions to democratic processes, while important, are insufficient; she and we should, like Sen, give a much more robust role to democracy conceived as an inclusive and deliberative process.

Philosophical dialogue and public deliberation

Nussbaum rightly sees an important role for philosophical theorizing about questions of social justice and good development. Everyday ideas are often "jumbled and unexamined,"[44] and people's preferences are frequently infected by traditional beliefs, self-deception, and their efforts to adapt to a grim reality.[45] Moreover, our everyday notions are often riddled with defective past theories, such as utilitarianism. Through critical scrutiny, conceptual clarification, argument with ourselves, and immersion in concrete problems, normative and systematic theory can overcome these deficiencies and provide a coherent and policy-relevant system of ethical principles and prescriptions.[46]

Dialogue, argues Nussbaum, is also important. With respect to the contents and status of her list, Nussbaum consistently has advocated and practiced a conception of philosophical dialogue. She endorses a cross-cultural inquiry in which philosophers and others – through "participatory dialogue"[47] – construct a consensus on what it means to be human and to live well. Participants in this inquiry consult their own experience, the stories and self-understandings of their respective groups, and the insights of other groups and dialogue partners. International interdependence, boundary crossings, and the transnational scope of issues of various kinds make it imperative to forge a widespread or "overlapping consensus" on – at least partial – human flourishing and related constitutional principles. The consensus, ideally, will match most people's considered judgments and common intuitions – regardless of their religious or metaphysical commitments – about the cross-cultural core of a "free-standing"[48] conception of at least the basic dimensions of human flourishing. In areas in which an international consensus has not yet formed, for example whether plants and nonhuman animals have intrinsic or only instrumental value, Nussbaum does not take a stand.[49]

Nussbaum has practiced what she preaches. For example, she has responded to criticisms by fellow philosophers, and now emphasizes that her list does not offer necessary and sufficient conditions for being human or for human flourishing, but rather "central" capabilities.[50] Moreover, perhaps due to her new post (starting in 1995) at the University of Chicago Law School and to her discussions with Chicago law professor Cass Sunstein, among others, her later lists have included legal rights as institutional protections for the valuable capabilities. Finally, she argues that her discussions with Indians and especially women's groups have led her to make changes to the initial lists: "The primary changes are a greater emphasis on bodily integrity and control over one's environment (including property rights and employment opportunities), and a new emphasis on dignity and non-humiliation."[51] Not only has Nussbaum apparently learned from dialogue with philosophers and a wider public, especially poor Indian women, she also in turn believes that philosophy should value and contribute to "public deliberation":

Philosophy asks for public deliberation instead of the usual contest of power. It asks us to choose the view that stands the test of argument, rather than the view that has the most prestigious backers; the view that gets all the details worked out coherently and clearly, rather than the view whose proponents shout the loudest. At its best, its conceptual fussiness is profoundly practical: only if things are worked out in all their detail will we know whether we really do have the alternative that can stand up to objection better than another, and sometimes the fatal objection to a view emerges only after considerable probing. It makes sense for public deliberation to take account of these apparently fussy debates, because this is how we think through what we have to do, see what we really want to stand for.[52]

I wholeheartedly agree with Nussbaum on the potential reciprocity between philosophical dialogue and public deliberation. In fact, I would go further and urge that she view her list not as something to be directly enshrined in constitutions but as a stimulus for public debate in the construction, interpretation, modification, and application of constitutional principles. I would note, however, that Nussbaum tends to collapse "public deliberation" into philosophical dialogue. Of course, important similarities (and fruitful interaction) obtain between, on the one hand, philosophical dialogue, and, on the other hand, public discussion and deliberation that leads to policy choice. Both aspire to uncoerced and overlapping consensus. Both involve the give and take as well as the rational scrutiny of arguments. But while philosophical dialogue aims solely at the truth or at least at reasoned agreement on beliefs and values, in democratic deliberation fellow citizens deliberate over, decide on, and bind themselves to problem-solving policies that (most) all can accept.

Although Nussbaum herself has learned from citizen debates and concerns, she offers "fussy" philosophical argumentation and a coherent normative view or list as an improvement on everyday beliefs and arguments. In contrast, Sen makes it very clear that philosophical theorizing in general and "the framework of capabilities" in particular cannot displace public (citizen) reasoning and that Nussbaum's "canonical list" threatens to do just that:

Nussbaum has discussed the importance of identifying an overarching "list of capabilities," with given priorities, in a more Aristotelian way. My own reluctance to join the search for such a canonical list arises partly from my difficulty in seeing how the exact lists and weights would be chosen without appropriate specification of the context of their use (which could vary), but also from the disinclination to accept any substantive diminution of the domain of public reasoning. The framework of capabilities, as I see it, helps to clarify and illuminate the *subject matter* of public reasoning, which can involve epistemic issues (including claims of objective importance) as well as ethical and political ones. It does not – and cannot – displace the need for public reasoning.[53]

Constitution-making

Nussbaum boldly proposes her list to the global community with the intent that the list and argumentation, especially the appeal to equal human dignity, will "provide the philosophical underpinning for an account of basic constitutional principles that should be respected and implemented by the governments of all nations, as a bare minimum of what respect for human dignity requires."[54] Her intent is that political agents in particular countries will use her list to shape public policy in general and their country's basic constitutional principles in particular.

With one exception, which I discuss presently, Nussbaum does not pause to consider the process of constitution-making and the role that citizens and their representatives can and should play in this process. No mediation seems to exist between the philosopher's articulation of the capabilities or human rights list and their embodiment in a nation's constitution.

At one point, however, Nussbaum sensibly affirms that the nation should make or change its own constitution, thereby converting Nussbaum's philosophical list into constitutional guarantees. Rather than seeking to impose her list on a nation, Nussbaum *recommends* that the nation itself deliberate – informed by her list – and decide on or amend their own constitution:

> It would be inconsistent if a defender of the capabilities approach, with its strong role for democratic politics and political liberty, were to seek an implementation strategy that bypassed the deliberations of a democratically elected parliament. Thus at this point the approach is recommended as a good idea to politicians in India or any other nation who want to make it the basis of national or local policy . . . In a case such as India's, if the Constitution is going to change, it will ultimately have to be because the people of India choose such a change. Capabilities theory would be a prescription for tyranny if it bypassed the nation.[55]

In this passage Nussbaum gets it exactly right as far as she goes, although one would like to see her spell out her conception of the deliberative processes by which a constitutional convention should frame, or a parliament should alter, its constitution. How should philosophers propose, and citizens and their representatives respond, so that there is genuine give and take among equal participants rather than a short-circuiting of national self-determination? What stance should Nussbaum take if citizens reject her list in whole or in part? Is she not going too far when she declares that a society that fails – regardless of its wealth – to guarantee her ten capabilities, at some level, to all its citizens, cannot be fully just?[56] What is unclear and deserves attention is the extent to which a country like the USA is morally justified in using non-deliberative methods, such as economic or military sanctions, to assure a nation's success in making or reforming a particular kind of constitution. What is morally permissible for capability philosophers to say, and for democratic nations and international agencies (committed to central capabilities or basic rights) to do, to get recalcitrant governments to entrench capability and rights guarantees, including the right of citizen participation, in their constitutions? Going beyond mere recommendation and even strong commendation, Nussbaum entertains – especially when there are "egregious violations of human dignity" – "the use of economic and other strategies to secure compliance."[57] I hope to take up these questions in future work on democratization. What mixtures of coercion, negotiation, and deliberation can and should be used, and at what stage in a democratic transition, such that the process is efficient and peaceful as well as respecting the dignity of all citizens and their ownership of their own institutions?[58]

Constitutionally constrained democracy

Once capability guarantees are in place, Nussbaum also attributes a role – albeit an insufficiently robust role – to democratic decision-making in specifying and implementing capability norms. Since the late 1980s, Nussbaum has insisted that it is up to each community to "specify" and implement her list in its own way, including deciding on the threshold for each central capability. Initially she called this permissible pluralism "local specification": "The Aristotelian must aim at some concrete specification of the general list that suits, and develops out of, the local conditions. This will always most reasonably be done in a participatory dialogue with those who are most deeply immersed in those conditions."[59]

In her more recent writings she describes this feature of her list as "multiple realizability."[60] The list's very general items "can be more concretely specified in accordance with local beliefs and circumstances," and citizens and, presumably, judges can contribute to a determination of the threshold of each central capability. They do so by working "toward a consensus for political purposes . . . within each constitutional tradition, as it evolves through interpretation and deliberation."[61]

However, although she leaves a role for democratic processes to specify and design strategies for implementing her list, Nussbaum refuses to permit a governing body to prioritize, weigh, or outweigh central capabilities. In the light of her normative principles and list, a nation's constitution would include capability "guarantees" that a government is bound to enforce. Nussbaum does say that there should be a "strong role for democratic politics and political liberty" in certain areas left open by her list. But in fact she leaves open few such areas.

One decision that she does give to democratic processes to resolve concerns "the thorny issues of institutional competence raised by the clash between the legislative and judicial branches." Admitting that she is "agnostic" on this "clash," Nussbaum states that "each nation must resolve those particular issues on its own, in the light of its own traditions and constitution."[62] She should also add to this list of tough issues the similar question of whether or not the theory of the "unitary executive," a theory that permits the US President to circumvent the statutes, is morally or constitutionally justified.

Another topic about which Nussbaum looks not to her own intuitions, normative theory, or proposed constitutional principles but to "the democratic processes of a nation"[63] is whether (or the extent to which) a government is justified in being paternalistic in relation to certain individual choices. For example, to what extent, if any, should a community prohibit actions in which a person freely chooses to risk or surrender a central capability? Should the person's exercise of her central capability for choice trump her equally central capability for bodily integrity and healthy functioning, especially when the loss of the capability may be irreversible? For example, should the state prohibit freely selling oneself into slavery, consensual genital mutilation, the consensual surrender of reproductive capability, free participation in very violent or risky sports, and the unregulated purchase of dangerous medicines and drugs? Although Nussbaum makes it clear that she favors – "up to a point" – governmental "interference with choice" in such matters, she does recognize that "all these issues are controversial because they do raise legitimate concerns about paternalism"[64] and that other people may have different views as to where to draw the line with respect to legitimate government intervention.[65]

In these kinds of cases Nussbaum admits that a democratic polity can and should decide democratically and deliberatively how to balance goods that conflict and about whose balancing people are not in agreement. Her mistake is in failing to see that there are many more areas in which a democratic community will have to decide how to weigh conflicting goods and strike a fair balance between different conceptions of their appropriate weights.

Even with respect to these areas of democratic decision-making, Nussbaum assumes that a fundamental incompatibility exists between constitutionalism and democracy: the more you have of one, the less you have of the other. Either democratic (majority) votes are completely unconstrained by moral or constitutional principles, or constitutions – based on philosophically established principles – stringently check and limit the democratic will. I believe this assumption is mistaken. A constitution can and should not only protect certain capabilities (rights) but also secure and mandate venues for democratic and deliberative decision-making in the various branches of government and their relation to "the people." As Cass Sunstein puts it:

Against those who see a continuing conflict between constitutional law and democracy, I urge that there need be no such conflict at all. Whether a constitution conflicts with democracy depends on what kind of constitution and what kind of democracy we seek. In a deliberative democracy, one of the principle purposes of the constitution is to protect not the rule of the majority but democracy's internal morality, seen in deliberative terms. A system in which many people cannot vote or vote equally, or in which some people have far more political power than others, violates that internal morality.[66]

Supreme Court Justice Stephen Breyer offers just such a view of the US Constitution. Although, he argues, the Constitution certainly provides guarantees for "liberty of the moderns," that is, various protections against government intrusions in the lives of citizens, the Constitution also embodies a commitment to "the liberty of the ancients." This "active liberty" is, argues Breyer, "the freedom of the individual citizen to participate in the government and thereby to share with others the right to make or to control the nation's public acts."[67] For Breyer, "the Constitution is not a document designed to solve the problems of a community at any level – local, state, or national." It is, rather, a document that "trusts people to solve those problems themselves" and "creates a *framework* for a government that will help them do so."[68] The perspective of "active liberty," when put in proper balance with "modern liberty," will enable judges to interpret a legal text in a way that "will yield a better law – law that helps a community of individuals democratically find practical solutions to important contemporary social problems."[69] Unmistakably resonant in this jurisprudential view are both Dewey's ideal of democracy and Sen's ideal of citizen agency as ethically justified dimensions of collective problem-solving.

I share Nussbaum's concern for constitutional protection for the most vital and basic capabilities, for I would not want to see a mere majority vote deprive some minority of its freedoms. Yet I am reluctant to ascribe to philosophers the job of prescribing a "canonical list of rights" and to Supreme Court justices the task of authoritative interpretation of a constitution that supposedly enshrines the philosophers' norms. For each of these moves seems motivated, in the words of Jeremy Waldron, "to put that canon beyond the scope of political debate and revision."[70] It is indeed important to welcome philosophical critique and construction and to avoid the tyranny of the majority, but it is equally desirable not to succumb to the possible tyranny of the philosopher king or to that of nine (or five!) judges. The best way to avoid the tyranny of the majority requires deliberative democracy in three ways. First, although they might advance philosophical argument or include citizen-philosophers, group members – acting directly or through their representatives – should deliberate about, decide on, and ratify their own constitution. Second, a constitution, if decided deliberatively and fairly, likely would provide guarantees that both protect everyone and that (most) everyone could accept, and that in any case would be subject to revision following public deliberation. Third, a point that Nussbaum misses, a democratic and just constitution would itself establish and encourage multiple venues for participatory and deliberative democracy.

Among other things, such democratic venues would provide citizens the opportunity and responsibility to scrutinize constitutions, constitutional rulings, and judicial review. In so doing citizens exercise their own agency in deciding collectively their values and their policies. Lists of capabilities or human rights that citizens have reason to value may still play an important role. But rather than functioning beyond the reach of deliberative and popular bodies, these lists should be viewed as generic topics or menus for discussion or specific proposals for democratic bodies and citizens to discuss.

Returning to the question of what sort of list is compatible with deliberation, I agree with Sen that the issue between Nussbaum and himself is not that of "to list or not to list." The issue is: what sort of list for what purpose? If the list is subject to additions and corrections as well as a tool for stimulating, elevating, deepening, or broadening public discussion, well and good. If the list is determined prior to public deliberation and dogmatically shuts off debate, such a list is appropriate for the starting line-up for a soccer team but not for self-governing citizens trying to solve problems that have emerged in their particular social context:

> My skepticism is about fixing a cemented list of capabilities that is seen as being absolutely complete (nothing could be added to it) and totally fixed (it could not respond to public reasoning and to the formation of social values). I am a great believer in theory, and certainly accept that a good theory of evaluation and assessment has to bring out the relevance of what we are free to do and free to be (the capabilities in general), as opposed to the material goods we have and the commodities we can command. But I must also argue that pure theory cannot "freeze" a list of capabilities for all societies for all time to come, irrespective of what the citizens come to understand and value. That would be not only a denial of the reach of democracy, but also a misunderstanding of what pure theory can do, completely divorced from the particular social reality that any particular society faces.[71]

Why does Nussbaum put so much emphasis on a nation's constitution rather than, as does Sen, on democratic processes and citizen participation? There are, I believe, at least two reasons.

First, as we have seen, she fears that a democratic majority – when unconstrained by a rights-guaranteeing constitution – will ride roughshod over individual or minority rights. One of the virtues of an inclusive and deliberative democratic process is the likelihood that the minority concerns will be at least partially embodied in the group's decision. If not, as I shall argue further, in Part IV, the solution is more and not less democracy. Nussbaum has surprisingly little to say in her writings about democracy,[72] and what she does say tends to identify democracy with decision-making by simple majorities unconstrained by constitutions.[73] More awareness of the recent innovations in democratic theory and experiments in democratic practice might break the hold on her uncritical acceptance of minimalist democracy.

A second reason for Nussbaum's skepticism about democratic processes is her view on "trade-offs." On Nussbaum's account, a society's task, especially that of its government, is to promote and protect the central capabilities by ensuring that each citizen is able to get over a basic threshold with respect to each and every capability on Nussbaum's list. Although there is a plurality of central capabilities, a society cannot and should not decide among them or rank them. For, Nussbaum claims, these central capabilities are of equal moral urgency, and more of one can never make up for less of another:

The list is, emphatically, a list of *separate components*. We cannot satisfy the need for one of them by giving a larger amount of another one. All are of central importance and all are distinct in quality. The irreducible plurality of the list limits the trade-offs that it will be reasonable to make, and thus limits the applicability of quantitative cost-benefit analysis.[74]

How should we assess this "no trade-offs" reason for constraining democratic deliberation? I accept that there is a plurality of equally valuable capabilities and that more of one does not compensate for less or the loss of another. That said, it does not follow that there are not – in addition to decisions with respect to specification and implementation – important normative decisions that individuals and groups can and should make concerning the contextual ranking and sequencing of capabilities that they have reason to value. Sometimes there are insufficient resources or opportunities to promote (equally) all the valuable capabilities. Then what? Nussbaum's consistent answer over the years is to transform the world so that each capability can be fully or sufficiently protected.[75] In response to the reasonable objection that sometimes this win-win solution is (at least in the short run) practically impossible, Nussbaum resigns herself to the "tragic character" of some choices. Such choices are tragic in the sense that, especially when they push citizens below a capability threshold, they cause real harm by "slighting" a distinctive good.[76]

There is, however, another, less tragic, and democratic solution: a democratic body can deliberate and decide – when it cannot obtain all good things, at least not at once – to give priority to some capabilities over others or prioritize some valuable capabilities in such a way that many (if not all) are satisfied to some extent, but some more than others. As political theorist William A. Galston says, "The most difficult political choices are not between good and bad but between good and good."[77] How, for example, should a community weigh – when they conflict – the good of security and the good of civil liberties, or the good of protecting endangered species versus the good of increasing economic opportunity? One virtue of deliberative democracy is that it offers a process by which clashing goods can be dealt with in such a way that a reasonable balance between goods and viewpoints can be forged. Good reasons exist, which I consider in Chapter 9, why a community's selection and weighting of valuable capabilities and their thresholds should be made democratically, following a process of deliberation, rather than through appeal to a philosopher or other expert.

Individual freedom and plural specification

Finally, Nussbaum attempts to soften her constitutionalism by affirming individual freedom and "plural specification." The former means that one can decide whether to avail oneself of government provisioning of central capabilities. The latter means freedom "to specify each of the components [of the list] more concretely, and with much variety, in accordance with local traditions, or individual tastes."[78] Hence, not only does Nussbaum open some policy space for democratic decisions; she also celebrates the individual's capability and right to decide (within limits) her own course of life. Based on the liberal idea of "the citizen as a free and dignified human being, a maker of choices,"[79] she affirms, especially by elevating the capability of "practical reason," the individual's freedom to shape her own life:

Politics here has an urgent role to play, providing citizens with the tools that they need, both in order to choose at all and in order to have a realistic option of exercising the most valuable functions. The choice of whether and how to use the tools, however, is left up to the citizens in the conviction that this is an essential aspect of respect for their freedom. They are seen not as passive recipients of social patterning but as dignified free beings who shape their own life.[80]

One of the ways open to these active citizens is that of the central capability of controlling their environment, including "being able to participate effectively in political choices that govern one's life; having the right of political participation, protections of free speech and association."[81]

There is much with which to agree in these passages, but it is notable that Nussbaum's focus is on *individual* agency to shape one's life through personal choice rather than on the *collective* choice of political values (for instance, valued capabilities and functionings) and policies. Although

Nussbaum does include in her central capabilities the individual's capability and right to participate politically, the emphasis is on the individual's political rights rather on two themes increasingly prominent in Sen. Sen emphasizes each citizen's "social commitment" to deliberate and decide policy together as well as the important role of political freedom in furthering public debate, rational scrutiny of options, and *social* choice of priorities: "One of the strongest arguments in favor of political freedom lies precisely in the opportunity it gives citizens to discuss and debate – and to participate in the selection of – values in the choice of priorities."[82]

Nussbaum does ample justice to one side of the "two-way relation" between individual freedom and societal arrangements, namely, the way in which social arrangements and political actions can and should "expand individual freedoms." She misses, however, Sen's more capacious perspective in which individual freedoms "make the social arrangements more appropriate and effective."[83] Sen is convinced that "the direction of public policy can be influenced by the effective use of participatory capabilities by the public."[84] Whether deliberating collectively as citizens of a polity or as members of an association, individuals acting collaboratively and through public discussion shape their preferences and arrive at remedies to practical problems.

We drive home the difference between Sen and Nussbaum on this point in relation to Nussbaum's one-sided interpretation of a recent idea of Sen's. In "Freedom and Needs," Sen says: "Political rights are important not only for the fulfillment of needs, they are crucial also for the formulation of needs. And this idea relates, in the end, to the respect that we owe each other as fellow human beings."[85] Nussbaum interprets this passage as meaning exclusively that each citizen has the right to decide on her own needs and whether to avail herself of government provisioning. Sen, however, by the "constructive role" of "basic political and liberal rights," *also* means that "our conceptualization of economic [and other] needs depends crucially on open public debates and discussions, the guaranteeing of which requires insistence on basic political liberty and civil rights."[86]

Concluding remarks

In one of Sen's most recent books,[87] he and co-author Jean Drèze make even clearer the difference between Sen's democratic approach to popular valuation and an approach, like Nussbaum's, which gives more priority to philosophical reflection and valuation. Sen and Drèze distinguish between democratic ideals, institutions, and practices. It is certainly important to defend democratic *ideals*. These ideals are elements in the comprehensive idea of democracy as government of, by, and for the people – a conception of government that contrasts with government of, by, and for kings, philosophers, or other elites. These ideals include "freedom of expression, participation of the people in deciding on the factors governing their lives, public accountability of leaders, and an equitable distribution of power."[88] Going from "basic intents" to institutions, the two authors affirm "such institutional arrangements as constitutional rights, effective courts, responsive electoral systems, functioning parliaments and assemblies, open and free media, and participatory institutions of local governance (such as panchayats and gram sabhas)."[89]

Something more is needed, argue Drèze and Sen, than democratic ideals and institutions. A strong or deep democracy is composed of people who make democracy "work,"[90] who "practice"[91] democracy by engaging in public action and voicing concerns in various ways, such as voting, street protests, organizing political parties and civic movements, and monitoring governmental action. Without the "practice" of democracy, democratic institutions will function "at variance with the democratic ideals."[92] With democratic practice on the part of citizens, the "quality of democracy" improves. And a crucial aspect of democratic practice is that citizens evaluate freedoms and forge together common values:

> The practice of democracy gives the citizens an opportunity to learn from each other, and can also profoundly influence the values and priorities of the society. Even the idea of "needs" (including the understanding "economic needs"), which is often taken to be fixed and well-defined, can respond to public discussion and exchange of information, views and analyses. In this sense, democracy has a *constructive importance,* in addition to the intrinsic value it has in the lives of the citizens and an instrumental role in political decisions. Value formation is as much a democratic activity as is the use of social values in the determination of public policy and social response.[93]

In this chapter I have argued that Nussbaum's "route" to evaluating capabilities and functionings is to balance her bold normative list and her strong constitutionalism with *some* provisions, on the one hand, for philosophical dialogue, democratic constitution-making, and democratic processes within a constitutional polity, and, on the other hand, for freedom of individual choice. I have also argued that the door that she opens for democracy in each of the areas can and should be opened wider and that Sen helps us see how this might be done. In Chapter 9, I argue that the theory and practice of deliberative democracy has much to offer Sen in his effort to renovate democratic theory, improve democratic institutions, and deepen democratic practice. I argue that respecting people's dignity and agency requires not only, as Nussbaum contends, that they be free as individuals to form their own conception of the good life; it also requires that people have the right and responsibility to form collective values and decide practical policies together.

In my thirty years teaching, writing, and applying development ethics, I have been continually stimulated, enlightened, and provoked by the capability orientation, especially the versions that Sen and Nussbaum have contributed to development theory and practice. In the three chapters of Part II, I have sought to share the results of my evolving engagement with this approach to development ethics. I have analyzed both similarities and differences between these two thinkers with respect to their evaluations of alternative normative perspectives in development (Chapter 4), their concepts of agency, functioning, and capability (Chapter 5), and their ways of evaluating capabilities and functionings in development (Chapter 6). I have probed each position for weaknesses as well as strengths and have sought to work out an assessment that strengthens the capability orientation. In the two chapters of Part III, I apply development ethics and my favored version of the capability orientation to the problems of global consumption and hunger. In Part IV, I argue further for the fruitful convergence of the capability orientation and the theory and practice of deliberative democracy.

NOTES

This chapter has not appeared previously. It has benefited from comments by Verna Gehring, Lori Keleher, and David Wasserman.

1. Amartya Sen, "Human Rights and Capabilities," *Journal of Human Development*, 6, 2 (2005): 158.
2. Martha Nussbaum, *Women and Human Development: The Capabilities Approach* (Cambridge: Cambridge University Press, 2000), 83.
3. Amartya Sen, "The Standard of Living," in *The Standard of Living: The Tanner Lectures on Human Values*, ed. Amartya Sen, J. Muellbauer, Ravi Kanbur, K. Hart, and Bernard Williams (Cambridge: Cambridge University Press, 1987), 107; see also Amartya Sen, *Inequality Reexamined* (Cambridge, MA: Harvard University Press, 1992), 44–6.
4. Amartya Sen, *Commodities and Capabilities* (Amsterdam: North-Holland, 1985), 32.
5. Ibid., 48.
6. For two examples of Nussbaum's list prior to the mid-1990s, see Nussbaum, "Human Capabilities, Female Human Beings," in *Women, Culture and Development*, ed. Martha Nussbaum and Jonathan Glover (Oxford: Oxford

University Press, 1995), 83–5; and "The Good as Discipline, the Good as Freedom," in *Ethics of Consumption: The Good Life, Justice, and Global Stewardship*, ed. David A. Crocker and Toby Linden (Lanham, MD: Rowman & Littlefield, 1998), 318–20. (Although the last paper appeared in 1998, Nussbaum presented it in a conference in 1994.) Nussbaum sets forth, with little variation, her more recent list in Martha Nussbaum, "Capabilities and Human Rights," *Fordham Law Review*, 66 (1997): 273–300, reprinted in *Global Justice and Transnational Politics*, ed. Pablo De Greiff and Ciaran Cronin (Cambridge, MA, and London: MIT Press, 2002); *Sex and Social Justice* (Oxford: Oxford University Press, 1999), 41–2; *Women and Human Development*, 78–80; "Capabilities as Fundamental Entitlements," *Feminist Economics*, 9, 2–3 (2003): 41–2.

7. For criticisms of Nussbaum's early "essentialism," in which a person's having each of the listed capabilities is necessary for being human or for human flourishing, see Susan Wolf, "Martha C. Nussbaum: Human Capabilities, Female Human Beings," in *Women, Culture and Development*, ed. Martha Nussbaum and Jonathan Glover, 107–9; and David A. Crocker, "Functioning and Capability: The Foundations of Sen's and Nussbaum's Development Ethic, Part 2," in ibid., 172–3.

8. Up to the mid-1990s, Nussbaum advocated and practiced a two-step normative procedure and generated a separate list for each. The first step in constructing an account of good human functioning was to work out an "outline sketch" of being human, a "thick vague conception of the human being" or "the shape of the human form of life." The second step, the thick vague conception of good human functioning, goes further and provisionally identifies, in a more determinate but still general way, the most important or "basic human functional capabilities," "the totality of functionings that constitute the good human life." The source of the first phrase is "Non-Relative Virtues: An Aristotelian Approach," *Midwest Studies in Philosophy*, 13 (1988): 38–9, and "Aristotelian Social Democracy," in *Liberalism and the Good*, ed. Bruce Douglass, Gerald Mara, and Henry Richardson (London and New York: Routledge, 1990), 205–6, 217–24; Nussbaum formulates and discusses the second step in, for example, "Aristotelian Social Democracy," 225–34. Although there are still residues of this two-step sequence in Nussbaum's recent writings, the first step is now de-emphasized and does little, if any, independent work (see "The Good as Discipline, the Good as Freedom," 317–18; *Sex and Social Justice*, 39–40; *Women and Human Development*, 73).

9. Nussbaum, "Capabilities as Fundamental Entitlements," 42.

10. Ibid., 40.

11. See, for example, *Women, Culture and Development*, ed. Martha Nussbaum and Jonathan Glover (Oxford: Clarendon Press; New York: Oxford University Press, 1995); Jerome M. Segal, "Living at a High Economic Standard: A Functionings Analysis," in *Ethics of Consumption*, ed. Crocker and Linden, 345–54; *Feminist Economics*, 9, 2–3 (2003); and Carol C. Gould, *Globalizing Democracy and Human Rights* (Cambridge: Cambridge University Press, 2005), 57–8.

12. Nussbaum, *Women and Human Development*, 5, 56, 73–4.
13. Ibid., 72–3, three footnotes omitted.
14. Ibid., 5.
15. Ibid., 76.
16. Ibid., 5; see also 12–13, 74, 188–90, 246–7, 250–2, 274–5.
17. Ibid., 12.
18. Ibid., 5.
19. Ibid., 190; see also 221–2, 275.
20. Ibid., 275.
21. See Jesús Conill, *Horizontes de economía ética* (Madrid: Editorial Tecnos, 2004), esp. 178–88.
22. David Wasserman, "Disability, Capability, and Thresholds for Distributive Justice," in *Capabilities Equality: Basic Issues and Problems*, ed. Alexander Kaufman (New York and London: Routledge, 2006), 229. See also Martha Nussbaum, *Frontiers of Justice: Disability, Nationality, Species Membership* (Cambridge, MA: Harvard University Press, 2006).
23. Nussbaum, "Aristotelian Social Democracy," 217.
24. See David A. Crocker, "Functioning and Capability: The Foundations of Sen's and Nussbaum's Development Ethic," *Political Theory*, 20, 4 (1992): 595–9; "Functioning and Capability: The Foundations of Sen's and Nussbaum's Development Ethic, Part 2," in *Women, Culture and Development*, ed. Nussbaum and Glover, 69–80.
25. See Jesús Conill, "Bases éticas del enfoque de las capacidades de Amartya Sen," *Sistema*, 171 (2002): 47–64.
26. Nussbaum, *Women and Human Development*, 74.
27. Crocker, "Functioning and Capability, Part 2," 174–6. See Nussbaum's 1995 list in "Human Capabilities, Female Human Beings," 83–5.
28. David Alexander Clark, *Visions of Development: A Study of Human Values* (Cheltenham, and Northampton, MA: Edward Elgar, 2002), 71–3.
29. Martha Nussbaum, "Nature, Function, and Capability: Aristotle on Political Distribution," *Oxford Studies in Ancient Philosophy*, supp. vol. (Oxford: Clarendon Press, 1988), 152. Quoted by Sen in "Capability and Well-Being," in *The Quality of Life*, ed. Martha Nussbaum and Amartya Sen (Oxford: Oxford University Press, 1993), 46.
30. Sen, "Capability and Well-Being," 47.
31. A good analogy would be Robert Nozick's distinction between "the general outlines of a theory of justice in holdings" and a specific theory of justice in holdings: "the general outlines of the theory of justice in holdings are that the holdings of a person are just if he is entitled to them by the principles of justice in acquisition and transfer, or by the principle of rectification of injustice (as specified by the first two principles). If each person's holdings are just, then the total set (distribution) of holdings are just. To turn these general outlines into a specific theory we would have to specify the details of the three principles of justice . . . I shall not attempt that task here": Robert Nozick, *Anarchy, State, and Utopia* (New York: Basic Books, 1974), 153. Another analogy would be John Rawls's distinction between a *concept* of justice, those kinds of normative principles whose role is to provide the

distribution of the benefits and burdens of fair social cooperation, and a particular *conception* of justice, that is, any proposal of *specific* principles to govern just distributions: John Rawls, *A Theory of Justice*, rev. edn. (Cambridge, MA: Harvard University Press, 1999), 5. Both Nozick and Rawls could say that *any* specific theory consistent with the general approach is permitted but not required by that approach.

32. Sen, "Human Rights and Capabilities," 158. See also Sudhir Anand and Amartya Sen, "Human Development Index: Methodology and Measurement," in *Readings in Human Development*, ed. Sakiko Fukuda-Parr and A. K. Shiva Kumar (New Delhi: Oxford University Press, 2003), 114–27.
33. Sen, "Capability and Well-Being," 47.
34. Ibid.
35. Sen, "Human Rights and Capabilities," 160.
36. Nussbaum, *Women and Human Development*, 13.
37. Sen, "Capability and Well-Being," 49; *Inequality Reexamined*, 42–4.
38. Sen, *Inequality Reexamined*, 44.
39. Sen, "Capability and Well-Being," 49.
40. Ibid., 48.
41. Sen, *Development as Freedom* (New York: Knopf, 1999), 20.
42. Ibid., xiii–xiv.
43. Sen, "Capability and Well-Being," 49; *Development as Freedom*, 66.
44. *Women and Human Development*, 35.
45. See Nussbaum, *Women and Human Development*, ch. 2.
46. See ibid., 298–303, for a nice statement of this conception of the role of philosophy.
47. Nussbaum, "Human Capabilities, Female Human Beings," 94. I omit a footnote that refers to Martha Chen's development project in Bangladesh and its use of Paolo Freire's method of "participatory dialogue" (Martha Alter Chen, *A Quiet Revolution: Women in Transition in Rural Bangladesh* [Cambridge, MA: Schenkman, 1983]).
48. Nussbaum, *Women and Human Development*, 83.
49. Ibid., 157.
50. See Crocker, "Functioning and Capability, Part 2," 172–3; Susan Wolf, "Comments on Nussbaum's 'Human Capabilities, Female Human Beings,'" in *Women, Culture and Development*, ed. Nussbaum and Glover, 105–15; Jerome M. Segal, "Living at a High Standard of Living," 342–65.
51. Nussbaum, *Women and Human Development*, 78, n. 82. Some of Nussbaum's critics argue that her academic interchanges are largely restricted to like-minded colleagues, and that in her discussions with poor women she does not worry sufficiently that poor women may be intimidated by her academic stature and tell her (Nussbaum) what she wants to hear.
52. Ibid., 300.
53. Sen, "Elements of a Theory of Human Rights," *Philosophy and Public Affairs*, 32, 4 (2004): 333, n. 31. Sen makes the same point in almost the same words in "Human Rights and Capabilities," 157.
54. Nussbaum, *Women and Human Development*, 5; cf. 51, 116.
55. Ibid., 104.

56. Nussbaum, "Capabilities as Fundamental Entitlements," 42.
57. Ibid.
58. See Thomas Carothers, *Aiding Democracy Abroad: The Learning Curve* (Washington, DC: Carnegie Endowment for International Peace, 1999); *Critical Mission: Essays on Democracy Promotion* (Washington, DC: Carnegie Endowment for International Peace, 2004).
59. Nussbaum, "Human Capabilities, Female Human Beings," 94.
60. Nussbaum, *Women and Human Development*, 77.
61. Ibid.
62. Nussbaum, *Women and Human Development*, 202. Two pages later Nussbaum says: "I remain agnostic about the proper role of legislature and the judiciary in this evolution [of boundary-fixing between these two branches]; the resolution of such institutional questions depends on contextual features about the nature of democratic traditions in each country" (ibid., 204). Notice that the work to be done here seems to be done by (legal?) interpreters of a nation's constitution and "democratic traditions" and not by public deliberation.
63. Ibid., 95.
64. Ibid.
65. Sen, I argued in Chapter 5 and will reiterate in Chapter 10, would describe these choices as ones between agency freedom, on the one hand, and well-being capabilities or functionings, on the other.
66. Cass R. Sunstein, *Designing Democracy: What Constitutions Do* (Oxford: Oxford University Press, 2001), 10.
67. Stephen Breyer, *Active Liberty: Interpreting Our Democratic Constitution* (New York: Knopf, 2005), 3.
68. Ibid., 134.
69. Ibid., 6. See also E. J. Dionne, "Talking Sense on Court Choice," *Washington Post* (November 23, 2004): A 29.
70. Jeremy Waldron, "A Right-Based Critique of Constitutional Rights," *Oxford Journal of Legal Studies*, 13, 1 (1993): 19. See also Waldron, *Law and Disagreement* (Oxford: Oxford University Press, 1999), Part III.
71. Sen, "Human Rights and Capabilities," 156.
72. No entry for "democracy" exists in the subject index of *Women and Human Development*, *Sex and Social Justice*, or *Frontiers of Justice*, but Nussbaum entitles one section in *Sex and Social Justice* "Justification and Implementation: Democratic Politics" (101–5).
73. In *Women and Human Development*, Nussbaum worries that without constitutional guarantees a majoritarian democracy may harm the capabilities and opportunities that future generations would have either to enjoy nature or nonhuman species (94) or to choose their own religion or speech (160). In a recent article, however, Nussbaum departs from democratic minimalism and appreciates that "a good democracy" fosters "responsiveness and interactivity" among citizens who think critically, deliberate together, and imaginatively consider alternative social possibilities. See "Education and Democratic Citizenship: Capabilities and Quality Education," *Journal of Human Development: Alternative Economics in Action*, 7, 3 (2006): 391.

74. Ibid., 81.
75. See Nussbaum, "Aristotelian Social Democracy," 212. See Crocker, "Functioning and Capability, Part 2," 178–80.
76. For a compelling argument that Nussbaum fails to justify her exclusive trichotomy of "no trade-offs" or "change the world" or "accept tragedy," see Wasserman, "Disability, Capability, and Thresholds for Distributive Justice," 228–32.
77. William A. Galston, *Liberal Pluralism: Implications of Value Pluralism for Political Theory and Practice* (Cambridge: Cambridge University Press, 2002), 34.
78. Nussbaum, "Human Capabilities, Female Human Beings," 94.
79. Nussbaum, "Capabilities and Human Rights," 134.
80. Ibid., 135 (footnote omitted citing Sen, "Freedom and Needs," 38).
81. Nussbaum, *Woman and Human Development*, 80.
82. Sen, *Development as Freedom*, 30.
83. Ibid., 31.
84. Ibid., 18. Happily, Nussbaum is beginning to reach for a more balanced view on the relation between individual critical thinking and social deliberation when in a 2006 article she applauds Socrates' mission of promoting "the examined life": "But he [Socrates] defended his activity on the grounds that democracy needs citizens who can think for themselves rather than simply deferring to authority, who can reason together about their choices rather than just trading claims and counter-claims": "Education and Democratic Citizenship," 388.
85. Sen, "Freedom and Needs," *New Republic*, 10, 17 (1994): 38.
86. Sen, *Development as Freedom*, 148.
87. Jean Drèze and Amartya Sen, *India: Development and Participation*, 2nd edn. (Oxford: Oxford University Press, 2002).
88. Ibid., 347.
89. Ibid.
90. Sen, *Democracy as Freedom*, 154–5.
91. Drèze and Sen, *India*, 347–79.
92. Ibid., 351.
93. Ibid., 25.

Part III

Strengthening and applying the capability approach

7   Agency, responsibility, and consumption

If development ethics is to be more than an academic exercise, it must confront urgent human problems. Sometimes the ethicist begins with moral dilemmas and searches for relevant ethical principles. Sometimes the ethicist applies to a new quandary principles that have proven helpful in grasping and resolving other moral issues or dilemmas.

The list of urgent practical challenges is lengthy, but at or near the top would be those challenges addressed in the next two chapters: over-consumption and hunger. Many lives go very badly because some people in both the South and the North consume too much or the wrong kind of goods and services. One result is climate change, which endangers the planet and all its inhabitants. Others in both the North and the South suffer and even die from lack of food and other necessities. Moreover, in a globalizing world, that some have more than they need is sometimes the cause of others having much less than they need to have the real opportunity for at least a minimally adequate life.

The two chapters of Part III are efforts to understand and provide a normative – yet policy-relevant – framework to help understand and resolve these problems of over-consumption and under-consumption, such as hunger. How should the development ethicist grasp and judge over-consumption as well as hunger and other deprivations in the global North and South? Do richer individuals and nations have moral obligations either to alter their consumption patterns or to provide food aid and development assistance to countries and individuals suffering from hunger and other deprivations? In so, under what conditions and at what costs? In Denis Goulet's apt phrase, over-consumption and under-consumption are global, national, and local challenges that "put development ethics to the test."[1] Can development ethics, especially when informed by the capability approach, contribute to the formation of ethically justified and responsible responses to these problems?

In this chapter I engage the capability approach with the "discourse ethic" of the Spanish philosopher Adela Cortina to generate an ethical principle relevant for assessing consumption practices in both the global North and South and to propose a guide for responsible action. The result, a further elaboration of my agency-focused version of the capability approach, shows that the capability approach – contrary to the judgment of some critics – can provide an adequate account of ethical responsibility, including the duties of Northern consumers with respect to the developing world.[2]

Building on the capability approach

In her book appropriately entitled *Por una ética del consumo: La ciudadanía del consumidor en un mundo global* (For an Ethic of Consumption: Consumer Citizenship in a Global World),[3] Cortina has given the international community the most comprehensive ethical assessment available of current consumption practices, their causes, and their consequences. She offers this consumption ethic as one application of a general ethical outlook that clarifies and defends ethical principles and proposes – in the light of these principles – an account of the duties and rights of consumers as well as some guidelines for public policy. Her book, she hopes, will contribute to the search for "an ethic of consumption based on the values that ought to orient the tasks of humanity in this third millennium."[4] Unlike my earlier formulation of a *prudential* version of the capability approach and its application only to North American consumption,[5] Cortina explicitly aspires to a cross-cultural *ethic* of responsibility relevant for issues of international development and global justice.

Cortina correctly recognizes that Sen himself has offered neither a consumption ethic nor a complete ethical theory.[6] She also realizes what many miss, that Sen provides resources for constructing *various* ethical outlooks and that these resources both open doors and provide some guidance about the features of an ethical outlook as well as an ethic of consumption.[7] What does Cortina mine from the capability lode?

First, and perhaps most importantly, Cortina argues that Sen's emphasis on human freedom rather than on commodities starts us off on the right track. Although keenly aware of the ways in which other people and our socially acquired beliefs, inclinations, and values condition us, Cortina repeatedly stresses that humans are moral agents and that they have (or should have) freedom – depending on both external and internal conditions – with respect to what they buy, maintain, consume, give to others, and use up.[8] Because people's consumption choices affect not only themselves but others near and far (in both space and time), and because it is important that any reasonable ethic assess the effects of our actions (on both ourselves and others), we need an ethics of responsible consumption.[9] A prudential approach to consumption ill-advisedly abstracts from many aspects of our life in the world. If we focus exclusively or in the wrong way on the consumption choices in relation to our own well-being, we fail to take into account our *moral* obligations to others and, I would argue, to ourselves.

Cortina correctly sees that Sen's carving out of the evaluative space of freedoms (capability) and functions (functioning) enables him to advance beyond "commodity fetishism" without falling into anti-materialism. The market goods and services that we consume and give to others to consume certainly are important, but only as means to our freedom to be and act in ways that we have reason to value – including, but not limited to, securing our own well-being. We should choose goods that liberate us (and others) from domination and necessity of various sorts and enable us and others to be and act as we choose, even when we choose to sacrifice our well-being to some cause.

Second, crucial for Cortina in this context is one freedom: the freedom to be master of one's own life, one's own boss (*su propio señor*).[10] To be master of one's own life is to be self-determining not only with respect to one's conduct but also with respect to one's moral commitments and beliefs. The autonomous person determines her principles and conduct for herself rather than having the "choice" made by someone else or some external or internal force.

In working out her consumption ethic, Cortina correctly grasps what many interpreters and critics alike miss – that Sen affirms and gives a fundamental role to the freedom that Sen calls "agency." Recall Chapter 5, in which I discussed Sen's ideal of agency in relation to the individual's (or group's) freedom for and achievement of deliberation, decision, and effective action in the world. Capabilities, as those freedoms or opportunities we have reason to value, are important not only because we value them but also because they enable us to exercise our agency. Cortina usually eschews the term "agency" because the Spanish translation (*agencia*) too readily suggests travel agencies (*agencies de viajes*), spies (*agentes*), or a boss's lackey.[11] She correctly recognizes that her concept of "autonomy" is close to Sen's ideal of agency. For Cortina, in relation to consumption choices, we realize our autonomy not only when we independently and reflectively choose one consumption good over another, but also when we choose our moral commitments, including our consumption ethic.[12]

The concept of agency – which I find in Sen and want to defend – adds an additional element: the agent's self-determined choice and resultant action make some difference in the world. Person are agents to the extent that they are able to scrutinize critically their options, themselves decide (rather than have the decision made by someone else or some external or internal force), act to realize their purposes, and have an impact on the world. In my interpretation of Sen throughout this volume, I emphasize this notion of agency, and argue that it has become more prominent in his recent writings, and that it offers us an important ethical principle for evaluating development success and failure. Cortina finds much to agree with in the agency-focused capability approach.

One question that Cortina and her colleague Jesús Conill take up, in the effort to strengthen the capability approach, is the question of priority between, on the one hand, agency freedom (and achievement) and, on the other hand, well-being freedom (and achievement).[13]

Furthermore, Cortina, like Sen, accepts two implications of a commitment to agency: anti-perfectionism and, with some qualification, anti-paternalism. It is not up to philosophers to prescribe authoritatively to others *the* correct conception of the good life, or for legislators to impose on citizens one conception of the flourishing life. Cortina affirms:

In this type of substantive freedom [the capability to choose for oneself a conception of the good life in community], concrete persons choose what functioning they desire to exercise in order to carry out their vital projects. It is not a "perfectionist ethic" that lays out a model of the good life, but a liberal ethic that leaves open the choice of the happy life. But neither is this ethic an "ethic of negative freedom" or one of "procedural freedom." Rather it is committed to the capability of persons themselves acting (*comprometida con la capacidad de sí hacer de las personas*).[14]

Third, in Sen's own answer – "Equality of basic capabilities" – to his 1979 question, "Equality of what?," Cortina finds language to articulate a fundamental principle in her ethic of responsibility: "an obligation to empower those found in situations of poverty, to strengthen their capacities in such a way that they can choose the functionings that they consider valuable."[15] Cortina accepts the prudential account of valuable capabilities, but only if it is construed as a platform for self-determination and public discussion and is supplemented in important ways. Her project is to extend the prudential focus on one's own self to other-directed moral obligation. Rather than make (a list of) capabilities the end of the story, Cortina – like Sen – understands well-being capabilities, to be discussed presently, as a platform that makes possible the exercise of agency. Because all humans are equal in dignity, we have certain moral obligations to each of them. One such obligation is to (try to) provide the conditions, including commodities and other material conditions, for all people to have those freedoms (capabilities) necessary to be able to be in charge of their own lives or have autonomy.

Strengthening the capability approach

Cortina, we have seen, accepts Sen's "Equality of what?" question and builds on his answer: "Equality of basic capabilities." However, she and her colleague Jesús Conill also take a step that Sen does not take and ask a new question: "Capabilities for what?"

Sen, I argued in Part II and especially Chapter 5, sets forth well-being and agency as both intrinsically good and as instrumentally important for each other. Our well-being, which includes both freedoms (capabilities) and achievements (functionings), has to do with our own lives going well or the attaining of what Sen sometimes calls 1 "personal advantage." Sen, we have seen, also contends that human beings have another descriptive and normative dimension: they are agents who usually can and should deliberate, make their own decisions, act, and effect change in the world. To be a full agent is to design and run one's own life rather than be subjected to fate, impersonal structures, the will of others, or internal whims.

For Sen, both the well-being and the agency dimensions are normatively important. We have good reason to value intrinsically the freedoms and achievements that constitute our own well-being, and we also treasure as intrinsically good our freedom to choose and act as designers of our own lives. These two good aspects converge when we ourselves decide to benefit ourselves, for instance by deciding to expand our well-being capabilities or to realize them in our activities. An individual is free to choose to promote and protect *only* his own well-being. An individual, however, can and sometimes should choose in such a way that he subordinates his own well-being to persons, groups, or causes beyond himself, such as his family, his business, his country, or social movement. People can and do exercise their agency in all sorts of ways, sometimes enhancing their well-being but other times intentionally or unintentionally reducing their well-being. The extreme is the hunger striker or suicide bomber who sacrifices her life for her cause.

Does Sen view either aspect as more important than the other? I believe not, although Sen could be clearer on this point. We have good reason, Sen affirms, to value intrinsically both our well-being and our agency. It is important not only that an individual agent decide for herself but also that the exercise of agency effectively promote or protect well-being – the agent's and that of others. Democratic bodies, I shall argue in Chapter 9, should be judged not only by their engaging in inclusive and deliberative decision-making but also by their expanding opportunities for well-being.

Each aspect – agency and well-being – may be instrumentally important for the other. I often know better than others what makes my life go well – for instance, what gives me satisfaction. An inclusive and deliberative democratic body, I will argue in Part IV, is more likely than either autocratic rulers or technical experts to make decisions that protect the well-being of all. Likewise, without a basic level of well-being, it is difficult for a person or group to have or exercise (full) agency. Such is the fate both of those individuals starving, in great pain, or paralyzed by fear, and of those groups composed of such individuals.[16] Without agency, persons and groups lack the capacity to steer their lives in advantageous ways or, in short, to avoid or mitigate the slings and arrows of outrageous fortune. For the very young, those severely incapacitated, or the very old, agency is not yet, or is no longer, a possibility; and the best to be attained (usually with the help of others) is a high level of functioning. For individuals displaced from their homes and subsisting in refugee camps, well-being levels may be too low to exercise collective agency. For morally responsible adults and self-determining groups, however, each of the two aspects is not only intrinsically good, but instrumentally valuable for the other.

It is precisely at this point that Cortina and Conill seek to move Sen's capability and agency approach in a (more) Kantian direction and give agency a *normative* priority over well-being. Both Cortina and Conill insist that we ask "Why capabilities?" or "Capabilities for what?"[17] Their answer is that there is and should be a normative asymmetry between well-being and agency. Although both well-being (achievement and freedom) and agency (achievement and freedom) may be viewed as goods in themselves, agency is more important, for to choose well-being over agency (or vice versa) is itself an exercise of agency. In this way Cortina and Conill seek to ground (*fundamentar*) capabilities (well-being freedoms) and functionings (well-being achievements) in what Sen calls agency and Kant calls moral freedom, autonomy, or rational agency.[18] This "grounding" is not an effort to *deduce* a moral first principle from a self-evident starting point. It shows, rather, that the choice – between, on the one hand, freedom as self-determination and, on the other hand, well-being freedoms (capabilities) or well-being achievements (functionings) – is a fundamental choice that should itself be an act of moral freedom.

Self-determining free acts and the potential capability (in the case of children) or actual capability (in the case of adults) for such choice are the basis of our dignity and worth as human beings. Due to our moral freedom, each human being is, at least potentially or by remembrance (in the case of the very old), an end in itself and not merely a means or tool for someone else's projects. Cortina and Conill claim, then, to have made Sen's commitment to human agency more explicit and to show that it presupposes the moral priority of agency over well-being (whether capabilities or functionings).[19] We might then call this ultimate freedom to exercise our agency – to be masters of our own lives – the capability of capabilities, a meta-capability, or a super-capability. We might also say it is what makes us persons.

How should we assess this argument for the normative priority of agency over well-being? The best response, it seems to me, would be to agree that the choice of agency over well-being is itself an act of agency, but to argue that this priority is a *causal* one and does not entail that agency is normatively superior to well-being any more than the reverse is proved by the causal dependence of agency on some minimal level of well-being.[20] I would also argue (and I believe Sen would agree) against the absolute normative priority of agency over well-being because without their equal moral urgency we would lack any basis for criticizing an autonomous individual's taking her own life (as a selfish escape from moral duties to the well-being of others and even herself), or a democratic body making decisions that harmed a minority or failed to protect the well-being of all.

Sometimes, of course, agency should trump well-being. It would be wrong for governmental officials to force-feed an imprisoned hunger striker who has freely decided to protest against prison abuse by starving himself to death. But sometimes well-being should trump agency, for instance when the state prohibits the sale of certain weapons (because they threaten others' well-being as well as agency) or addictive drugs (because they cause ill-being as well as loss of agency).

Whether we conceive of agency and well-being as of equal moral weight or give normative (in contrast to causal) priority to the former over the latter, what, in general, are the political, economic, and social implications of the importance of agency? Negatively, it means that individuals and groups have at least a *prima facie* duty neither to subject others to their will through coercion, manipulation, or deception, nor to submit – irreversibly or completely – to someone else's will or to social conditioning. Positively, the affirmation of moral freedom means we have at least a *prima facie* duty to promote and protect other human beings and groups as masters of *their* own lives rather than as our (or someone else's) subjects, vassals, or slaves. The commitment to moral freedom would also imply a *prima facie* duty to promote our own agency and that of others in relation to inner compulsions and autonomy-eroding behavior.

With echoes of aristocratic practices of lordship but with an egalitarian commitment to elimination of bondage, Cortina interprets, with a Kantian twist, both national and global citizenship: "A citizen is one who is his own master (*su propio señor*) together with his equals in the heart [*seno*] of the city."[21] Such a view nicely articulates Sen's view of agency-oriented development, expressed in the following passage: "Expansion of freedom is viewed, in this approach, both as the primary end and the principal means of development. Development consists of the removal of various types of unfreedoms that leave people with little choice and little opportunity of exercising their reasoned agency."[22]

Cortina applies her Kantian-inspired outlook to the issue of consumption and consumer choice. Human beings, both as individuals and in groups, can and should exercise their freedom in deciding *whether* to consume, *what* to consume, and *how much* to consume. In each case, an important and sometimes overriding consideration will concern the extent to which the consumption choice expresses and promotes individual and collective autonomy. Morally responsible agents should take non-agency considerations into account, such as their duties to the well-being of others, and this point implies that the strengthening of Sen's capability approach need not go so far as asserting the *normative* priority of agency over well-being. Ironically, an absolute and normative priority of agency over well-being would limit individual and collective agency, for absolutizing agency would prevent choosing well-being instead of agency (or sacrificing short-term agency for long-term agency).

Cortina seeks to strengthen the capability approach in a second way. She does so by defending an account of individual and social responsibilities. What explicitly moral or ethical responsibilities do individuals have in their personal consumption choices? And what responsibilities do groups of individuals and governments have and how should they exercise their moral freedom or agency in exercising their responsibilities? As we shall see, even the process by which an individual decides on her own major consumption choices is a social process that should involve concern for and, in at least some cases, deliberation with others.

One general criticism of Sen's capability approach has been that it provides little, if any, account of moral responsibility. It is true that until recently Sen has largely neglected this aspect of ethics. Some materials for an account of obligation certainly exist in Sen's writings, and he himself is beginning to make use of them.[23] One way he does so is to connect widely valued capabilities and functionings to the concept of human or moral rights, which he in turn conceives of as tools to protect and promote those capabilities and functionings that people have reason to value.[24] We have good reason to value being alive and having the freedom to live a long life; and, hence, it is important to affirm that we and others have a moral and legal right to life.[25] We have good reason to value running our own lives, and thus we and others have a moral right not to be enslaved. In turn, the human right to life, to other well-being functionings and freedoms, and to agency are the bases for affirming that other individuals and societies have duties to respect those rights. The rich have a duty to feed the starving as well as the duty not to kill. Moreover, our own moral freedom or agency is presupposed when we decide on and accept certain commitments and responsibilities (for ourselves and others):

An approach to justice and development that concentrates on substantive freedoms inescapably focuses on the agency and judgment of individuals; they cannot be seen merely as patients to whom benefits will be dispensed by the process of development. Responsible adults must be in charge of their own well-being; it is for them to decide how to use their capabilities. But the capabilities that a person does actually have (and not merely theoretically enjoys) depend on the nature of social arrangements, which can be crucial for individual freedoms. And there the state and the society cannot escape responsibility.[26]

Although he has begun to tackle the issue of individual and societal responsibilities, Sen himself has not set forth a theory of moral obligation, analogous to that, say, of philosophers Henry Shue[27] or James W. Nickel,[28] nor has he directly or explicitly taken up the issue of consumer responsibilities.[29] And the prudential account, as we have seen, intentionally defers or brackets the issue of our responsibilities to others when we make consumption choices. An account that attends only to the individual's own well-being, as I developed in my earlier essay on consumption, although important, is incomplete precisely because it declines to advance beyond self-interest, even enlightened self-interest, to consider what individuals owe to others and what groups owe to others.

To strengthen and apply our agency-focused capability approach, I turn now to Cortina's account of, on the one hand, consumer responsibilities and rights and, on the other hand, societal and state responsibilities. With respect to what we buy and either use or give to others, what are our responsibilities and our rights? What does it mean to engage in morally responsible consumption? What sorts of consumption choices are morally permissible and impermissible? What sorts, if any, are morally obligatory? What duties do governments and other groups have with respect to consumption choices and practices?

Cortina does not prescribe to consumers a "thick" or detailed conception of the good, one to which everyone's consumption choices should conform. Rather, she proposes a conception of consumption that is right and just regardless of one's conception of the good life – regardless, for example, of whether religion, art, science, business, sports, or leisure is at the top of one's hierarchy of valued activities. Responsible consumption, for Cortina, is consumption that is autonomous, just, co-responsible, and happiness-generating. Let us examine each feature in turn. These norms provide at least criteria for what is permissible and impermissible. It is not so clear whether or when they also enjoin positive obligations.

Autonomous consumption

The autonomous consumer, contends Cortina, "takes the reins" (*toma las riendas*)[30] of his or her own consumption. It is a nice metaphor, for it captures the important idea that I (rather than other people) should take the reins of my own consumption mount. I should be in control rather than being dragged around by my possessions or my consumer passions. The metaphors of "taking the reins," like that of "taking charge" and "being the author of one's own life," are suggestive. What, more precisely, does Cortina mean by autonomy (and its opposite)?

For Cortina, autonomous consumption contrasts most obviously and correctly with addictive buying or consuming. In addictive consuming I cannot live without this drug, this alcoholic beverage, this medicine. I can't stop buying (begging, borrowing, or stealing) and consuming the commodity to which I am addicted. Rather than being in charge of my life, I have lost control. I succumb to physical "cravings" or "drives," to various "pushes" and "pulls." I may realize gradually, in spite of my attempts to rationalize and deceive myself, that I do have a consumer addiction. In this circumstance, I may still have sufficient autonomy to figure out a way to free myself from my addictive behavior. For instance, I may make it inconvenient or difficult for me to enter a situation of temptation, or I may seek professional help, play some other passion off against my entrenched consumer passions,[31] or, more generally, find some modern equivalent to Ulysses' ordering his sailors to forcibly restrain him from answering the sirens' calls.

These cases are fairly easy ones for the principle of autonomous consumption. We have an obligation, presumably a moral obligation to ourselves as agents, both to refrain from those consumption choices that result in addiction and to develop, perhaps through other consumption choices, the skills, habits, and moral strength to regain or protect our inner control.

Where does Cortina stand in relation to cases in which we make consumer choices in the context of current advertising and fashionable consumer practices, especially when the latter are displayed by individuals whom we admire or envy, or with whom we want to keep up? What does the norm of autonomous consumption prescribe with respect to consumption practices that are mildly addictive or what philosopher Bradford S. Hadaway calls "grooves of habituated behavior" that seem to bypass if not override our autonomy? Is there anything that can be done to strengthen or restore autonomous consumption when our lapses are less than addiction? How might we recognize less than fully autonomous conduct? And how strong is the duty to refrain from or protect against non-autonomous consumer conduct?

Cortina establishes the parameters to answer this question, but leaves some problems unresolved. On the one hand, societal practices or conventional values and beliefs do not, at least normally, completely *determine* our consumption. On the other hand, we unthinkingly permit advertising, current practices and beliefs, and our consumption inclinations, habits, and passions to more or less reduce the range of our options. Advertising gives some information about options but also withholds information and often makes exaggerated or false claims. I am not forced or mechanically determined to buy certain clothes, but if I want to appear in public without shame I am limited in what I can choose to wear. I am not fatalistically driven to participate in the orgy of holiday buying, giving, and receiving, but holiday gift exchange does seem to constrain autonomy as well as give opportunity to express love and friendship. Many of my consumption choices are more a matter of unthinking habit than of any autonomous choice.

Cortina's basic strategy in relation to these sorts of non-autonomous consumption is to identify various ways in which individual consumers can gain fuller information about product features, the norms that are influencing them, and the likely consequences of continuing current and habitual consumer practices. Then, armed with this information, we are able to take the reins of our personal consumption rather than make uninformed decisions or ones unknowingly influenced by unconscious motives or habitual practices. We have a duty to protect and enhance our own autonomy by investigating our customary motives as well as the features and likely affects of using different products:

The consumer . . . is not sovereign, but in principle has the possibility of being "autonomous," that is, of taking the reins of his consumption, which requires that he becomes aware of personal motivations, societal beliefs, and societal myths; knows how to decode advertising; discovers assumptions from his earliest socialization; is familiar with different styles of life capable of conferring a dignified social identity; and, is aware of the impact of his consumption choices on his own life and on the lives of other human beings.[32]

Enhanced information and self-awareness certainly contribute to our exercising our duty to be or become autonomous consumers. Some unanswered questions, however, remain. Do not habitual consumers need more than enlightenment about commodities and their motives? Could a consumer aspiring to more autonomy in fact weaken her agency by spending excessive time studying *Consumer Reports* and shopping "comparatively?" Should not ways be found, often with the aid of others, to strengthen one's agency freedom to resist consumer temptation? One approach to gaining such moral strength would be to resolve to deepen one's commitment to the norm of just consumption, to which I now turn.

Just consumption

For Cortina, responsible consumption is *just* as well as autonomous.[33] Cortina's ethic is an ethic of responsibility that sets forth imperatives in relation to the effects our consumption choices are likely to have on others. As we have seen, her criticism of a prudential approach to consumption is that it fails to consider others at all or does so only insofar as consumption by others impacts our own consumer choices and redounds to our own benefit or harm. For Cortina, in contrast, we have, in our consumer choices, direct and significant duties to other people, our institutions, and the environment. Just consumption choices assume the equal dignity of all human beings, present and future, and seek to take as many as possible into account.[34] We are morally responsible not merely for our own well-being and our own autonomous consumption, for justice requires that we and our society be responsible – in our consumption and other choices – for the autonomy and well-being of others as well.

This ethic of just consumption has relevance for public policy as well as for personal conduct. A just society, in its consumption policies as well as in other ways, is one that promotes the autonomy and well-being of its citizens and protects them from domination by others and other forms of deprivation. In addition to being imprudent, the veteran drug user is egregiously irresponsible when he consumes cocaine in the presence of impressionable and admiring youths. The drug consumer, like the drug dealer who gives an adolescent his first hits, is violating a moral duty not to harm. This duty to others is also dramatically illustrated by our responsibility not to feed another's addiction or lead the reforming addict "into temptation."

Our positive duty to help can take diverse forms. We contribute to agencies that help addicts recover. As citizens, acting through both consumer associations, such as Consumers Union, different levels of governments, and the media, we improve and disseminate unbiased information about options for consumer choice and ways of protecting autonomy in the face of consumer habits. For example, citizen action can result in legislation that requires drug companies to reveal the ingredients and dangers of various medications. Investigative reporters disseminate concerns of researchers and government agencies that a given medication has unforeseen and negative side-effects.[35] Government agencies, such as the US Food and Drug Administration, test products, such as medications, both before and after they are released on the market. As a result, unsafe products may never make it to the marketplace or may be recalled on the basis of consumer complaints and further testing. Consumer associations exercise citizen responsibility when they test and rate products and scrutinize advertising claims, thereby reducing the dangers of manipulative or deceptive advertising. Citizens increasingly discharge their consumer responsibilities by using the internet to evaluate and rate such goods and services as electronic equipment, books, restaurants, hotels.[36] Parents, friends, and social critics have the duty – at least through dialogue and possible interventions – to get others and themselves to better understand and be in control of their consumption motives. Again, however, it would be appropriate if Cortina paid more attention to ways in which citizens might increase their moral strength in promoting or protecting their own just consumption as well as that of others.

Do citizens, acting through their governments, have the right and duty either to prohibit the production, sale, or consumption of certain goods and services or to regulate them on such grounds as the age of the consumer or the frequency and amount of use? Although Cortina addresses this important topic only in passing, her basic idea is that a democratic community has the responsibility to deliberate and decide on what production, sale, and consumption is to be permissible, what is to be regulated, and what is to be prohibited altogether. Autonomy-promoting *regulation* and *prohibition* would take into account the risks of various consumption choices with respect to irreversibly weakening autonomy or subverting it altogether. The sale and purchase of strongly and irreversibly addictive substances, at least, should be strongly regulated (especially to minors), if not prohibited.[37] The sale and purchase of slaves, including child prostitutes, should be prohibited altogether as incompatible with human autonomy and dignity.

From cases such as these, Cortina formulates a general and negative norm for just consumption: "Any form of consumption is unjust that does not promote equal development of people's basic capabilities."[38] What does she mean? That "basic" qualifies "capabilities" alerts us to the fact that Cortina is *not* proposing a strict egalitarianism in which the state should ensure that everyone has exactly the same level of all capabilities. Not only would the implementation of this policy be inordinately expensive, but it would unjustly restrict the freedom of many to consume above the required line. To have one's *basic* capabilities guaranteed is to have a secured *threshold* or *adequate* amount of the *most important* freedoms or opportunities. What we buy from or give to others as well as what the government (or some non-state group) guarantees to others by way of in-kind goods or income – these commodities should promote such capabilities as being able to live a reasonably long, decently healthy, and adequately fed life in contrast to a life in which one has no choice but to die young or be ill-fed, ill-clothed, and chronically sick. An example would be governmentally supplied or subsidized malaria-preventing mosquito nets. To promote these opportunities is to offer them, protect them once obtained, and restore them if lost. The concept of "basicness" has to do with the individually and socially relative *amount* of commodities needed to realize an *adequate* level of the valued capabilities. And individuals and democratic communities may judge the acceptable threshold of valued capabilities on the basis, among other things, of whether or not citizens are thereby enabled to be at or over a minimum of political power. Why is having the apparel to appear in public without shame important? One reason is that such a capability enables people, if they so choose, to be and act as citizens. In Chapter 9 I return to this issue and in Chapter 10 I defend against objections to this equal-opportunity egalitarianism.

On this view, the amount and kind of food or basic income to be provided to citizens of one's own or other countries (world citizens) varies in relation to what capabilities would be chosen by them as needed in order to be authors of their own lives both individually and collectively. Commodities are instrumentally important as means to capabilities that people choose. Capabilities are both important in themselves and a platform not only for choosing one's own style of life but also for participating in public debate about consumption norms and other matters.

What sort of goods and services, by way of illustration, do people need in order to be citizens? At this point Cortina seeks to apply – as a test for consumption choices – her notion of *equality* of basic capabilities and autonomy by employing several versions of a Kantian principle of universalizability.[39] Although I cannot address the question further, some of these versions seem to be less an application of Kant's distinctive non-consequentialist ethic and more an effort to fuse a commitment to universality (not making an exception for yourself) with an ethic of responsibility (for consequences).

The first version of universalizability that Cortina employs is that citizens should consume in such a way that if everyone performed the same action the result would not destroy or risk destroying nature, for such destruction would end (human) life – and the pursuit of all human purposes – as such.[40] This formulation explicitly refers to the consequences likely if everyone made the same consumption choices. If everyone in the world owned and drove a car, would the emissions connected with petroleum consumption doom nature and humankind? Kant himself arguably would not examine practical consequences but rather would ask if there were something logically self-defeating or incomprehensible about universalizing the "maxim" of one's consumption choice.

Second, Cortina formulates a consumption-relevant principle of universalizability in a way that affirms equal freedom (of capabilities and autonomy): "consume in such a way that you always, and at the same time, respect and promote the freedom of all humanity, yourself as well as others."[41] A practical implication of the second formulation is that when I make a consumption choice, I should not exempt myself from moral obligations I insist apply to others. For example, it is morally impermissible for me to insist that everyone have a car that gets 40 miles per gallon but permissible to make an exception for myself and own an SUV that gets only 8 miles per gallon. My agency and capability freedoms are important, but no more so (and no less so) than those of others.

Applied to consumption choices, many consumption decisions would be blocked if the agent took into account their likely effects on the autonomy and well-being of *all* those affected and not, as does the prudential account, merely on oneself. Individually and collectively reducing consumption levels in the USA and other affluent countries, especially in relation to luxury goods, would free up resources and time that could be used to protect and promote basic capabilities and agency in poor countries. Buying and giving simulated rather than real gold earrings would lessen both environmental damage and labor exploitation caused by gold-mining operations.[42] Buying "fair trade" coffee, which benefits a worker-owned, democratically managed coffee cooperative in Costa Rica, is clearly better than buying coffee from a company with notorious labor and environmental practices.

Cortina applies a third formulation of Kantian universalizability, the "Kingdom of Ends" formula, to consumption norms and choices: "Take upon yourself (*asume*), together with others, the norms of a consumption life style that promote your freedom and that of all persons, making possible a universal Kingdom of Ends."[43] In explaining this rather abstract and austere "test" for consumption choices and norms, Cortina explains that those that inhabit this kingdom are precisely beings of intrinsic worth, ends-in-themselves, who can decide for themselves to transcend their own self-interest and respect the autonomy of others. To live in this kingdom is to choose to consume in ways that "respect each and every human being as ends-in-themselves," that "promote each person's liberty and projects for a happy life," and that "never interfere with other human beings."[44] The commodities I choose should serve human freedom, both mine and that of others. By "freedom" (*libertad*) here Cortina means – as does Sen with his concept of "agency" – the intrinsically good capability to decide for oneself (autonomy) and, especially, to choose *one's own* style of life (self-realization). To live in this Kingdom of Ends (with other beings who are also ends-in-themselves) also means that my choices must be compatible with the free choices of others.

In this third formulation, Cortina also emphasizes that what should be sustainable and universalizable are not isolated actions but *entire* forms of life and the norms informing them. It is not enough that family members diligently recycle bottles, cans, and newspapers and yet each drive a car, especially one that is fuel-inefficient. Taking account of those in poor countries as equal citizens in the Kingdom of Ends, Cortina applies the principle to automobiles:

> For just consumption, then, it is important to emphasize sustainable, adoptable, and universalizable *styles of life* rather than isolated norms. The principle of "one car per person" is unjust because it destroys nature and is then a positional good, a good that one cannot universalize because it results in a zero-sum game, that is, one in which if some have the good then others cannot have it. The solution is not to get rid of cars altogether but to reduce consumption of cars in rich countries and elevate it in poor countries. To do so requires that rich countries come up with forms of life that may be extended [to other countries].[45]

By "reducing the consumption of cars in rich countries," Cortina appears to mean both "fewer cars" and "more efficient cars." In urging that the consumption of cars be increased in poor countries, she recommends "more cars." She also believes that rich countries should improve auto gasoline efficiency and devise other vehicle energy sources (ethanol and electricity) not only because of the *directly* beneficial environmental impact but also because rich country breakthoughs in auto energy efficiency and alternative modes of transportation might be replicable in poor countries.

Cortina's proposal seems eminently reasonable, but on closer inspection it is not clear how to put it into practice. On one application of her third universalizability test, I should choose what sort of car to own (or some alternative mode of transportation) in relation to the predicted consequence of everyone doing likewise. The stock criticism of Kantian universalizability is that the moral force of the imperative depends on how one describes the choice situation. Does the description take into account that both my wife and I live close enough to our jobs to walk or bike? Does it take into account that public transportation is some distance away and does not always go where we want to go? Even if this problem can be resolved, there exists the problem of either judging the self-defeating character or forecasting the negative results of everyone in the world making the same consumption choice.

Cortina, we have seen, briefly examines several options with respect to the universalizability of buying and using a car. Given that autos (and their production) use up both renewable and nonrenewable natural resources, produce emissions that befoul the air, contribute to global warming, and eventuate in wrecked and worn-out cars, the options in car purchasing seem to include at least the following:

(1) My wife and I should walk and ride bicycles instead of driving cars, and so should anyone else (in reasonably good health) in the world. Here we would change our consumption to match that of many poor people in the developing world.[46]
(2) My wife and I should give up one (or both) of our two cars and only own a car that is small, light, and either petroleum efficient or powered by alternative energy. All families in the world should have the same sort of car, which would result, by some yet to be specified mechanism, in many poor families getting a car for the first time but result, unless new technologies save the day, in a large increase in fuel consumption and pollution.[47]
(3) My wife and I should keep our two cars, even those that are large, heavy, guzzle gas, and burn oil, and every family in the world should (have the freedom to) have the same sort of car.

Employing her Kantian tests, Cortina clearly and rightly rules out (3): "the earth does not have sufficient resources to universalize the model of the American Dream."[48] And, we have responsibilities to future generations, responsibilities that (3) completely ignores. Cortina seems, however, undecided between (1) and (2) and does not consider the possible variations or combinations of these two. She recommends more cars in poor countries and fewer (inefficient) cars in rich countries, but she also challenges rich countries to invent more environmentally friendly modes of transportation. Overcoming this vacillation would seem to depend on our knowing the extent to which each of the three choices (and their variations and combinations) exhausts limited environmental goods and inflicts environmental damage and, therefore, damage (the loss of capability and agency) to present and future persons. Yet to know what these impacts would be requires knowing what new or substitute resources might be found or invented, and what technological break-throughs might occur to make cars less environmentally harmful, enable societies to dispose of them and clean up their messes more efficiently, and devise more environmentally sustainable modes of transportation. And of course the choice of each of the three options would have to take into account the various benefits and other costs – for oneself and others – that result from each option. Maybe the best scientific predictions about likely future environmental risks enable us to rule out some extreme options (a fleet of SUVs per family) and even some currently acceptable options (typical American autos). We do not seem to have, however, the crystal ball we would need to have reasonable beliefs about if and when our consumption choices, if universalized, would result in surpassing the earth's carrying capacity or unfairly reducing others' freedom.

Several ways exist to respond to the crystal ball problem. One would be to return to the Kantian tradition and adopt an interpretation of Kant's ethics that depended not on forecasts of the future but rather on showing the logically self-defeating character of some choices. The choice of renting a stretch limousine made by Sherman McCoy (a character in Tom Wolfe's *The Bonfire of the Vanities*) would be ruled out because everyone's making the same choice would defeat his goal of distinguishing himself. A second way to respond to future uncertainty, given what we reliably know now, is to employ some sort of presumptive precautionary principle.[49] A third way, not necessarily at odds with the second, is to invoke democratic procedures. Cortina's third consumption norm, co-responsibility, provides exactly this assistance. Democratic bodies on all levels can and should grapple with how best to universalize in our current contexts.

Co-responsible consumption

Consumption that is fully justified, contends Cortina, is co-responsible (*corresponsable*) or "expressive of solidarity" (*solidario*) as well as autonomous and just.[50] On the surface this norm seems merely to repeat that *all* humans, at least those with the actual capacity, have the responsibility not to make non-autonomous or unjust consumption choices and help others to so refrain. (As I shall point out later, it is less clear if Cortina's norms prescribe other positive duties.) More, much more, is involved, however, and this norm brings us to the heart of Cortina's dialogical and deliberative ethic of consumption. Although very general, the norm of co-responsible consumption has relevance for both individual and collective consumption.

With respect to my individual consumer choices, I – as a national and world citizen – have an obligation to enter into dialogue with others. I have the duty to do so not only to help me determine which consumption choice is best for me but also which would best fulfill the norms of autonomous and just consumption. I may be short-sighted or blind on all counts and you, my friend, trusted salesperson, consumer reporter, may supply crucial information or help me reprior-itize my values. The decision is up to me, but thanks to you – the information or ethical challenge you supply – I buy soccer shoes that the manufacturer and supplier certify have not been made in sweat-shops or by child labor. Often the advice we receive differs, and we must weigh it and decide. It remains prudent as well as morally res-ponsible to weigh the pros and cons with others, including the experts (if there are any). We are most likely to arrive at an ethically correct result when our interactions with others involve reason-giving and critical deliberation.

With respect to collective choices on the desirability of certain goods and services, democratic bodies on all levels have the responsibility to decide when to intervene with market "forces" to encourage or discour-age (through tax incentives), regulate, or prohibit the buying and selling of certain goods and services.[51] Citizens have the right and duty to (help) make decisions on matters that affect them. Presumably, one exercises this right through such means as dialogue with political representatives and the activities of consumer organizations that gather information, evaluate consumer practices, and promote certain consumer policies in public discussion.

Furthermore, co-responsible consumers not only individually and collectively take into account the impact of their consumption choices and practices on other people as well as on themselves; they also work to "empower" those affected to make their interests and concerns known. If democratic decision-making is to be just, it must be inclusive, which requires that those without a "voice" be regularly part of demo-cratic deliberation and have an influence on collective decision and action. Having a place at the democratic table, however, while necessary, is not sufficient if those participants in democratic deliberation are unable to deliberate as equals. They may lack deliberative skills or sufficient economic well-being to have the time and energy to partici-pate. Hence, co-responsible consumers seek to enact educational and economic policies that promote the deliberative participation and influence of those most adversely affected by typical consumer – and production – practices:

It is a moral obligation, an indispensable ethical presupposition for any meaningful dialogue concerning the justice of forms of consumption, to empower those affected, to promote those basic capabilities that permit them to be real interlocutors in a dialogue about that which affects them . . . Unless the participants in the dialogue have participatory skills and stand as much as possible in relations of symmetry [of power], no expert is able to say what form of consumption is just.[52]

This responsibility to empower all those affected extends not only to others in one's own nation but also to citizens of other countries. Good development practices empower those in other countries, especially those affected by the consumption practices of Northern consumers, to tell their story and have their say in various national and global forums.[53]

It is in democratic deliberation on local, national, and global levels, with inclusive and empowered participation of all affected, that co-responsible consumers can and should decide about which types of consumption choices should count as autonomous and just. It is not that everybody always decides about everything in some big (virtual) global encounter, but that democratic bodies on different levels take into account in their deliberations the decisions of other bodies. The weaknesses we found in other versions of universalization may be overcome by the deliberative version with which Cortina concludes her discussion: "Adopt (asume), together with others, styles of life that promote the capability of people to defend dialogically their interests, do not endanger the sustainability of nature, and promote associations and institutions that labor in this direction."[54]

Happiness-generating consumption

The fourth and final aspect of Cortina's norm for ethically justified consumption is that such consumption should make the consumer happy.[55] What, however, is happiness and why is it important?

Cortina seems to employ two different concepts of happiness, and each contributes to her evaluation of consumption choices. First, she accepts and affirms a conventional notion of happiness – as experienced "satisfaction" with the way things are going – and then argues that above a certain level, consumption is a poor source of happiness.[56] This notion is the one that social scientists, such as Robert Lane, and economists of happiness, such as Richard Easterlin, Robert H. Frank, and Carol Graham, among others, employ in their research.[57] On this view, happiness or, better, "satisfaction" or "subjective well-being" is what people report on questionnaires and interviews when asked how happy or satisfied they are with the way their lives are going. Here (reported) satisfaction contrasts with (reported) depression or frustration.

Given this everyday (and social scientific) meaning of happiness, Cortina sees her job as ethicist as that of drawing on scientific research and driving home the claim that above a certain level of consumption, no link exists between such things as social success and consumer goods, on the one hand, and personal satisfaction, on the other. Even more, she cites available evidence (which has increased since she wrote her book) that what brings people satisfaction, joy, or pleasure in life is not having more or better consumer goods but better friendships, marriages, working relationships, and leisure time.[58] Although shopping for, owning, and consuming goods sometimes can be "fun," the empirical evidence is that whatever enjoyment these activities bring is transitory and frequently is accompanied by or quickly results in dissatisfaction when one realizes that there is far more to be had or that someone else is more successful. In particular, Cortina appeals to Juliet Schor's finding that many Americans report that they are trapped in a frustrating circle of "work-spend-consumption-credit."[59] To break out of this "squirrel cage"[60] of perpetually unsatisfied consumer desires, Cortina takes up Schor's recommendations of ways to "downshift."[61] However, Cortina wisely recognizes, as does Jerome M. Segal, that it is much easier for the upper-middle-class professional to answer the call for a "simple life" than it is for someone with few resources and threatened by the lack of a reliable living wage.[62]

Cortina recognizes one complication in strategies based on this first conception of happiness. Recognizing that satisfaction is one humanly important value, she is sympathetic with Luis Camacho's point that the North might learn much from "the millions of poor people [who] live at very low levels of consumption" and yet still find "laughter and joy"[63] in their lives. Yet, she rightly worries that such a point might be used to undermine efforts to reduce poverty, especially in the South. She would agree with Sen about the value of happiness even (or especially) when it is experienced by a deprived and hopeless person upon receiving an alm or other "small mercy." But, like Sen, she worries that this happiness may hide from consumers and governments alike the lucky recipient's deprivations, such as poor health and domination by others. Additionally, the happiness brought by the small mercy may cause the rich to ignore the poor and occasion the poor passively to accept their lot.

The second concept of happiness that Cortina employs is happiness not as experienced satisfaction or a mental state of pleasure but as an

Aristotelian combination of good character and good luck. The Greek word for happiness, *eudaimonia*, observes Cortina, literally means good *daimōn* or good character.[64] Good character, says Cortina, consists most importantly of two virtues: lucidity and practical wisdom or good sense (*cordura*). The lucid consumer is aware of her consumer habits and motives, especially ones that tend to be obsessive or addictive. Such awareness may help the consumer – often with the assistance of others – to reduce or outwit the power of these motives. For example, the lucid "consumer" of the sport of soccer recognizes that no spectator will see the soccer field any better if *all* stand up at their seats and that there needs to be some arrangement – more effective than shouts of "Down in front!" – to get everyone to remain seated.[65] Lucidity also enables the consumer to evaluate the claims of advertising and assess relevant commodities and the consequences of their consumption. Finally, lucidity about causal chains enables the responsible consumer to develop reasonable beliefs about which consumption choices clearly benefit needy producers, especially in poor countries, and which ones clearly lower their chances to live a decent life.

In addition to lucidity, Cortina convincingly extols the human excellence of what she calls *cordura*. More than prudence with its exclusive focus, direct or indirect, on self-interest, *cordura* is that kind of wise self-control that retains prudence's middle way between excess and defect but extends moderation to get the proper balance, on the one hand, between one's own well-being and that of others, and, on the other, between human appropriation and conservation of nature's bounty. Cortina gives the example of choosing goods that are durable, energy efficient, and easily reparable. Consistent with her consumer ethic would be purchasing from companies that lead their industries in socially responsible business practices.

A combination of lucidity and ethically infused practical wisdom would result in the reform of consumption practices. With respect to holiday gift-giving, an extended family might adopt a variant of the common university departmental practice of each member drawing a name and giving a Christmas gift only to that one colleague. Rather than giving Christmas gifts to every family member, an extended family might decide – through democratic deliberation, of course – that each nuclear family would give gifts to three members of other family units, whose names they had drawn, from among these units. In the interest of greater austerity, a spending cap might be put on all gifts. In the interest of filial piety, grandparents might be permitted to go beyond their allotments and give gifts to *all* their grandchildren. A more radical reform would be – in the name of the family member – to purchase a cow for a poor farm family in a developing country, or giving a portion or even the entirety of the family's holiday gift budget to a charity.

Extended to the whole society, it would be wise to follow Frank's recommendation and have high taxes on luxury items such as McMansions, luxury cars, and elegant clothing.[66] The standard for social success would be lowered for everyone, and the money saved could be spent on goods, such as Cortina's book on consumption, and services more conducive to the well-being and autonomy of all. If the tax monies were earmarked for environmental clean-up and aid to poor communities at home and abroad, we would display the many facets of *cordura*.

How adequate is Cortina's conception of consumer good character or virtue? Both lucidity and a golden-mean-informed practical reason are compelling candidates for any such ideal. I would suggest that she supplement her list, however, with an additional virtue, namely, what philosopher Bradford Hadaway calls "moral strength" or "successful self-governance."[67] Not only do responsible consumers require insight into the causes and consequences of various consumption choices and an ability to find a middle way between excess and deficit and between self-regarding and other regarding choices. Ethically responsible consumers also require the ability and courage to extirpate their addictions, weaken encrusted consumer habits, and resist advertising's allure. If we are to be or become agents, authors of our own life, we must control our own motivational life by finding, in Hadaway's felicitous phrases, "bulwarks against" and "tools to uproot" those compulsions and inclinations that undermine our agency. One way to do so is to (re)commit ourselves to the ideal of equal agency and, thereby, respect ourselves as well as others.

Although she does not do so, we can bring together Cortina's two senses of happiness, namely, satisfaction and good character. When citizens are lucid, wise, and (I would add) morally strong in their lives as autonomous, just, and co-responsible consumers, they are also likely – with luck – to experience the satisfaction that comes from doing the right thing.

National and global citizens

Cortina culminates and weaves together the threads of her ethics of consumption with Part V, entitled "Being a Citizen in a Global World" and consisting of two chapters, "The Citizenship of the Consumer" and "Cosmopolitan Economic Citizenship."[68] Her work on the ethics of citizenship, one of the most novel and important aspects of Cortina's ethics and political philosophy, has great relevance for international development ethics.[69] It is beyond the scope of this chapter to take up her notion in detail, but I would leave her consumption ethic incompletely analyzed if I failed to mention some salient points.

First, human beings are citizens as well as consumers. Moreover, these are not two separate spheres of human life but instead are roles that do and should intertwine. To be a citizen is to be one's own master – together with one's equals (other citizens) – in making basic decisions with respect to life together in community. Whatever persons are affected by the community, even those who are members of other communities, have some kind or level of citizenship rights and duties in that community. The community can be as narrow as the family or neighborhood and as broad as the global community. For instance, even (or especially) people in Iraq, because they are so deeply affected by US policy, would be *moral* citizens – in contrast to legal citizens – of the United States.

Second, Cortina contends that consumer-citizens, whether locally, nationally, or globally, have both rights and duties with respect to consumption. The most general right (and duty) is that of publicly deliberating and helping decide consumption policies. Communities at every level face the question of what consumer goods to produce and make available, and those affected by these policies have the moral right to have a say in the making of policies that encourage, permit, regulate, or prohibit the sale and use of specific consumer goods. A globalized world economy makes available both unsafe and safe food, gold jewelry from both environmentally irresponsible and responsible mines, costly as well as cheap HIV-AIDS medication, regulated and unregulated armaments, coerced and non-coerced sex workers. Citizen-consumers have the right (and duty) to influence consumption policies with respect to these and many other goods.

Cortina also proposes more specific consumer rights, ones that she finds nicely articulated in John F. Kennedy's 1962 Consumer Bill of Rights.[70] These include: (1) the right to be protected from unsafe goods, such as spoiled food and cars that explode after rear-end collisions; (2) the right to information about a commodity's proper usage, risks, and benefits; (3) the right to have consumer options rather than one choice or no choice at all; (4) the right to be heard by, on the one hand, those who produce goods, and, on the other hand, those who make and enforce laws. We would also add two consumer rights that Cortina does not mention in this context but are implied by her book, and in any case connect to consumer duties, to be presently discussed. Consumer-citizens have the right – within limits constrained by their resources and duties to others – to buy and use what they want and live their own conceptions of the good life.[71] They also have the right to a certain level of goods and services so as to be able to exercise their duties as citizens.

Citizen-consumers, contends Cortina, have responsibilities as well as rights. Each should take responsibility for her own consumption decisions, refraining from consumption choices that are not autonomous, just, co-responsible and happiness-producing, and pursuing consumption choices that fulfill or, at least, do not violate the four criteria. Each citizen is also responsible for influencing community consumption policies. Accordingly citizens should join with other citizens in public discussion, form consumer groups, and establish other channels to influence public consumption policy. How and why might consumers be motivated to shoulder these – often demanding – consumer responsibilities? Although we can do no more than touch upon this important topic, Cortina bites the bullet (as I did above in advocating the virtue of moral strength and the importance of a commitment to agency) and declares that "ethical conviction is the best motor: consumer groups become aware that they are citizens and they ought to try to change, both personally and institutionally, forms of consumption for the sake of reasons of justice and happiness."[72] Although she does not reject arguments, such as those of Frank, that changing our levels and types of consumption would make us happier, she puts more weight on reconstructing our notion of happiness to include concern for others (as well as ourselves) and finally appeals to our commitments to justice.

Governments and other institutions on all levels, including global institutions, also have responsibilities. However important are individual and group consumer responsibilities, governments and society have responsibilities too. Poorer and richer countries alike, the former with the right kind of help from the latter, are responsible to be sure that all those affected by their policies have real opportunities to be responsible themselves. Such responsibility, including consumer responsibility, requires that all people be able to lead decent lives, and, thereby, be active citizens. The kinds and levels of goods and services will vary from place to place and time to time. Governments, however, are co-responsible to ensure that everyone is empowered to have a minimum level of capability and roughly equal agency. Although the following passage from Sen's *Development as Freedom* does not occur in a context in which Sen addresses consumption policy, it is relevant for the consumption responsibilities that Cortina advocates:

The substantive freedoms that we respectively enjoy to exercise our responsibilities are extremely contingent on personal, social, and environmental circumstances. A child who is denied the opportunity of elementary schooling is not only deprived as a youngster, but also handicapped all through life (as a person unable to do certain basic things that rely on reading, writing and arithmetic). The adult who lacks the means of having medical treatment for an ailment from which she suffers is not only prey to preventable morbidity and possibly escapable mortality, but may also be denied the freedom to do various things – for herself and others – that she may wish to do as a responsible human being. The bonded laborer born into semislavery, the subjugated girl child stifled by a repressive society, the helpless landless laborer without substantial means of earning an income are all deprived not only in terms of well-being, but also in terms of the ability to lead responsible lives, which are contingent on having certain basic freedoms. Responsibility *requires* freedom.[73]

Governments of developing countries share responsibility in assuring that their people have basic capabilities and agency. Rich countries, however, not only have a "backup" co-responsibility when a poor country is unable to deliver the goods and assure basic capabilities. Developed countries and societies also are obligated to alter their own consumer practices insofar as they have negative effects on the developing world, including the frustrating "demonstration effect" of luxury consumption. Such governmental (and other institutional) responsibility does not entail that either Sen or Cortina is advocating a "nanny" or paternalistic state. Rather they both urge that we understand that responsible consumption can occur only when states and institutions at all levels create "more opportunity for choice and for substantive decisions for individuals who can then act responsibly on that basis."[74]

Cortina concludes by suggesting additional means – beyond a change in values and the right sort of development assistance – that enable governments and other institutions to exercise their responsibilities. Among them are (1) the transfer of technology that is appropriate and does not cause dependency on the donor; (2) the elimination of trade protectionism that prevents Southern producers from competing with heavily subsidized Northern producers;[75] and (3) the experimentation with and dissemination of styles of life, such as Segal's "graceful simplicity," that promise the realization of Cortina's principles. She also urges that governments, private corporations, and international consumer and other civil society groups come together to forge a "Global Pact on Consumption" that would play a similar role in focusing global attention on the opportunities and the danger in current consumption practices that other global agreements have done with respect to production, poverty, and inequality.[76] The aim is to deliberate together "to design and make operative recommendations to promote just, autonomous, and happy consumption."[77] Although Cortina does not suggest it, the deliberative process in forming such a pact would surely cover such consumption items as handguns and other armaments; addictive drugs;

medicine and preventative measures for AIDS, malaria, and other diseases; sex tourism; body parts, such as kidneys; and food and water consumption – to mention only a few. What sorts of consumption should global and national bodies encourage, permit, regulate, and prohibit? And by what means? The challenge would be to find ways in which the rich nations and individuals could reduce their irresponsible consumption in ways that guarantee that poor nations and people have opportunities for well-being and agency.

Assessment and further challenges

Cortina's ethic of consumption is by and large compelling. It successfully builds on and strengthens Sen's capability approach to development and development ethics. I have argued that Cortina's consumption ethic can both incorporate the insights of a prudential consumption ethic and advance beyond it. Cortina gives us, among other things, a way to employ the capability approach to criticize over-consumption as well as under-consumption and to sketch out the consumer responsibilities of individuals, nations, and the global community.

Cortina's consumption ethic is work in progress, and nine topics (several of which I have identified above) deserve further attention. First, more work is needed on consumption responsibilities – their source, nature, relations, and limits. What, more precisely, is the moral force of Cortina's proposed norm prescribing autonomous, just, co-responsible, and happiness-generating consumption? Does Cortina intend that her four norms or four parts of one norm prescribe both negative duties (duties to refrain from action) and positive duties (duties to perform positive actions)? It seems clear that it is morally impermissible for me to buy and consume what violates any of the four norms; for instance, what undermines my autonomy or that of others. Is it also morally required and not merely praiseworthy for me to consume in such a way that I promote consumption that fulfills or promotes the four norms? If Cortina accepts that her norm implies both negative and positive duties, what is her view on the relative weight of the negative and positive duties? If I fulfill my negative duties and refrain from norm-violating consumption, how strong is the additional demand to perform positive acts of autonomous, just, co-responsible, and happiness-producing consumption? Am I doing just as much moral wrong when I fail to help (promote responsible consumption) as I do when I hurt (indulge in irresponsible consumption). For instance, is my duty not to snatch away life-saving food or withdraw autonomy-enhancing education stronger than my duty to contribute food aid to the starving and education to the ill-informed? How much time, money, and effort should I spend in finding out the best way to exercise my positive consumption duties, especially if it takes time away from my other responsibilities? Is the answer with respect to the relative weights of negative and positive duties the same or different with respect to each of the four parts of the consumption norm? For example, in making a consumption choice is the weight of my duty to make others happy (relative to my duty not to make them unhappy) stronger or weaker than the weight of my duty to make others autonomous (relative to my duty not to make them addicted)?

Second, closely related to the question of the relative weights of negative and positive consumption duties is the question of the relative weights of the four norms themselves and what to do when the norms point in different directions. Clearly, trade-offs may exist between consumption choices that, for example, promote agency and those that promote basic capabilities, consumer dialogue, or happiness. The gift of a computer that makes my son happy may feed his internet compulsions, harm his health, or take him away from public deliberation. Presumably, each of the four norms is not an absolute (exceptionless) norm but a rebuttable normative presumption or *prima facie* obligation that may be overridden by an even stronger duty in a particular situation. When the four duties do *not* converge on one consumption choice – and, happily, sometimes they do – are there any priority rules? And if not, how should the responsible consumer decide?

Third is the question of whether in consumption we have *moral* duties to *ourselves* as well as to other people, institutions, and the environment. It would be worth addressing whether Kant's "formula of humanity" of the categorical imperative ("act in such a way that you treat humanity, whether in your own person or in the person of another, always at the same time as an end and never simply as a means") implies that human agents in their consumption choices have a *moral* obligation to develop and protect their *own* autonomy, basic capabilities, co-responsibility, and happiness as well as that of other persons.[78] The prudential account exclusively attends to the agent's well-being, but appeals to enlightened self-interest rather than to any moral duties to himself or herself. Cortina's ethic of consumption emphasizes our obligations to others, the environment, and institutions. A fully adequate consumption ethic is one that includes some *moral* responsibility for our own agency and well-being in consuming.[79] Although we too readily embrace the advertising pitch that says "you owe it to yourself" to buy X, sometimes the point indeed may apply. That we have presumptive moral obligations to ourselves would be something that Cortina's happy/virtuous consumer might discern, especially when that virtue includes the moral strength to protect one's autonomy from consumer passions and manipulative advertising.

A fourth issue that would benefit from more attention would be whether Cortina's consumption ethic presupposes a moral psychology or theory of the self and, if it does, whether she should explicitly clarify and defend it. On the one hand, she seems to be assuming that human beings are more or less conditioned but not completely determined by both external and internal forces. Human beings often have some power to shape their environment and control themselves. Our consumption choices are not or do not have to be – if we take control of our lives – the mere effects of external causes and internal drives, passions, habits, and inclinations. Persons as agents can prevent impulses and inclinations from robbing them of control; they can decide on, or at least modify or lessen (or increase), the strength of their inclinations and, thereby, coordinate them.

To make sense of this power, is it necessary to move beyond metaphors, such as "taking charge," "being one's own boss," and "running one's own life," and defend a philosophical theory of the self? And if the latter, what are the options? Must one posit a Kantian transcendental ego that operates "from above," against, or instead of our "empirical" motivations? Or is there a way of understanding inner control without falling into a *metaphysical* dualism? Worth investigating here would be the resources of non-metaphysical interpretations of Kant's own view(s) as well as other theories of the self, such as those of Harry Frankfurt and Amartya Sen, in which agents have more or less freedom to prioritize and coordinate their various inclinations, affiliations, and roles.[80]

A fifth question that merits further reflection is how far governments on different levels can legitimately go in encouraging, discouraging, regulating, and prohibiting different forms of consumption. Like Sen, Cortina is concerned both to protect and promote individual freedom to choose lifestyles that people have reason to value and to protect against damage to people and the environment. More work is needed to understand how governments can achieve the right balance between these sometimes conflicting commitments. When, if at all, and why should a government *prohibit* certain levels or kinds of goods and services – assault rifles, cocaine, foods, medicine, pornography, cigarettes, prostitution, political lobbying, campaign contributions – from sale, purchase, or consumption? When should certain goods and services be available but governmentally *regulated* with respect to amount of the commodity, age of the consumer, a doctor's authorization, and so forth? When should certain goods, such as McMansions, McYachts, and gasoline, be legally available for purchase and use but highly taxed (as an incentive to decrease consumption and dependence on, for example, Middle Eastern oil)? When, if ever, should the state require certain acts of consumption, for example vaccinations of schoolchildren or the force-feeding of hunger strikers?

Sixth, Cortina, in addressing the impact of Northern consumption on the South, has contributed significantly to development ethics and to cross-cultural discussions concerning responsible consumption. She recognizes and draws on debates about the shape and limits of responsible consumption that are occurring in both industrialized and developing countries throughout the world. And she appropriately worries about the demonstration effect of American consumption patterns – fuel-inefficient cars, throwaway electronic devices, McDonalds fast food – as they spread around the globe. Although she rightly points out many cases in which Northern consumption patterns harm the developing world, she might also consider the way that Northern consumption choices either have little effect on the South or benefit the South, even (or especially) those who are most vulnerable.

Counter Culture Coffee, for example, markets "Sanctuary Shade Grown Coffee" in high-end food markets in the USA.[81] Located in North Carolina, this US company buys and roasts coffee from small Latin American producers, such as the cooperatives Cerro del Fuego in Costa Rica and Organic Cooperative of San Ramón in Matalgalpa, Nicaragua. The North Carolina Crop Improvement Association certifies that Sanctuary coffee is organic; other groups certify that it is "fair trade" and "shade grown."[82] Not only does the taste of shade-grown coffee appeal to many coffee-drinkers, but, claims Counter Culture Coffee, shade-grown coffee farms along the routes of migratory songbirds "provide a safe haven for songbirds, as well as a variety of indigenous flora and fauna." Moreover, Counter Culture Coffee donates 10 percent of the proceeds from each bag of Sanctuary Coffee to the National Fish and Wildlife Foundation (NFWF), a group that claims to support habitat conservation in Latin America and migratory bird projects in the USA.

The responsible consumer would like to have independent confirmation of Counter Culture Coffee's claims and the reliability of the various certifying organizations.[83] Yet, if the claims survive scrutiny and if the Latin American coffee-growers include small producers, then we would have a good example of "win-win" consumption. Although Northern consumers must pay a premium for specialty coffee, they benefit from high-quality coffee, protect migratory songbirds, and provide earnings for small Latin American producers and protection for Latin American flora and fauna. Sometimes good things *do* go together, and the responsible consumer is obliged to inform herself about and contribute to this convergence.

Seventh, although consumption is important, it is not everything. Morally irresponsible consumption is not the cause of all the world's problems, nor would morally responsible consumption in either the North or the South be their sole cure. Just as earlier investigators and pundits often mistakenly paid attention to productivity, population, environment, or ethnicity each in isolation from the others and from consumption, so there is a danger of a one-sided focus on consumption patterns to the exclusion of other social factors and institutions. An ethics of consumption is meant to supplement and not replace such inquiries as an ethics of population, an environmental ethics, and an ethics of employment and poverty reduction. An ethics for consumption should not substitute for an ethics of aid and a consideration of the obligations of the rich to improve global justice and aid poor countries and individuals. An ethic of consumer responsibility is only one – largely neglected – part of an ethic of personal conduct and both national and global arrangements. Cortina recognizes this point, but she could do more to connect her analysis and evaluation of consumption with an analysis of national and global economic productivity, employment, and foreign aid.

Although she raises the question of whether altered Northern consumption patterns would be bad for domestic employment and poverty reduction, she needs to go more deeply into these topics. What responsibilities would national governments have if their high taxes on gasoline put domestic auto-makers out of business and their employees out a job? Similarly, although she recognizes the positive roles that rich country foreign aid and development assistance can and should play in poor regions (my topic in the next chapter), she (and we) should address the *relative* impacts of even the most responsible Northern consumption, private philanthropy, and public foreign aid. Both empirical research and ethical assessment are called for to evaluate, for example, one of Katha Pollitt's New Year's "resolutions for liberals":

> Don't think your lifestyle can save the world. I love slow food! I cook slow food! I shop at farmers' markets, I pay extra for organic, I am always buying cloth bags and forgetting to bring them to the supermarket. But the world will never be saved by highly educated, privileged people making different upscale consumer choices. If you have enough money to buy grass-fed beef or tofu prepared by Tibetan virgins, you have enough money to give more of it away to people who really need it and groups that can make real social change.[84]

Eighth, although she does consider consumption patterns in other times and places,[85] Cortina could enrich her account considerably if she attended to current consumption debates in the developing world.

What we see in many developing countries is that citizens and social critics scrutinize rich country consumption patterns and poor country emulation of these patterns.[86] Sometimes American consumerist values are uncritically embraced; sometimes they are passionately rejected. Not infrequently, as Charles Mann points out, people around the world want what Americans have but they also want to be "aggressively themselves – a contradictory enterprise."[87] Most promising as a way to avoid such contradictions is the occurrence throughout the world of critical discussion, public deliberation, and social experimentation about how much is enough, what consumption is appropriate, and what are the consumer responsibilities of government and citizens alike.[88] Such debate also can contribute to the process and achievement of the Global Consumption Pact that Cortina recommends.

Finally, although she affirms the importance of social dialogue and public deliberation about consumption, her work on consumption would be strengthened if she further developed her conceptions – in relation to consumption policy – of the nature, process, location, structure, and limits of democratic practices and social agency (*protagonismo*). Cortina clearly recognizes how important it is that public deliberation exists concerning consumption as well as production, but a clearer idea of the strengths and weaknesses of various kinds of deliberative and other sorts of democratic practices is essential. For example, I worry that her concept of citizen agency lacks sufficient balance between deliberating, making decisions, and having an influence on decisions. Can and should citizens be involved in some ways in the making of decisions as well as deliberating about them and influencing those who decide in their stead? Moreover, I am not clear about the kinds of claims that Cortina views as appropriate in democratic deliberation. Does she admit expression of self- and group interest as well as proposals for the common good? Does she think that venues for public deliberation should be capacious enough to include professions of religious faith or should these religious claims be filtered out by "public reason" and a civic ethic? In Part IV, I argue that a similar lacuna, which I hope to fill, exists in Sen's work. My hope is that the version of deliberative democracy I develop in later chapters can provide a way to improve both Sen's and Cortina's work and contribute to their further convergence.

NOTES

This chapter greatly benefited from discussions in the fall of 2005 with colleagues and students at the University of Valencia. I am grateful to Jesús

Conill, Adela Cortina, Eddie Crocker, Daniela Gallegos, Des Gasper, Bradford S. Hadaway, Daniel Levine, Lori Keleher, Verna Gehring, and Martin Urquijo for helpful comments on earlier drafts. Cortina's and Hadaway's incisive and extensive comments were especially useful, and I hope to do them justice, if not in this chapter, then in subsequent publications.

1. Denis Goulet, "World Hunger: Putting Development Ethics to the Test," *Christianity and Crisis* (May 26, 1975): 125–32. This article, which originated as a paper at the World Food Conference at Yale University early in 1975, was reprinted in *Sociological Inquiry*, 45, 4 (1975): 3–9.

2. For the argument that the capability approach has not provided – and, perhaps, cannot provide – an ethic of consumption and, particularly, an ethic that would criticize "consumerism, the unending addictive quest for satisfaction through purchases," see Des Gasper, *The Ethics of Development: From Economism to Human Development* (Edinburgh: Edinburgh University Press, 2004), 181. See also John Cameron and Des Gasper, "Amartya Sen on Inequality, Human Well-being and Development as Freedom," *Journal of International Development*, 12, 7 (2000): 985–8.

3. Adela Cortina, *Por una ética del consumo: La ciudadanía del consumidor en un mundo global* (Madrid: Taurus, 2002).

4. Ibid., 40.

5. David A. Crocker, "Consumption, Well-being, and Capability," in *Ethics of Consumption: The Good Life, Justice, and Global Stewardship*, ed. David A. Crocker and Toby Linden (Lanham, MD: Rowman & Littlefield, 1998), 366–90.

6. Cortina, *Por una ética del consumo*, 203.

7. Ibid., 204.

8. Ibid., 29, 136, 179–80, 234.

9. I cannot take up here the interesting question of whether consumption choices have more extensive and long-lasting consequences on poor countries than do other kinds of "Northern" choices, such as legal, military, production, or development aid decisions.

10. Ibid., 139, 174, 217, 224–7, 248, 303.

11. Conversation, November 23, 2005.

12. Cortina, *Por una ética del consumo*, 207, 217, 227. Flavio Comin has suggested that one might prefer "autonomy" over "agency" for the reason that autonomy suggests that a person determines his conduct by his own highest values or moral principles while agency suggests only that the person acts on purpose and for a purpose but not necessarily on the basis of cherished values or principle. This is one conception of autonomy, but it is not Cortina's or Sen's ideal of agency. It is true that in one passage Cortina suggests something like this sense of autonomy when she says that "'substantive liberty' consists above all in wanting what is valuable in itself above and beyond one's egoistic self-interest" (*Por una ética del consumo*, 242). Stephen Darwall would classify this specific sense of autonomy as either "personal autonomy" (the agent determines his conduct "by his own most highly cherished values") or "moral autonomy" (the agent determines his conduct "in accord with his own moral convictions or principle"): "The Value of Autonomy and

Autonomy of the Will," *Ethics*, 116, 2 (2006): 264. Cortina's considered view of autonomy, however, is a more robust one in which the agent determines his own principles of action as well as his own conduct (in the light of those principles). Cortina's conception of autonomy and Sen's ideal of agency are the same as political theorist Rob Reich's ideal of an autonomous person: "The conception of autonomy I defend refers to a person's ability to reflect independently and critically upon basic commitments, values, desires, and beliefs, be they chosen or unchosen, and to enjoy a range of meaningful life options from which to choose, upon which to act, and around which to orient and pursue one's life projects": Rob Reich, *Bridging Liberalism and Multicultuarlism* (Chicago: University of Chicago Press, 2002), 105.

13. Jesús Conill, "Capacidades humanas," in *Glosario para una sociedad intercultural*, ed. Jesús Conill (Valencia: Bancaja, 2002); *Horizontes de economía ética* (Madrid: Editorial Tecnos, 2004), esp. 141–98. See also Marta Pedrajas Herrero, "El desarrollo humano en la economía ética de Amartya Sen," doctoral thesis, Faculty of Philosophy, University of Valenica, 2005), ch. 4.

14. Cortina, *Por una ética del consumo*, 213.

15. Ibid., 214.

16. If a poor person could exercise *no* agency, then an important justification for an inclusive democracy would be undermined. Flavio Comin helped me see this point.

17. Cortina, *Por una ética del consumo*, 224–27; Conill, *Horizontes de economía ética* 32, 173–82, 190–4.

18. For an interpretation of Kant's notion of rational agency in relation to both recent interpretations of Kant and the issue of Northern consumption, see Bradford S. Hadaway, "Subsistence Rights and Simplicity," a paper presented at the First International Politics and Ethics Conference, University of Southern Mississippi – Gulf Park, Long Beach, Mississippi, March 24–5, 2005.

19. Cortina, *Por una ética del consumo*, 227.

20. I owe this point to discussions with Bradford S. Hadaway.

21. Cortina, *Por una ética del consumo*, 139. See also "La tradición del republicanismo aristocrático," in *Republicanismo y educación cívica: ¿Más allá del liberalismo?*, ed. Jesús Conill and David A. Crocker (Granada: Editorial Comares, 2003), 57–72.

22. Sen, *Development as Freedom*, xii. It is true, as Flavio Comin remarks in a personal communication, that this passage conceives development as removing unfreedoms and expanding *freedoms* or *capabilities*. I contend, however, that with his reference to "reasoned agency" Sen is also expressing the importance of that capability – I would say "super-capability" – in terms of which individuals and groups themselves decide on and prioritize freedoms or capabilities that they have reason to value.

23. See Sen, *Development as Freedom*, 90–3, 216–19, 225–6, 282–9; Sabina Alkire, *Valuing Freedoms: Sen's Capability Approach and Poverty Reduction* (Oxford: Oxford University Press, 2002), 99–100; Polly Vizard, *Poverty and Human Rights: Sen's "Capability Perspective" Explored* (Oxford: Oxford University Press, 2006), 78–91.

24. Amartya Sen, "Elements of a Theory of Human Rights," *Philosophy and Public Affairs*, 32, 4 (2004): 315–56, esp. 328–30. See also Sen, *Development as Freedom*, 230–1.

25. For this argument to go through, one needs a premise of moral equality or impartiality. Otherwise the conclusion that I should be concerned for others would follow only if and when I would benefit. In Chapter 9, I argue that Sen should make this assumption of moral equality explicit in his argument for the intrinsic value of democracy. That Sen himself makes this egalitarian assumption is suggested when he says that our responsibilities to help as well as not to harm others "is not so much a matter of having exact rules about how precisely we ought to behave, as of recognizing the relevance of our shared humanity in making the choices we face" (Sen, *Development as Freedom*, 283). Also relevant is his remark, when discussing the importance of moral and legal rights, that "human rights are seen as rights shared by all – irrespective of citizenship – the benefits of which everyone *should* have" (ibid., 230).

26. Sen, ibid., 288. It should be noted that this passage and the section of *Development as Freedom* entitled "Interdependence between Freedom and Responsibility" address our responsibilities for ourselves rather than responsibilities to others. Sen briefly takes up the issue of responsibility to others, especially in the field of business ethics, in ibid., 261–81.

27. Henry Shue, *Basic Rights: Subsistence, Affluence, and US Foreign Policy*, 2nd edn. (Princeton: Princeton University Press, 1996); "Mediating Duties," *Ethics*, 98, 4 (1988): 687–704; "Solidarity among Strangers and the Right to Food," in *World Hunger and Morality*, 2nd edn., ed. William Aiken and Hugh La Follette (Upper Saddle River, NJ: Prentice-Hall, 1996), 113–32; Henry Shue, "Thickening Convergence: Human Rights and Cultural Diversity," in *The Ethics of Assistance: Morality and the Distant Needy*, ed. Deen K. Chatterjee (Cambridge: Cambridge University Press, 2004), 217–41.

28. James W. Nickel, *Making Sense of Human Rights*, 2nd edn. (Oxford and Malden, MA: Blackwell, 2007); "How Human Rights Generate Duties to Protect and Provide," *Human Rights Quarterly*, 15 (1993): 77–86.

29. Especially relevant for constructing an ethic of consumption from Sen's writings is Amartya Sen, "The Living Standard," *Oxford Economic Papers*, 36 (1984): 74–90. Excerpts from this essay, together with two postscripts – bearing on consumption – from two of Sen's later essays appear as "The Living Standard," in *Ethics of Consumption*, ed. Crocker and Linden, 287–311.

30. Cortina, *Por una ética del consumo*, 280. Cortina treats autonomous consumption most extensively in ibid., 234–41.

31. See Hadaway, "Subsistence Rights and Simplicity," 14–21.

32. Cortina, *Por una ética del consumo*, 280.

33. See esp. ibid., 241–48.

34. Ibid., 197.

35. See, for example, a *Washington Post* article that reports mounting evidence that certain widely used antibiotics and anti-heartburn medications make consumers more susceptible to a bacterial stomach infection known as *Clostridium difficile* or *C.diff.*: Rob Stein, "Stomach Bug Mutates into

Medical Mystery," *Washington Post* (December 29, 2005), A 1, 9. We must distinguish, of course, between, on the one hand, responsible journalism that reports scientific research and expert concerns and, on the other hand, reporting that outstrips the evidence and either exaggerates or minimizes consumer risk.

36. In a personal communication, Daniel Levine observes that some online reviewers have gained respect as reliable evaluators of certain kinds of products.

37. I leave open the question of whether the sale and consumption of various addictive drugs should be criminalized.

38. Cortina, *Por una ética del consumo*, 222.

39. Ibid., 242–8.

40. Ibid., 245.

41. Ibid., 246.

42. Jane Perlez and Kirk Johnson, "Behind Gold's Glitter: Torn Lands and Pointed Questions," *New York Times* (October 24, 2005), A 4; "Tangled Strands in Fight Over Peru Gold Glitter" (October 25, 2005), <http://query.nytimes.com/search/query?srcht=s&srchst=m&vendor=&query=%22environment%22&submit.x=48&submit.y=17>. See also Andrea Perera, "Controversy Surrounding Gold Mining Grows as Jewelers, Indigenous Community Leaders Speak Out," *Oxfam Exchange* (Spring 2006). One may visit <www.nodirtygold.org> and sign the No Dirty Gold pledge to end destructive mining practices.

43. Cortina, *Por una ética del consumo*, 248.

44. Ibid., 247.

45. Ibid., 248.

46. Des Gasper suggest a variant to (1) in which we supplement our regular walking and bike-riding with occasional use – when weather is bad or destinations are far – of taxis and public transportation. In mountain terrain, cycling would take a back seat, so to speak, to walking and some motorized transport.

47. Combining features of options (1) and (2) would result in walking and biking as the default mode of transportation, with our fuel-efficient car being used in bad weather or to travel longer distances (not served by public transportation).

48. Cortina, *Por una ética del consumo*, 230.

49. Des Gasper has suggested this point.

50. Cortina, *Por una ética del consumo*, 249–55.

51. Ibid., 139.

52. Ibid., 250.

53. Ibid., 253.

54. Ibid., 254–5. This democratic-deliberative alternative to the "crystal ball" problem would have to make it more reasonable to believe that democratic decision-making would yield more reliable answers (and that citizen deliberative capacities can be acquired) than our best estimates of the consequences of various consumption choices. I owe this point to personal conversations with Daniel Levine.

55. Cortina, *Por una ética del consumo*, 255–61.

56. See, for example, ibid., 233.

57. See Richard A. Easterlin, "Will Raising the Incomes of All Increase the Happiness of All?," *Journal of Economic Behavior and Organization*, 27 (1995): 35–48; Robert H. Frank, *Luxury Fever: Why Money Fails to Satisfy in an Era of Excess* (New York: Free Press, 1999), esp. ch. 9; Carol Graham and Stefano Pettinato, *Happiness and Hardship: Opportunity and Insecurity in New Market Economies* (Washington, DC: Brookings Institution Press, 2002).

58. See Robert E. Lane, *The Market Experience* (New York: Cambridge University Press, 1991), ch. 26; "Does Money Buy Happiness?" *Public Interest*, 111 (Fall 1993), 59, 61; "The Road Not Taken: Friendship, Consumerism, and Happiness," in *Ethics of Consumption*, ed. Crocker and Linden, 218–49; *After the End of History: The Curious Fate of American Materialism* (Ann Arbor: University of Michigan Press, 2005). See also Frank, *Luxury Fever*, esp. ch. 5.

59. Cortina, *Por una ética del consumo*, 113–14, 308. See Juliet B. Schor, *The Overspent American: Upscaling, Downshifting, and the New Consumer* (New York: Basic Books, 1998), ch. 6. See also Schor, *The Overworked American: The Unexpected Decline of Leisure* (New York: Basic Books, 1992).

60. See Jerome M. Segal, "Living at a High Economic Standard: A Funtionings Analysis," in *Ethics of Consumption*, ed. Crocker and Linden, 361, 363.

61. For "downshifting" trends in Australia and the UK, see Clive Hamilton, *Growth Fetish* (London: Pluto Press, 2004).

62. Cortina, *Por una ética del consumo*, 308–9. See Jerome M. Segal, *Graceful Simplicity: Toward a Philosophy and Politics of Simple Living* (New York: Henry Holt, 1999).

63. Luis Camacho, "Consumption as a Topic for the North–South Debate," in *Ethics of Consumption*, ed. Crocker and Linden, 559. See Cortina, *Por una ética del consumo*, 311.

64. Cortina, *Por una ética del consumo*, 255.

65. See Robert H. Frank, *Choosing the Right Pond: Human Behavior and the Quest for Status* (New York: Oxford University Press, 1985); Judith Lichtenberg, "Consuming Because Others Consume," in *Ethics of Consumption*, ed. Crocker and Linden, 155–75.

66. See Frank, *Luxury Fever*, esp. ch. 17.

67. See Hadaway, "Subsistence Rights and Simplicity," 14–24.

68. Cortina, *Por una ética del consumo*, 265–90.

69. See also Adela Cortina, *Ciudadanos del mundo: Hacia una teoría de la ciudadanía* (Madrid: Alianza, 1997); *Alianza y contrato: Política, ética, y religión* (Madrid: Trotta, 2001).

70. Cortina, *Por una ética del consumo*, 270.

71. Ibid., 170.

72. Ibid., 266.

73. Sen, *Development as Freedom*, 284. Cf. Cortina, *Por una ética del consumo*, 316.

74. Sen, *Development as Freedom*, 284.

75. Further work is needed to investigate the extent to which lowering trade barriers for producers in the South would lower prices for Northern consumers and enrich large transnational producers, but fail to benefit local populations in developing countries.

76. Cortina, *Por una ética del consumo*, 316.
77. Ibid., 322.
78. Immanuel Kant, *Grounding for the Metaphysics of Morals*, 3rd edn., trans. James W. Ellington (Indianapolis, IN: Hackett, 1993), 429. On pp. 244–5 above, I quoted and discussed Cortina's gloss (for consumption choices) of the "formula of humanity" version of Kant's categorical imperative. See also Cortina, *Por una ética del consumo*, 246.
79. See Hadaway, "Subsistence Rights and Simplicity."
80. In his suggestive and incisive paper, Hadaway draws on the following recent interpretations of Kant: Henry E. Allison, *Kant's Theory of Freedom* (Cambridge: Cambridge University Press, 1990); Marcia Baron, *Kantian Ethics Almost Without Apology* (Ithaca, NY: Cornell University Press, 1995); Stephen Engstrom, "The Inner Virtue of Freedom," in *Kant's Metaphysics of Morals: Interpretive Essays*, ed. Mark Timmons (Oxford: Oxford University Press, 2002); Barbara Herman, *The Practice of Moral Judgment* (Cambridge, MA: Harvard University Press, 1993); and Nelson Potter, "Duties to Oneself, Motivational Internalism, and Self-Deception in Kant's Ethics," in *Kant's Metaphysics of Morals*, ed. Timmons, 371–89. Harry Frankfurt's seminal essay is "Freedom of the Will and the Concept of a Person," *Journal of Philosophy*, 68, 1 (1971): 5–20. For recent work on autonomy, see *Personal Autonomy: New Essays in Personal Autonomy and Its Role in Contemporary Moral Philosophy*, ed. James Stacey Taylor (Cambride: Cambridge University Press, 2005). For Sen on identity and freedom, see "Reason Before Identity," Romanes Lecture, Oxford University, November 17, 1998; "Beyond Identity: Other People," *The New Republic*, 223/5 (2000): 23–30; *Identify and Violence: The Illusion of Destiny* (New York: W. W. Norton, 2006).
81. <www.counterculturecoffee.com>.
82. According to the "Grounds for Change" website, certified organic coffee "is grown without the use of chemical pesticides and fertilizers, thereby assuring the health of the soil, forest and farmers"; "certified fair trade coffee gives farmers a better standard of living and producer cooperatives are guaranteed a minimum fair price for their crop"; and "shade grown coffee protects migratory bird habitat and reduces clear-cutting in tropical rainforests as well as enhancing flavor": <www.groundsforchange.com>.
83. For an evaluation of the reliability of various agencies and their approaches to organic certification, see *Consumer Reports* (February 2006).
84. Katha Pollitt, "Happy New Year!," *Nation* (January 22, 2007), 10.
85. See, for example, *Por una ética del consumo*, ch. 2.
86. See Norman Myers and Jennifer Kent, *The New Consumers: The Influence of Affluence on the Environment* (Washington, DC: Island Press, 2004).
87. Charles C. Mann, "Betting the Planet," in Peter Menzel and Charles C. Mann, *Material World: A Global Family Portrait* (San Francisco: Sierra Club Books, 1994), 9.
88. See, for example, David A. Crocker, Luis Camacho, and Ramón Romero, "Globalization, Changing Consumption Patterns, and Human Development: The Cases of Costa Rica and Honduras," Background Paper for United Nations Development Programme, *Human Development Report 1998*.

In this chapter I focus on the scourge of hunger. Whether due to emergencies caused by natural calamities, such as tsunamis, drought, or locust infestation, or to chronic lack of food, world hunger shocks the moral conscience. "Hunger continues to be," asserts the Hunger Task Force of the Millennium Development Project, "a global tragedy."[1] What are the facts about food and global hunger?

More than enough food exists worldwide for everyone to have enough to eat. Food aid scholars Christopher B. Barrett and Daniel G. Maxwell state the relatively undisputed facts at the outset of their important volume *Food Aid After Fifty Years: Recasting Its Role*: "Enough food is produced globally to meet every person's dietary requirements adequately. In 2000, the world enjoyed a daily per capita supply of more than 2,800 kilocalories and 75 grams of protein, more than enough to keep every man, woman, and child well nourished."[2]

Food availability, however, does not result in nutritional well-being for all. Although estimates depend on definitions of hunger and nutritional adequacy, the Food and Agriculture Organization (FAO) of the United Nations estimated in 2004 that in 2000–2 approximately 852 million, or one sixth of the world's people, did not have enough to eat.[3] Although most of the world's hungry people live in Asia (Bangladesh, China, India, and Indonesia), fully 30 of the world's 190 or so countries – two-thirds in sub-Saharan Africa – have insufficient food to provide their inhabitants with 2,100 calories per person per day. Sixty nations in the world have insufficient food supplies to afford their citizens the widely accepted standard of 2,350 calories per person per day.[4] According to the Millennium Development Project's task force on hunger, 5.5 million children die each year from malnutrition-related causes, and 134 million children are underweight, 34 million of whom live in sub-Saharan Africa.[5]

These figures, of course, are only averages; many persons in these food-deficit countries get much less to eat per day, and a few enjoy much more. At least half the people in ten countries, seven in sub-Saharan

Africa, are malnourished. In four of these sub-Saharan African countries, two-thirds or more of the population lack adequate food. Even high-food-consumption countries, such as the USA, in which people consume on average 3,772 calories per day, have 38 million people who don't get enough to eat, many of them in minority populations. However, the overwhelming majority of hungry people (815 million) live in poor or developing countries rather than in transition countries (28 million) or "developed" countries (9 million). Although the world made progress in the period from 1990–2 to 1995–7 in reducing by 27 million the numbers of hungry people, two-thirds of this gain was wiped out from 1995–7 to 2000–2. It is all too clear that the world is not on track to achieve the Millennium Development Goal of halving the world's hungry by 2015.[6]

How have philosophers and other development ethicists responded to these and earlier facts of global hunger? In Chapter 1, I argued that throughout the 1970s and early 1980s, often in response to Garrett Hardin's "lifeboat ethics," initially Peter Singer and subsequently other analytically trained philosophers addressed the issue of world hunger and moral obligation of the rich to help the hungry.[7] They argued that affluent nations and individuals do have a positive obligation to send food aid (foodstuffs and money) to distant and hungry people, and they spent the bulk of their efforts in exploring the nature, basis, and limits of this obligation. These thinkers paid scant attention to food aid policies of rich countries or development policies in poor countries. And they mostly neglected the efforts of poor countries to feed and develop their own people. If these philosophers had critically scrutinized food aid policies of the 1970s, they would have found that the form food aid had taken since its inception a quarter of a century earlier was increasingly – as food policy scholars and practitioners at the time were beginning to argue – morally problematic and in desperate need of reform. It was becoming all too clear that sending surplus US grain and other food commodities, while only a negligible help to US farmers and maritime and commercial interests, often failed to get to the hungry. Even worse, when recipient governments sold ("monetized") the so-called "program food aid" in local markets, these markets became glutted, prices for locally grown food precipitously declined, and small farmers stopped producing and themselves went hungry.[8] Moreover, government officials often "appropriated" the food or the money it yielded for their own purposes. In short, scholars and activists were coming to recognize that merely sending food or money to the distant hungry failed to bring about – and even undermined – long-term and sustainable development (however defined).

One such scholar-activist was the late Denis Goulet, the pioneer (at least in English-speaking countries) of development ethics. Influenced by the French development thinker and planner Louis Joseph Lebret, Goulet began his career in the late 1950s and early 1960s as a grassroots activist and researcher among "communities of struggle" in Lebanon, Algeria, Brazil, and several other developing countries. His ethical concerns about development originated in his own direct engagement with human misery as well as with some of the early critics of what Goulet called "assistentialism," the post-World War II idea that "rich nations could help war-damaged and, later, poor nations industrialize by transferring investment capital, food and other supplies to them."[9]

It may have been a blessing that Goulet lacked familiarity at that time with analytic philosophy and with Singer's challenge to philosophers. Influenced instead by the fairly progressive social teachings of the Catholic Church, the (more radical) theology of liberation, and the ethically infused existentialism of the Algerian-French philosopher Albert Camus, Goulet was relatively immune to analytic philosophy's fixation on abstract arguments that rich countries had obligations to provide food aid. Likewise, he was able to recognize that much of the popular and professional debate in the early 1970s about hunger and food aid ran the risk "of seeing world development simply as a matter of food aid to starving nations or of compensatory financial assistance to offset inflationary price rises."[10] In a 1975 article, aptly titled "World Hunger: Putting Development Ethics to the Test," Goulet clearly and presciently saw that hunger was but a symptom of deeper causes, including bad development, and that food aid by itself was always in danger of being a soothing palliative that failed to address root causes:

Hunger is merely one dramatic symptom of a deeper ill: the persistence of national and international orders that foster distorted development. Consequently, the problem is not met *solely* by boosting food aid or by cutting births, but, ultimately, by creating new ground rules governing access to the world's productive resources.

Societies now powerless must gain such access *upstream* – at the production end – and not merely *downstream* – at the distribution end – if an equitable, dynamic and liberating form of world development is to appear.[11]

Amartya Sen was another development thinker whose approach transformed the Hardin–Singer debate from that of food aid to (good) development. Building on his work since the late 1950s in economics, evaluation, and development, in 1981 Sen published his seminal *Poverty and Famines: An Essay on Entitlement and Deprivation.*[12] In this volume, which decisively broke with the view that the (main) cause of famine was lack of food (and food aid), Sen argued that eliminating famines and reducing chronic malnutrition require not merely food aid but a deep and broad approach to national and global development. Although he did not address Singer's challenge, Sen – in contrast to Goulet – critically engaged and employed the tools of analytic moral and sociopolitical philosophy as well as those of political economy.

Catching up with this recasting of food aid, a few analytically trained philosophers in the mid-1980s began to reframe the ethics of famine relief – "Do rich countries have a moral duty to aid the global hungry?" – and insert it in a more comprehensive ethics of and for development. Just as Sen and others reframed and enlarged food aid to become only one tool in promoting development, so philosophers, sometimes under Sen's influence, incorporated an ethics of famine relief into a more comprehensive ethics of development.

My main claim in this chapter is that many philosophical and policy discussions of acute hunger and chronic malnutrition committed and still commit what Whitehead called "the fallacy of misplaced concreteness."[13] Philosophers, policymakers, and citizens still abstract one part – food aid – from the whole complex of hunger, poverty, and bad development, and proceed to consider that part in isolation from other dimensions.[14] Just as cutting-edge food aid and development scholars, policymakers, and practitioners have done, philosophers should refocus and then broaden their attention with respect to the complex causes, conditions, and cures of hunger. Otherwise, we will have an incomplete and distorted picture of both the facts and the values involved. Instead of continuing virtually exclusive preoccupation with the moral basis for aid from rich countries to famine victims in poor countries, development ethicists should join the most progressive food aid scholars, development economists, and policymakers and shift their emphasis (1) from moral foundations to interpretative and strategic concepts, (2) from famine to persistent malnutrition, (3) from remedy to prevention, (4) from food availability to food entitlements, (5) from food entitlements to capability and agency, and (6) from capability and agency to development as freedom. This last progression will take us beyond even the best recent work on world hunger and development aid. My intent is not to reject the first term in each pair but to subordinate them to the more fundamental and comprehensive second terms. Overall, the progression I favor conceives an ethics of food aid as a part of a more basic and inclusive ethics for development.

From moral foundations to interpretative and strategic concepts

Are affluent states and their citizens morally obligated to send food or money for food to the hungry and starving in other countries? Is such aid morally required, permissible, or impermissible? This was the question that philosophers and many others asked in the 1970s. The answers ranged from the extreme claim that such aid was morally required, even if it impoverished the donors, to the contrary extreme that such aid was morally reprehensible (and stupidly imprudent) because it did more harm than good, while middle-of-the-road views held that it was permissible and even admirable to give aid, but not wrong to refrain from so doing.

A few in the 1980s and many more in the middle of the first decade of the new millennium, however, perceived the problem of "world hunger and moral obligation" differently. When we see pictures – whether in the media or on the cover of ethics anthologies – of an emaciated child crouching on desiccated or water-saturated soil, the question "Do we have a duty to help?" seems beside the point. Of course we should help. The moral imperative, once we know the facts, is clear and compelling. The Food and Agricultural Organization's (FAO) 2004 report on global food insecurity is unusual only in its succinctness: "In moral terms, just stating the fact that one child dies every five seconds as a result of hunger and malnutrition should be enough to prove that we cannot afford to allow the scourge of hunger to continue. Case closed."[15]

We should not take seriously those philosophers and others who insist that we refrain from assisting until a (conclusive) theoretical or moral argument is found to justify the view that the rich in the North and West should help the poor in the South or East. To be sure, in the light of our concomitant obligations to aid our families, friends, and compatriots, a place for moral debate exists with respect to *how much* assistance morality or enlightened prudence requires us to give distant people.[16] And in some contexts it can be valuable to consider whether the rich have *any* moral obligations to the distant poor.

Among such contexts are university seminar rooms or public forums in which it is argued that foreign aid is unjustified, since it is not in the donor country's national interest, and national interest is the only legitimate basis for aid. This argument's first premise, of course, can often be shown to be false. Sometimes, perhaps often, prudential arguments lead to the same conclusion as the best moral arguments. When such convergence occurs, the moral argument may be important in bolstering the prudential argument. It is when prudential and moral considerations fail to converge that the moral arguments for or against aid may become not only theoretically but also practically important.

Usually, however, we see no good reason to doubt that we owe *something* to the distant poor and hungry, if we can be reasonably sure that our help will alleviate – or help the hungry themselves alleviate – their immediate misery and improve their long-term prospects. For most citizens and many philosophers, the obstacle in the way of supporting aid to distant peoples is not so much skepticism about the existence of a convincing moral argument as pessimism about practical results. It could be, of course, that aid skeptics cast their argument in prudential or effectiveness terms because they are uncomfortable with publicly arguing that their country has no moral duty to help (or has a moral duty not to help). One reason for this discomfort may be that the skeptic knows he is out of step with the widely held commitment that affluent states and citizens should help those in dire straits.[17]

Unfortunately, preoccupied as they were with the task of establishing a moral basis for aid to distant people, most analytically trained philosophers in the 1970s and early 1980s evinced negligible interest in institutional and practical issues. They seemed to believe that if they could resolve the foundational questions, the rest would be easy; the rational – on its own – would become real. It is true that Will Aiken and Hugh La Follette in their 1977 anthology, *World Hunger and Moral Obligation*, did challenge their readers to consider: "If one ought to help the hungry, how should one help?"[18] However, the volume's essays almost completely failed to address the best ways to diagnose and remedy the problem of world hunger.

As we saw in Chapter 1, one partial exception to the prevailing lack of interest in practical issues was Peter Singer, the philosopher who initiated the debate. Although Singer seems to advocate individual donations of food or money as the best way to fulfill an affluent person's duty to combat the suffering of distant people, upon closer inspection Singer argues compellingly that potential donors are obligated to find the most effective way or ways to do their duty. He also goes so far as to list a few broad types of aid or other actions – from population control, economic security, and agricultural assistance, to voting, socially responsible consumption, and working for organizations. And we must look beyond saving of a life now and see if there is reason to believe that such rescue will "do more than perpetuate the cycle of poverty, misery, and high infant mortality."[19] However, what Singer has never done, other than express an occasional preference for one possible means over another, is to assess the advantages and disadvantages – moral and otherwise – of the various options for aid and development. Nor has he adequately investigated – by himself or in collaboration with others – the national and global causes of hunger and other deprivations.

It might be objected that analysis of the causes and cures of world hunger is a purely factual, empirical, or technical matter to which philosophers and other ethicists cannot contribute. Yet I would argue that facts and values cannot be separated so easily. Let us distinguish two ways in which facts and values are entangled.[20]

First, as Dewey was well aware, different descriptive, interpretative, and explanatory concepts and categories have different practical consequences for investigators and public actors alike. And among those consequences are some that we should morally applaud and others that we should morally condemn. For example, a widely held concept of famine includes the idea that famine amounts to excessive mortality due – principally if not exclusively – to food shortages. One reason to reject this concept is that it has had morally disastrous effects. On the one hand, this notion has delayed interventions until people started dying in large numbers, when earlier interventions might have saved many. Such was the case, for example, in Niger in the summer of 2005.[21] On the other hand, this definition of famine implied that the cure was always and only more food, when in fact the problem – arguably, one of justice – was often a hungry household's *access* to food.[22]

A second way in which values are linked to facts is that we discern ethically salient features of facts on the basis of our moral values.[23] Ethical reflection, whether the work of philosophers or of non-philosophers, plays not only a critical role in assessing consequences and a guiding role in prescribing actions but also an *interpretative* role in relation to social reality and change. An ethic, of course, does propose norms for assessing present social institutions, envisaging future alternatives, and assigning obligations for getting from the present to the future. An ethic, finally, provides a basis for deciding how agents should act individually or collectively in particular circumstances. What is equally important and frequently neglected, however, is that a normative vision also informs the ways we discern, describe, explain, and forecast social phenomena. How we "read" the situation, as well as how we describe and classify it, will be, to some extent, a function of our value commitments and even our moral sensitivities.[24] For instance, if we ask, "How is India doing?," we are seeking an empirical analysis of what is going on in that country. Alternative ethical perspectives will focus on distinct, though sometimes overlapping, facts: hedonistic utilitarians attend to pleasures and pains; preference utilitarians select preference satisfactions and dissatisfactions (or per capita productivity and consumption); human rights advocates emphasize human rights compliances and violations; and Rawlsians investigate the distributions of "social primary goods" such as income, wealth, liberties, and opportunities. In each case the ethic provides a lens to pick out what counts as morally relevant information. One value of intellectual dialogue between different ethical perspectives and democratic deliberation among diverse citizens is that in "give and take" we learn to see the world in new and different ways. Moreover, as Sherman says, "how to see becomes as much a matter of inquiry (zetêsis) as what to do."[25]

Amartya Sen, Jean Drèze, Martha Nussbaum, and others, as I showed in Part II above, offer the capability perspective as an important part of the effort to understand and combat world hunger and other deprivations. Capability theorists employ their ethical concepts and commitments to appraise social institutions and guide policy formation and actions.[26] To accomplish this task they defend explicit ethical principles and have begun to assign moral responsibilities.[27] The capability perspective, however, also yields distinctive ways of perceiving world hunger and understanding its empirical causes and attempted cures. With its emphasis on "the commodity commands [entitlements] and basic capabilities that people enjoy,"[28] the capability approach interprets and supplies a rationale for broadening the investigative focus from food aid for famine victims to the most important (and modifiable) causes, conditions, consequences, and remedies of endemic hunger and other privations.[29] As Drèze and Sen argue, "seeing hunger as entitlement failure points to possible remedies as well as helping us to understand the forces that generate hunger and sustain it."[30] In this chapter I emphasize the interpretative contribution of Drèze and Sen's capability approach – or, better, "the agency-oriented capability approach" – and argue that this normative perspective helps justify both a broader and a more focused perspective on world hunger.

In the first decade of the twenty-first century, philosophical reflection on world hunger remains important. After Ethiopia, Kampuchea, Sudan, Somalia, and Rwanda in the 1980s and 1990s, and Niger, North Korea, Sudan, and South Asia in the present or recent past, however, increasing numbers of philosophers are appropriately less concerned with morally justifying aid to the distant hungry and more concerned with the conceptual and ethical dimensions of understanding hunger as well as local, national, and global policies for successfully combating it.

From famine to persistent malnutrition

Philosophers, like policymakers and the public, typically have paid excessive attention to famine and insufficient attention to impending famine, acute hunger following natural or human disasters, or persistent malnutrition.[31] Both acute hunger, including famine, and endemic malnutrition are forms of hunger in the sense of "an inadequacy in dietary intake relative to the kind and quantity of food required for growth, for activity, and for maintenance of good health."[32] Famine, other forms of acute hunger, and chronic hunger, however, differ in character, cause, consequence, and cure. Although some acute hunger, such as that following a tsunami, is an event largely caused by a specific natural or human disaster, a famine is a "slow-onset disaster"[33] and as much a process as an event. Although its outbreak may be abrupt and dramatic, "involving acute starvation and sharp increase in mortality,"[34] the complex causes reach back in time. During famines, some people avoid starvation and death by selling valuable assets, such as their cattle. To take this response to impending starvation into account, perhaps, the best working definition of famine is that of famine and food scholar Peter Walker: "Famine is a socio-economic process which causes the accelerated destitution of the most vulnerable, marginal and least powerful groups in a community, to a point where they can no longer, as a group, maintain a sustainable livelihood."[35]

Like epidemics and natural disasters, such as earthquakes, droughts, pestilence, and hurricanes, famine makes a sensational topic for the evening news or fundraising rock concerts and often stimulates an outpouring of governmental and private donations. Yet famine and other forms of acute hunger, although more dramatic, account for only about 10 percent of global hunger.[36] Chronic hunger, which governments and people more easily ignore, accounts for the rest.[37]

Chronic hunger, persistent nutritional deprivation, has somewhat different and deeper causes than famine (and other forms of transitory hunger) and is harder to eradicate. The consequences of persistent hunger – severe incapacitation, chronic illness, and humiliation – may be worse than death. And chronic hunger is itself a killer, since hunger-weakened persons are especially prone to deadly diseases such as malaria, diarrhea, and pneumonia. If we are concerned about the misery and mortality caused by famine and other kinds of acute hunger, we should be even more exercised by the harms caused by persistent malnutrition. Drèze and Sen recognize that strategies to combat famine and persistent malnutrition also differ:

To take one example [of diverse strategies in responding to transitory and endemic hunger], in the context of famine prevention the crucial need for speedy intervention and the scarcity of resources often call for a calculated reliance on existing distributional mechanisms (e.g. the operation of private trade stimulated by cash support to famine victims) to supplement the logistic capability of relief agencies. In the context of combating chronic hunger, on the other hand, there is much greater scope for slower but none the less powerful avenues of action such as institution building, legal reforms, asset redistribution or provisioning in kind.[38]

Famine and chronic malnutrition do not always go together. Nations – for instance, India since independence and Haiti in 1994 – have been free of famine and yet beset by endemic malnutrition, including micro-nutritional deficiencies. In the late 1950s and early 1960s, China achieved a reasonably high level of nutritional well-being and yet in 1959–62 was stricken by calamitous famines. To be exclusively preoccupied with famine, afflicting only 10 percent of the hungry, is to ignore the chronically hungry and the food insecurity in countries not prone to famine. To be focused on chronic hunger, on the other hand, may blind a country to impending famine. Food security requires concern with combating these two types of hunger.

As important as is the distinction between these two varieties of food deprivation, we must neither exaggerate the differences nor fail to recognize certain linkages in both causes and cures. Not only are famine and chronic malnutrition both forms of hunger, but they have certain common causes and interlinked remedies. Both can be understood as what Drèze and Sen call "entitlement failures" and "capability failures" (of which more presently).

As with many other problems, institutions matter. A nation with the right sort of basic political, economic, and social institutions – for instance, stable families, adequate infrastructure, certain kinds of markets, public provisions, a democratic government, a free press, and nongovernmental organizations – can prevent and remedy both sorts of hunger more readily than a society without the right set of interlocking institutions. The appropriate response to both forms of hunger usually includes some kind of governmental action. Moreover, some of the best short- and long-term approaches to famine prevention – remunerated public employment and, more generally, sustainable development – build on and often intensify effective ways of addressing persistent malnutrition.[39] By contrast, the most common emergency action to combat famine, the herding of people into relief camps in order to dole out free food, jeopardizes long-term solutions by disrupting normal economic activities, upsetting family life, and creating breeding grounds for infectious diseases. Relief camps, in contrast to what Sen calls "the employment route," also undermine people's agency and, thus, are at odds with the capability approach's moral commitments. Later in this chapter, we return to the norm of agency and its policy implications.

From remedy to prevention

Whether concerned with abrupt, transitory, or chronic hunger, philosophical ethicists typically emphasized – and often continue to do so – the moral response to *existing* hunger problems rather than the prevention of *future* ones.[40] An important early exception was Onora O'Neill, who clearly addressed the question of pre-famine as well as famine policies.[41] On the basis of an expanded conception of the duty not to kill others, O'Neill argued that we have a duty to adopt pre-famine policies that ensure that famine is postponed as long as possible and is minimized in severity. Such pre-famine policies, O'Neill argued, must include both a population policy and a resources policy, for "a duty to try to postpone the advent and minimize the severity of famine is a duty on the one hand to minimize the number of persons there will be and on the other to maximize the means of subsistence."[42]

O'Neill's approach, however, unfortunately assumes that famines cannot be prevented altogether, only postponed and minimized. This supposition flies in the face of recent historical experience. Drèze and Sen summarize their findings on this point when they observe: "There is no real evidence to doubt that all famines in the modern world are preventable by human action . . . many countries – even some very poor ones – manage consistently to prevent them."[43] More positively and perhaps too optimistically Sen asserts: "Famines are, in fact, so easy to prevent that it is amazing that they are allowed to occur at all."[44] Nations that have successfully prevented impending famines (sometimes without outside help) include India (after independence), Cape Verde, Kenya, and Botswana.[45] Often effective is the regeneration of "the lost purchasing power of hard-hit groups" through "the creation of emergency employment in short-term public projects."[46]

It is also possible to prevent much chronic hunger, if not eliminate it altogether. We must combat that pessimism – a close cousin of complacency – that assures us that the hungry will always be with us, at least in the same absolute and proportionate numbers.[47] One of the great achievements of Drèze and Sen is to document, through detailed case studies of successes in fighting hunger, that "there is, in fact, little reason for presuming that the terrible problems of hunger and starvation in the world cannot be changed by human action."[48] What is needed, among other things such as political will, is a forward-looking perspective for short-term, middle-term, and long-term prevention of both types of hunger.

Unfortunately, efforts to *remedy* world hunger – especially acute hunger – far outweigh those long-term development approaches that would *prevent* future hunger. The authors of *Halving Hunger* observe that in Ethiopia's 2003 famine USAID spent $500 million on emergency food aid "compared with $50 million for development programming in agriculture, health, nutrition, water, and sanitation put together."[49] As we shall see, what is called for is a better balance between remedy and prevention as well as responses to food emergencies that at least do not undermine long-term development and, if possible, promote it.

From food availability to food entitlements

Moral reflection on the prevention and relief of world hunger must be expanded from food productivity, availability, and distribution to what Sen calls food "entitlements." Popular images of famine relief emphasize policies that, in Garrett Hardin's words, "move food to the people" or "move people to food."[50] In either case, the assumption is that lack of food is the sole or principal cause of hunger. For more than fifty years the conventional wisdom has been that it is greater agricultural productivity (and population controls) that will reduce if not eliminate hunger, and that famine "relief" is a technical problem of getting food and starving people together in the same place at the same time. It is obviously true that lack of food is one cause of hunger. Much hunger, however, occurs even when people and ample food – even peak supplies – are in close proximity. A starving person may have no access to or command over the food that is in the shop down the street. Force or custom may exclude a Dalit (untouchable) from the queue of people waiting for food handouts.

When famine strikes a country, a region, and even a village, often enough food exists in that locale for everyone to be adequately fed. Recent research makes it evident that since 1960 there has been sufficient food to feed the world's people on a "near-vegetarian diet" and that "we are approaching a second threshold of improved diet sufficiency (enough to provide 10 percent animal products)."[51] Accordingly, it is often said that the problem is one of *distribution*. This term, however, is ambiguous. Purely spatial redistribution is insufficient and may not be necessary. Sen reminds us that "people have perished in famines in sight of much food in shops."[52] What good distribution of food should mean is that people have *effective* access to or can acquire food (whether presently nearby or far away). Hence, it is better to say that the problem of hunger, whether transitory or persistent, involves an "entitlement failure" in the sense that the hungry person is not able to gain access to food or lacks command over food. What is important is not just the food itself but also whether particular households and individuals have operative "entitlements" over food. The distinction between households and individuals is important, for households as units may have sufficient food for the nourishment of each family member, yet some members – usually women or girls – may starve or be chronically malnourished due to entitlement failures.

We must be careful here, for Sen's use of the term "entitlement" has caused much confusion and controversy. Unlike Robert Nozick's explicitly normative or prescriptive use of the term,[53] Sen employs "entitlement" in a predominantly descriptive way, one relatively free of moral endorsement or criticism, to refer to a person's actual or operative command, permitted by law (backed by state power) or custom, over certain commodities.[54] A person's entitlements will be a function of (1) that person's *endowments*, for example what income, wealth (including land), goods, or services (including labor) she has to exchange for food; (2) *production possibilities*, related to available technology and knowledge; (3) *exchange opportunities*, for instance the going rate of exchange of work or money for food; (4) *legal claims* against the state, for instance rights to work, food stamps, or welfare; and (5) nonlegal but *socially approved and operative rules*, for example the household "social discipline" that mandates that women eat after and less than men.[55] A person with little more than labor power and unable – due to primitive technology and knowhow (either to produce food or something else to exchange for food) – may have insufficient money to buy food at famine-induced prices and no claim on government employment or welfare programs.

Generally speaking, an entitlement to food would be the actual ability, whether *morally* justified or not, to acquire food by some legally or socially approved means – whether by producing it, trading for it, buying it, or receiving it in a government feeding program. A Hutu child separated from his family may be morally justified in stealing a meal from a Tutsi food supply center, but he has no legal claim or other social basis for *effective* access to the food. In Sen's sense, then, the child lacks an entitlement to that food.

To view hunger as an entitlement failure commits one neither to the position that hunger is *never* due to food scarcity nor to the position that the same set of causes *always* explains hunger. Sometimes a fall in food production, due perhaps to natural disaster or civil conflict, is a factor contributing to acute or chronic hunger. Rather, the entitlement theory of hunger directs one to examine the various links in a society's "food chain" – production-acquisition-consumption or availability-access-utilization – any or all of which can be dysfunctional and contribute to an entitlement failure.[56] A production failure, due to wars, earthquakes, drought, or pests, will result in an entitlement failure for those small farmers "whose means of survival depend on food that they grow themselves."[57] When food is abundant and even increasing in an area, landless laborers may starve because they have insufficient money to buy food, no job to get money, nothing of worth to trade for food, or no effective claim on their government or other group.

Conceiving hunger as an entitlement failure also may help us see ways of preventing impending famines and ways of remedying actual famines – ways we might miss with other ethical lenses. What is needed is not only food but institutions in which people can "enjoy" entitlements, that is, institutions that protect against entitlement failures and restore lost entitlements. Moving food to hungry people may *not* always be necessary, for the needed food already may be physically present. The problem, in this case, is that some people cannot gain access to it. Even worse, increasing food availability in a given area may increase the hunger problem. Direct delivery of free food, for instance, can send market food prices plummeting, thereby causing a disincentive for farmers to grow food. The result is a decline not only in their productivity but also in their own food entitlements.

Moreover, even though necessary, food by itself is not sufficient to prevent or cure famine if people never had entitlements to food or lost what they had previously. And it may be that the best way to ensure that people have the ability to command food is not to give them food itself, but rather to provide cash relief or cash for work. Such cash "may provide the ability to command food without directly giving the food."[58] Moreover, such cash may have the effect of increasing food availability, for the cash may "pull" private food traders into the area in order to meet the demand.

One deficiency of the "food availability" approach to hunger is that it is purely aggregative, that is, concerned solely with the amount of food in a given area summed over the number of people. Thus, this view has inspired a simplistic and inconclusive debate between, on the one hand, "Malthusian optimists," those who think that *the* answer to the "world food problem" is more food, and, on the other hand, "Malthusian pessimists," those who think the only answer is fewer people.[59] Another – more deadly – consequence is that data concerning food output and availability often lull government officials and others into a false sense of food security and thereby prevent them from taking measures to prevent or mitigate famine. As Sen observes, "The focus on food per head and Malthusian optimism have literally killed millions,"[60] and "the Malthusian perspective of food-to-population ratio has much blood on its hands."[61]

Sen's approach, in contrast, focuses on the command over food on the part of vulnerable occupation groups, households, and, most importantly, individuals.[62] It recognizes that although food and food productivity are indispensable for famine prevention and remedy, much more than food is needed. According to Sen, an approach to hunger that attended exclusively to food and even entitlements to food would stop short of the fundamental goal – to reduce human deprivation and contribute to human well-being and agency.

From food and food entitlements to capability and agency

Different moral theories understand human well-being and the good human life in diverse ways. Capability theorists, for reasons that I examined and evaluated in Chapters 4–6, choose the moral space of two kinds of freedom and achievement: (1) agency freedom and achievement, and (2) those well-being freedoms (capabilities) and achievements ("functionings") that people have reason to value. Capability proponents argue that these moral categories are superior to other candidates for *fundamental* concepts such as resources or commodities, utilities, needs, or rights. Although they do have a role in a complete moral theory and approach to world hunger, these latter concepts refer to "moral furniture" that is in some sense secondary. Commodities are at best *means* to the end of valuable functions and freedoms to so function. Access to – or command over – these commodities fails to address the problem that what benefits one person may harm or have a trivial impact on another person. Utilities are only one among several good functionings and may "muffle" and "mute" deprivations. Moral or human rights, arguably, are not free-standing but are best defined in relation to valued freedoms and achievements.[63]

Recall what capability theorists mean by the term "functioning": a person's functionings consist of his or her physical and mental states ("beings") and activities ("doings"). The most important of these functionings, the failure of which constitutes poverty and the occurrence of which constitutes well-being, "vary from such elementary physical ones as being well-nourished, being adequately clothed and sheltered, avoiding preventable morbidity, etc., to more complex social achievements such as taking part in the life of the community, being able to appear in public without shame, and so on."[64]

A person's capability, I argued in Chapter 6, is that set of functionings *open* to the person, given the person's personal characteristics ("endowment") as well as economic and social opportunities. An alternative formulation is that the general idea of capability refers "to the extent of freedom that people have in pursuing valuable activities or functionings."[65] From the capability perspective, to have well-being, to be and do well, is *to function* and *to be capable of functioning* in ways people have reason to value.

Given the plethora of capabilities and functionings open to individuals and groups, who is to decide which ones are valued and which ones are disvalued? As we saw in Part II, especially in Chapter 6, Sen employs the concept of agency precisely at this point to affirm that *people themselves* – rather than philosophical, scientific, or political guardians – should make their *own* decisions about their individual and communal well-being. To exercise agency is to deliberate, decide, act (rather than being acted upon by others), and make a difference in the world – sometimes enhancing one's own well-being and sometimes not. Although always more or less constrained by conditioning factors, individuals and groups are self-determining when their behavior is not merely the result of internal or external causes, when they do not enact a script set by someone or something else, but, rather, are the authors of their own individual or collective life. As individual and collective agents we decide how to respond to inner urges, external forces, and constraining circumstances, and whether or not to enhance or sacrifice our well-being to some higher cause. If we choose our own individual or communal well-being, we still must deliberate and decide which valued capabilities are most urgent and how they should be weighted and sequenced in relation to one another and to other normative considerations. As agents we also act more or less effectively in the world, making it different than it was before. Although agents may get assistance from others without their agency being compromised, this aid must respect and promote agency or autonomy. As development ethicist David Ellerman reminds us, ethical assistance "helps people help themselves."[66] Let us apply these normative conceptions of well-being (capability and functioning) and agency to further understand, assess, and combat world hunger.

Sen and Drèze give four reasons for moving beyond *actual* food entitlements to a perspective on hunger that includes both well-being (capability and functioning) and agency: (1) individual variability; (2) social variability; (3) diverse means to nourishment; and (4) nourishment as a means to other good goals. Let us briefly consider each.

Individual variability

The capability approach recommends itself in the debate on hunger and food security because it makes sense of and insists on the distinction between, on the one hand, food accessibility and even food intake and, on the other hand, being nourished or free to be nourished. The focus is not merely on food in itself, legal or customary command over food, or even on food as ingested. Rather the capability approach emphasizes food and the access to food as *means* to be well nourished and to have the freedom to be well nourished. Exclusive attention to food, food entitlement, and food intake neglects importantly diverse impacts that the same food can have on different human beings and on the same individual at different times.[67] A particular woman at various stages of her life "requires" different amounts and types of food, depending on her age, her reproductive status, and her state of health. More generally, higher food intake at one time may compensate for lower or no intake at other times without it being true that the person is ever suffering from nutritional distress or malfunctioning. In the hours leading up to and during a marathon, a marathoner undergoes nutritional deprivation, but that same runner may "load up" on carbohydrates the day before the race and enjoy a celebratory repast afterwards.

Instead of identifying hungry people simply by a lack of food intake and mechanically monitoring individuals or dispensing food to them according to nutritional requirements, the focus should be on nutritional *functioning* and those "nutrition-related capabilities that are crucial to human well-being."[68] A person's energy level, strength, weight, and height (within average parameters that permit exceptions), the ability to be productive, and capacities to avoid morbidity and mortality – all valuable functionings or capabilities to function – should supplement, and may be more significant with respect to nutritional well-being than, the mere quantity of food or types of nutrients.[69]

Various measurements of the human body, especially of children, are particularly good ways of measuring degrees of deficient nutritional functioning. "Wasting," which occurs when a child's weight is low for its height, indicates an acute condition due to recent starvation or disease. "Stunting," which takes place when a child's height is low for its age, is a chronic condition due to sustained under-nutrition and – although not immediately life-threatening – indicates poor prospects for long-term physical and cognitive growth. In Ethiopia's Anhara region, for example, 56 percent of the children under five are either stunted or severely stunted.[70] Finally, being "underweight," having a low weight-for-age, is intermediate between wasting and stunting and may be due to recent inadequate food intake, past under-nutrition, or poor health.[71]

Social variability

In addition to differences in individual bodily activities and physical characteristics, the capability approach is sensitive to differences in socially acquired tastes and beliefs with respect to foods.[72] That is, the capability perspective recognizes that these tastes and beliefs can also block the conversion of food to nutritional functioning. Attempts to relieve hunger sometimes fail because hungry people are unable, for some reason, to eat nutritious food. For example, the taste of an available grain may be too different from that to which they are accustomed. Evidence exists that people who receive extra cash for food sometimes fail to improve their nutritional status, apparently because they choose to consume nutritionally deficient foods. If food is to make a difference in people's nutritional and wider well-being, it must be food that the individuals in question are generally willing and able to convert into nutritional functioning. This is not to say that food habits cannot be changed. Rather, it underscores the importance of nutrition education and social criticism of certain food consumption patterns. If people find food distasteful or unacceptable for other reasons, even nutritious food to which people are entitled will not by itself protect or restore nutritional well-being.

Diverse means to being well nourished

If one goal of public action is to protect, restore, and promote nutritional well-being, we must realize that food is only one means of reaching this goal.[73] A preoccupation with food transfers as the way to address impending or actual hunger ignores the many other means that can serve, and may even be necessary for achieving, the end of being (able to be) well nourished. These include "access to health care, medical facilities, elementary education, drinking water, and sanitary facilities."[74] To sharpen the point, it is not just that food is necessary but insufficient for nutritional well-being. Rather, if *food* is to make its contribution (to nourishing people), other factors are needed as well. To achieve nutritional well-being, a hungry, parasite-stricken person needs not only food but also medicine to kill the parasites that cause the malabsorption of consumed food. A disease-enfeebled person who is too weak to eat requires medical care as well as food. An Achean youngster orphaned by the tsunami disaster and wandering in the hills may be ignorant of what to eat and what not to eat. Without clean water, basic sanitation, and health education, recipients of nutritious food aid may succumb to malaria, cholera, dysentery, and typhoid before having the chance to be adequately nourished. Such was the fate of many, especially the very young and very old, in the weeks and months following the South Asian tsunami of December 26, 2004. Barrett and Maxwell, leading scholars on food aid, put this often neglected point well: "food aid often has the desired nutritional and health effects only when it is part of a complete package of assistance."[75]

In particular situations, the best way to combat famine may not be to dispense food at all but to supply remunerated jobs for those who can work and cash for those who cannot.[76] The evidence is impressive, and should be congenial to free-market liberals, that an increase in hungry people's purchasing power often pulls food into a famine area, as private traders find ways of meeting the increased demand.[77] Committed to the ideal of agency, donors – except in extreme emergencies – will eschew rescue camps and food handouts and find ways to enable people to stay in their familiar surroundings and feed themselves or earn the income to do so. As Sen remarks:

> The employment route also happens to encourage the processes of trade and commerce, and does not disrupt economic, social and family lives. The people helped can mostly stay on in their own homes, close to their economic activities (like farming), so that these economic operations are not disrupted. The family life too can continue in a normal way, rather than people being herded into emergency camps. There is also more social continuity, and furthermore, less danger of the spread of infectious diseases, which tend to break out in the overcrowded camps. In general, the approach of relief through employment also allows the potential famine victims to be treated as active agents, rather than as passive recipients of government handouts.[78]

Although Sen should qualify his argument, his point does *not* imply that food aid is never justified. As Barrett and Maxwell argue, food aid is appropriate when a humanitarian emergency exists, local food is scarce, markets fail (people have no money or private food suppliers fail to respond to demand), and government provisions (of money or jobs) are inadequate.[79] Under these extreme circumstances, distributing food to needy but passive recipients may be indispensable (not sufficient) to avert massive and severe capability failure. Such would seem to have been the case with respect to at least 35,000 children in Niger in August 2005.[80]

In sum, famine and chronic hunger are prevented and reduced through strategies that protect and promote entitlements, valuable capabilities, and citizen agency. In the next section, we will return to the hunger-fighting role of national development strategies and international development initiatives. At this juncture, the crucial point is that direct food delivery is only one means and often not the best means for fighting world hunger. The capability approach helpfully interprets and underscores this point when it insists that public and private action can and should employ an array of complementary strategies to achieve the end of nutritional well-being for all. Committed to agency as well as valuable capabilities, the capability approach insists that local and national communities have "default" responsibility for selecting and implementing hunger-reducing strategies as well as for prioritizing them in relation to one another and to other development goals. Help from other nations and global institutions should play a supplementary or backup role – when local and national institutions are unable or unwilling to attack hunger effectively.

Food as a means to other good goals

The capability approach helps widen our vision to see that the food that hungry people command and consume can accomplish much more than giving them nutritional well-being. Nutritional well-being is only one element in human well-being; the overcoming of transitory or chronic hunger also enables people and their governments to protect and promote other ingredients of well-being. Being adequately nourished, for instance, contributes to healthy functioning that is both good in itself and indispensable to the freedom to avoid premature death and fight off or recover from disease. Having nutritional well-being and good health, in turn, is crucial to acquiring and exercising other capabilities that people have reason to value, such as being able to learn, think, deliberate, and choose, as well as to be a good pupil, friend, householder, parent, worker, or citizen. A recent report on malnutrition in Ethiopia observes that those who survive malnutrition face bleak prospects, as do their countries that depend on their productivity:

Almost half of Ethiopia's children are malnourished, and most do not die. Some suffer a different fate. Robbed of vital nutrients as children, they grow up stunted and sickly, weaklings in a land that still runs on manual labor. Some become intellectually stunted adults, shorn of as many as 15 I.Q. points, unable to learn or even to concentrate, inclined to drop out of school early.[81]

Similarly, as I argued in the last chapter, an agency-focused capability approach reinforces the commonsense point that too much food or an unbalanced diet – for example, a surplus of calories or deficit in proteins, vitamins, and minerals – limits what persons can do and be. Obesity, due to an excess of junk food consumption and a lack of exercise, besets children in New Delhi[82] as well as New Rochelle.

Because good food and food entitlements can have so many beneficial consequences in people's lives, creative development programs and projects find ways in which people can link, on the one hand, food assistance, distribution, access, and utilization, to, on the other hand, the generation or protection of other valuable activities and freedoms.[83] Because nutritional deficiencies affect fetal and infant development, pregnant and lactating women (and their infants) acquire food supplements in health clinics. Since hungry children do not learn well and certain nutritional and micronutrient deficiencies result in visual and cognitive impairment, school children eat nutritionally balanced and micronutrient-fortified school meals. In addition to these measures, the Millennium Project appropriately recommends that schools "provide take-home rations as an incentive for school attendance."[84] "Food for work" programs establish close links between nutritional well-being and socially productive activity. Just as work can be paid for in either food or cash – with which food can be purchased – so entitlements to and consumption of food can result in greater productivity. Similarly, while nutritional deficits force people to struggle to survive, leaving them scant time or energy to be politically active, adequate nourishment makes possible sustained political involvement – both a component of well-being and an exercise of agency. Moreover, the provision of meals in communal projects and political activity can function as an incentive for participation in those activities. The food dispensed in these ways – whether in health clinics, schools, work projects, or political activities – additionally can promote long-term development insofar as the food is grown locally or regionally rather than in developed countries.[85]

A word of caution, however, is in order. Just as ethics and ethical codes sometimes function to promote or be a cover for corruption and other morally problematic practices, so much food aid may cause or camouflage human ill-being. Ballyhooed food drops in Afghanistan and Iraq have harmed houses and people and diverted attention from the civilian casualties ("collateral damage") resulting from US military intervention. Food aid may result in and cover up human ill-being as well as be a means to various dimensions of human well-being. Such risks make it all the more important to keep our eyes on development ends as well as means.

From capability and agency to development as freedom

Nutritional well-being, then, is both constitutive of and a means to human development conceived as both well-being and agency, both freedoms and achievements. And human development is or should be the ultimate purpose of socioeconomic development. Hence, a more comprehensive approach to world hunger will explicitly aim for good development. The dichotomy of famine relief or food aid, on the one hand, and long-term development, on the other, does more harm than good. As Drèze and Sen observe: "The nature of the problem of hunger – both famines and endemic deprivation – calls for a broader political economic analysis taking note of the variety of influences that have a bearing on the commodity commands and basic capabilities that people enjoy."[86]

The alleged dilemma between "relief" and "development" is a much exaggerated one, and greater attention should be paid to the positive links between the best sort of famine prevention and emergency relief, on the one hand, and development ends and means, on the other.[87]

One of the ends (as well as means) of development should be to eliminate hunger. Among the Millennium Development Goals, to which 191 countries agreed in 2002, is that of halving global hunger by 2015.[88] The overwhelming majority of US citizens not only embrace these goals but "support the idea that the US should not only try to help alleviate hunger, but should also address the long-term goal of helping poor countries develop their economies," especially through educational programs and improved opportunities for women and girls.[89] Moreover, impressive evidence exists that genuine socioeconomic development is in fact the best prevention and long-term cure for hunger.[90] If such is the case, then attempts to understand and eradicate hunger must also be included in the effort to explain and achieve development. As noted in the last section, this is not to say that emergency food aid should cease or take a back seat to rehabilitation and development. Rather, action taken to relieve both short-term and long-term hunger should be executed from a "developmental perspective."

Although defensible development strategies may differ in diverse contexts, comprehensive empirical investigations of development successes and failures reveal some common – although quite general – features in developmentally structured food strategy. Drèze and Sen observe:

> It is not hard to see what is needed for the elimination of endemic undernutrition and deprivation. People earn their means of living through employment and production, and they use these means to achieve certain functionings which make up their living. Entitlements and the corresponding capabilities can be promoted by the expansion of private incomes on a widespread basis, including all the deprived sections of the population. They can also be promoted by extensive public provisioning of the basic essentials for good living such as health care, education and food. Indeed, participatory growth and public provision are among the chief architects of the elimination of endemic deprivation – illustrated amply by historical experiences across the world. The basic challenge of "social security" (in the broad sense in which we have used this term) is to combine these instruments of action to guarantee adequate living standards to all.[91]

Development goals, means, and obstacles must be viewed as political and social as well as economic. A country should not be called fully developed, no matter how high are its rates of economic growth, if it lacks good governance and fails to be reasonably democratic. China should not be said to be more developed now than twenty years ago simply because it has increased its economic productivity. At best China could be said to exhibit developmental improvement along only some variables. A society has not realized its highest potential if it makes economic progress but does not progress in political freedoms and rights. Moreover, political and cultural factors can promote the achievement of more narrowly construed economic goals, such as the guarantee of "adequate living standards to all."

Even when the proximate causes of famine lie outside the country, one of the deepest causes of famine, Sen persuasively argues, is "the alienation of the rulers from those ruled." The starkest examples are authoritarian China in 1959–62 and Sudan since 1985. Moreover, citizen agency and participation, political pluralism, and democratization often have beneficial effects on preventing and combating hunger and achieving other economically related goals. One of Drèze and Sen's greatest contributions is to point out the role of democratic openness, political pluralism, adversarial politics, and a free press in preventing famine and overcoming chronic hunger. As Sen has famously noted, "no famine has ever taken place in the history of the world in a functioning democracy – be it economically rich (as in contemporary Europe or North America) or relatively poor (as in post-independence India, or Botswana, or Zimbabwe)."[92]

It is not sufficient to note a correlation between democracy and famine prevention. One must also supply a plausible causal story for *how* democracy prevents famines. Sen offers two such causal factors. First, in a multiparty democracy with contested elections, governmental leaders – if they want to be reelected – have a political incentive to avert famine. If they fail to prevent famine by acts of omission or commission, the "accusing finger"[93] of public criticism can result in an early departure from the public stage. In contrast, in a nondemocracy, especially an authoritarian state, famine is unlikely to dislodge or undermine a government or its leaders: "if there are no elections, no opposition parties, no scope for uncensored public criticisms, then those in authority don't have to suffer the political consequences of their failure to prevent famines."[94] Reinforcing these political disincentives are personal disincentives. Why should the governmental and military authorities in an authoritarian state worry about famines? In addition to being protected from electoral change, they will never *themselves* suffer from this lack of food or well-being.

A second explanation for democracy's important role in preventing famine concerns information. Opposition parties, a free and investigative press, and public discussion contribute to riveting governmental attention on impending famines, revealing the scope of the problem, and communicating effective solutions. In contrast, hunger intensifies and famine erupts due to press censorship, bureaucratic filtering out of bad news from below, and a government being misled by its own optimistic propaganda. Sen drives the point home: "I would argue that a free press and an active political opposition constitute the best early-warning system a country threatened by famines can have."[95] More and better information, however, is not sufficient. Also important are the broad-based commitments of national, bilateral, and multilateral organizations to give voices to the hungry or, better, enable such voices to be included and heard. The World Food Programme summarizes the evidence from many South Asian countries:

> Giving the disadvantaged hungry poor a voice requires more explicit public action [than merely international financial institutions sharing knowledge]. This is especially true for women, children, and minorities, who are not able to sufficiently express their needs and views in public and in the political arena. Advocacy for the food insecure in a democratic society means raising awareness amongst decisions makers, publishing important findings, raising funds for financing interventions, building networks of concerned individuals and organizations, creating consensus on objectives and means of food assistance, and also establishing a vision for the future.[96]

If we keep the language of development as shorthand for beneficial change, it has become evident, as I examine in more detail in later chapters, that good national and subnational development requires certain sorts of regional and global institutions and is undermined by other types. Although the nation-state remains an important unit of development – and sometimes the most important unit – regional and global institutions also have significant roles to play in combating hunger and enabling development. National development and the relations among various countries should be considered in the context of global forces and institutions, such as transnational corporations, bilateral trading pacts, the Bretton Woods financial institutions, and the United Nations system. The UN World Food Programme has been an especially important global player in promoting food aid for development as well as development for "food security."[97] Overcoming both acute and chronic hunger is both an end and a means of good global development. Local and national development can contribute to and benefit from global development.

Understanding and sustainably reducing hunger require a developmental perspective in which national and global development is understood as the solution to human deprivation and powerlessness. This perspective should include invariant but general goals and context-specific economic and non-economic strategies. Development, as beneficial societal change, applies to the structure and interaction of subnational, national, and global institutions.

It is a step forward that the norm of agency protection and agency promotion is beginning to inform the choice of general strategies to promote nutritional well-being. Those food security strategies that have proven to be most effective include strong components of citizen participation. The World Food Programme, for example, summarizes lessons learned from food security strategies in several South Asian countries: "Participatory approaches should be used in the selections and design of activities. The systematic involvement of beneficiaries is a precondition of sustainability."[98] Likewise, Barrett and Maxwell clearly recognize that the new rights-based approach to food aid and development requires that donors and governments take seriously the right of hungry people to participate in making decisions that affect them: "While participation has long been a 'good word' in development and humanitarian work, the emergent approach demands the right of people to participate in decisions and choices about meeting their food security requirements."[99] Agency freedoms and achievement are among the means as well as the ends of ethically based development. Even the Millennium Development Project, which overall has a top-down, economic growth, and technocratic emphasis, recognizes that hunger alleviation projects fail if local communities do not participate in defining food security problems and implementing solutions. Adopting what the Project calls "a people-centered approach," *Halving Hunger* unequivocally asserts: "Any strategy to reduce hunger must therefore have as a central tenet the empowerment of the poor through full participation in decision-making and implementation."[100] The report recommends that national experts train local citizens to be agricultural and nutrition paraprofessionals, field workers, and dialogue facilitators or animators.[101] It also recognizes that "consultation" is not enough and that ordinary citizens or their representatives must be involved through "dialogue" in defining food security needs and costs, determining priorities, and implementing decisions.[102]

Yet the Millennium Development Project's occasional anti-elitist appeal to community dialogue and decision-making seems to be merely populist rhetoric in relation to its fundamentally technocratic and top-down approach. The report rightly advocates dialogue and decision-making that include all stakeholders, the rich and powerful as well as the poor and food insecure. And the document correctly reflects the concern that various elites might capture or dominate national and local deliberations. Yet the report offers no institutional designs to mitigate, let alone eliminate, this danger of elite capture or to provide regular channels for citizen deliberation and choice. Except for a vague reference to "representatives of civil society," the report's list of stakeholders is tilted toward local, national, and global elites:

Key stakeholders include ministries of agriculture, health, social services, environment, water, transport, commerce, planning, and finance and the government body responsible for food aid. They also include representatives of civil society, the private sector, banks, and other financial institutions, and the donor community, including multilateral and bilateral institutions.[103]

Moreover, while the document calls for "good governance," it defines this fashionable buzzword largely in relation to transparency and the rule of law and refrains from any mention of the "D" word – "democracy."[104] If we take citizen agency seriously in relation to hunger and other capability failures, then public discussion and democratic decision-making must be institutionalized at national and global as well as local levels. I return to these issues in Part IV.

From the ethics of aid to an ethics for development

The implication of my argument thus far is that the ethics of food assistance should be incorporated within and subordinated to an ethics of and for development at all levels – local, national, and global. International development ethics evaluates the basic goals and appropriate strategies for morally desirable social change. No longer fixated on the stark options of earlier debates – food aid versus no food aid, aid as duty versus aid as charity – development ethics asks instead what kind of aid is morally defensible and, even more fundamentally, what sort of national and global development food assistance *should* foster.

As early as the mid-1950s, development economists have been examining the developmental impact of different kinds of food aid and trying to design famine relief and development assistance that would contribute to rather than undermine long-term development goals.[105] Yet, in the 1970s, analytic philosophers such as Peter Singer, and others, such as Garrett Hardin, by and large failed to refer to the nuanced debate that had been going on for more than twenty years. Furthermore, as one expert on food aid remarks, "many of them did not feel it important to become more than superficially familiar with the technical or institutional aspects of food production, distribution, or policy."[106] As happens all too often, the owl of Minerva – Hegel's image for the philosopher – takes wing at dusk and "comes on the scene too late to give . . . instruction as to what the world ought to be."[107]

Moreover, when philosophers did try to analyze development, they usually emphasized development *aid* that rich countries provided to impoverished recipients (rather than the development *goals* that poor countries set and pursued *for themselves*), or how rich country policies caused food deficits in poor countries. By the mid-1980s, however, ethicists – as we saw in Chapters 1 and 2 – became increasingly aware that they could not talk about morally justified or unjustified development aid from the standpoint of outside donors without first talking about the "beneficiary's" own development philosophies, goals, strategies, leadership, and will. One marked advantage of the agency and capability ethic is that it puts its highest priority on a nation's intellectual and institutional capability for *self*-development without denying the role of outsider intellectual and practical help.

In earlier chapters I showed that a new field or cross-boundary discipline – international development ethics – has emerged to evaluate existing development paths and identify better ones. This new field is practiced in ways that differ markedly from the earlier ethics of famine relief. Rather than being predominantly if not exclusively the work of white males from rich and English-speaking countries, as was the case in the initial ethics of famine relief, international development ethics is an inquiry that includes participants from a variety of nations, groups, and moral traditions, all of whom seek an international consensus about problems of international scope. It has become evident that policy analysts and ethicists – whether from "developing" countries or "developed" countries – should neither uncritically impose alien norms nor simply accept the operative or professed values implicit in a particular country's established development path. Rather, as I have argued elsewhere, cultural insiders, cultural outsiders, and insider-outsider hybrids should engage in an ongoing and critical dialogue that includes explicit ethical analysis, assessment, and construction with respect to the ends and means of national, regional, and global change.[108]

Moreover, development ethics, as I argued in Part I and have illustrated in this chapter, is interdisciplinary rather than exclusively philosophical. It eschews merely abstract ethical reflection and Olympian pronouncements and instead relates – in a variety of ways – values to relevant facts about hunger and other deprivations. Development ethicists, as we have seen in Goulet's and Sen and Drèze's work on hunger, evaluate (1) the normative assumptions of different development models, (2) the empirical categories employed to interpret, explain, and forecast the facts, and (3) development programs, strategies, and institutions.

Development ethics straddles the theory/practice distinction. Its practitioners are informed by as well as engage in dialogue with policy-makers and development activists. Instead of being an exclusively academic exercise, development ethics (in which theorists and practitioners cooperatively engage) assesses the moral costs and benefits of current development policies, programs, and projects as well as articulate alternative development visions.

In this chapter I have not only drawn on the work of development ethicists with respect to acute, hidden, and chronic hunger and ways of combating it, but I have also analyzed and evaluated more recent academic and policy work on hunger, food aid, and development. We have seen that the Millennium Development Project's *Halving Hunger* advocates a "people-centered approach" to eliminating global hunger and poverty but compromises this perspective with a predominantly technocratic and paternalistic strategy. The best scholars in the field of food aid, Barrett and Maxwell, freely acknowledge the pivotal role of Sen and their indebtedness to Drèze and Sen's approach to understanding and combating global hunger. Although they fail to grasp adequately the normative and human rights dimensions of Drèze and Sen's work on hunger and development, Barrett and Maxwell themselves assume a normative rights-based approach to nutritional well-being and development. They affirm the right to food as part of a package of human rights and, as we saw above, acknowledge the importance of hungry people's right to participate in making those decisions that affect them. In future work I shall consider the relations between the agency-focused capability approach and various explicitly rights-based approaches to world hunger and other forms of poverty. Especially important will be investigating who has responsibility for reducing hunger and how strong this obligation is in the face of competing duties.

Barrett and Maxwell offer compelling evidence that various donor interests unrelated to combating hunger have dominated and distorted food aid for fifty years.[109] Among these non-developmental aims, which have resulted in less food aid getting to recipients than otherwise would have been the case, are those of supporting US farm prices, dumping farm surpluses, maintaining the US maritime industry, and advancing US geo-strategic interests. If the US Food for Peace program purchased food in food-impoverished countries or their nearby neighbors, US farmers, millers, and shippers would lose money, but food would arrive more quickly in hunger-stricken countries and the purchases would benefit the local economies.[110] When US food aid has failed to free itself from its many masters and to combat hunger directly, US aid has been top-down, inefficient, and often not received by those that need it most.

I applaud Barrett and Maxwell's critique of US food aid, their emphasis on a right to food security and citizen participation, and their resultant recasting of food aid from an emphasis on donor interest to a "recipient-oriented food aid system."[111] I urge, however, in keeping with their emphasis on participation rights, that Barrett and Maxwell join development ethicists in abandoning recipient and beneficiary language and replacing it with the language of agency and deliberative participation. Just as I argue that Sen has appropriately supplemented his earlier emphasis on capability and functioning with his more recent underscoring of agency and public discussion, so I encourage food aid scholars like Barrett and Maxwell to jettison the residue of beneficent paternalism and embrace the fuller implications of "agency-oriented human development" – the expansion of *both* agency and well-being freedom. One role of development philosophy is to identify the most promising conceptual, institutional, and strategic advances, criticize what limits these advances from flowering more fully, and articulate a vision of even more progressive ends and means.

Much, of course, remains to be done in applying development ethics to understanding and reducing world hunger. One task, already mentioned, is to consider the merits of a rights-based approach to hunger and the allocation of duties to fulfill the right not to be hungry. Another task is a *detailed* analysis and ethical assessment of the *specific* hunger-reducing strategies and tactics proposed by the World Food Programme, *Halving Hunger*, and Barrett and Maxwell, *Food Aid After Fifty Years*. Such scrutiny and evaluation would draw on what I have offered in this chapter – a reframing, in the light of the capability and agency approach to development, of the philosophical and policy debates concerning world hunger and food aid.

Concluding remarks

Famine, food aid, and the ethics of famine relief remain – as they were in the early and mid-1970s – pressing personal, national, and global challenges. Philosophers and other ethicists can play a role in meeting these challenges and thereby reducing world hunger. This goal is best achieved, however, when the questions of world hunger and moral obligation are reframed and widened. I have argued that development ethicists, policymakers, and citizens must emphasize (1) interpretative and strategic concepts instead of moral foundations, (2) persistent malnutrition instead of famine, (3) prevention rather than treatment of hunger, (4) food entitlements instead of food availability, (5) human capability and agency rather than food and entitlements, and (6) local and national self-development rather than external food aid and development assistance. My intent is not to reject the second term in each pair but to subordinate each of them to the first terms – concepts at once more fundamental and comprehensive.

Overall, the refocusing I advocate has conceived an ethics of food aid as part of a more basic and inclusive ethics for development. Since the best long-term cure for hunger is good national and global development, we must put emergency and project food aid in a developmental perspective and incorporate an ethics of famine relief into an ethics of and for national and global development. With the capability approach to agency-oriented development, we can supplement a focus on food with an emphasis on agency and capability as the means and ends of development as freedom. To avoid the fallacy of misplaced concreteness is not to eschew abstractions but to place them in their proper relation to one another and to the concrete world of facts and values.

NOTES

This chapter considerably expands and modifies my essay "Hunger, Capability, and Development," in *World Hunger and Morality*, 2nd edn., ed. William Aiken and Hugh La Follette (Upper Saddle River, NJ: Prentice-Hall, 1996), 211–30. I am grateful to the editors for comments on the original essay and to Verna Gehring, Hugh La Follette, and Michael Taylor for very helpful criticisms of a draft of the present chapter. I gave the original paper at the University of Maryland, the University of Costa Rica, Yale University, and St. Mary's College, Maryland.

1. UN Millennium Project Task Force on Hunger, *Halving Hunger: It Can Be Done* (London, and Sterling, VA: Earthscan, 2005), 1.
2. Christopher B. Barrett and Daniel G. Maxwell, *Food Aid After Fifty Years: Recasting Its Role* (London: Routledge, 2005), 6. At 260, n. 10, Barrett and Maxwell cite the Food Balance Sheets, available from the Food and Agriculture Organization (FAO) of the United Nations through FAOSTAT: <http://apps.fao.org>.
3. Food and Agricultural Organization of the United Nations, *Food Insecurity in the World 2004* (Rome: FAO, 2004), 6. See also L. C. Smith, "Can FAO's Measure of Chronic Undernourishment Be Strengthened?" *Food Policy*, 23, 5 (1998), 425–45; Barrett and Maxwell, *Food Aid After Fifty Years*, 7–8; UN Millennium Project Task Force on Hunger, *Halving Hunger*, 1.
4. Barrett and Maxwell, *Food Aid After Fifty Years*, 8.
5. UN Millennium Development Project, *Halving Hunger*, 18, 35.

6. Food and Agricultural Organization of the United Nations, *The State of Food Insecurity in the World 2004*, 6.
7. For the most important essays and anthologies in the 1970s and 1980s addressing world hunger and moral obligation, see above, ch. 1, nn. 20, 22, and 23. Some of the seminal early papers as well as more recent studies appear in *World Hunger and Morality*, ed. Aiken and La Follette.
8. See Barrett and Maxwell, *Food Aid After Fifty Years*, esp. ch. 2.
9. Denis Goulet, "World Hunger: Putting Development Ethics to the Test," *Christianity and Crisis* (May 26, 1975): 125.
10. Ibid.
11. Ibid., 125–6.
12. Amartya Sen, *Poverty and Famines: An Essay on Entitlement and Deprivation* (Oxford: Clarendon Press, 1981).
13. Alfred North Whitehead, *Science and the Modern World* (New York: Macmillan, 1925), 200.
14. Although it is beyond the scope of this chapter, the same claim could be made about other sorts of emergency assistance, such as medical supplies, clothing, housing materials, cattle, and agricultural inputs.
15. Food and Agriculture Organization of the United Nations, *The State of Food Insecurity in the World 2004*, 4. Two other recent studies of combating hunger and promoting food security – Barrett and Maxwell, *Food Aid After Fifty Years*, 111–18; and UN Millennium Project Task Force on Hunger, *Halving Hunger*, ch. 1, 32–4 – affirm that countries and citizens have moral obligations to alleviate hunger and poverty, but these same studies refrain from developing any moral arguments for this conclusion. The Program on International Policy Attitudes (PIPA) at the University of Maryland found in 2001, as it had in 1995 and 1999, that with respect to US citizens "overwhelming majorities" – almost 80 percent in all three polls – "are supportive of efforts to alleviate hunger and poverty – much more so than for foreign aid overall." Insofar as Americans have reservations about aid, it is not because they believe it lacks moral justification, but because they worry that US aid money ends up "in the pockets of corrupt officials and programs overseas," that aid programs "lack effectiveness" and help authoritarian regimes to violate human rights, and that America gives too much unilateral aid rather than working through multilateral or private channels: PIPA, "Americans on Foreign Aid and World Hunger: A Study of US Policy Attitudes" (February 2, 2001); see PIPA, "Americans on Addressing World Poverty" (June 30, 2005). The PIPA reports are available online at <www.pipa.org> and were accessed on January 24, 2006.
16. See, for example, Catherine W. Wilson, "On Some Alleged Limitations to Moral Endeavor," *Journal of Philosophy*, 90 (1993): 275–89; Garrett Cullity, "International Aid and the Scope of Kindness," *Ethics*, 105 (1994): 99–127; and *The Moral Demands of Affluence* (Oxford: Clarendon Press, 2004); Peter Singer, *One World: The Ethics of Globalization*, 2nd edn. (New Haven and London: Yale University Press, 2004); "Poverty, Facts, and Political Philosophies: Response to 'More than Charity,'" *Ethics and International Affairs*, 16 (2002): 121–4; "Achieving the Best Outcome: Final Rejoinder," *Ethics*

and International Affairs, 16, 1 (2002): 127–8; and "What Should a Billionaire Give – and What Should You?," *New York Times Magazine* (December 17, 2006); Andrew Kuper, "More Than Charity: Cosmopolitan Alternatives to the 'Singer Solution,'" *Ethics and International Affairs*, 16 (2002): 107–20; Pablo Gilabert, "The Duty to Eradicate Global Poverty: Positive or Negative?," *Ethical Theory and Moral Practice*, 7 (2004): 537–50; Dale Jamieson, "Duties to the Distant: Aid, Assistance, and Intervention in the Developing World," *Journal of Ethics*, 9 (2005): 151–70; Mathias Risse, "What We Owe to the Global Poor," *Journal of Ethics*, 9 (2005): 81–117; Judith Lichtenberg, "Famine, Affluence, and Psychology," in *Singer Under Fire*, ed. Jeffrey Schaler (Chicago: Open Court, forthcoming). The most important recent anthology on aid to the distant poor is *The Ethics of Assistance: Morality and the Distant Needy*, ed. Deen Chatterjee (Cambridge: Cambridge University Press, 2004). It is interesting but regrettable that this volume, which includes Peter Singer, "Outsiders: Our Obligations to Those beyond Our Borders" (11–32), abstracted so much from the question of "hunger" and "food aid" that neither term appears in its short index. It is beyond the scope of this chapter to consider the best way to think about our general duty to assist others and the nature and weight of our particular duty to aid the foreign needy.

17. My views in the last two paragraphs are indebted to conversations with Hugh La Follette.

18. *World Hunger and Moral Obligation*, ed. William Aiken and Hugh La Follette (Englewood Cliffs, NJ: Prentice-Hall, 1977), 10.

19. Singer, *One World*, 2nd edn., 189.

20. For a recent and nuanced treatment of the issues, one that draws fruitfully on some of Amartya Sen's early papers on value judgments, see Hilary Putnam, *The Collapse of the Fact/Value Dichotomy and Other Essays* (Cambridge, MA, and London: Harvard University Press, 2002).

21. Isabel Teotonio, "When Children are Too Weak to Cry," *Toronto Star* (August 6, 2005), A 9.

22. See Stephen Devereux, *The Theories of Famine* (London: Harvester Wheatsheaf, 1993), chs. 2 and 13; Alex De Waal, *Famine Crimes: Politics and the Disaster Relief Industry in Africa* (London: James Currey; Bloomington, IN: Indiana University Press, 1997).

23. I owe the idea of perceiving or discerning "ethical salience" to Nancy Sherman, *The Fabric of Character: Aristotle's Theory of Virtue* (Oxford: Clarendon Press, 1989), 28–44. See also Martha Nussbaum, *Love's Knowledge: Essays on Philosophy and Literature* (New York and Oxford: Oxford University Press, 1990), esp. chs. 2 and 5.

24. For a discussion of how ethical principles constrain what counts as relevant and irrelevant factual information, see Amartya Sen, "Well-being, Agency, and Freedom: The Dewey Lectures 1984," *Journal of Philosophy*, 82 (1985): 169–84; *Inequality Reexamined*, 73–5; *Development as Freedom*, 54–62, 92–4. Sherman discusses the way in which the agent's "reading of the circumstances" may be influenced by his or her moral or immoral character; see *The Fabric of Character*, 29. To prevent misunderstanding, I am not claiming that one's ethical lenses structure the facts like cookie-cutters shape dough.

Rather, different ethical lenses focus on different aspects or properties of the factual field. Just as switching ethical lenses can reveal hitherto neglected but important facts, so deeper immersion in the facts of the matter, for instance awareness of the "facts of famine," can help change our ethical judgments. We need both new and better ways of looking at the world, which ethics provides, as well as deeper and broader experience of human deprivation and achievements.

25. Sherman, *The Fabric of Character*, 30.

26. See especially Sen and Drèze's works on hunger and food aid in The World Institute for Development Economics Research (WIDER) series Studies in Development Economics: Jean Drèze and Amartya Sen, *Hunger and Public Action* (Oxford: Clarendon Press, 1989); *The Political Economy of Hunger*, 3 vols.: I: *Entitlement and Well-being*; II: *Famine and Prevention*; III: *Endemic Hunger*, ed. Jean Drèze and Amartya Sen (Oxford: Clarendon Press, 1990).

27. See Amartya Sen, "The Right Not to be Hungry," in *Contemporary Philosophy: A New Survey*, II (The Hague: Martinus Nijhoff, 1982), 343–60.

28. Drèze and Sen, *Hunger and Public Action*, 273.

29. Just as one's focus can be too narrow, so it can also be so broad as to be disabling. Blaming or praising such large formations as capitalism, socialism, industrialism, globalization, or Northern and Western imperialism commits fallacies of hasty generalization and over simplification that deter examination of the complex of causes that are both specific and alterable in the short, medium, and long run. I owe this point to discussions with James W. Nickel.

30. Drèze and Sen, *Hunger and Public Action*, 24.

31. Although Aiken and La Follette, the editors of the 1977 anthology *World Hunger and Moral Obligation*, did distinguish famine and chronic hunger (see p. 1), they and the anthology's other contributors attended almost exclusively to famine victims rather than those who were chronically hungry or suffering malnutrition following natural disaster.

32. Sara Millman and Robert W. Kates, "Toward Understanding Hunger," in *Hunger in History: Food Shortage, Poverty, and Deprivation*, ed. Lucile F. Newman (Oxford, and Cambridge, MA: Blackwell, 1990), 3. Notice that this definition of hunger is significantly different from one popular meaning of hunger, which the UN Millennium Project Task Force on Hunger characterizes as "the subjective feeling of discomfort that follows a period without eating": *Halving Hunger*, 19. Millman and Kates's definition is similar to the World Bank's (1986) and World Food Summit's (1996) definition of food insecurity as the absence of food security, defined as "access by all people at all times to sufficient food for an active and healthy life": see World Bank, *Poverty and Hunger: Issues and Options for Food Security in Developing Countries* (Washington, DC: World Bank, 1986); Food and Agricultural Organization of the United Nations, "Rome Declaration on World Food Security and World Food Summit Plan of Action," (1996). The importance of "activity" and an "active and healthy life" fits well, we shall see, with the ideal of agency-oriented development.

33. John Osgood Field, "Understanding Famine," in *The Challenge of Famine: Recent Experience, Lessons Learned*, ed. John Osgood Field (West Hartford,

CT: Kumarian Press, 1993), 20. See also Barrett and Maxwell, *Food Aid After Fifty Years*, 111.

34. Drèze and Sen, *Hunger and Public Action*, 7.
35. Peter Walker, *Famine Early Warning Systems: Victims and Destitution* (London: Earthscan, 1989), 6; cited in Devereux, *The Theories of Famine*, 16, 181.
36. Perhaps to focus more attention on chronic hunger, scholars and policy analysts increasingly replace the concept of famine with that of acute or transitory hunger, rather than subsuming the former into the latter. It is noteworthy that neither the Millennium Project Task Force on Hunger, *Halving Hunger*, nor Barrett and Maxwell, *Food Aid After Fifty Years*, has entries for "famine" in its glossary. In 2005, reporters increasingly used the "F" word to describe conditions in Niger in which 3.6 million people in 3,000 villages were at risk. Among those most needy were an estimated 192,000 children, 32,000 of whom were severely malnourished in the sense that they required "special feeding and medical assistance": Teotonio, "When Children are Too Weak to Cry," 9. Teotonio reported that "Ethiopia, Burkina Faso, and Mali . . . are facing similar predicaments."
37. The authors of *Halving Hunger* helpfully distinguish "hidden hunger" from both the acute and chronic varieties. On this account, hidden hunger is due to a lack of essential micronutrients, such as vitamins A and B, and minerals and other nutrients, such as iron, iodine, and folic acid. If they consume adequate calories and protein, those suffering from such deficiencies may appear well nourished. Hence, in contrast to famine and other forms of acute hunger, hidden hunger – even more than chronic hunger – is often off national and global radar screens. See Millennium Development Project Task Force on Hunger, *Halving Hunger*, 2; and Michael Wines, "Malnutrition is Cheating Its Survivors, and Africa's Future," *New York Times* (December 28, 2006), A 1.
38. Drèze and Sen, *Hunger and Public Action*, 7–8. Of course, in extreme emergencies, such as the tsunami in December 2004 or Katrina's devastation of New Orleans in August 2005, "existing distributional mechanisms" may themselves be destroyed and speedy emergency and external relief, such as national or international distribution of rations, are called for.
39. Ibid., 158.
40. This failing, of course, is unique neither to philosophers nor to the issue of combating hunger. I owe this important point to Hugh La Follette.
41. Onora O'Neill, "Lifeboat Earth," in *World Hunger and Moral Obligation*, ed. Aiken and LaFollette, 161–4.
42. Ibid., 163.
43. Drèze and Sen, *Hunger and Public Action*, 47.
44. Sen, *Development as Freedom*, 175 (endnote omitted). See also ibid., 179.
45. See Drèze and Sen, *Hunger and Public Action*, ch. 8; Field, "Understanding Famine," 21.
46. Sen, *Development as Freedom*, 179.
47. Since 1965, the proportion of hungry people in the world has declined from 33 percent to 18 percent in 2005. See Millennium Development Project Task Force on Hunger, *Halving Hunger*, xv.

48. Drèze and Sen, *Hunger and Public Action*, 276.
49. *Halving Hunger*, 97. This Millennium Project Task Force on Hunger cites two USAID studies: USAID, "Ethiopia – Drought: Fact Sheet #17 (FY 2003)" (Washington, DC: Bureau for Democracy, Conflict, and Humanitarian Assistance, Office of US, Foreign Disaster Assistance, 2003); and USAID, "Ethiopia: Complex Health/Food Insecurity Emergency Situation Report #1 (FY 2004)" (Washington, DC: USAID, 2004).
50. Garrett Hardin, "Lifeboat Ethics: The Case Against Helping the Poor," in *World Hunger and Moral Obligation*, ed. Aiken and LaFollette, 19.
51. Robert W. Kates and Sara Millman, "On Ending Hunger: The Lessons of History," in *Hunger in History*, 404. See also Barrett and Maxwell, *Food Aid After Fifty Years*, 6.
52. Amartya Sen, "The Food Problem: Theory and Practice," *Third World Quarterly*, 3 (July 1982): 454.
53. Robert Nozick, *Anarchy, State and Utopia* (New York: Basic Books, 1974), esp. ch. 7.
54. It would be interesting to consider to what extent Sen's avowedly descriptive use of "entitlement" also has a prescriptive "charge" (suggested when Sen says that people "enjoy" entitlements), and whether, as La Follette has contended in conversation, Sen should be more explicit about this prescriptivity. Sen states that "the entitlement of a person stands for the set of different alternative commodity bundles that the person can acquire through the use of the various legal channels of acquirement open to someone in his position": "Food, Economics and Entitlements," in *The Political Economy of Hunger*, I: *Entitlement and Well-being*, ed. Drèze and Sen. In *Development as Freedom*, 9, Sen says: "What we have to concentrate on is not the total food supply but the 'entitlement' that each person enjoys: the commodities over which she can establish her ownership and command." For an incisive clarification and defense of Sen's notion of entitlement and its application to famine, see Siddiq Osmani, "The Entitlement Approach to Famine: An Assessment," in *Choice, Welfare, and Development: A Festschrift for Amartya K. Sen*, ed. Kaushik Basu, P.K. Pattanaik, and K. Suzamura (Oxford: Clarendon Press; New York: Oxford University Press, 1995), 253–94, esp. 254–60.
55. See Drèze and Sen, *Hunger and Public Action*, 10–11; Amartya Sen, *Inequality Reexamined* (New York: Russell Sage Foundation; Cambridge, MA: Harvard University Press, 1992), 149–50; Barrett and Maxwell, *Food Aid After Fifty Years*, 109. Charles Gore shows that Sen has gradually expanded his concept of entitlement to include nonlegal – primarily household – rules, but persuasively argues that Sen needs to go further in recognizing the ways in which "socially approved moral rules" may be extra-legal and even anti-legal. See Charles Gore, "Entitlement Relations and 'Unruly' Social Practices: A Comment on the Work of Amartya Sen," *Journal of Development Economics*, 29 (1993): 429–60.
56. Barrett and Maxwell, *Food Aid After Fifty Years*, 110.
57. Amartya Sen, "Food Entitlements and Economic Chains," in *Hunger in History*, ed. Millman and Kates, 377.

58. Amartya Sen, "Food, Economics and Entitlements," in *The Political Economy of Hunger*, I: *Entitlement and Well-being*, ed. Drèze and Sen, 43.

59. Sen, "The Food Problem," 447–51. Cf. Drèze and Sen, *Hunger and Public Action*, 24–5; and "Food, Economics, and Entitlements," 35–6.

60. Sen, "The Food Problem," 450. Cf. Amartya Sen, *Poverty and Famines: An Essay on Entitlement and Deprivation* (Oxford: Clarendon Press, 1981); and *Resources, Values and Development* (Oxford: Blackwell; Cambridge, MA: Harvard University Press, 1984), chs. 18, 20.

61. Sen, *Development as Freedom*, 209.

62. Drèze and Sen, *Hunger and Public Action*, 30–1.

63. That the capability orientation is more basic than or superior to a sophisticated human rights approach – either in general or in relation to the challenge of world hunger – introduces questions beyond the scope of the present volume. Resources for answering these questions occur in Amartya Sen, "The Right Not to be Hungry"; "Elements of a Theory of Human Rights," *Philosophy and Public Affairs*, 32, 4 (2004): 315–56; "Human Rights and Capabilities," *Journal of Human Development*, 6, 2 (2005): 151–66; and Martha Nussbaum, "Capabilities and Human Rights," in *Global Justice: Transnational Politics: Essays on the Moral and Political Challenges of Globalization*, ed. Pablo De Greiff and Ciaran Cronin (Cambridge, MA: MIT Press, 2002), 117–49; "Capabilities as Fundamental Entitlements: Sen and Social Justice," in *Feminist Economics*, 9, 2–3 (2003): 33–61. See also Barrett and Maxwell, *Food Aid After Fifty Years*, ch. 6; and the essays by Xiaorong Li, James W. Nickel, and Henry Shue on human rights approaches to world hunger in *World Hunger and Morality*, 2nd edn., ed. Aiken and La Follette. For an excellent treatment of the ways in which the capability approach and the international human rights regime support each other, see Polly Vizard, *Poverty and Human Rights: Sen's Capability Perspective Explored* (Oxford: Oxford University Press, 2006).

64. Sen, *Inequality Reexamined*, 110.

65. Drèze and Sen, *Hunger and Public Action*, 42.

66. David Ellerman, *Helping People Help Themselves: From the World Bank to an Alternative Philosophy of Development Assistance* (Ann Arbor: University of Michigan Press, 2005).

67. Some recent work on food security draws on Drèze and Sen and captures this point in distinguishing the *utilization* of food from the *availability of* and *access to* food. See, for example, World Food Programme, *Enabling Development: Food Assistance in South Asia* (Oxford: Oxford University Press, 2001), ch. 1; and Barrett and Maxwell, *Food Aid After Fifty Years*, 109–11.

68. Drèze and Sen, *Hunger and Public Action*, 14.

69. See ibid., 41. For a more detailed and technical discussion of these issues by nutritionists who are sympathetic with the capability approach, see *Nutrition and Poverty*, ed. S. R. Osmani (Oxford: Clarendon Press, 1992).

70. Wines, "Malnutrition is Cheating Its Survivors," 41.

71. See World Food Programme, *Enabling Development*, 215.

72. In *The World of Consumption* (London: Routledge, 1993), esp. 148–93, Ben Fine and Ellen Leopold criticize theories that overemphasize either the

physical characteristics or the "socially constructed" meanings of foods, thereby neglecting the complex structure of food systems or chains as "systems of provision." In "The Capability Approach: A Theoretical Survey," *Journal of Human Development*, 6, 1 (2005): 93–114, Ingrid Robeyns insightfully emphasizes the social context (social institutions, social and legal norms, other people's behavior, environmental factors) in the conversion of goods and services into capabilities and in the choice of which capabilities to realize in functionings.

73. Drèze and Sen, *Hunger and Public Action*, 267.
74. Ibid., 13.
75. Christopher B. Barrett and Daniel G. Maxwell, "Recasting Food Aid's Role," *Policy Brief* (August, 2004), 6. See also the same authors' *Food Aid After Fifty Years*.
76. Drèze and Sen, *Hunger and Public Action*, 121.
77. Ibid., 88–93.
78. Sen, *Development as Freedom*, 177–8.
79. Barrett and Maxwell, *Food Aid After Fifty Years*, 123–4. Cf. UN Millennium Development Project Task Force on Hunger, *Halving Hunger*, 148.
80. Teotonio, "When Children are Too Weak to Cry."
81. Wines, "Malnutrition is Cheating Its Survivors."
82. Somini Sengupta, "India Prosperity Creates Paradox: Many Children are Fat, Even More are Famished," *New York Times* (December 31, 2006), A 8.
83. See John Osgood Field and Mitchel B. Wallerstein, "Beyond Humanitarianism: A Developmental Perspective on American Food Aid," in *Food Policy: The Responsibility of the United States in the Life and Death Choices*, ed. Peter G. Brown and Henry Shue (New York: Free Press, 1977), 234–58; *The Challenge of Famine*, ed. Field; World Food Programme, *Enabling Development*.
84. UN Millennium Development Project Task Force on Hunger, *Halving Hunger*, 142, 196–9.
85. For arguments that the emergency food aid should come from local or regional sources in order to stimulate local or developing country agriculture and marketing systems, see UN Millennium Development Project Task Force on Hunger, *Halving Hunger*, 142, 148, 199–200; and Barrett and Maxwell, *Food Aid After Fifty Years*, 15–16.
86. Drèze and Sen, *Hunger and Public Action*, 273.
87. Ibid., 67; see also 119.
88. UN Millennium Development Goals website: <www.un.org/millennium goals>.
89. PIPA, "Americans on Foreign Aid and World Hunger."
90. See Field, "Understanding Famine," 11, 19–22. Cf. Sen's claim that "there can be little dispute that economic and social development tends to reduce fertility rates": Amartya Sen, "Population: Delusion and Reality," *New York Review of Books*, 61, 15 (September 22, 1994), 65.
91. Drèze and Sen, *Hunger and Public Action*, 267.
92. Sen, *Development as Freedom*, 16. See also ibid., 15, 51–3, 155–7, 178–86; and Drèze and Sen, *Hunger and Public Action*, 210–15, 263–4.

93. Sen, *Development as Freedom*, 171.
94. Ibid., 180.
95. Ibid.
96. World Food Programme, *Enabling Development*, 183.
97. See D. John Shaw, *The UN World Food Programme and the Development of Food Aid* (Houndsmills and New York: Palgrave), esp. 5 and 9.
98. World Food Programme, *Enabling Development*, 150; see also 182–3, 192.
99. Barrett and Maxwell, *Food Aid After Fifty Years*, 117.
100. UN Millennium Development Project Task Force on Hunger, *Halving Hunger*, 64. See also 90, 185–9.
101. Ibid., 17, 189, 191, 194.
102. Ibid., 17, 64, 80, 85, 185–7.
103. Ibid., 187.
104. *Halving Hunger* cites approvingly, but does not argue for, two studies advocating participatory processes: Robert Chambers, A. Pacey, and Lori Ann Thrupp, *Farmer First: Farmer Innovation and Agricultural Research* (London: ITDG, 1989); and Sakiko Fukuda-Parr, C. Lopes, and K. Malik, *Capacity for Development: New Solutions to Old Problems* (London: Earthscan and United Nations Development Programme, 2002). Although *Halving Hunger* does draw on some ideas in Barrett and Maxwell's recent work, the Millennium Project Task Force on Hunger completely ignores Barrett and Maxwell's strong stress on citizen participation to combat hunger and bad development. Moreover, conspicuous by absence are references to the extensive literature on "participatory development" or deepening democracy. Not surprisingly, the index to Jeffrey Sachs's predominantly top-down and technocratic *The End of Poverty: Economic Possibilities for Our Time* (New York: Penguin, 2005) has no entries for "participation" or "democracy" and only one entry for "democratization, Africa."
105. For a good account, with full references, of controversies in the 1950s, 1960s, and 1970s concerning US food aid and development policy, see Anne O. Krueger, Constantine Michalopoulos, and Vernon W. Ruttan, *Aid and Development* (Baltimore and London: Johns Hopkins University Press, 1989); *Why Food Aid?*, ed. Vernon W. Ruttan (Baltimore and London: Johns Hopkins University Press, 1993), esp. 37–129; David Halloran Lumsdaine, *Moral Vision in International Politics: The Foreign Aid Regime, 1949–1989* (Princeton: Princeton University Press, 1993); Barrett and Maxwell, *Food Aid After Fifty Years*, esp. ch. 2. For a comprehensive evaluation of aid's effectiveness, and a proposal for its reform, see Roger C. Riddell, *Does Foreign Aid Really Work?* (Oxford: Oxford University Press, 2007).
106. *Why Food Aid?*, ed. Ruttan, 66.
107. Georg W. F. Hegel, *Hegel's Philosophy of Right*, trans. T. M. Knox (Oxford: Oxford University Press, 1952), 12–13.
108. "Insiders and Outsiders in International Development Ethics," *Ethics and International Affairs*, 5 (1991): 149–73.
109. See Barrett and Maxwell, *Food Aid After Fifty Years*, esp. ch. 5.

110. Dan Charles, "New Plan Calls for Buying Aid Foods Outside US," *All Things Considered*, National Public Radio (March 7, 2007). The 2007 US debate about food aid has split humanitarian groups. Some, such as Oxfam and Catholic Relief Services, favor purchasing food aid in hunger-stricken countries and their neighbors in order to save "time, money, and lives." Others, such as World Vision, are concerned about long-term food availability, and have become unlikely bedfellows with US agricultural, milling, and maritime interests that stand to lose money in proportion to US purchases of local food. The latter position arguably overemphasizes food availability and underemphasizes aid that makes a difference in lives of people who are hungry.

111. In *Food Aid*, Barrett and Maxwell entitle ch. 6, their most explicitly normative chapter, "Edging Towards a Recipient-Oriented Food Aid System."

Part IV

Deliberative democracy, participation, and globalization

9 The capability approach and deliberative democracy

In this chapter I argue for three claims. First, Sen's normative assumptions – the concepts of agency, capability, and functionings, which I analyzed, evaluated, and applied in earlier chapters – enable him to argue persuasively for democracy's three-fold importance. Second, Sen's capability approach to social ethics and international development requires democracy conceived as public discussion as well as fair and free elections. Third, Sen's conception of democracy and democratically oriented development would be fruitfully enriched and specified by explicitly drawing on some features of the theory and practice of what is called "deliberative democracy." I discuss and evaluate recent work on the nature, merits, challenges, and limits of deliberative democracy and argue that this perspective is an important resource for the capability approach in its efforts to deepen democracy, design participatory institutions, and make democracy central to development challenges of our times. In the next chapter, I apply a deliberative version of the agency and capability approach to local development projects. In the volume's last chapter, I show how development ethics would employ this approach in arguing for the democratization of globalization as well as the globalization of democracy.

Sen's capability approach and democracy

Sen's normative assumptions enable him to argue for democracy's three-fold importance and that, in turn, democratic discussion and decision-making are not only permitted but also required by his normative vision. Although democratic decision-making has been a background theme in much of Sen's earlier work, it is especially in *Development as Freedom*,[1] "Democracy as a Universal Value,"[2] (with Jean Drèze) *India: Development and Participation*, 2nd edn.,[3] and *The Argumentative Indian: Writings on Indian History, Culture, and Identity*[4] that Sen makes explicit his commitment to democracy conceived as public discussion and democratic decision-making.

Agency and well-being; freedom and achievement

In Chapter 5 above, I offered a detailed interpretation of the normative "foundation" of Sen's capability and agency approach to development, namely, his cross-cutting distinctions of agency and well-being, on the one hand, and achievement and freedom, on the other.

One is an agent when one deliberates and decides for oneself, acts to realize one's aims, and, thereby, makes some intentional difference in the world. Depending on the traits of a person, for example whether they are cognitively impaired, a person has more or less agency. Depending on the setting, humans are more or less free to exercise their agency. Sen appeals to our considered judgments that it is good for people to reason about, make conscious decisions about, and be in charge of their own actions rather than being mere pawns in a cosmic, natural, or social chess game. Among the options for human action is that of promoting or protecting those ways of living and freedoms (functionings and capabilities) that the agent has reason to value, such as adequate health and the freedom for good health. The well-being with which an agent is concerned may be her own or that of other people. I may be an agent in promoting, ignoring, or undermining my own well-being or that of other people. When I exercise my agency to help others or when others exercise theirs in order to help me, the help may either focus on the recipient's agency (to help himself), or cause the one helped to be a passive recipient. The contrast with being an agent is that of a person acted upon, without say or control, by other persons or impersonal forces.

What is democracy?

Given the moral space of agency, both freedom and achievement, and well-being (both capabilities to function and functionings), how does Sen argue for democracy? On the level of nation-state governance, Sen argues that democratic governance is important for intrinsic, instrumental, and what he calls "constructive" reasons.[5] Before analyzing and evaluating each of these justifications and relating them to Sen's key ethical notions, it is important to grasp Sen's normative definition of democracy:

What exactly is democracy? We must not identify democracy with majority rule. Democracy has complex demands, which certainly include voting and respect for election results, but it also requires the protection of liberties and freedoms, respect for legal entitlements, and the guaranteeing of free discussion and uncensored distribution of news and fair comment. Even elections can be deeply defective if they occur without the different sides getting an adequate opportunity to present their respective cases, or without the electorate enjoying the freedom to obtain news and to consider the views of the competing protagonists. Democracy is a demanding system, and not just a mechanical condition (like majority rule) taken in isolation.[6]

This definition of democracy is normative in the sense that it sets forth what Sen calls the "ideals" of democracy, in contrast to its "institutions" and its "practice," and portrays democracy as a "demanding system" of governance. To supplement Sen's account of the demanding ideal of democracy, I offer a scalar account of the concept. Democracy is a more-or-less rather than an either/or affair. Groups are more or less democratic or, perhaps better, function more or less democratically along four dimensions: breadth, depth, range, and control.[7]

Democracies differ with respect to *breadth*. In the early days of the USA, democracy was very narrow, for only white male landowners had the vote. More demanding is an inclusive democracy in which there is "widespread actual participation, including the most disadvantaged," and an "equitable distribution of power."[8]

Democracies also differ with respect to *depth*. In shallow democracies, citizens – if they vote at all – do little more than vote. Deeper democracy requires modes of participation in addition to balloting and majority rule, for example free discussion and the give and take of opposing arguments. It is especially with this aspect of democracy that the theory and practice of deliberative democracy has made its greatest contribution.

As we shall see in Sen's argument for democratic government's constructive importance, democracies differ both with respect to the *range* of questions that citizens should democratically decide and with respect to the *kinds* of institutions that are democratic. Finally, the dimension of *control* in democracy concerns the extent to which citizens make or influence decisions and the extent to which these decisions make a difference in the world. The dimension of control or influence is important, for the group that "rules" may be inclusive, address many sorts of issues through many channels, and address them in a variety of ways, including discussion, and yet have no influence over the decision or no impact on the world. The more "the people," whoever they are, actually rule, influence decisions, and control their affairs, the more fully do we have a fully functioning democracy.[9]

Democracy's intrinsic value

First, Sen argues that democracy is intrinsically good because it enables citizens to participate politically and this freedom is something people have reason to value intrinsically. Democracy and political and civil rights have, says Sen, "*direct* importance in human living associated with basic capabilities (including that of political and social participation)": "Political and social participation has *intrinsic value* for human life and well-being."[10] Opportunities for political participation as well as actual participation help make our lives go well, and "to be prevented from participation in the political life of the community is a major deprivation."[11]

Sen might be criticized here for smuggling into his liberalism a conception that the good life or even the best life is one of political engagement. That objection, however, would assume that Sen identifies well-being and human flourishing, which he does not. Sen's concept of well-being refers to personal advantage, one's life going well, and not to a life of realizing one's "highest" potentials. Moreover, it is the freedom for political participation that Sen emphasizes and not the activity itself. Our lives go less well when we are prevented from political activity even if we would not choose it. Another objection might be that, far from contributing to personal advantage, political activity is for many either boring or burdensome (or both). Sen's point, however, is not about the joys of political activity so much as about the loss that comes from being excluded from participation.

Let us push further. One reason why being prevented from political involvement is bad is that it means that someone makes decisions for me, someone else runs my life. Yet surprisingly, although he – as we saw above – does defend the ideal of agency, Sen does not appeal to agency in his intrinsic argument for democracy. He does not say that democracy is intrinsically important because in democracy citizens exercise their agency as well as having the freedom to do so. As an agent I decide, act, and make a difference in the world rather than having no effect or being merely the recipient of someone else's decision and action. Sen can and should say that democracy is intrinsically valuable because democracy provides each citizen with agency freedom and, often, agency achievement insofar as democracy provides its citizens with opportunities to shape public policies and select their leaders. Good development provides social arrangements, including democratic processes, in which human beings are free – directly or indirectly – to express their agency, "shape their own destiny," "be in charge of their own well-being,"[12] and effect change:

Social arrangements, involving many institutions (the state, the market, the legal system, political parties, the media, public interest groups, and public discussion forums, among others) are investigated in terms of their contribution to enhancing and guaranteeing the substantive freedoms of individuals, seen as active agents of change, rather than passive recipients of dispensed benefits.[13]

In democratic self-rule, agency freedom and achievement are collective as well as individual. Consider the Huaorani, a small Indian tribe that lives in the Ecuadorian Amazon. This formally pristine region is undergoing rapid change due to oil exploration and extraction, environmental degradation, and new settlers seeking land and work. It is also a region with newly protected areas, politically significant alliances among Indian tribes, partnerships with the government and oil companies, and new opportunities, such as ecotourism. A long-time resident of the area remarks on the Huaoranis' right to be among the agents of their own change:

Change is inevitable. The Huaorani cannot avoid change. The real question is, on what terms will change occur? The right the Huaorani have – a basic moral right that all people have – is to be allowed to evolve their own cultural tools for dealing with change, rather than having that change imposed upon them.[14]

Another observer of the Huaorani notes that in one of their villages (Quehueire Ono), the Huaorani have decided on a creative mixture of old and new:

[The stack of written documents that a Huaorani association had produced in its first two years of operation] suggested that while it would be tempting to see Quehueire Ono as a return to tradition that would be inaccurate. If anything, Quehueire Ono represented a Huaorani synthesis: a traditional way of living enhanced by certain modern tools that offered access to an *abundancia* not found in the forest and on which, increasingly, they had come to depend. That is, *cowode* [non-Huaorani] abundance. And in what must be considered a rat's nest of paradox and irony, one of the most valued of these new tools was literacy.[15]

Sen, I believe, would judge the "Huaorani synthesis" less as paradoxical and more as a creative outcome of people collectively exercising their agency – their human right to decide together what parts of their traditional life to abandon, what parts to retain, what parts to adapt, and how to supplement or modify their traditional life with new ideas. Although he employs the language of capabilities at the start of the following passage, he finally and appropriately makes his normative point in the language of action or agency:

We come back again to the perspective of capabilities: that different sections of the society (and not just the socially privileged) should be able to be active in the decisions regarding what to preserve and what to let go. There is no compulsion to preserve every departing lifestyle even at heavy cost, but there is a real need – for social justice – for people to be able to take part in these social decisions, if they so choose.[16]

In effect we see the materials from which Sen can and should construct an argument – based on the value or dignity of agency – for the intrinsic worth of democratic processes: democracy embodies or expresses individual and collective agency; agency is intrinsically valuable (because it is one basis for human dignity); so, democracy is intrinsically valuable.

This Huaorani case also suggests that Sen should add or make explicit a third dimension in arguing democracy's intrinsic value. That dimension is moral equality. We have reason to value democracy as inherently good because it assumes that all adult members of the group are equal with respect to their worth or dignity, and this worth is related, among other things, to their agency. Apart from whatever good consequences it may have, democracy is intrinsically important because it treats members of the group as having *equal* status, freedom, and agency.[17] Although Sen does not explicitly offer this egalitarian argument for democracy's intrinsic worth, it is clear that he believes that "equitable distribution of power"[18] is among the democratic ideals. He can also appeal to the link between agency and the process aspect of freedom discussed above: democracy is justified because it provides a fair and equitable procedure for social choice. In a democracy, citizens have agency or process freedom: they are "free to invoke and utilize procedures that are equitable."[19]

In summary, implicit in Sen's work is a complex argument – appealing to human well-being, agency (dignity), the process aspect of freedom, and equality – for the intrinsic worth of democracy and the inclusion of democratization in development. Daniel Little, in a volume heavily indebted to Sen and Nussbaum, felicitously combines the three components to argue for the intrinsic value of democracy in development:

Is democracy a morally important institution? Should we include democratiza-tion within the set of fundamental values and goals of development? Democracy is a crucial aspect of human freedom. Fundamentally, it is a good thing because it facilitates free human choice and furthers the good of political participation. Democracy is a necessary component of the individual's ability to live freely and autonomously. And democracy is a political form that pays appropriate heed to the inherent worth and dignity of the person. Thus, democracy is a central constituent of the individual's ability to live freely and autonomously as a human being.[20]

Democracy's instrumental value

Democracy, Sen contends, is also instrumentally good. Democracies have the good consequences of not warring against each other, and in bad times democracies are more responsive than nondemocracies to the importance of protecting human agency (voice) and well-being: "Democracy has an important *instrumental* role in enhancing the hearing that people get in response to their claims to political attention (including the claims of economic needs)."[21] Although a benevolent dictator may listen to "his" people and respond compassionately to their needs, he is likely to insulate himself from popular demands. Although narrow democracies may exclude the voices of the poor, and thin democracies may restrict participation to voting, distributive justice is more likely to occur in even a formal or minimal democracy than in a nondemocracy.[22]

A citizen's freedom not to starve, Sen argues and as we discussed in Chapter 8, frequently benefits from the "protective power of democracy."[23] Democracy is especially valuable in times of crisis. A free press, for example, may identify a pressing human problem such as an immanent famine and, before it becomes a reality, "demand appropriate public action."[24] Or, following a disaster, such as the tsunami of December 26, 2004, or the hurricane that struck New Orleans in August, 2005, a region is more likely to prevent or mitigate a disaster if and when citizens have the freedom to press their demands for compensation and future security. In a democratic country, government officials have an incentive – if they want to be reelected – to pay attention to what people want and demand.

Democracy's constructive value

Finally, Sen argues that democratic governance is "constructively" good insofar as it provides institutions and processes in which people can learn from each other and "construct" or decide on the values and priorities of the society:[25] "Value formation is as much a democratic activity as is the use of social values in the determination of public policy and social response."[26] In this third and most original of his three arguments for democracy, Sen identifies an aspect of the capability approach to which the theory of deliberative democracy may contribute by offering a principled account of the processes groups should employ to decide certain questions and form their values. What, more precisely, are these sorts of social choices? Although Sen has never listed these choices in one place, an inspection of his writings reveals at least the following:

(1) *The choice of agents and participants.* Who should be a member of the group and who or what is to make (further) choices? Should the group make its own choices and make them deliberatively or should it choose to have some other agent or authority make them? Like most participatory and deliberative theorists, Sen assumes that people who are most affected by a decision should make the decision.

(2) *The choice of the process of decision-making.* Just as individuals can make their own decisions in many ways (such as coin-flipping, whim, appeal to authority, appeal to expertise, critical reflection), so groups

have a choice from among several collective decision-making proced-ures, including some form of democratic decision-making. Sen has devoted much of his work over the course of his career to the rational scrutiny of various social choice processes.[27]

(3) *The choice of agency versus well-being.* When the community's choice to make its *own* decisions (rather than have someone else make them) is likely to reduce the well-being of its members or vice versa, it faces a fundamental decision not only about agency but also of agency versus well-being. This choice is the social version of an individual's choice between what Sen calls the opportunity aspect of freedom, which con-cerns capabilities for functionings, and the process aspect of freedom, which concerns agency and process:

A person may, in a specific case, have more direct control over the levers of operation and yet be less able to bring about what she values. When such a divergence occurs, we can go in somewhat different directions. We may, in many cases, value real opportunities to achieve certain things no matter how this is brought about ("don't leave the choice to me, you know this restaurant and my tastes, you should choose what I would like to have"). But we may also value, in many cases, the process of choice ("I know you can express my views much better than I can, but let me speak for myself").[28]

A society also has a choice between helping its members achieve their agency goals, such as by building a statue to some citizen's hero, or, in contrast, by "mak[ing] sure that no one has to starve, or fail to obtain medical attention for a serious but eminently treatable ailment."[29] If there were only two options (and Sen rejects such a dichotomy), is it better to have a "nanny state" in which the state and its experts both run the show and provide for basic need satisfaction of its passive citizens, or a government in which citizens exercise political agency but achieve a lower level of well-being? Sen's own judgment is clear, but the decision of the relative weights of agency versus well-being is one that groups must often make:

The alternative to an exclusive reliance on individual responsibility is not, as is sometimes assumed, the so-called nanny state. There is a difference between "nannying" an individual's choices and creating more opportunity for choice and for substantive decisions for individuals who can then act responsibly on that basis.[30]

In Chapter 7, I argued that Sen himself – with good reason, I believe – does not give normative priority to either agency or well-being. Each is important to supplement and correct the other. At this juncture, how-ever, the point is that sometimes a group must decide between agency and well-being or what balance to strike between them.

(4) *The choice between functioning and capability.* Within the "space" of well-being, a community sometimes must choose between a functioning, such as its members being made healthy now (through curative medicine), and a capability, such as being made free from ill health (through preventative medicine). Decisions concerning aid to immediate versus future victims of massive natural disasters often have this character. Sen himself is generally critical of those approaches, which he calls collectively BLAST ("Blood, Sweat, and Tears"), which sacrifice current generations to future ones.[31]

(5) *The choice between functionings (or capabilities) now and functionings (or capabilities) in the future.* A community with scant food may have to decide between present and future ill functioning, such as being ill-nourished now and being ill-nourished in the future. A militant group in a repressive society may forgo public protest now in order to be free to engage in it in the future.

(6) *The choice and weighting of* valuable *capabilities and functionings.* As I argued in Chapter 6, once in the "space" of capabilities and functioning, individuals and communities can exercise their agency and decide on those capabilities and functionings that are most valuable, those that are less valuable, those that are trivial, and those that are evil. I also argued in Chapter 6 that Nussbaum conceives of the philosopher's task as that of constructing – on the basis of her intuitions and through critical dialogue with others – an objective but incomplete and revisable list of valuable capabilities to be embodied in the nation's constitution.[32] The role that Nussbaum gives to the philosopher and a constitution Sen gives to the society or group itself. For Sen, a society has the freedom and responsibility to choose which capabilities and functionings are most valuable and to weigh or prioritize them for diverse purposes in different contexts. This additional topic for collective choice is justified because, for Sen, we have reason to want to be free of *ex ante* priority rules, algorithmic formulae of rationality,[33] or even a "unique blueprint for 'the just society.'"[34] Such weightings would "lock" a group prematurely "into one specific system for 'weighting' some of these competitive concerns, which would severely restrict the room for democratic decision-making in this crucial resolution (and more generally in 'social choice,' including the variety of processes that relate to participation)."[35]

(7) *The choice of* basic *capabilities and thresholds.* Not only can a society select certain capabilities as ones that it generally or in a particular situation has more reason to value than others, but also it can – for certain purposes – designate some capabilities as *basic.* Sen first employed his notion of "basic" capabilities in the 1979 Tanner Lectures,

and the term's meaning has been difficult to pin down.[36] Sen's clearest definition of a "basic capability" occurs in a footnote in *Inequality Reexamined*: "[A basic capability is] the ability to satisfy certain elementary and crucially important functionings up to certain levels."[37] This exercise, of course, requires that the community decide on a threshold or level, taking into account its level of prosperity and expected external assistance. It is in this context that Sen argues that a community can define what it means by the (basic) needs that social arrangements should meet: "Even the idea of 'needs' (including the understanding of 'economic needs'), which is often taken to be fixed and well-defined, can respond to public discussion and exchange of information, views and analyses."[38]

(8) *The choice between* basic *capabilities and expansion of* all *valuable capabilities*. Alkire correctly identifies a further choice that is only implicit in Sen's writings but one that communities sometimes face, namely between the promotion of basic capabilities and the expansion of all valuable capabilities or freedoms. Alkire remarks: "[This choice] allows commendation of activities that may be expected to meet basic needs. But it also allows a community to choose to leave some basic needs unmet."[39]

This discretionary power, with respect to constitutional guarantees, is exactly the sort of thing that Nussbaum's constitutionalism, which I criticized in Chapter 6, intends to block.[40]

(9) *The choice to specify general capabilities and functionings*. Suppose that a group selects certain capabilities and functionings as valuable and even basic; it is still free to *specify* or *interpret* its selections in certain ways. It can, as both Nussbaum and Henry Richardson argue, reason collectively about ends by specifying these capabilities and functionings, making them more precise.[41] The capability to appear in public without shame can be specified differently in the Costa Rican rainforest than in the Norwegian tundra.

(10) *The choice of distributive and other values*. Communities also can and should choose distributive and other values, how to interpret them, and how to prioritize them. Among the values open for a community to decide is that of just or fair distribution (strict equality, a Rawlsian difference principle, proportionate shortfall from one's potential, capability to be above a threshold, non-dominance). But, while important, justice once decided, contends Sen, is not everything, and a community has the freedom to decide to value and sometimes prioritize other values such as efficiency (the maximizing of the sum of individual advantage no matter how distributed),[42] social cohesion, social stability, social tranquillity (freedom from anxiety-producing choices), and compensation for bad luck.[43]

Sen makes the same fundamental point for each of these ten kinds of choice. Each type – including the choices of who should make the choices and how they should do so – confronts groups from the local to the global level. It is clear, as we have seen, that for Sen "public scrutiny and criticism" have a role to play in these valuational debates and that such debate "is a crucial part of the exercise of democracy and responsible social choice."[44] Rather than authorizing rule by philosophers, other experts, or a mere aggregation of citizen preferences, Sen endorses public discussion and democracy.

This emphasis on public reason should change how we engage in the theory and practice of "development" as well as how we think about equality and justice. Sen's own answer to his famous question "Equality of what?" is not only an equality of democratically decided basic capabilities but also, and just as importantly, equality of agency or process freedoms.[45] As a result, rather than offering one theory designed to best the others or to yield a definitive blueprint of "the just society," Sen takes the ball away from philosophical theory and kicks it to an agency-oriented conception of democratic decision-making. In an important passage, already partially quoted, Sen states:

> At the level of the pure theory of justice, it would be a mistake to lock prematurely into one specific system of "weighting" some of these competitive concerns [such as "weights" to be given to various capabilities or to aggregative versus distributive concerns], which would severely restrict the room for democratic decision making in this crucial resolution (and more generally in "social choice," including the variety of processes that relate to participation). Foundational ideas of justice can separate out some basic issues as being inescapably relevant, but they cannot plausibly end up, I have argued, with an exclusive choice of some highly delineated formula of relative weights as being the unique blueprint for "the just society."[46]

Sen contends that "the struggle for democracy around the world . . . is the most profound challenge of our times," but that the conception of democracy is often excessively narrow.[47] In addition to balloting, which can be an enormous achievement, Sen maintains that democracy should be understood, following John Rawls, as "the exercise of public reason."[48] Sen continues that "this more capacious concept [of democracy] includes the opportunity for citizens to participate in political discussions and so to be in a position to influence public choice."[49]

But what does Sen mean by public scrutiny and public reason? How does he conceive of the process of public valuational and policy discussion? What, more precisely, are his views on democratic decision-making as a kind of "responsible social choice?" Who should engage in this process, in what venues, and how should they do so – in ways consistent with Sen's basic value commitments?

Although he gives us hints, it is precisely at this point that Sen needs to go further. Alkire correctly identifies what is missing:

The problem is that, although Sen regularly refers to the need for explicit scrutiny of individual and social goals, for reflectiveness, value judgment, practical reason, and democratic social choice, he chooses not to specify the possible range of procedures by which valuational issues are to be resolved or by which information on valuations is to be obtained.[50]

Sen himself recognizes that the literature on deliberative democracy provides a resource for addressing these questions of democratic procedures and principles. When discussing the "practice of democracy" in both democratic and nondemocratic regimes, Sen observes that people must seize the participatory opportunities that exist. Then he adds that whether or not people take advantage of these opportunities "depends on a variety of factors." In a formal democracy, these factors would include "the vigor of multiparty politics" while in a nondemocracy or predemocracy the role of opposition parties may be important. Another and related factor, presumably in all societies, would be "the dynamism of moral arguments and value formation."[51] Then, in an endnote to this statement, Sen interestingly continues: "An important factor [in people seizing democratic opportunities] is the reach of deliberative politics and of the utilization of moral arguments in public debates."[52] Sen immediately proceeds to cite leading examples of the then current (1999) works on deliberative democracy.[53] However, although Sen opens the door to an explicit engagement between the capability approach and deliberative democracy, he has only begun to venture through it.

Sen's strong endorsement of democratic "practice," and his distinguishing it from democratic ideals and institutions, are part of his claim that the latter do "not serve as an automatic remedy of ailments as quinine works to remedy malaria."[54] Democracy is not, as the first Mayor Daley allegedly said about another matter, a "pancreas." In addition to the important role of democratic values and institutions, democratic citizens must "make democracy work" by committing themselves to and engaging in the "practice" of democracy. Yet, we must add, although it is true that deliberative politics has an important role in the "practice" of democracy, the *theory* of deliberative democracy can enrich the ideals of democracy, shape new institutional devices, and guide citizens in the practice of democratic deliberation. Or so I shall argue.

Deliberative democracy

Sen's capability approach can benefit from recent work on deliberative democracy. By considering the way certain deliberative democracy theorists pose and answer questions concerning the purpose, conditions, process, outcomes, and limits of deliberation, we (and Sen) may find resources to enrich his democratic turn in social and development ethics. Moreover, at least one deliberative democracy theorist, James Bohman, has adapted some of Sen's ideas to solve problems within deliberative democracy.[55] It may be, then, that engaging Sen and deliberative democracy will prove beneficial in both directions.

What is deliberative democracy? It is the theory and practice of a model of democracy that emphasizes the exchange of reasons in the making of democratic decisions. As a working conception, I adopt the influential 1999 definition by John Rawls:

> The definitive idea for deliberative democracy is the idea of deliberation itself. When citizens deliberate, they exchange views and debate their supporting reasons concerning public political questions. They suppose that their political opinions are not simply a fixed outcome of their existing private or nonpolitical interests. It is at this point that public reason is crucial, for it characterizes such citizens' reasoning concerning constitutional essentials and matters of basic justice.[56]

The deliberative democracy literature – both for and against – has in recent years become a cottage industry. It is a heterogeneous literature that sports both different versions and diverse criticisms of deliberative democracy, and some of the former have been formulated to meet some of the latter. In the present chapter I have insufficient space to analyze in a systematic way the merits and weaknesses of the various versions or criticisms, although occasionally I will take sides in particular controversies. Rather, my aim here is to identify several key ideas in the deliberative democracy movement that yields an explicitly deliberative democratic version of the capability approach.

First, I take up the question of the purpose of deliberation, and then, second, explain three ideals that seem to me to be especially important, namely, reciprocity, publicity, and accountability. Third, drawing on these ideals, I explore answers to the question "Who deliberates?" Fourth, I address the question of background conditions that enable group members to deliberate. Fifth, I follow Henry Richardson's reconstruction of the process of deliberation to emphasize that a deliberative group reasons together about what ought to be done by, among other things, forming joint intentions. Finally, I consider the personal capacities and virtues of deliberators.

Deliberative aims

A popular conception of both actual and ideal democracy is that democracy is a government that holds regular, competitive elections in which the candidate or issue with the most votes wins.[57] A somewhat more robust, but still rather minimalist, definition conceives democratic politics as entailing "a rule of law, promotion of civil and political liberties, free and fair election of lawmakers."[58] The general task of deliberative democrats is to start with the idea that democracy is rule by the people and then deepen and broaden the conception of "rule" by stressing a kind of inclusive and public discussion and by extending popular rule to at least some nongovernmental associations.

If such is the goal of deliberative democrats, then how do they understand the aims of deliberative discussion and decision-making? Two aims stand out. First, deliberation aims to identify and solve *concrete* problems or to devise general policies for solving specific problems. Second, deliberation's goal is to provide a fair way in which free and equal members of a group can overcome their differences and reach agreement about action and policy.

In introducing *Deepening Democracy: Institutional Innovations in Empowered Participatory Governance*, a volume that presents and evaluates four case studies in deliberative democracy, editors Archon Fung and Erick Olin Wright nicely capture the practical or problem-solving orientation of deliberative democracy:

> The first distinctive characteristic of the cases . . . is that they all develop governance structures geared to quite concrete concerns. These experiments, though often linked to social movements and political parties, differ from both in that they focus on practical problems, such as providing public safety, training workers, caring for habitats, or constructing sensible municipal budgets. If these experiments make headway on these issues, then they offer a potential retort to widespread doubts about the efficacy of state action. More importantly, they would deliver goods to sectors of society that are often most grievously denied them.[59]

Rawls, in the definition of deliberative democracy cited above, emphasizes a public use of reason to decide "constitutional essentials and matters of basic justice." Sen so far has stressed that public discussion enables group members collectively to scrutinize and improve their individual and shared values. In contrast, political scientists Fung and Wright propose that what they call "empowered participatory governance" "extends the application of deliberation from abstract questions over value conflicts and principles of justice to very concrete matters such as street paving, school improvement, and habitat management."[60]

One advantage of this Deweyan "problem-solving" approach, so far not evident in Sen's work, is that it enables scholars to evaluate institutional experiments in deliberative decision-making and "explore strategies to improve its quality."[61] Another advantage is that the practical orientation of deliberative democracy offers a way to achieve deliberative democracy's second goal of fairly reducing disagreement among group members: "This practical focus also creates situations in which actors accustomed to competing with one another for power or resources might begin to cooperate and build more congenial relations."[62] Emphasizing deliberative democracy as a problem-solving method does not rule out Sen's focus on value formation, for sometimes groups need to go beyond immediate problems to broader and less specific issues. Exclusive focus on, say, street paving might weaken the deliberative character of the group once the streets are paved. And solving the problem of potholes may not occur unless the group resolves the deeper problems of redistributive taxation. Yet, as we shall see presently, Fung and Wright's stress on public deliberation as practical problem-solving cautions group members to avoid ascending to value commitments when such ascent polarizes the group or jeopardizes practical agreements.

Deliberative democracy is a collective device not only to solve concrete problems but also to make fair decisions. Here fairness means that *each* member is treated with respect in that each member has the right to make his voice heard and to contribute to the final decision.

A group informed by this second deliberative aim contrasts with a group in which many – the poor or ethnic majorities or minorities – are excluded from the decision-making process. A deliberatively democratic group also contrasts with a group that practices a democratic procedure that is merely aggregative. In aggregative democracy, preferences or interests are formed in private and then expressed and added together in public. The aim of aggregative democracy is to elicit these private and unscrutinized preferences and additively combine them. If all the members prefer the same policy or objective, everyone gets what they want. In the usual cases where group members differ – sometimes radically – in their preferences, mere aggregation means either that the majority (or the option with the most votes) wins or there is no non-arbitrary winner due to voting "cycles."[63] In the former case, minority views lose out altogether and a danger of majority tyranny over the minority exists. In the latter case, the lack of a non-arbitrary winner seems to doom democracy and lead to some kind of authoritarianism. Aggregative social choice, as Sen himself sees it, seems to be "inevitably arbitrary or irremediably despotic."[64]

In the version of deliberative democracy that I favor, the focus of collective choice is not on preferences (what members want to do) or beliefs (what members believe about the world) but on joint and shared intentions to strive for certain goals and enact certain policies.[65] The point of deliberation is to provide a fair way for morally free and equal group members to cooperate together and forge – through the give and take of proposals, reasons, and criticisms – a reasoned agreement about their goals, values, policies, and actions. As a result, deliberative democracy publicly "transforms" rather than merely aggregates preferences.[66] Or, more accurately, in order to solve a common and practical problem, group members together make and rationally scrutinize competing proposals for policies and respectfully hammer out mutually acceptable intentions for action.

Rather than presupposing a preexisting agreement, deliberative democracy assumes that citizens disagree – sometimes deeply and bitterly – about what is to be done. It offers public deliberation as the process by which citizens – who initially disagree and may continue to do so – may generate a social choice. As Gutmann and Thompson put it, "recognizing that politics cannot be purged of moral conflict, it [deliberative democracy] seeks a common view on how citizens should publicly deliberate when they fundamentally disagree."[67] Without clarifying his views of public reason or explaining the process of public discussion, Sen also recognizes that such discussion begins in a context of disagreement:

The ideal of public reasoning is closely linked with two particular social practices that deserve specific attention: the tolerance of different points of view (along with the acceptability of agreeing to disagree) and the encouragement of public discussion (along with endorsing the value of learning from others).[68]

Deliberative ideals

A further contribution of deliberative democracy – especially Gutmann and Thompson's version – to Sen's capability approach consists of clarifying and defending three principles that should regulate collectively reasoned agreements: reciprocity, publicity, and accountability. The ideal of *reciprocity* prescribes that each group member make proposals and offer justification in terms that others can understand and could accept: "Deliberative democracy asks citizens to justify public policy by giving reasons that can be accepted by those who are bound by it."[69] Each would do so knowing that the others will do likewise. Reciprocity is an apt term, for it suggests that each make an appropriate response to a good received:[70] "The 'good received' is that you make your claims on terms that I can accept in principle. The 'proportionate return' is that I make my claims on terms that you can accept in principle."[71]

The aim, presupposing that the group involves cooperation among equal and free members, is to form an agreement that is mutually acceptable. Ideal deliberators build on whatever common commitments they share or come to share in order to reduce their disagreements. In such reciprocity, each does more than passively tolerate or grudgingly put up with the – perhaps despised – views of others, for each critically engages with the others, making accommodations and sometimes deep compromises in order to fashion something all or most can endorse.

The ideal of *publicity* likewise is important, and Gutmann and Thompson's ideal helps us flesh out Sen's reference to "public" discussion and the importance of "rich" information for rational choice. Publicity demands, among other things, that each member be free to engage (directly or by representation) in the deliberative process, that the process be transparent to all (rather than being done, as Habermas would say, "behind their backs"), and that each know that to which she is agreeing or disagreeing. Sometimes, of course, publicity must be set aside in favor of secrecy, but publicity should be the presumption and any general limits to publicity should issue from public deliberation.

A third ideal for deliberation is that of *accountability*. Each group member is accountable to all (and not to himself or herself alone) in the sense of giving acceptable reasons to the others. It should not be thought that deliberative democracy concerns only face-to-face groups in which all are directly present in the give and take of reasons. In larger-scale deliberative forums, representatives, officials, or leaders "who make decisions on behalf of other people, whether or not they are electoral constituents, should be accountable to those people."[72] Although a representative's constituents do not directly participate in the course of parliamentary deliberation, constituents rightly hold accountable those who represent them, and the former thereby indirectly express their agency in the deliberative process of forming joint intentions. Moreover, owing to publicity, constituents can both monitor the course of deliberation and the group's eventual decision, and through their representatives intervene in the former and challenge the latter. Institutions also can be designed that provide both representatives and represented with regular opportunities to reason together about issues and what stands the representative might take. Such efforts, I argued in Chapter 5, close the gap between direct agency (participatory democracy) and indirect agency (representative democracy).

Accountability extends then not only to one's fellow group members and their subgroups, and not only to those one represents, but also to those in other groups who are bound by the group's decisions or affected by its actions. Deliberative democrats differ over whether these persons – affected by the group but not members of it – deserve an accounting or even should have a voice or some other role in the decisions that affect them. Each of two contiguous groups may gain a voice in the deliberations of the other by scaling up to form a more inclusive group or by forming a new higher-level and overlapping representative group to address mutual problems (for instance, a joint committee of the US House and the Senate or an inter-county committee for two adjacent counties).

Who should deliberate?

This last point about voice enables us to identify a third contribution that deliberative democracy can make to Sen's version of the capability approach. If we are to emphasize deliberation and some conception of the ideals that might guide the process of deliberation, then we must answer two related questions: which groups should practice deliberative democracy and, within the deliberating groups, which members (and perhaps nonmembers) should deliberate and decide? These are large and difficult questions, and all I can hope to do in this chapter is to identify them, urge defenders of the capability approach to take them up, and encourage proponents of deliberative democracy to contribute to their resolution.

I first address the question of the scope or reach of deliberative democracy. The most radical answers would be monistic, for they would either affirm or deny that deliberative democracy should be the ideal for every governmental and nongovernmental group at levels from the local to the global. John Dewey, for example, distinguishes between "democracy as a social ideal and political democracy as a system of government." As an ideal or "form of life," democracy for Dewey would be "barren and empty save as it is incarnated" in all types of "human relationships":

The idea of democracy is a wider and fuller idea than can be exemplified in the state even at its best. To be realized it must affect all modes of human association, the family, the school, industry, religion. And even as far as political arrangements are concerned, governmental institutions are but a mechanism for securing to an idea channels of effective operation.[73]

For a radical deliberative democrat, *all* groups that currently operate on nondemocratic or anti-democratic principles should be targets for internally adopted or externally promoted deliberative democracy. This list would include families, including patriarchical ones; small-scale income generation projects in Afghanistan; associations, such as Augusta National Golf Association; governments (at all levels), such as Iran; international institutions, such as the World Bank; and global institutions, such as the Roman Catholic Church. The trouble with this perspective is that it fails to respect what William Galston calls "the expressive liberty" of groups to conduct their affairs according to, if they so choose, non-deliberative and nondemocratic principles and practices.[74]

A less radical alternative would be to affirm that democracy, in general, and deliberative democracy, in particular, has limits, for example in scientific inquiry, judicial review, sports teams, traditional religious communities, or private golf clubs. Democratic deliberation, however, is relevant for, on the one hand, democratic politics and such governing institutions as legislative bodies and administrative agencies, and, on the other hand, for nongovernmental groups whose members view themselves as free and equal and engaged in a cooperative enterprise. Even this less radical first-level position that affirms the limits of public deliberation might appeal to democratic deliberation on a second or meta-level. On this second-level approach, the clashes between groups – whether democratic or nondemocratic – as well as the scope and limits of deliberative democracy should themselves be settled by democratic deliberation. Democratic deliberation would, like the turtles mythically alleged to support the universe, "go all the way down." Are there any nondeliberative bases for challenging the results of deliberation?

Although we might agree that deliberation is an intrinsic good, because it enables people to exercise their agency, we must decide when to employ deliberation on the basis of some other principle. Some evidence exists, for example, that a manipulative elite sometimes uses deliberation as a means of dominating others. If so, a group might choose deliberation or a theorist might propose it only if deliberation did not result in domination.[75] If one dimension of "rule by the people" is "effective voice" or influence over decision-making and impact on the world, then these outcomes sometimes may be brought about most effectively not by deliberation but by non-deliberative means such as bargaining, political maneuvering, clientalism, and agitation.[76] Understanding both deliberation and non-domination or effective power as sometimes coincident and sometimes competing intrinsic values seems to be entirely compatible with Sen's value pluralism. It does not respond fully to Galston's challenge of whether respect for "expressive liberty" requires noninterference with and respect for a hierarchical group based on relations of obedience to authority.

Who has the best answer to the question of the limits and applicability of deliberative democracy (and to the second-level question of who should decide)?[77] It is not yet clear, but capability proponents should take up these issues and the various proposals. Which groups should be deliberatively democratic and who should decide this question (and how) regarding the scope of democratic deliberation? These questions raise such further questions as: which members of groups should engage in deliberation?

Some deliberative groups have formed already, some are in the process of formation, and sometimes unaffiliated individuals decide to form a deliberative group. Who in the group – or outside it – should have an (equal) opportunity to deliberate and vote? Should there be a minimum threshold of cognitive ability, perhaps with age as a proxy? Can one forfeit one's right to participate by committing a felony?[78] Should legal or illegal immigrants have a voice but not the right to vote, or should the right to vote be extended only to citizens? Should different levels of citizenship exist? More generally, should those outside the group have a voice in deliberations and a right to vote? What, if anything, should qualify someone to join a citizens' forum whose task is to address a contentious issue such as damming a pristine river or preventing snowmobilers from entering a wilderness used by cross-country skiers? Can anyone interested join the group? Is it first come first served? What if more skiers than snowmobilers attend? How small should the decision-making group be and who should decide?

One answer to these kinds of questions is to give responsibility to the deliberative body itself and to allow it to debate and decide who should be a member. That answer, however, is not completely satisfying, for it already, perhaps arbitrarily, excludes people from deliberation. Alternatively, one might say that anyone *affected* by the group should have a role in its deliberations and decisions, but that might give someone halfway around the world the same deliberative and decision-making status as those in the group. Perhaps these outsiders should be consulted for their views, but should they be treated as equal members with the right to decide? Are Gutmann and Thompson right when they say that "if representatives are accountable to their moral constituents as well as their electoral constituents, deliberative democracy should create forums in which citizens of foreign countries could present their claims and respond to the counterclaims of our legislators"?[79] Should protesters in Washington, DC, not only be listened to or consulted, but also be given a vote in the World Bank proceedings about debt forgiveness? The fact that a rose cultivation project in Pakistan affects neighbors (some neighbors were envious of the rose cultivators' success) does not seem to entail that the neighbors should be included in the group's discussions and decisions.[80] Again, on a second-order level, should group membership be decided democratically or in some other way, and, if the later, does this option undermine democracy? Shapiro and Hacker-Cordón call this "a chicken-and-egg problem that lurks at democracy's core,"[81] and Shapiro more recently observes: "Questions relating to boundaries and membership seem in an important sense prior to democratic decision making, yet paradoxically they cry out for democratic resolution."[82] Once more, these are pressing questions being debated by deliberative and other democratic theorists. Democratic capability theorists could benefit from the controversy and perhaps contribute to its resolution.

Enabling conditions

A fourth way in which deliberative democracy can contribute to the capability approach is to help identify background and institutional conditions that are presupposed by – or, better, conducive to – a group's democratic deliberation. These conditions coincide with, and reinforce, institutional arrangements that Sen himself advocates. That they are conducive to democratic deliberation only provides additional justification for their instrumental importance. Richardson has helpfully identified what he calls "institutions needed to preserve the background justice of democratic deliberation,"[83] especially with respect to the normative equality (to be discussed presently) of deliberators within or between groups. Where these conditions do not exist – because the potential deliberators live in dictatorships, in racist and anti-poor oligopolies, or in failed states beset by civil war – democratic deliberation may exist in underground venues or employ non-deliberative means but be exceedingly vulnerable.[84] What, then, are the conditions that contribute to democratic deliberation?

Equal political liberty

Equal political freedoms, contends Richardson, means among other things that "each citizen is to enjoy the same freedoms of speech, assembly, and political participation."[85] A less demanding idea of political equality is that each citizen is able to be at or above a threshold of minimally adequate political functioning.[86] These freedoms, based on an ideal of moral equality of persons, contribute to deliberator equality and deliberative democracy in local, national, and global venues. These liberties or civil and political rights must be protected and not merely be part of the legal code. Sen concurs: "one of the strongest arguments in favor of political freedom lies precisely in the opportunity it gives citizens to discuss and debate – and to participate in the selection of – values in the choice of priorities."[87]

Equality before the law

This condition affords the same fundamental constitutional rights to each citizen, regardless of ethnicity, religion, class, education, or sexual preference. More generally, this background condition means that no one is justified in claiming to be above the law and no one is beneath the protection of the law. This condition has been and continues to be especially important in the practice of religious freedom and toleration.

Economic justice

Economic poverty, inequality, and concentration of wealth can impede if not doom people's freedoms and deliberative participation. As Jean Drèze and Sen argue:

Large sections of the population have very limited opportunities to speak for themselves. The daily struggle for survival leaves them with little leisure to engage in political activity, and efforts to do so sometimes invite physical repression. Lack of formal education and access to information restricts their ability to intervene in public discussions and electoral debates, or to make effective use of the media, the courts, and other democratic institutions. Lack of adequate organizations further enhances this political marginalization.[88]

Hence, it is important to create conditions in which people have the real opportunity to advance to at least a level of minimally adequate well-being. Only then would people be able *individually* and *collectively* to choose the lives they want to lead. Moreover, too great a gap in economic and social power between the rich and the poor would result in the political domination of the former over the latter.

Procedural fairness

Richardson's final background condition for equality among deliberators and deliberative democracy is that "the process of democratic debate and decision must itself be structured so as to allow each person a fair chance to participate and to counteract to a degree the potential influence of disparities in economic and political power."[89] Different measures – to provide fair chances and reduce the threat of elite capture – will be appropriate in different contexts. Campaign finance reform, an abolition of the US Electoral College, and reform of registration and voting procedures would lessen inequality in US national elections. Requiring that at least one third of members of Afghanistan's legislature be women is an egalitarian institutional device; enforced limits on deliberator speaking time is yet another.

Two objections might be made to the deliberative democrat's appeal to these background conditions. First, does not deliberative democracy presuppose a radical and morally problematic egalitarianism? Second, a "chicken-and-egg" problem, does not this view imply that a deliberative democracy society must already be just (have equal political power and economic opportunity) if deliberative democracy is to "work" and promote justice? If such demanding conditions must be in place *before* deliberative democracy is possible, then deliberative democracy is unreasonably utopian, for the conditions are either impossible or unlikely to obtain.[90]

How should we respond to these objections? The first criticism, one that charges deliberative democracy with an unacceptable egalitarianism, I will take up in the concluding section of the next chapter. To the second charge – that deliberative democracy is unrealistic utopianism – I respond now in four steps. First, it is important to concede that deep economic and other inequalities beset actually existing democracies. For example, an overriding concern of the United Nations Development Programme's 2004 report on Latin American democracies is that although most of the region's nations have abandoned authoritarianism in favor of democracy, the regions exhibit worsening poverty and inequality.[91] In unjust conditions, economic and political elites often capture democratic institutions and procedures and use them to protect and even to intensify their social dominance.[92] The result is frequently disillusionment with democracy.

Second, although formal or minimalist democracies often do badly in reducing poverty and inequality, autocracies at the same economic levels do as badly and often worse than their democratic counterparts. Employing a fairly minimalist definition of democracy,[93] Halperin et al. present impressive evidence that democracies and democratizing states on average do a better job than authoritarian states in reducing poverty and inequality.

Third, as Iris Young – following Frank Cunningham and his notion of a "democratic fix"[94] – argues, "in formally democratic societies with serious injustices it must be possible to promote social changes towards greater justice through democratic means."[95] Halperin et al. explain this possibility and the "democratic advantage" on the basis of even a minimalist democracy's accountability, allocation of opportunity, openness (including access to information), stability, and ability to learn.[96] Rather than a country first achieving certain enabling conditions for democracy and then achieving democracy, the country may gradually achieve the "enabling conditions," for instance greater political liberty and economic equality, *by means of* democracy. Sen puts it aptly: "A country does not have to be deemed fit *for* democracy; rather, it has to become fit *through* democracy."[97]

Fourth, the potential for democracy's reducing political and economic inequality is even greater when a society – in the light of a firm grasp of democratic values – moves beyond formal or minimalist democracy to deepen and broaden its democratic institutions. The cure, then, for the deficiencies of democracy is not some nondemocratic system but more and better democracy. John Dewey put it extremely well in 1927:

> We object to the common supposition of the foes of existing democratic government that the accusations against it touch the social and moral aspirations and ideas which underlie the political forms. The old saying that the cure for the ills of democracy is more democracy is not apt if it means that the evils may be remedied by introducing more machinery of the same kind as that which already exists, or by refining and perfecting that machinery. But the phrase may also indicate the need of returning to the idea itself, of clarifying and deepening our apprehension of it, and of employing our sense of its meaning to criticize and re-make its political manifestations.[98]

The theory and practice of deliberative democracy constitute precisely an attempt to rethink the ideal and institutions of "rule by the people." We need not assume that Richardson's background conditions must be fully attainable or completely in place before roughly free and equal group members can engage in injustice-reducing deliberation. In spite of political and economic inequalities, with the help of what Fung and Wright call "self-conscious intentional design efforts,"[99] such as training in public speaking and reason-giving, people *in and through* the deliberative process itself may reduce their differences and promote justice as they together forge answers to practical problems. In deliberative venues, as "schools of democracy," they may learn (to deliberate justly) by doing (deliberating justly).[100] What occurs is a "virtuous circle" in which a deepening democracy improves conditions that enable further democratization.

Gianpaolo Baiocchi submits evidence that one of the important experiments in deliberative democracy, that of participatory budgeting in Porto Alegre, Brazil, has had the outcome of reducing member inequalities and the occurrence of domination:

> Despite significant inequalities among citizens, the didactic features of the [Porto Alegre] experiment have succeeded in large part in offsetting these potentials for domination. This confirms the expectations of democratic theorists who, while

assuming that persons may come to deliberative settings with certain inequal-ities, expect that over time participation will offset them.[101]

The Porto Alegre experiment also shows that the participatory budgetary exercise itself has been "highly redistributive,"[102] contribut-ing to the conditions that in turn help enable deliberative democracy. Deliberative democracy often results in the bringing about of conditions that in turn contribute to more egalitarian distribution and deliberation. This point reinforces and gives empirical support to Drèze and Sen's point that there is a "virtuous circle" of "achieving greater equity," on the one hand, and citizen participation or "democratic practice," on the other: "A reduction of inequality both contributes to democratic practice and is strengthened by successful practice of democratic freedoms."[103] The conditions for deliberative democracy can be built through the practice of such democracy.

As important as these four responses are, I now think it is too glib – in the face of criticisms of (deliberative) democracy – merely to say that "the solution for the ills of (deliberative) democracy is more (delibera-tive) democracy." Much depends on what obstacles are in the way of (further) democractization. When there is good will on the part of all deliberators and no serious economic, educational, or other inequalities, then more democracy may do the job. But the less good will there is, especially when accompanied by severe inequalities, non-deliberative methods may have a limited role. Among these methods would be political pressure, public shaming, and appeal to experts.[104]

The process of deliberative democracy

A fifth contribution that deliberative democracy can make to the capability approach is to make the latter more concrete and detailed with respect to its account of the process of public discussion and decision-making. It is at this point that the recent work of Henry Richardson becomes particularly relevant. One of Richardson's innova-tive contributions to deliberative democracy is to recast the under-standing of the deliberative democratic process from a focus on preferences – regardless of whether simply aggregated or transformed through discussion – to a focus on partially joint intentions and shared ends for concrete action.[105] One advantage of the intention/action perspective is that it enables us to see deliberation as a kind of practical reasoning in the sense that deliberators reason together about what the group (and they as individuals) ought to do. The aim is to agree on, or fashion together, not beliefs about the world or convictions about ultimate values but a plan or policy (end plus means) about which all (or most) can agree and on which all can act in order to realize it.

I turn now to Richardson's modeling – in terms of reasoning about and deciding on partially joint intentions – of "collective, political deliberation by individual reasoners with potentially distinct views."[106] For Richardson, joint intentions are the outcome of a four-stage process of "formulating proposals; discussing their merits; coming to an informal agreement; and converting informal agreement into official decision."[107] It is appropriate that Richardson designates each stage with a gerund, for public deliberation is a practice or complex action, structured by norms, whose outcome is a joint intention to act (or an agreement to disagree).

Formulating proposals

If, instead of deliberation, social choice were merely the aggregation of private preferences, we might just vote or consult preferences in a relevant focus group. Or a cost-benefit economist might collect our preferences and those of others, and ask about willingness to pay for a benefit and accept compensation for a burden. Or we might forsake mere aggregation and either defer to some wise person or expert or obey a dictator or religious leader with respect to what the group should do. If we had nothing but a fair procedure, each of us might try to outdo other group members by influencing them more than they influence us. Finally, a group might try to eliminate deliberation by uncritically appealing to the nation's constitution or its judicial interpreters.

Richardson, however, reframes our group task as that of reasoning together to fashion an answer to what collectively we ought to do. We begin when one (or a subgroup) among us makes a proposal to the rest. Even prior to that initial proposal, a point that Richardson neglects, it may be useful for the group to brainstorm about the nature of the problem it faces and some possible solutions.[108] At this initial stage, wide participation is appropriate to guard against a skewed identification of the problem at hand or which of several problems is most urgent. Whatever problem is identified or proposed solution is offered, individuals – and not some big collective deliberator or general will – are the agents.

It is appropriate to express private preferences or desires, especially when a person or subgroup argues that its interests should be treated (more) fairly. Jane Mansbridge insightfully insists that such expressions of self-interest have an important role in democratic deliberation: "As participants in deliberation, we cannot understand ourselves or others, or work out just resolutions to many conflicts, if we cannot formulate relatively accurately and express relatively well some conception of our own narrow self-interest."[109] Deliberation does not require that deliberators become so impartial that they are not able to claim fair treatment of their interests. As we saw in Chapter 7, such a balance between one's interests and those of others requires lucidity, about my interests and those of others, and practical wisdom about getting a just balance.

Although the proposal may (or may not) express private preferences or desires, the act of proposing what *we* ought to do is a *public* act, the performance of which the others are aware of and the content of which others can grasp. Each and every group member is free to make proposals, for each has equal status as a source of claims and as a group member. I face other group members not (merely) as enemies to be hated, persons to be disapproved of, or rivals to be bested, but (also) as fellow citizens in a cooperative scheme. In spite of our differences, the ideal of reciprocity, as well as my respect for each member's dignity and autonomy or agency, demand that what I propose to others is something that they understand (no foreign languages in the absence of translators; no technical jargon) and either do or could accept (given appropriate reasons). I also would require the same from them.

Finally, although my proposal is about what we should do together, to make the proposal honestly is also to indicate my willingness to do my part in carrying out the plan and my promise to do so if my proposal gains acceptance. The making of such a promise, of course, would be contingent, negatively, on encountering no unforeseen obstacles as well as, positively, on others (who accept the proposal) freely agreeing to do their parts. The making of one proposal often results in the making of additional proposals, whether they are modifications of the first or rivals to it. This brings us to stage 2.

Arguing the proposals' merits

In deliberative democracy, those who make proposals give reasons for the actions or policies they favor, and the members engage in a deliberative give and take to identify the strengths and weaknesses of the proposal. Here it is important to connect the notion of a proposal with the concept of intention as a sort of means–end package.

In making a proposal I offer reasons, hopefully ones that have some "uptake" (Bohman), for its acceptance (and perhaps reasons for my reasons). Other group members do not just listen to or record my proposals (as vote-counters might register my vote, as interviewers might record my expression of willingness to pay, or as focus group members might acknowledge my opinion). Rather, each member has the opportunity to scrutinize rationally both means and ends. Others may defend my proposed action but as a means to additional or alternative ends.

Or they may reject my proposal in favor of what they take to be a better means; they may reject my intention altogether and propose different actions and ends. Agreeing with Jürgen Habermas,[110] Richardson criticizes exclusive reliance on instrumental thinking that takes ends as given and reasons only about the most efficient or effective means. Practical reasoning should assess ends, for we often differ on and decide about not only "know-how" but also "know-whether." Going beyond Habermas, Richardson gives an account in stage 3 of how, more specifically, we can reason about ends.

Such assessment of ends often leads back to what Richardson calls "final ends" – ends which are valued in themselves (whether or not they are also valued instrumentally).[111] One way to interpret these final ends is as different interpretations of a public good, not as something independent waiting to be discovered but as something to be hammered out or agreed to through discussion. Democratic deliberation, however, need not and often should not push back (or down) to one's *ultimate* ends in the sense of those highest goals in one's goal hierarchy. The principle of reciprocity requires that I offer only reasons that my fellow deliberators can understand and accept, and ascending to ultimate ends or reasons often prevents the group from forming an intention to act.

Here Richardson departs from Gutmann and Thompson's notion of "public reason," however; for, unlike them, Richardson[112] permits deliberators to *supplement* (not *replace*) their publicly accessible reasons and values with a public profession of their ultimate values – for instance, religious values – presumably when these ultimate values may help other members understand where a person is "coming from."

Richardson's view is a promising third way between (1) Habermas's view[113] that there should be *no* restrictions on the content of what is offered in public deliberation, and (2) Rawls's contention[114] that the idea of "public reason" should filter out whatever other citizens are unable to accept.[115] To respect my fellow citizen I should welcome his (or her) attempt to *clarify or explain* (not justify) his proposal (and its reasons), even if that means he does so by appealing to matters he knows I cannot accept. To respect and tolerate me, it is permissible that he profess belief in God's will as a way of helping me understand his proposal, but if he knows I am a non-religious person, he should not offer this profession as a way to *justify* his proposal. To do so would be to disrespect me as one he knows to be non-religious. If I argue that a particular action (if not "everything") is permitted because God does not exist, not only does my conclusion not follow from my premise but my premise also is one with no chance of being accepted by the theist and one that, in fact, disrespects him or her.[116]

Coming to an informal agreement

In Richardson's account of deliberation, the first two stages give the deliberators an abundance of riches. Group members may offer competing proposals about what to do, but the proposed actions and reasons (ends and values) submitted may be significantly, even radically, different. How does Richardson's version of deliberative democracy deal with these differences? How can the many, especially when heterogeneous, be reduced to a one that yields unitary collective action? Here is one place where deliberative democracy advances beyond balloting and majoritarian democracy because, in stage 3, deliberation includes several ways in which (most) group members (both majority and minorities) respectfully and tolerantly cooperate together to forge a joint intention.

One way to form a joint intention, contends Richardson, is to agree on the same action and policy and yet agree to disagree on its justifications: "We may all agree on what ought to be done but each have quite different reasons for coming to this conclusion."[117] Cass Sunstein terms an agreement of this sort an "incompletely theorized agreement on particular outcomes."[118] It is, I believe, a particularly effective way to practice tolerant deliberation in the face of deep valuational disagreement.

Alternatively, we may seek out intermediate final ends that lead to the same policy but do not rank high in our hierarchy of ends, and in any case we refuse to advance together to the realm of potentially divisive or "hot button" higher-order final or ultimate ends.[119] Or, we may deliberate about two competing final ends, at least one of us showing the other that there is good reason to be guided by the hitherto neglected end. We may agree on a final end, disagree on its specification, and through give and take come to agree on one of the competing specifications or together invent a new and more comprehensive specification that does justice to both sides. Furthermore, deliberators may creatively and collectively fashion a new and higher-order end that can be specified in two complementary lower-order ends. Finally, and most radically, through what Richardson calls "deep compromise," ends can be refashioned rather than held as fixed: "Deep compromise, by contrast [with "bare compromise," which is only a change in means] is a change in one's support of policies or implementing means that is accompanied and explained or supported by a change in one's ends that itself counts as a compromise."[120]

The joint intention (whether or not combined with justifying reasons) that is agreed to is not just a set of individual intentions to perform a similar action. Rather, it is an agreement to do something together, and this "togetherness" means that: "(1) each of the parties intends to do his or her part as required by the joint plan; (2) each of the parties believes that the joint action can be carried out if enough do their parts; and (3) these intentions and beliefs are common knowledge."[121]

Why would fellow deliberators want to adopt one of these ways to handle disagreement about ends, especially that of deep compromise? Richardson offers two plausible motivations. First, through increased information that discussion brings to light, one or more members may become convinced that the limited available means require a change of ends or that past attempts to realize a given end have resulted in unintended and unanticipated effects that now should be avoided.[122] Richer information about facts leads to refashioning of values. Second, deliberators, as free and equal partners informed by the ideals of reciprocity and toleration in a fair cooperative enterprise, are obliged to be responsive to and – within limits – to accommodate one another's ends.[123] More work is needed on the limits of toleration, especially in relation to dogmatically held or intolerable – for instance, racist or sexist – ultimate beliefs.

Does this affirmation of an obligation based on a debt of gratitude "pull a normative rabbit out of a positive hat?," asks Richardson.[124] Not if we accept the principle of reciprocity and the notion that "I, in turn, owe you" is a fitting response when you assume a burden or bestow on me a benefit. A balance obtains between self-interest and obligation.

Converting informal agreement into official decision

Majoritarian democracy emphasizes majority vote and downplays or neglects public discussion leading up to the vote. In contrast, deliberative democracy emphasizes the first three stages of the deliberative process and views majority vote as one means to obtain official conversion (stage 4) of the informal mutual agreement already achieved (stage 3). Rather than an aggregator of preferences, voting in deliberative democracy is a "closure device"[125] that expresses or acknowledges acceptance of a proposal and commitment to a joint intention, including one's role in executing it. Sometimes in face-to-face groups voting is a mere formality, for it is readily apparent that most if not all members have already agreed to a joint intention. The informal agreement is acknowledged and in a sense ratified, for example when a Quaker-style moderator formulates what he or she takes to be "the sense of the meeting" and no one objects. At other times, especially in large and even nationwide groups, a vote indicates that more members are for than against a proposal (or more are for one proposal rather than another). Those in the majority will have tried but failed to accommodate sufficiently the minority to the joint intention, making it partially rather than completely joint. There are deliberative disagreements as well as deliberative agreements. Minorities, however, can often accept the results insofar as the process was fair – they had their say – and the majority tried to accommodate (and perhaps partially succeeded in accommodating) what turned out to be minority views. The result is a *partially* joint intention that gains legitimacy from a fair substantive process – even though not everyone voted for it or some voted against it.

The extent to which Dewey anticipated this view of the relation of deliberation to the majority vote is astonishing:

The man who wears the shoe knows best that it pinches and where it pinches, even if the expert shoemaker is the best judge of how the trouble is to be remedied . . . A class of experts is inevitably so removed from common interests as to become a class with private interests and private knowledge, which in social matters is not knowledge at all. The ballot is, as often said, a substitute for bullets. But what is more significant is that counting of heads compels prior recourse to methods of discussion, consultation and persuasion, while the essence of appeal to force is to cut short resort to such methods. Majority rule, just as majority rule, is as foolish as its critics charge it with being. But it never is *merely* majority rule. As a practical politician, Samuel L. Tilden, said a long time ago: "The means by which a majority comes to be a majority is the more important thing": antecedent debates, modification of views to meet the opinions of minorities, the relative satisfaction given the latter by the fact that it has had chance and that the next time it may be successful in becoming a majority . . . The essential need, in other words, is the improvement of the methods and conditions of debate, discussion and persuasion.[126]

Some participatory democrats reject voting because it allegedly violates the rights of the losing side(s) and sets people – as competitors – at odds with one another. Instead, the participatory democrats urge that deliberation continue until there is absolute consensus or complete unanimity. Then everyone in fact would get what they want, people would not be set at odds with one another, and a majority would not tyrannize a minority. In fact, rule by consensus can be more tyrannical than majority voting, for a dissenter or a small number of dissenters can block a decision to make changes. As Richardson points out, the consequence of rule by consensus is that the status quo, no matter how unjust, is "unduly privileg[ed]."[127] Furthermore, as Gutmann and Thompson observe, a decision on when to use majority rule and other decision rules, such as the unanimity rule in juries, executive action, or parental authority, should itself be a matter of public deliberation rather than imposed by the individual or faction that controls the agenda.[128]

Several reasons converge to make Richardson's four-stage process both morally attractive and an appropriate specification or consistent development of some of Sen's commitments. First, the positive valuation of the *outcome* of the deliberative process – a partially joint intention – is coupled with the positive evaluation of the *process* itself. Just as a soccer team committed to fair play wants not only to win, but to win fairly, so a deliberatively democratic community values not only a joint intention but also the fair process by which group members generate that intention. Richardson's stages are a nice illustration of Sen's notion of a "'comprehensive outcome' that incorporates inter alia the process through which the 'culmination outcome' [the joint intention] comes about."[129] Second, the so-called "impossibility" or arbitrariness of combining individual preferences into a social function may be avoidable if deliberators are conceived as fashioning – with the help of richer information and in and through the giving and sifting of proposals and reasons – (partially) joint intentions and (sometimes) shared ends.

Third, Richardson's focus on joint intentions enables us to avoid the equally unpalatable extremes of, on the one hand, collapsing individual deliberators into one organic deliberator or, or the other hand, elevating individual intentions to the detriment of joint intentions. Richardson's insight is that joint intentions grow out "of what each of us, as distinct individuals, think [*sic*] ought to be done,"[130] but also intertwine or overlap in such a way as to enable us to act in concert, with each of us having responsibilities to do her share. Another way of making the point is to say that that Richardson has found a "way of conceiving of public decision-making that is at once sufficiently cognitive to make it truly deliberative and also sufficiently responsive to the positions of individual citizens to count as democratic."[131] Finally, Richardson's account of the course of practical reasoning enables him to do justice to the way in which deliberation usually builds on present commitments but also – through deep compromise and innovation – may creatively forge novel purposes that at least a majority of participants can endorse.

Deliberator capacities and virtues

So far I have explored the resources of deliberative democracy for understanding the aims, ideals, groups and group membership, background conditions, and process of deliberation. In another essay, I have also addressed the important questions of the kinds of persons who would make competent and virtuous deliberators and the way these skills and virtues might be brought about.[132] Here it must suffice to say that, without participants with the "right stuff," the deliberative approach to democracy might not manifest respect for persons, result in mutually acceptable decisions, or promote justice. As Drèze and Sen remark, democracy requires, in addition to the democratic ideals and institutions of (deliberative) democracy, citizens who "make democracy work."[133]

Concluding remarks

A frequent criticism of the relevance of Sen's capability approach for global, national, regional, and local development is that it leaves too many evaluative issues unresolved. Enlisting the resources of deliberative democracy, I sought in this chapter to strengthen Sen's appeal to democracy as public discussion and argued that groups and communities themselves, on all levels, have the primary responsibility to resolve these evaluative issues and should do so democratically and deliberatively. Sen contends both that "the value of public reasoning applies to reasoning about democracy itself" and, following Dewey, that "the defects of democracy demand more democracy not less."[134] The resultant public debate about the ends and means of democracy, democracy promotion, and deliberative participation in development will, one hopes, also contribute to meeting our greatest national and global challenge – developing deeper, more inclusive, and more resilient democratic institutions and ways of life. In the next chapter, I take up this challenge with respect to local development, and in the volume's final chapter I address the challenge in relation to globalization and global institutions.

NOTES

This chapter adapts my essay "Sen and Deliberative Democracy," in *Capabilities Equality: Basic Issues and Problems*, ed. Alexander Kaufman (New York: Routledge, 2006), 155–97. For helpful comments – not all of which are yet addressed adequately – on earlier drafts, I thank Sabina Alkire, Jay Drydyk, Verna Gehring, Douglas Grob, Laura Antkowiak Hussey, Lori Keleher, Judith Lichtenberg, Christopher Morris, Joe Oppenheimer, Henry Richardson, and the late Iris Marion Young. An early version of the chapter contributed to a World Bank project, which I codirected with Sabina Alkire, entitled "Responding to the Values of the Poor: Participation and Aspiration" (February, 2002–December, 2003). I gave presentations based on the chapter at the Philadelphia Area Philosophy Consortium, St. Joseph's University; Fundación Nueva Generación Argentina; Centro de Investigaciones Filosóficas, Argentina; Michigan State University; University of Maryland; and the 4th Conference on the Capability Approach, University of Pavia, Italy, September 5–7, 2004.

Ethics of Global Development

1. Amartya Sen, *Development as Freedom* (Oxford: Oxford University Press, 1999).
2. Amartya Sen, "Democracy as a Universal Value," *Journal of Democracy*, 10, 3 (1999): 3–17. See also Amartya Sen, "Democracy and Its Global Roots," *The New Republic*, 229, 4 (2003): 28–35.
3. Jean Drèze and Amartya Sen, *India: Development and Participation*, 2nd edn. (Oxford: Oxford University Press, 2002).
4. Amartya Sen, *The Argumentative Indian: Writings on Indian History, Culture, and Identity* (New York: Farrar, Straus & Giroux, 2005). See also Amartya Sen, *Identity and Violence: The Illusion of Destiny* (New York and London: W. W. Norton, 2006).
5. See Sen, "Democracy as a Universal Value," 148; *Development as Freedom*, 9–11; Drèze and Sen, *India*, 24–5.
6. Sen, "Democracy as a Universal Value," 9–10.
7. I borrow the terms "breadth," "depth," and "range" from Carl Cohen, *Democracy* (Athens, GA: University of Georgia Press, 1971). See also Svetozar Stojanović, *Between Ideals and Reality: A Critique of Socialism and Its Future*, trans. G. Sher (Oxford: Oxford University Press, 1973); and David A. Crocker, *Praxis and Democratic Socialism: The Critical Social Theory of Marković and Stojanović* (Atlantic Highlands, NJ: Humanities Press; Brighton: Harvester Press, 1983), 293, 299–300.
8. Drèze and Sen, *India*, 24, 347.
9. Due to the occurrence of "majoritarian tyrannies," one might be tempted to add another dimension to the strength of a democracy, namely, its making *just* decisions. Majoritarian tyranny can be wide and deep and range over many issues and institutions but make decisions that are unjust in content and consequence. Should we not build into the notion of democracy some notion of just decisions and consequences? Yes and no. Insofar as strong democracy presupposes an ideal of free and equal agents, equal political liberty and equality before the law, and at least rough economic justice, democratic institutions presuppose justice. Moreover, the more inclusive, wide-ranging, and deep democracy is, the more likely it is to make decisions that an independent critic might assess as just. However, no conceptual or practical guarantee exists that a strong democracy will also yield justice or avoid injustice. Rather, what justice should mean in that group's time and place will be decided (perhaps mistakenly) by the group itself. Although Jay Drydyk will not agree with these remarks, they owe much to his searching comments.
10. Sen, *Development as Freedom*, 148; and "Democracy as a Universal Value," 10.
11. Sen, "Democracy as a Universal Value,"10.
12. Sen, *Development as Freedom*, 288.
13. Ibid., xii–xiii.
14. Joe Kane, *Savages*, 2nd edn. (New York: Vintage, 1996), 75.
15. Ibid., 137–8.
16. Sen, *Development as Freedom*, 242; see also 241.
17. Daniel Little, *The Paradoxes of Wealth and Poverty: Mapping the Ethical Dilemmas of Global Development* (Boulder, CO: Westview Press, 2003), 222.

Little usefully clarifies two of the "tenets of normative democratic theory": "the universal citizenship principle" and "the liberty principle and the equality principle." The former holds that "All adult members of the collectivity ought to have the status of citizens (that is, there should be no restriction in political rights for different groups of people within the polity)." The latter affirms that "All citizens ought to have the broadest set of political rights and liberties possible, compatible with the extension of equal rights to all." For a similar argument based on national and world citizens' equal dignity and autonomy, see Adela Cortina, *Los ciudadanos como protagonistas* (Barcelona: Galaxy Gutenberg, 1999).

18. Drèze and Sen, *India*, 347.

19. Sen, "Elements of a Theory of Human Rights," *Philosophy and Public Affairs*, 32, 4 (2004): 336.

20. Little, *The Paradoxes of Wealth and Poverty*, 229. Another question with respect to the Huaorani in the context of Ecuador and the Amazon, of course, is how not only the Huaorani and other Amazonian tribes but also other affected groups – including the Ecuadorian government, other national governments, and the transnational oil companies – can and should decide collectively and fairly the fate of the region as well as reap the instrumental benefits of democracy. Who should come to the table, set the agenda, and deliberate about the ends and means of policy?

21. Drèze and Sen, *India*, 24.

22. Morton H. Halperin, Joseph T. Siegle, and Michael M. Weinstein, *The Democracy Advantage: How Democracies Promote Prosperity and Peace* (New York: Routledge, 2005). For additional arguments for and against the claim that democracy promotes justice, equality, efficiency, and freedom, see *Democracy's Edges*, ed. Ian Shapiro and Casiano Hacker-Cordón (Cambridge: Cambridge University Press, 1999); Larry Diamond, *Developing Democracy: Toward Consolidation* (Baltimore and London: Johns Hopkins University Press, 1999); Adam Przeworski, Michael E. Alvarez, José Antonio Cheibub, and Fernando Limongi, *Democracy and Development: Political Institutions and Well-Being in the World, 1950–1900* (Cambridge: Cambridge University Press, 2000); and Fareed Zakaria, *The Future of Freedom: Illiberal Democracy at Home and Abroad* (New York: W. W. Norton, 2003).

23. Sen, *Development as Freedom*, 43. See also Sen, *The Argumentative Indian*, 198–200.

24. Ibid., 150–1.

25. Sen, *Development as Freedom*, 152–3.

26. Drèze and Sen, *India*, 25.

27. Sen, *Rationality and Freedom* (Cambridge, MA: Harvard University Press, 2002).

28. Ibid., 10; and Sen, "Elements of a Theory of Human Rights."

29. Sen, *Inequality Reexamined* (Cambridge, MA: Harvard University Press, 1992), 70–1.

30. Sen, *Development as Freedom*, 284.

31. Amartya Sen, "Development Thinking at the Beginning of the 21st Century," in *Economic and Social Development into the XXI Century*, ed. Louis

Emmerji (Washington, DC: Inter-American Development Bank, 1997); cf. Sen, *Development as Freedom*, 35–6.

32. Martha Nussbaum, *Women and Human Development: The Capabilities Approach* (Cambridge: Cambridge University Press, 2000).
33. Sen, *Rationality and Freedom*, 49.
34. Sen, *Development as Freedom*, 287.
35. Ibid., 286.
36. See Sen, "Equality of What?," in *The Tanner Lectures on Human Values*, I, ed. Sterling M. McMurrin (Salt Lake City: University of Utah Press, 1980), 197–220.
37. Sen, *Inequality Reexamined*, 45, n. 19. This passage is evidence that Nussbaum is mistaken when she says, "Sen nowhere uses the idea of a threshold": Nussbaum, *Women and Human Development*, 12.
38. Drèze and Sen, *India*, 25; Sen, *Development as Freedom*, 153–4.
39. Sabina Alkire, *Valuing Freedoms: Sen's Capability Approach and Poverty Reduction* (Oxford: Oxford University Press, 2002), 195.
40. For Nussbaum, constitutional guarantees, for example for health care, are compatible with someone's freedom to forgo good health in order to realize some nonbasic capability.
41. Nussbaum, *Women and Human Development*, 77; and Henry Richardson, *Democratic Autonomy: Public Reasoning About the Ends of Policy* (Oxford: Oxford University Press, 2002), 104, 154, 214, 246.
42. Sen, *Inequality Reexamined*, 146–7.
43. Alkire, *Valuing Freedoms*, 92. Cf. the World Bank's *World Development Report 2006*, in which it is recognized that – although "equity" usually contributes to "efficiency" (and vice versa), at least in the long run – sometimes a nation must choose between "equity" and "efficiency": World Bank, *World Development Report 2006: Equity and Development* (New York: World Bank and Oxford University Press, 2005), 3, 10, 17.
44. Sen, *Development as Freedom*, 110. See also *ibid.*, 30.
45. Sen, "Equality of What?"
46. Sen, *Development as Freedom*, 286–7.
47. Sen, "Democracy and Its Global Roots," 28.
48. Ibid., 29.
49. Ibid.
50. Alkire, *Valuing Freedoms*, 13.
51. Sen, *Development as Freedom*, 155–6.
52. Ibid., 329, n. 9.
53. These include the following: Jürgen Habermas, "Three Normative Models of Democracy," *Constellations*, 1, 1 (1994): 1–10; Seyla Benhabib, "Deliberative Rationality and Models of Democratic Legitimacy," *Constellations*, 1, 1 (1994): 41–5; *Deliberative Democracy*, ed. James Bohman and William Rehg (Cambridge, MA: MIT Press, 1997); James Fishkin, *Democracy and Deliberation* (New Haven, CT: Yale University Press, 1971); Ralf Dahrendorf, *The Modern Social Contract* (New York: Weidenfeld & Nicolson, 1988); *The Good Polity*, ed. A. Hamlin and Philip Pettit (Oxford: Blackwell, 1989); Cass Sunstein, *The Partial Constitution* (Cambridge, MA: Harvard

University Press, 1993); and Amy Gutmann and Dennis Thompson, *Democracy and Disagreement* (Cambridge, MA: Harvard University Press, 1996). Among the most important volumes defending or evaluating deliberative democracy that Sen does not cite (many of which were published after 1999) are, in the order in which they appeared: James Bohman, *Public Deliberation: Pluralism, Complexity and Democracy* (Cambridge, MA: MIT Press, 1996); Joshua Cohen, "Procedure and Substance in Deliberative Democracy," in *Democracy and Difference: Contesting the Boundaries of the Political*, ed. Seyla Benhabib (Princeton: Princeton University Press, 1996); *Deliberative Democracy*, ed. Jon Elster (Cambridge: Cambridge University Press, 1998); *Deliberative Politics: Essays on Democracy and Disagreement*, ed. Stephen Macedo (Oxford: Oxford University Press, 1999); *Democracy's Edges*, ed. Shapiro and Hacker-Cordón; *Democracy's Value*, ed. Ian Shapiro and Casiano Hacker-Cordón (Cambridge: Cambridge University Press, 1999); *Democracy*, ed. Ellen Frankel Paul, Fred D. Miller, Jr., and Jeffrey Paul (Cambridge: Cambridge University Press, 2000); Iris Marion Young, *Inclusion and Democracy* (Oxford: Oxford University Press, 2000); Cass Sunstein, *Designing Democracy: What Constitutions Do* (Oxford: Oxford University Press, 2001); Henry Richardson, *Democratic Autonomy: Public Reasoning About the Ends of Policy* (Oxford: Oxford University Press, 2002); *Deepening Democracy: Institutional Innovations in Empowered Participatory Governance*, ed. Archon Fung and Erik Olin Wright (London: Verso, 2003); Ian Shapiro, *The State of Democratic Theory* (Princeton: Princeton University Press, 2003); Bruce Ackerman and James S. Fishkin, *Deliberation Day* (New Haven and London: Yale University Press, 2004); Archon Fung, *Empowered Participation: Reinventing Urban Democracy* (Princeton: Princeton University Press, 2004); Amy Gutmann and Dennis Thompson, *Why Deliberative Democracy?* (Princeton: Princeton University Press, 2004); and *The Deliberative Democracy Handbook: Strategies for Effective Civic Engagement in the 21st Century*, ed. John Gastil and Peter Levine (San Francisco: Jossey-Bass, 2005). In his 2004 essay "Elements of a Theory of Human Rights," 349, nn. 57 and 58, Sen cites Cohen (1996) and Gutmann and Thompson (1996) in relation to deliberative democracy and public reasoning, respectively.

54. Sen, *Development as Freedom*, 155.
55. Bohman, *Public Deliberation: Pluralism, Complexity and Democracy*.
56. John Rawls, *The Law of Peoples* with "The Idea of Public Reason Revisited" (Cambridge, MA: Harvard University Press, 1999), 138–9. Joshua Cohen, in an essay that helped launch the recent deliberative democracy movement, says: "By deliberative democracy, I shall mean, roughly, an association whose affairs are governed by the public deliberation of its members": "Deliberation and Democratic Legitimacy," in *The Good Polity*, ed. Hamlin and Pettit, 17. Cf. Amy Gutmann and Dennis Thompson's definition: "Deliberative democracy is a conception of democratic politics in which decisions and policies are justified in a process of discussion among free and equal citizens or their accountable representatives": *Why Deliberative Democracy?*, 161.

57. Adam Przeworski, "Minimalist Conception of Democracy: A Defense," in *Democracy's Value*, ed. Shapiro and Hacker-Cordón, 23–55; and Joseph Schumpeter, *Capitalism, Socialism, and Democracy* (New York: Harper, 1942).

58. Young, *Inclusion and Democracy*, 1–19.

59. Fung and Wright, *Deepening Democracy*, 16.

60. Ibid., 15.

61. Ibid., 13.

62. Ibid., 16.

63. "Cycling" refers to the way in which, as Sen puts it, "majority rule can be thoroughly inconsistent, with A defeating B by a majority, B defeating C also by a majority, and C in turn defeating A, by a majority as well": Sen, *Rationality and Freedom*, 68. See also Gerry Mackie, *Democracy Defended* (Cambridge: Cambridge University Press, 2003).

64. Sen, *Rationality and Freedom*, 69.

65. See Richardson, "Democratic Intentions," in *Deliberative Democracy*, ed. Bohman and Rehg, 349–82; and Richardson, *Democratic Autonomy*, 162–76.

66. Young, *Inclusion and Democracy*, 26.

67. Gutmann and Thompson, *Democracy and Disagreement*, 93.

68. Sen, "Democracy and Its Global Roots," 31.

69. Gutmann and Thompson, *Democracy and Disagreement*, 52.

70. Gutmann and Thompson rely on Lawrence Becker's concept of reciprocity as "making a proportionate return for good received"; see L. C. Becker, *Reciprocity* (London: Routledge & Kegan Paul, 1986), 73–144. The principle, however, may plausibly be pitched on a more abstract level to include proportionate responses to bads as well as goods received; see J. L. Crocker, The Upper Limits of Just Punishment," *Emory Law Journal*, 42 (1992): 1059.

71. Gutmann and Thompson, *Democracy and Disagreement*, 55.

72. Gutmann and Thompson, "Why Deliberative Democracy is Different," in *Democracy*, ed. Paul, Miller, Jr., and Paul, 161–80.

73. John Dewey, *The Public and Its Problems* (Athens, OH: Swallow Press, 1927), 143.

74. William A. Galston, *Liberal Pluralism* (Cambridge: Cambridge University Press, 2002).

75. Shapiro, *The State of Democratic Theory*, chs. 1 and 2.

76. Andrew D. Selee, "The Paradox of Local Empowerment: Decentralization and Democratic Governance in Mexico," PhD dissertation, University of Maryland, School of Public Policy, 2006.

77. Gutmann and Thompson discuss these issues in "Why Deliberative Democracy?" 116–38.

78. David Broder, "Endangered Suffrage," *Washington Post* (September 17, 2003), 27.

79. Gutmann and Thompson, "Democratic Disagreement," in *Deliberative Politics*, ed. Macedo, 273.

80. See Alkire, *Valuing Freedoms*, 271–7.

81. *Democracy's Edges*, ed. Shapiro and Hacker-Cordón, 1.

82. Shapiro, *The State of Democratic Theory*, 52.
83. Richardson, *Democratic Autonomy*, 88.
84. See Archon Fung, "Deliberation Before the Revolution: Toward an Ethics of Deliberative Democracy," *Political Theory*, 32, 2 (2005): 416.
85. Richardson, *Democratic Autonomy*, 88.
86. Bohman, *Public Deliberation*, 112, 24.
87. Sen, *Development as Freedom*, 30.
88. Drèze and Sen, *India*, 29; and Richardson, *Democratic Autonomy*, 88.
89. Richardson, *Democratic Autonomy*, 88.
90. Séverine Deneulin, "Promoting Human Freedom under Conditions of Inequalities: A Procedural Framework," *Journal of Human Development*, 6, 1 (2005): 75–92.
91. United Nations Development Programme, *La democracia en América Latina: Hacia una democracia de ciudadanas y ciudadanos* (Buenos Aires: Aguilar, Altea, Taurus, Alfaguara, 2004).
92. For a surprisingly forthright analysis of the reality of elite dominance over a disempowered majority and the danger of elite capture of measures to reduce this dominance, see World Bank, *World Development Report 2006*, 156–8, 175, 178–82.
93. Halperin *et al.* define democracies as "those countries that have met the relatively high standards of having instituted genuine checks and balances on executive power and created mechanisms for popular participation in the political process": Halperin, Siegle, and Weinstien, *The Democracy Advantage*, 66.
94. Frank Cunningham, *The Real World of Democracy Revisited* (Atlantic Highlands, NJ: Humanities Press, 1994).
95. Young, *Inclusion and Democracy*, 35.
96. Halperin, Siegle, and Weinstien, *The Democracy Advantage*, 146–51.
97. Sen, "Democracy as a Universal Value," 4.
98. Dewey, *The Public and Its Problems*, 143–4.
99. *Deepening Democracy*, ed. Fung and Wright, 23.
100. Compare ibid., 28, 32; Gianpaolo Baiocchi, "Participation, Activism and Politics: The Porto Alegre Experiment," in *Deepening Democracy*, ed. Fung and Wright, 56–8; and Drèze and Sen, *India*, 362–3.
101. Baiocchi, "Participation, Activism and Politics," 52.
102. Ibid., 67. See also World Bank, *World Development Report 2006*, 70–1.
103. Drèze and Sen, *India*, 357.
104. In "Deliberation Before the Revolution," 401–16, Fung convincingly argues that deliberative democrats may employ non-deliberative methods but only with the long-term goal of a deliberative society and when deliberative activists have first assumed good faith on the part of their opponents, have exhausted deliberative methods, and have limited their use of non-deliberative methods by a principle of proportionality.
105. Richardson, "Democratic Intentions," in *Deliberative Democracy*, ed. Bohman and Rehg, 349–82; and *Democratic Autonomy*, ch. 10.
106. Richardson, *Democratic Autonomy*, 162.
107. Ibid., 164.

108. Fung, "Deliberative Democracy, Chicago Style: Grass-roots Governance in Policing and Public Education," in *Deepening Democracy*, ed. Fung and Wright, 118.

109. Jane Mansbridge, "Practice-Thought-Practice," in *Deepening Democracy*, ed. Fung and Wright, 176; see also 179–83.

110. Jürgen Habermas, *The Theory of Communicative Action*, I: *Reason and the Rationalization of Society* (Boston, MA: Beacon Press, 1984).

111. Richardson, *Democratic Autonomy*, 12.

112. Ibid., 82.

113. Jürgen Habermas, "Reconciliation through the Public Use of Reason: Remarks on John Rawls's *Political Liberalism*," *Journal of Philosophy*, 92 (1995): 109–31.

114. Rawls, *The Law of Peoples*, 140–8.

115. Ibid. For an analysis of these two options and an argument for the second, see Oswaldo Guariglia, *Una ética para el siglo XXI: Ética y derechos humanos en un tiempo posmetafísico* (Buenos Aires: Fondo de Cultura Económica, 2001), 147–55.

116. Richardson correctly sees that Rawls himself is moving toward this "third way" in Rawls, *The Law of Peoples*, 121–80. In *Justice as Fairness: A Restatement*, which amounts to a final statement of the themes of his previous work, Rawls argues that people should be free to introduce their "comprehensive doctrines" into public debate as a means of "informing one another where they come from, so to speak, and on what basis they support the public political conception of justice": John Rawls, *Justice as Fairness: A Restatement*, ed. Erin Kelly (Cambridge, MA: Harvard University Press, 2001), 89. I discovered the passage in which Rawls makes this point only after I completed Chapter 9.

117. Richardson, *Democratic Autonomy*, 173.

118. Sunstein, *Designing Democracy*, 57.

119. Cf. Sen: "A consensus on public decisions may flourish so long as the exact grounds for that accord are not very precisely articulated": Sen, *Rationality and Freedom*, 558, quoted by Alkire, *Valuing Freedoms*, 92–3. See also Sunstein, *Designing Democracy*, 56–8; and "Agreement Without Theory," in *Deliberative Politics*, ed. Macedo, 123–50.

120. Richardson, *Democratic Autonomy*, 147.

121. Ibid., 165.

122. Sen, *Development as Freedom*, 256–61.

123. Richardson, *Democratic Autonomy*, 172.

124. Ibid.

125. Ibid., 204.

126. Dewey, *The Public and Its Problems*, 207–8.

127. Richardson, *Democratic Autonomy*, 205.

128. Gutmann and Thompson, *Democracy and Disagreement*, 32–3.

129. Sen, *Development as Freedom*, 27.

130. Richardson, *Democratic Autonomy*, 162.

131. Richardson, "Democratic Intentions," in *Deliberative Democracy*, ed. Bohman and Rehg, 359.

132. Crocker, "Sen and Deliberative Democracy," 187–90. For dialogical and deliberative skills and capacities, see Bohman, *Public Deliberation*; and "Deliberative Democracy and Effective Social Freedom: Capabilities, Resources, and Opportunities," in *Deliberative Democracy*, ed. Bohman and Rehg, 321–48. For the role of participatory education in promoting democratic critical thinking, seeing others as fellow (world) citizens, and narrative imagination, see Martha Nussbaum, "Education and Democratic Citizenship: Capabilities and Quality Education," *Journal of Human Development: Alternative Economics in Action*, 7, 3 (2006): 388–92. For the deliberative virtues of (mutual) respect, civic integrity, and civic magnanimity, see Gutmann and Thompson, *Democracy and Disagreement*, chs. 2–4.

133. Drèze and Sen, *India*, 347–52.

134. Sen, "Democracy and Its Global Roots," 34.

10 Deliberative participation in local development

In this chapter I aim to improve the theory and practice of participation in local, grassroots, or micro-development initiatives. Accomplishing this goal requires three steps. First, in order to clarify the different approaches to "participation" that have occurred in the last fifty years of development theory and practice, I discuss and enrich some classifications of types of participation, including those of Denis Goulet, J. N. Pretty, John Gaventa, Bina Agarwal, and Jay Drydyk. In relation to these accounts of participation, I propose and explain an ideal of deliberative participation derived from the theory and practice of deliberative democracy presented in the last chapter.

Second, in terms of these kinds of participation, and especially the ideal of deliberative participation, I analyze economist Sabina Alkire's recent efforts, in *Valuing Freedoms: Sen's Capability Approach and Poverty Reduction*, to apply Sen's theory to micro-projects. Although I find much to approve of in her approach to grassroots participation, I argue that it could be strengthened by features of deliberative participation.

Finally, I analyze and evaluate four objections that have been made to (1) Sen's democratic turn in his version of the capability approach, (2) the theory and practice of deliberative democracy, and (3) deliberative participation in local development. Critics find these allied accounts of robust democracy and citizen participation flawed by too much indeterminacy, too little autonomy, insufficient realism, and unjustified or unacceptable egalitarianism.

Before proceeding, it should also be noted that the chapter's focus on local democracy and grassroots development does not imply that local communities and development projects are the only or best place for deepening and democracy and citizen participation. Indeed, I would argue that the right kind of democratization should take place not only at the local level but also at regional, national, and global levels, and that efforts should be made to forge linkages among the various levels. In the next chapter my emphasis shifts to national and especially global democracy.

338

Participation in development

Since their inception after World War II, national and international initiatives to bring about "development" in "less developed" countries periodically have aspired to make development "participatory." More recently the term "empowerment" sometimes encompasses the idea that the recipients of "development" should participate in some way in the process or results of development. Often, however, what was meant by "participation" (and "empowerment") – while usually positive in meaning – was vague.[1] Somehow the recipients of development aid were to be involved in the process of beneficial change or "empowered" by it. Even when concepts of participation were precise, substantial differences have existed over the goals, "point of entry," agents, processes, causes, effects, value, and limits of "participation." More problematic is that the banner of "participation" has been waved over projects that were, at best, thinly participatory or, at worst, smokescreens for elite control. Several writers have recently exposed and excoriated a dark side, the anti-democratic side, of so-called participatory approaches and practices.[2] Jay Drydyk has ably analyzed and assessed these recent criticisms, and argued for a deeply democratic approach to participatory development.[3] Before drawing on and supplementing Drydyk's ideas, I want to approach the issue of participation and situate the ideal of deliberative participation in relation to some efforts to classify types of participation.

The late Denis Goulet, the widely acknowledged pioneer of development ethics, offers one such classification.[4] Throughout his career, most emphatically in his 1989 *World Development* article "Participation in Development: New Avenues," Goulet emphasized the principle of what he called "nonelite participation in development decision-making," or, more briefly, "nonelite participation."[5] The basic idea is that persons and groups should make their own decisions, at least about the most fundamental matters, rather than having others – government officials, development planners, development ethicists, community leaders – make decisions for them or in their stead. Authentic development occurs when groups at whatever level become subjects who deliberate, decide, and act in the world rather than being either victims of circumstance or objects of someone else's decisions, the tools of someone else's designs. Goulet, for example, applauds the Brazilian pedagogue Paulo Freire's agency-oriented ideal of participation:

For Freire, the supreme touchstone of development is whether people who were previously treated as mere objects, known and acted upon, can now actively know and act upon, thereby becoming subjects of their own social destiny. When people are oppressed or reduced to the culture of silence, they do not participate in their own humanization. Conversely, when they participate, thereby becoming active subjects of knowledge and action, they begin to construct their properly human history and engage in processes of authentic development.[6]

Goulet correctly recognizes that this commitment to non-elite participation does not get us very much beyond "participation" as a universally approved "buzzword" with either little content or, even worse, whatever content one wants to supply. Everyone is for "participation," but it turns out that in practice people often give the term very different meanings. Goulet makes additional headway in clarifying *his* normative concept of non-elite participation in two ways. First, he borrows Marshall Wolfe's 1983 working "operationalization" of the concept as it relates to development. Participation, says Wolfe, is "the organized efforts to increase control over resources and regulative institutions in given social situations, on the part of groups and movements hitherto excluded from such control."[7] Non-elite participation has to do with people's decision-making about and control over resources and institutions. Productive activity is not participatory unless the producer has a role in freely and intentionally shaping that activity. Second, recognizing that, even with this working definition, the term "participation" covers many different phenomena, Goulet helpfully distinguishes different *types* of participation on the basis of normative role, originating agent, scale, and "point of entry" in a group's decision-making process.

Popular participation, however conceived, can be either one goal of development, or only a means to other goals (such as economic growth), or both an end and a means. Similar to the agency argument for democracy that I developed in the last chapter, Goulet commits himself to popular agency as intrinsically valuable. Popular participation is a way in which people manifest their inherent worth. To respect and promote such participation is to respect the dignity of hitherto neglected or despised people: "Participation ... guarantees government's noninstrumental treatment of powerless people by bringing them dignity as beings of worth, independent of their productivity, utility, or importance to the state's goals."[8] Goulet also defends participation on instrumental grounds. The right kind of participation, at least its "upstream" variety, is likely to have good consequences in reducing poverty, expanding solidarity, and strengthening self-reliance.

Goulet also recognizes that participation occurs on different scales. Although the popular image of participation is either balloting in national elections or citizen face-to-face involvement in local governments or grassroots development projects, issues of participation of women arise in households, and citizen participation in addition to voting is possible in national and global governance structures. Throughout his career Goulet insisted that one of development's most important challenges is to find ways in which "micro" participation can be extended to venues of "macro" decision-making.

Furthermore, Goulet distinguishes three types of participation in relation to what he calls "the originating agent." The originator of development may be from "above," "below," or the "outside." Elite groups, acting "from above," sometimes establish non-elite participation on municipal or micro levels. Such occurred in 1989 in Porto Alegre, Brazil, when the Workers' Party set up the participatory budgeting process in that city of 1.5 million people.[9] Similarly, in 1996 in the Indian state of Kerala, the Left Democratic Front (LDF) coalition decentralized power and "empowered local government to a far greater degree than in any other Indian state."[10]

Participation can also originate from below when a local community or national sector spontaneously mobilizes and then organizes itself to resist exploitation or oppression or to solve an urgent problem. Underground neighborhood associations during Pinochet's dictatorship in Chile illustrate the former, and the spontaneous rise of associations of garbage-pickers (cartoneros) in Argentina after its 2001 economic collapse exemplifies the latter. William Easterly is a recent exponent of "home-grown" and "bottom" citizens searching for piecemeal and incremental solutions to local problems.[11]

External agents are Goulet's third type of originators of participation. Outsiders to the group, whether national or international, need not impose – from above – their views on the group, manipulate it, or coopt it. Rather, they may *facilitate* the participation of insiders. An important way to do so, one that the next chapter examines, is that outsiders, accepting the invitation of alien groups, may describe options available for insider choice. Temporary "pump-primers," the outside catalytic agents, help people help themselves. The outside agents stay only so long as the people are awakened "to their dormant capacities to decide and act for themselves."[12] Goulet is aware, as are some recent critics (noted above) of "participation," that each of the three ways of originating participation may go astray and weaken or undermine local control, if not result in outright domination. People from above and outside as well as insider leaders, often using the rhetoric of non-elite participation, may capture power and dominate the group. Examples of Goulet's point, arguably, are Venezuela's Hugo Chávez's *caudillo* (big boss)-like relation to his own people, and the USA's imposition of democracy on Iraq.

Finally, Goulet very helpfully classifies types of citizen participation according to the precise point in which non-elites are invited or insert themselves into a group's decision-making process: (1) initial diagnosis of the problem; (2) listing of possible solutions; (3) selecting one course of action; (4) preparing for implementation; (5) evaluating and self-correcting during implementation; and (6) considering the merits of further action. Goulet's classification of these non-expert entry points alerts us that the more citizens participate "upstream" in decision-making, the more fully people express their agency and the better the likely consequences with respect to social justice. However, when Goulet claims that "the quality of participation depends on its initial entry point," it is not correct that the entry point exclusively determines the quality of participation. As I note below, with respect to *each* of these times of entry, with the possible exception of the last one, various ways or modes of participation exist – some more active, deliberative, and influential than others.

We can supplement Goulet's classification in at least three ways. First, we can classify participatory arrangements, as we can quality of democracy, with respect to inclusiveness: how wide is the membership of the group? Agarwal, for example, assesses community forestry groups in both India and Nepal in relation to the extent to which they include or exclude women.[13] Other researchers examine the extent to which local development projects include other sectors of the community, especially the poor or the shunned.

Second, we should supplement Goulet's typology and, like Agarwal, investigate the causes of and impediments to different sorts of participation and participatory exclusions. "What," asks Agarwal, "determines participation?" With respect to the exclusion of women, for example, she identifies the following causal factors: formal rules that exclude women from group membership; social norms (such as gender segregation in public spaces; the gender division of labor, in which women's domestic duties leave them little time for public participation; gendered behavioral norms that emphasize "self-effacement, shyness and soft speech"); social perceptions that women are ill-equipped to participate; men's traditional control over community structures; and women's lack of personal property.[14]

Third, and for our purposes most importantly, we add to Goulet's typology by distinguishing *how* a group's non-elite members participate, especially in the group's decision-making. Here, drawing on and supplementing the classificatory work of Bina Agarwal, J. N. Pretty, John Gaventa, and Jay Drydyk,[15] I distinguish – from thinner to thicker – a spectrum of *modes* of participation in group decision-making:

(1) *Nominal participation:* The weakest way in which someone partici-
pates in group decision-making is when someone is a member of a
group but does not attend its meetings. Some people, of course, are
not even members. Some are members but are unable to attend,
because of other responsibilities, or are unwilling to attend, for
instance because they are harassed or unwelcome.

(2) *Passive participation:* In passive participation, people are group
members and attend the group's or officials' decision-making meetings, but passively listen to reports about the decisions that others
have already made. The elite tells the non-elite what the elite is
going to do or has done, and non-elite persons participate, like the
White House press corps, by listening and, at best, asking questions
or making comments.

(3) *Consultative participation:* Non-elites participate by giving information and their opinions ("input," "preferences," and even "proposals") to the elite. The non-elite neither deliberate among
themselves nor make decisions. It is the elite who are the "deciders,"
and while they may deign to listen to the non-elite, they have no
obligation to do so.

(4) *Petitionary participation:* Non-elites petition[16] authorities to make
certain decisions and do certain things, usually to remedy grievances. Although it is the prerogative of the elite to decide, the
non-elite have a right to be heard and the elite have the duty to
receive, listen, and consider, if not to heed. This participatory
model, like that of consultative participation, is often used in
traditional decision-making.

(5) *Participatory implementation:*[17] Elites determine the goals and main
means, and non-elites implement the goals and decide, if at all, only
tactics. In this mode non-elites do more than listen, comment, and
express. Like soccer players, they also make and enact decisions, but
the overall plan and marching orders belong to the coach.

(6) *Bargaining:* On the basis of whatever individual or collective power
they have, non-elites bargain with elites. Those bargaining are
more adversaries than partners. Self-interest largely if not exclusively motivates each side, and non-elite influence on the final
"deal" depends on what non-elites are willing to give up and what
concessions they are able to extract. The greater the power imbalances between an elite and non-elite, the less influence the non-eltite
has on the final outcome. An elite may settle for some loss now in
order to make likely a larger future gain. Alliances with and support
from actors outside and above tend to enhance non-elite bargaining
power.[18]

(7) *Deliberative participation:* Non-elites (sometimes among themselves and sometimes with elites) deliberate together, sifting proposals and reasons to forge agreements on policies that at least a majority can accept.

The further we go down the list, the "thicker" is the participatory mode in the sense of more fully expressing individual or collective agency. It requires more agency to attend a meeting than to be a stay-at-home member, and even more agency actively to comment or petition than merely to listen, accept others' decisions, or do what one is told. In both bargaining and deliberative participation, non-elite individuals and groups manifest even more robust agency because they are part of the decision-making process and not passive recipients of others' decisions.

It should also be noted that different kinds of participation are likely to differ with respect to their consequences. Of particular importance to the agency-focused capability approach is the extent to which non-elites are likely – through the different kinds of participation – to make a positive difference in the world, for example to promote human development. In a particular context, for example, some sort of non-deliberative participation, such as petitioning or bargaining, may be more efficacious than deliberative participation in promoting development as capability expansion and agency enhancement.[19] Moreover, a non-deliberative mode of participation now may play an important role in bringing about deliberative participation in the future.

How does Goulet stand with respect to these further classifications of participation? Goulet does emphasize that citizen "voice" or influence must make a difference in development policy and practice. With his concept of participation from below, Goulet argues that participation in micro venues of decision-making must scale up to macro arenas and confer "a new voice in macro arenas of decision-making to previously powerless communities of need."[20] As in his appeal to Marshall Wolfe's concept of participation as effective control over resources, Goulet improves upon some notions of deliberative democracy that seem content with talk and agreement even when not efficacious. Agency, as I have agreed with Sen, is not just making (or influencing) a decision, even when the decision is the outcome of deliberation. It is also effectively running one's own individual or collective life and thereby making a difference in the world.

Although Goulet does emphasize *effective* non-elite participation, his treatment of "deliberative participation" is relatively underdeveloped. It is true that Goulet endorses, in participation from above, what he calls "active dialogue"[21] between experts and non-elite participants. Moreover, he affirms the importance of "locating true decisional power in non-elite people, and freeing them from manipulation and co-optation."[22] What he does not do, however, is provide an account of the *process* by which people with diverse value commitments can and often should engage in a deliberative give and take of practical proposals and arrive at a course of action that almost all can accept. He rightly insists that the mere fact of consensus does not justify the consensus, since the "agreement" may be the result of elite manipulation.[23] He does not, however, discuss the dynamics of the process leading to a normatively compelling consensus. I intend the account of theory and practice of deliberative democracy, offered in the last chapter, to contribute to filling this lacuna.

Given our model of deliberative democracy as well as these various classifications of sorts of participation in development, let us now analyze and evaluate Alkire's approach to participatory development.

Alkire's participatory approach and deliberative participation

Amartya Sen's capability approach, I argued in Chapter 9, requires democracy conceived as "open public reasoning"[24] about matters of social concern. Sen himself urges that this deliberative ideal of democracy be built into our conception of the ends as well as the means of development, whether in "developed" or "developing" countries: "Such processes as participation in political decisions and social choice cannot be seen as being – at best – among the *means* to development (through, say, their contribution to economic growth), but have to be understood as constitutive parts of the ends of development in themselves."[25]

I now analyze and evaluate – as one way of promoting participatory development – Sabina Alkire's *Valuing Freedoms: Sen's Capability Approach and Poverty Reduction*. In this important book Alkire accurately interprets and skillfully applies Sen's capability approach to three micro socioeconomic development projects in Pakistan, each of which involves some sort of aid from above and outside. The three groups that constitute Alkire's Pakistan case studies – the loan-for-goats project with women from four villages near Senghar, Sindh; the Khoj literacy centers near Lahore; and the rose cultivation project in the village of Arabsolangi, Sindh – are all examples of non-public, local, and income-generation projects partially dependent on outside help from both an international development agent (Oxfam) and Pakistani nongovernmental organizations. Although this help does come from beyond the local community, Alkire's focus is on bottom-up and small-scale development.[26] In the three local development groups, local facilitators employed (and later helped assess) the value-laden participatory method, which I now analyze, assess, and strengthen.

Alkire supplements Sen's work with that of philosopher John Finnis.[27] The result is a novel approach to an outside development agent's decision on whether to continue funding an income-generating and community-building activity for which the group had received earlier support. Unique to this approach is the external funder's use of local facilitator-assessor-reporters to elicit, clarify, and then report on the groups' evaluations of the impact of the project funded earlier. I conclude that an ideal of deliberative participation, informed by the theory and practice of deliberative democracy, would strengthen Alkire's approach to local participatory development.

In her study, Alkire draws on and sometimes criticizes not only Sen's ideas but also the development literature concerning popular participation in development initiatives. Alkire's focus is on only one sort of development activity, and she is keenly aware that other participatory approaches may be called for in other contexts. Among these, I note, would be community-based natural resource management, where the resources to be managed sustainably are such things as forests, wildlife, water, and village councils.[28] What specific sort of development context does she address?

A global development agency, Oxfam, with the assistance of Pakistani nongovernmental organizations, had selected and invested in income-generating and community-building initiatives in three different grass-roots groups. The projects had been in operation for some time, and Oxfam wanted to assess how well the projects had done before deciding whether to continue funding them. Oxfam employs several established methodologies to evaluate success and failure. Among these are cost-benefit analysis and a form of social impact assessment (SIA) that emphasizes a contemplated intervention's anticipated social consequences, especially its negative impacts on human beings.[29] None of these methodologies, however, gave the groups themselves or their members much of a role. To remedy this deficiency, Alkire employed educated and local people – who, however, were not members of the communities studied – and provided Oxfam with a more robust participatory approach. The basic idea is that these evaluators elicited from the group members the latter's evaluations of the impact of the project on their lives. The results of this evaluation then supplemented the outcomes of the other methodologies. Hence, Oxfam, the ultimate decision-maker, was to have richer information with respect to *its* decision on whether or not to continue funding the projects and what sort of projects to fund in the future.

Alkire does not investigate or evaluate the process by which Oxfam itself makes decisions about what projects to fund. If she did, it would be important to know to what extent its decision-making was deliberative and to what extent, if any, representatives from the affected groups were involved at this higher level. Her focus rather is on the outsider-facilitated, backward-looking assessment exercise that the groups themselves perform. What role did the outsiders play, and did they intentionally or inadvertently communicate Oxfam preferences or interests? What role did the groups themselves and their members play? At what point did they enter the decision-making process, and how, exactly, did they participate?

The local facilitators (1) *elicited* the group members' value judgments about impacts of past projects; (2) *facilitated* the members' and groups' clarification, scrutiny, and ranking of those judgments; (3) *comparatively assessed and reported* to the funding institution the various groups' achievements; and (4) *reported* the funding body's assessments and funding decision back to the investigated groups.

Before briefly describing each role, it is important to underscore that Alkire is acutely aware of the importance of the outsider facilitators conducting the exercise in what she calls a "participatory manner":

To the greatest extent possible the facilitators or "assessors" wore simple clothing, used the local language, adapted the methodology flexibly to the situation, respected traditional and religious customs, organized the meeting at a convenient time and place, came with the attitude of informal learning and openness, encouraged quieter persons to speak more and dominant persons to speak less. They also spent time both prior to and after the meeting talking informally, gathering other information necessary for a full assessment, and addressing immediate problems in the activity.[30]

Alkire justifies these attitudes instrumentally insofar as they are likely to elicit "richer" and more accurate information than would arrogant, know-it-all "facilitators" with culturally insensitive attitudes. She could also make it clear that the outsiders – as both fellow human beings and guests – ethically owed this conduct to community members. Although the facilitators and group members did not constitute an ongoing group, something like the deliberative virtues of respect for autonomy, civic integrity (especially honesty), and civic magnanimity (especially openness) certainly apply.[31] Alkire rightly mentions one problem in this information-gathering phase, related to our ideal of civic integrity, namely what Robert Chambers calls "inadvertent ventriloquism."[32] In this kind of distorted communication, the person questioned tells the questioner just what the latter would like to hear. Some aspects of the "participatory manner," which Alkire approves of, would reduce this danger. Especially important in this regard would be the "informal talking" about the project, and what R. F. Fenno, Jr., calls "hanging out."[33] Assuming something like this "participatory manner" on the part of the outside facilitators, let us briefly analyze their four roles and assess them in relation to the deliberative ideals and process sketched in Chapter 9 and the type of participation discussed above.

Elicitation of value judgments

The facilitators – informed by an assessment framework of the "dimensions" of human development – came to the communities and interacted in various ways with their respective members. This framework is not a Nussbaum-type list that "select[s] those human capabilities that can be convincingly argued to be of central importance in any human life, whatever else the person pursues or chooses."[34] Recall that in Chapter 6 we discussed Nussbaum's list and her argument that it should be enshrined in every nation's constitution. Although a given polity, Nussbaum concedes, may *specify* the list according to its own traditions and culture, "the list is supposed to be a focus of political planning."[35] Nussbaum restricts her attention to constitutionally embodied and governmentally guaranteed entitlements. Alkire, like Sen himself and the position that I have taken in this book, has serious reservations about outsiders or even insiders using such a list on the local level. Even if freely specified, such a list risks removing from communities on every level the opportunity to decide for themselves what impacts they have reasons to value and disvalue, how to prioritize their various values, and what policies to adopt.

Alkire's outsiders, however, do not come with nothing, thereby leaving everything – the identification of topics as well as the making of assessments – to the group members. Why? Alkire answers: "Unsystematic public discussions and participatory exercises to date (at local and national levels) have often failed to consider key categories of valuable ends implicitly or explicitly."[36] On the basis of Alkire's synthesis of ideas from both Sen and Finnis, the outsiders did come with a conception of the multiple *dimensions* or categories of human development. It is in terms of this schema that the facilitators elicited value information. The facilitators did not *prescribe* ways of being and doing; instead they used the Alkire–Finnis dimensions to *stimulate* answers in relation to

certain categories or to *sort* the multiplicity of *elicited* value judgments
into what they call "basic reasons for acting":

Life/health/security
Knowledge
Work/play
Beauty/environment
Self-integration/inner peace
Religion
Empowerment[37]

What the outsiders elicit and the insiders provide and clarify – in terms
of these *types* of valued functionings and capabilities – are insider valuations of the changes that have occurred during the course of the project
and are perhaps attributable to it. In the field, the facilitators elicited
this information about value judgments in two ways. Initially, the outsiders used the dimensions as an "agenda for conversation"[38] and successively asked for value judgments under each of the above seven
rubrics. When this approach seemed too mechanical and to stifle a
free-flowing interchange, the facilitators used the categories differently.
After explaining "the general intent of the exercise (to think about the
full range of impacts of an activity, good and bad, anticipated and
unanticipated)," the facilitator would ask "a purely open question, 'what
valuable and negative impacts have you noticed?'"[39] After discussing the
impacts in thematic clusters, whether or not they fitted the dimensions,
the facilitator toward the end of a session would question whether the
group had any value judgments to make under any of the seven neglected categories. Quoting Finnis, Alkire remarks that this use of
the seven item menu "could catalyze the missing discussions by providing 'an assemblage of reminders of the range of possibly worthwhile
activities and orientations open to [a community].'"[40]

The difference between Nussbaum's prescriptive list and either version of Alkire's open menu approach is clear. In Nussbaum's account,
the list constitutionally mandates certain social goals and political planning, although Nussbaum encourages groups to *specify* the norms in
relation to its cultural context.[41] In Alkire's approach, the dimensions
"could usefully spark conversation"[42] about whether there have been
any impacts – good or bad – within a given category.

Alkire's approach to this point is notably different from the thinner
participatory modes discussed above. In *nominal participation* one par-
ticipates through mere group membership. In contrast the women in
Alkire's group evaluate their project. In *passive participation*, elites report
their decisions and non-elites passively listen and at best question and

comment; but the Pakistani women assess the strengths and weaknesses of their past projects.

Value clarification, scrutiny, and ranking

Facilitators did not just elicit information on valued or disvalued changes; they encouraged group members to participate in a deeper way, namely to scrutinize their choices, rank them by importance, and clarify and prioritize the underlying values they used in these rankings. Here, as in the first stage, a certain kind of social interaction among the group members took place. In the goat-loaning project, one member – valuing the empowerment on other issues that she believed resulted from the project – said: "We sit together . . . and whoever gives the best opinion, we do this."[43]

Given the focus on the past, the absence of much disagreement within relatively homogenous groups, and the absence of an emphasis on what ought to be done collectively, it might appear that there was no attempt on the part of either the insiders or the facilitators to convert the individual judgments and rankings into a social assessment of the past or a choice for future action. In fact, although the text could address this question more explicitly, the participants together seem to have ranked – in and through discussion – the various impacts of past projects as well as the basic values expressed.[44] Moreover, the facilitators themselves assessed the groups' assessments. Although I would like to find out more about these facilitator assessments, Alkire provides one crucial detail: "[One aim of the facilitator is] to assess impacts in such a way that the concerned community could (and did) reflect critically on *the relative value or desirability of different* impacts and formulate ongoing objectives (and on the basis of these select monitoring indicators)."[45] The group had an opportunity to react to and shape the report to be given to the funding institution. All too often outside development actors study a project and report on it to their superiors but rarely give the report to the community for assessment and revision. To do so is to deepen the participation of group members.

Reports to the external group

Following this second step, the facilitators reported the value information and rankings, which the women's groups had generated, to the external funding institution (Oxfam). Hence, the funders knew how the communities judged and weighed the impacts of the projects on their lives and something of what the communities viewed as their most important values. In addition, the facilitators – also called "assessors" – were responsible for comparing (employing common categories) the various projects that they investigated and, as noted above, performing their own (group-mediated) assessment of each project in relation to the others. The external funders took the insiders' information and assessments as well as the facilitators' comparative assessments, combined them with standard assessments such as cost-benefit analysis and social assessment techniques, and decided whether or not to continue funding a particular project. The final decision – to continue or discontinue funding – resided exclusively with the funding agency and not with the communities themselves. It would be interesting to know whether this decision was made in and through democratic discussion or in some other way. And were there not ways in which the communities could bargain or deliberate directly with the funders?

How does Alkire's approach to this point stand in relation to *consultative* and *petitionary participation*? As in consultative participation, the funding agencies consulted – through the mediation of the facilitators – the three groups about each group's evaluations of their own projects. Unlike engaging in mere consultation, Alkire's groups reached their evaluative conclusions through a deliberation process. Like consultation, however, the elite funders made the final decision about whether to continue funding. It is not clear, but it seems doubtful, that the Pakistani groups believed they had a *right* to be heard and petition. It would not be surprising, however, if the funders believed they had an obligation to elicit – through the facilitators – and take account of the groups' assessments prior to the funders' final decision. Going well beyond *implementation* of the funders' decisions, the groups had a role in influencing those decisions.

Although Alkire's account is silent on the matter, the communities may have had a deliberative role in initially deciding their needs and the focus – goats, roses, or something else – of their income-generating projects. Hence in this sense they were not treated as "passive recipients of the benefits of cunning development programs."[46] Still, in the evaluation of their past project, perhaps a fuller deliberative opportunity was missed. The external donors and the various communities (and perhaps the facilitators) could and arguably should have deliberated *together* about the projects' continuance.

Reports back to the communities

Outside investigators, even participatory ones, often neglect to return to the community to share with their informants the investigators' assessments and the donor's funding decisions.[47] Although Alkire provides scant details, the facilitators did share their and the funders' assessments with the communities themselves. Not only did this exercise provide the community with an occasion to assess critically the way the outside facilitators and funders evaluated the communities' achievements and failures, but each community also gained an opportunity "to formulate ongoing objectives."[48] Yet, just at this point, when we would like to hear much more, Alkire's account falls silent. For it is just here that another possibility emerges for the kind of four-stage deliberative participation discussed in the last chapter with respect to each group's decisions about the future. There is an understandable – yet avoidable – cause for this failure. The communities responded to the facilitators' reports and donor decisions in the local language rather than in Urdu, the language of the facilitators.[49] Part of the commended "participatory manner" that Alkire extols is that the facilitators communicate in the local language, yet apparently the facilitators were only able to speak in a language (Urdu) that only some of the group members spoke. Because of this deficiency, the ideal of reciprocity, discussed above, was seriously compromised. Of course, the communities also may have resorted to their own language to gain more ownership over the conversation,[50] but that possibility raises the question of whether facilitators should have been selected that could use the first local language and whether the communities might have acquired ownership through deliberative give and take.

What is significantly underdeveloped if not altogether missing in Alkire's capability-based reconstruction of participation is *the group's* deliberation on the initial projects, their assessments of past projects, their future objectives, and their response to the funders' decisions. Of course, in this exercise in grassroots evaluation and funding decisions, the emphasis was more on evaluating the past, the changes in capabilities and functioning, than in offering a collective procedure for deciding about the future. With respect to both past and future, however, Alkire says almost nothing about the process prior to deciding, especially if there were disagreements and how the group addressed them. We are eager to know more about the extent to which deliberation did take place within each group as well as between each group and the funders. If deliberative participation did not take place, could it and should it have done so? And what role might bargaining play in these deliberative processes?

One reason, perhaps, why Alkire did not address this issue is that social choice in the three groups proved relatively easy given that the groups were composed solely of women and were homogeneous in other ways. Males or group members of different castes surely would have made social choice more difficult and either called for deliberation or, perhaps, made it impossible.

Alkire is aware that work remains to be done on this issue of social choice. She candidly asks whether her facilitator-assessment methodology overcomes Social Impact Assessment's (SIA) alleged weakness of failing "to provide decision criteria"[51] and admits that her methodology leaves many issues about decision-making "unresolved."[52] For instance, Alkire concedes, the methodology "did not treat in depth the problem of combining this information [about valuable capability change] to reach a decision" or "what to do when one agent's choice is contested."[53] These are among the very issues that deliberative democracy attempts to answer. Finally, although Alkire adumbrates aspects of participation compatible with the ideal of deliberative participation worked out here, she rightly worries about some types of participation:

Participation may also *foster the common good*, by stimulating reflection and collective action on common issues, and helping bring into or keep in the picture people whose needs and interests might otherwise have been overlooked. It may also enable participants to act according to their *conscience*. At times the opposite could occur (as when a participatory decision fractures a community, or requires an individual to act against her conscience in order to implement it). Indeed, none of these potentially positive features may occur, which is why such scrutiny may be valuable.[54]

Alkire's participatory model, I conclude, would be improved by injecting a strong dose of deliberative participation, especially a version thereof that is sensitive to her concerns. Alkire herself recognizes the merit of addressing the deliberative interpretations of democracy:

This chapter does not engage with the very large current literature on public deliberation and democratic practice (both theoretical and empirical) which is directly concerned with these very same issues ["of participation (or decision by discussion)"] – not because this is not an important interface to work, but, to the contrary, because it is too important to be done improperly. I respectfully leave that task to others who are already engaged in it.[55]

One aim of the present and the preceding chapter, and, indeed, of the entire book, is to contribute to that task. Just as deliberative democracy theory can help Sen specify the concept, justification, and procedures of public discussion and democratic decisions, so deliberative aims, ideals, group membership, background conditions, and processes as well as the ideal deliberator capacities and virtues yield a theory and practice of deliberative participation relevant *inter alia* to small-scale, externally funded development projects for the destitute.[56] These communities, as collective agents of their own development, must often make choices about what they ought to do. In addition to clarifying and evaluating what has happened in the past, they may seek together to overcome their differences with respect to ends and means. An ethically defensible way of doing so is by putting into practice – sometimes with the assistance of outsiders – an ideal of deliberative participation informed by deliberative democracy. Then the favored definition of participation will include the italicized addition: "'Participation' refers to the process of discussion, information gathering, conflict, [*deliberation*,] and eventual decision-making, implementation, and evaluation by the group(s) directly affected by an activity."[57]

One way to strengthen Alkire's approach becomes clear when it is compared with Fung and Wright's model of Empowered Participatory Governance (EPG). In EPG, the grassroots or neighborhood deliberative sites are both linked together horizontally, and coordinated, monitored, and improved vertically, by district-wide intermediate bodies: "These central offices can reinforce the quality of local democratic deliberation and problem-solving in a variety of ways: coordinating and distributing resources, solving problems that local units cannot address by themselves, rectifying pathological or incompetent decision-making in failing groups, and diffusing innovations and learning across boundaries."[58]

The functions of these intermediate bodies are reiterated by a higher-order body that has "colonize[d] state power and transform[ed] formal governance institutions."[59] Some functions of Alkire's donor institutions and facilitators, such as funding and assessment, indeed have parallels in EPG. But EPG goes further. Funding, with few strings attached, comes from the state government rather than from international or national nongovernmental organizations. Local (neighborhood) groups are not isolated from one another but send democratically elected representatives to higher levels, and higher levels in turn coordinate, monitor, and build deliberative and other capacities in lower levels, including the capacity (and virtue) of accommodating the views of those with whom one disagrees. Resources, ideas, and skills are shared both horizontally and vertically in a comprehensive network of both direct and representative municipal government in which citizens and their representatives deliberate to solve common and practical problems. Majorities, the evidence tends to show, do not tyrannize minorities if and when all forge an agreement for effective action that at least partially embodies minority concerns and which most all can accept.

Objections

Many criticisms have been launched against the theory and practice of deliberative democracy in general and against deliberative participation in local, national, and global development.[60] Critics have charged, for example, that deliberative democracy is too rationalistic and orderly for the messy and passionate worlds of democratic politics and participatory development promotion, worlds that do not conform to the alleged tranquillity of the philosophy seminar. Others have claimed, in spite of protests to the contrary, that deliberative democrats still think in terms of face-to-face and local group interactions and tend to see national deliberation as "one big meeting." Still others have claimed that the ideal deliberators are those who ignore their own interests and grievances and ascend to an impossible and ethically undesirable realm of Rawlsian impartiality.

I think these particular criticisms have been or can be met. One way to do so, which I have employed in this and the preceding chapter, is to defend a version of deliberative democracy designed to overcome problems found in earlier versions.[61] Another way is to look at actual experiments in deliberative democracy and consider what the evidence shows. Empirical evidence often reveals that the allegedly bad effects of deliberative democracy in fact do not happen, happen much less than is supposed, or may be eliminated through better institutional designs.

Other criticisms or worries, however, continually surface among those sympathetic to the capability approach, deliberative democracy, or the convergence of the two currents on the ideal of deliberative participation. The first objection, the "indeterminacy criticism," accepts deliberative democracy's egalitarianism but says that Sen's ideal of democracy as public discussion is insufficiently determinate, would reproduce and even accentuate existing economic and other inequalities, and, therefore, would be bad for women, minorities, and poor people. In contrast, the second criticism, "the autonomy criticism," argues against deliberative democracy on the basis that the latter allegedly puts too many constraints on a society's decision-making. The third criticism accepts deliberative ideals in development but argues that they are totally unrealizable in our unjust world and that, therefore, we should not strive for deliberative institutions. Unlike the first three criticisms, the fourth objection, the inequality objection, challenges the agency-focused capability approach and deliberative democracy on the basis that their strong egalitarian and democratic commitments are unlikely to be shared by most people. Let us state and evaluate each criticism.

The indeterminacy objection

The "indeterminacy criticism" assumes, as do Sen and most deliberative democrats, that economic, political, and, more generally, social power is distributed very unequally in the world. This asymmetry of power afflicts groups at all levels – local, national, and global. To ascribe unconstrained agency, autonomy, or self-determination to groups themselves is to guarantee that the asymmetries will be reproduced when the group decides and acts. Rather than mitigate, let alone eliminate, these power imbalances, deliberative institutions and procedures at best have no effect and at worst accentuate unacceptable inequalities. Unconstrained democratic bodies will perpetuate and even deepen minority suppression or traditional practices that violate human rights. People with elite educations and well-traveled families tend to excel in debate; men are often thought to be better deliberators or are permitted more speaking opportunities than women; and the poor, the ill-educated, and the newly arrived immigrant will lose out in what is supposed to be a fair interchange of reasons and proposals.

Instead of invoking democratic agency, the objection continues, what is needed is a prescriptive philosophical theory of the good life or human rights to be embodied in every nation's constitution. Some freedoms are good (for instance, freedom from rape and for sexual equality) and some are bad (for instance, freedom to exploit and rape). With constitutional mandates that protect human rights or good freedoms, democratic bodies will not reproduce power inequities but rather will ensure that the human capabilities, valuable freedoms, and human rights of all people, especially those with lesser social power, will be protected.[62]

In the following lengthy passage, Martha Nussbaum makes this indeterminacy objection, assuming in her formulation not economic inequalities but gender inequalities:

[Sen and I have differed on the issue of] the importance of endorsing unequivocally a definite list of capabilities for international society.[*] Like the international human rights movement, I am very definite about content, suggesting that a particular list of capabilities ought to be used to define a minimum level of social justice, and ought to be recognized and given something like constitutional protection in all nations . . . Now of course some human rights instruments, or my capabilities list, might be wrong in detail, and that is why I have continually insisted that the list is a proposal for further debate and argument, not a confident assertion. But is it quite another thing to say that one should not endorse any definite content and should leave it up to democratic debate in each nation to settle content. In the sense of implementation and concrete specification, of course, I do so: no nation is going to be invaded because its law of rape gives women inadequate protection against spousal violence[*] . . . Sen's opposition to the cultural defense of practices harmful to women seems to me to be in considerable tension with his all-purpose endorsement of capability as freedom, [*] his unwillingness to say that some freedoms are good and some bad, some important and some trivial.

When we think about violence against women, we see that democratic deliberation has done a bad job so far with this problem . . . I view my work on the capabilities list as allied to their [the international women's movement] efforts, and I am puzzled about why definiteness about content in the international arena should be thought to be a pernicious inhibition of democratic deliberation, rather than a radical challenge to the world's democracies to do their job better.[63]

I have four problems with Nussbaum's argument. First, in comparing democratic decision-making with a democracy constitutionally constrained by her list, she compares failures of "actually existing" democracies with alleged successes of democracies in which not only is her list constitutionally embodied but the constraints actually result in compliance with constitutional norms. This recalls the equally unfair comparison of ideal capitalism with actually existing socialism (or the reverse). One can compare the ideal competitors with other ideal competitors or the actual social formations with "really existing" rivals, but not actual democratic decision-making with ideal, list-informed, constitutional democracies. It is important to observe that fine philosophical theories of justice and splendid constitutions do not – by themselves – guarantee that a society is just or law-abiding. Asymmetries of power can be just as inimical to the rule of philosophers or the rule of law as it is to rule by the people.

Second, I fully endorse Nussbaum's challenge to democracies to "do a better job." But one way to do so is by becoming more robust democracies, ones that are more inclusive, that tackle rather than duck important issues, and both offer opportunities for and promote a higher quality of citizen participation. It is not quite right to say that the only solution to a defect in democracy is more and better democracy. Non-deliberative and even nondemocratic methods sometimes may be used to bring about or protect a democracy as such and deliberative democracy in particular. We deliberative democrats, however, have good reason to believe that it is precisely in making democracies more democratic – along the four dimensions I propose above – that democracies are most likely to make decisions that provide the very protections, including that of minorities, that Nussbaum rightly deems important. As Sen reminds us, both agency (the *process* aspect of freedoms) and capability (the *opportunity* aspect of freedom) are intrinsically important, and each can contribute to the other. The importance of promoting and protecting well-being freedoms should not, however, weaken our commitment to the at least equal importance of fair agency freedom and achievement.[64]

Third, Nussbaum's "constitutionalism" gives insufficient weight to the role that democratic deliberation plays in the formation, interpretation, and change of constitutions. Although constitutional conventions, and the larger public discussion of which they are a part, involve much power politics – interest-based politicking, lobbying, and negotiation – such conventions also illustrate the very deliberative features captured in the model of deliberative democracy. Moreover, although more or less difficult to alter, constitutional democracies have procedures for constitutional amendments. Finally, although Nussbaum leaves ample room for a democratic body "specifying" her list, this exercise would not be sufficiently robust. It does not permit, as it should, a democratic body to decide that in its particular situation personal security is more important (right now) than health care (or vice versa). Democratic bodies, at whatever level, must often decide not merely between good and bad but also between good and good in particular situations. To block all trade-offs within her list is not only to limit the agency of democratic citizens, but also to prohibit their achieving increments of good in those situations where all good things do not go together.[65]

It is precisely because of the importance of self-determination that federal constitutions increasingly devolve a certain range of decisions (and resources to implement them) to state or municipal democratic bodies.[66] Similarly, outside funders, such as Oxfam in Alkire's cases, often provide the resources and then require that local development projects make their own decisions on their ends and means. Perhaps drawing on the Brazil case, Goulet in 1989 recognized that agents from above and from the outside could initiate robust citizen participation in local development.

A fourth problem with Nussbaum's statement of the "indeterminacy objection" relates to her assumption about the respective roles of normative theorizing, constitutions, and democratic decision-making. Nussbaum, as we observed in Chapter 5, has changed her list over the years, often responding to criticism. And she says of her current list that she puts it forward not as a "confident assertion" but as "a proposal for further debate and argument." Yet, she continues to propose that (something like) her list will be enshrined more or less intact in constitutions, which, then, should be the new touchstones of normative correctness. It is better, I submit, to resist the impulse to absolutize any of the three – normative theory, political constitutions, and democratic bodies. Rather, we should see them in ongoing dialectical tension and mutual criticism. For each can make serious mistakes, and each can be improved by listening to the other. Nussbaum hit the right note when she describes her list as "a proposal for debate." Such debate should take place among and between constitutional framers, judges, and democratic bodies at all levels. Constitutional advances, like democratic experiments, can in turn correct the one-sidedness of normative theorizing.

It might be argued that neither Nussbaum's criticism of democracy (without a constitutionally enshrined list) nor my four replies confront a deeper problem with democracy. Democratic bodies – whether or not constitutionally constrained (Nussbaum) and whether or not inclusive, wide-ranging, deep, and effective – can make unjust decisions, ones inimical to the well-being of minorities or even majorities. The notion of agency might be taken to imply that everybody, including slave-owners or white racists, could do whatever they wanted and not be constrained by a commitment to the well-being of others. Democracy is but a tool to effect justice in the world, and when it fails to do so it must be criticized in the light of the intrinsically good end of justice.

It is true that the democrat is committed not only to agency as intrinsically good and as expressed in democratic procedures but also to reduction of injustice. She believes that one good way – but not the only way – to promote and protect everyone's well-being and freedom is by an inclusive, deliberative, and effective governance structure based on the *equal* agency and agency freedom of all. Robustly democratic institutions are venues in which both free and *equal* citizens express their agency through a fair process. This process is not fair if some are excluded from participating or if the minority (or majority) does not accommodate both the agency and concerns of the majority (or minority). The solution is often to improve the democratic body along one or more of the dimensions of breadth, range, depth, or control. For instance, citizen petitioning of officials or non-deliberative protests might be more effective than deliberation in influencing decisions. Better ways may be found to ensure that power asymmetries are more effectively neutralized and that everyone has a voice.

Yet democracy, while intrinsically good, is not everything; and sometimes democrats concerned with justice will have to bypass or suspend it to prevent or remove some great injustice. It does not follow that we need a *theory* of justice or a philosophical list of capabilities or entitlements to tell us when to choose well-being outcomes over agency-expressing democratic process. And the choice of justice over democracy is or should itself be an expression of agency (rather than someone else's choice). What follows, rather, is that our commitments to both equal agency and adequate well-being for all should lead us to criticize democratic processes both when they fail to be sufficiently democratic and when they fail to deliver on their promise of justice.

The autonomy objection

The autonomy criticism criticizes both Sen's democratic turn and deliberative participation because they allegedly impose on a community a rigid, autonomy-threatening model of democratic and deliberative aims, ideals, processes, and virtues. What if a society would rather keep to its past traditions of hierarchical decision-making rather than democratic decision-making based on an assumption of free and equal citizens? What if a local community decides to reject outside development assistance if and when this assistance is tied to inclusive deliberation? If we genuinely embrace Sen's ideal of agency and deliberative democracy's ideal of being in charge of one's own (collective) life, should we not respect a group's decision to be nondemocratic and even antidemocratic? Should not we respect what Galston calls the group's "expressive liberty" to choose and live a communal life that prizes obedience to top-down authority?[67]

There are two responses to this argument, both of which presuppose the value of agency. The first response challenges the assumption that everyone in the group is in agreement with the "will" or "decision" of the group.[68] In fact it may be that a small elite has decided on hierarchical rule and has imposed that decision through force, fear, manipulation, or custom on the remaining members of the community. It should not be assumed that this elite, which is well served by hierarchical practices, speaks for everyone. Moreover, the only way it could be known whether everyone freely agreed with the leaders or the culture of obedience would be for people to have the real chance to decide for themselves and engage with their fellows in public discussion on the merits of different forms of governance. Part of an individual's having the freedom to decide for or against the nondemocratic way of life would be having information about alternatives and being able, if she chose, to exercise critical scrutiny of claims and counter-claims. Some features of democracy, then, would be necessary for a people (and not just their leaders) freely to decide to reject democratic freedom and deliberation.

The second response bites the bullet and accepts that most members of a group knowingly, voluntarily, and freely decide to reject democracy and deliberative participation. Those members who disagree should have the right and means to exit from the group, and democratic groups would have a duty to give them refuge and a new life. What about those who decided to stay and continued in oppose democratic and deliberative modes? I think the only consistent answer for the defender of agency is to accept this decision (as long as it was not imposed). There might be some suspicion that conditions for a free choice really did not exist – that people were still being forced or conditioned to accept non-freedom. But, at some point, reasonable doubt should be satisfied. Then the proponent of autonomy regretfully respects the group members' autonomous choice no longer to exercise their agency. The leaders, presumably, accept the will of the people and agree to stay in charge.

This second response is also the basis for answering the specific objection that democracy is incompatible with autonomy. More specifically, this version of the autonomy objection argues that public discussion, which Sen endorses, violates autonomy, and so does – even more so – deliberative democracy's package of aims, ideals, four-stage procedure, and citizen virtues. Although she does not herself accept this objection and indeed tries to show that it does not undermine her own proposal for a political procedure based on Nussbaum's "thick, vague" theory of human good, Deneulin formulates the autonomy criticism (before attempting to answer it):

Letting policy decisions be guided by a certain procedure of decision-making is inconsistent with the demands of human freedom, and inconsistent with the spirit of democracy itself. Indeed, by assessing the quality of how people decide about matters that affect their own lives in the political community through evaluating to what extent their decisions have respected certain requirements, one deeply infringes on their freedom. People are somehow not allowed to exercise their political freedom the way they wish.[69]

Deneulin's formulation does not quite get the objection right, for the term "letting policy decisions be guided" is too lax. Better for the autonomy objection to say, as Deneulin does later in the quoted passage, that freedom is infringed because "people are somehow not allowed to exercise their political freedom the way they wish." Sen, so the objection goes, is imposing public discussion on people. Deliberative democrats are forcing people to participate in inclusive, wide-ranging, deep, and inclusive democracy. The autonomy criticism sounds like the little boy who plaintively asked his "free school" teacher in 1970: "Do we have to do whatever we want to do again today?" "Do we," asks the autonomy critic, "have to engage in public discussion and democratic deliberation if we choose not to?"

Again, the answer is: "No, you don't have to, but this option is open to you." Similarly, to decide to accept the aims, ideals, procedures, and virtues of deliberative democracy is not an abrogation of freedom as long as one has other options and one makes one's own decisions (or the group does) to embrace, modify, or reject deliberative democracy. The point is illustrated by the decision to compose within the musical blues tradition. One is not forced to compose or sing the blues. Other musical genres are available. Once one uses one's freedom to be a bluesman or blueswoman, however, there are certain blues conventions that composer-performers from Robert Johnson and Bessie Smith to B. B. King have observed. Freedom goes further, however, for the blues composer, guitarist, or vocalist can creatively modify and supplement the blues format. Likewise, deliberative democrats offer their model not as something to impose on groups, but as something they have putative reason freely to accept and modify as they see fit.

Moreover, as I argued above and in the previous chapter, there may sometimes be good reasons to reject or postpone rather than employ deliberative and other democratic methods. Employing deliberation may sometimes be too costly with respect to other values, such as non-domination or group solidarity. The women in Alkire's micro-development projects may decide collectively to defer to one of their leaders. To decide autonomously not to express group agency in deliberation is itself a manifestation of agency or autonomy. The problem for both Sen and the deliberative democrats comes when someone, a tyrant or *jefe máximo*, or something else, an unscrutinized tradition or the "force of circumstance," makes the decision for the group. Then the group is not in charge of its own life, and individual and group agency has been sacrificed.

The realism objection

Many people respond initially to the ideals of robust democracy in general and deliberative participation in particular. They end up rejecting the latter, however, because it is too utopian or "idealistic," too much concerned with "what ought to be" and too far removed from "*actual* world conditions."[70] Deliberative democrats must take this objection very seriously, but I believe it can be answered. Let us initially make a distinction between two versions of the realist objection, both of which appeal to asymmetry of economic, political, or social power as a premise. One criticism says that due to power asymmetries, it will be impossible to advance from our present unjust world of thin democracies to the symmetric conditions presupposed by robust democracy. The other version says that even if deliberative democracy or participation were somehow established it would soon reinforce and even deepen power imbalances.

The most effective refutation of the impossibility version of the realist objection is to point to actually existing deliberative institutions. It is surprising how rarely self-described realists examine the *actual* world that they hold up as a touchstone for normative truth. If they did, they would find that there are hosts of deliberative institutions around the world.[71] It is true that many of these are at the neighborhood or city level, although Kerala's renovated Panchayat system functions in an Indian state of 32 million people. It is also the case that many of these institutions are fairly recent, and should be termed experiments rather than sustained institutions. Moreover, much more research is needed about what sorts of impact these institutions have had on people's lives and their surrounding societies.[72] Finally, the efforts to democratize existing democracies and development practices vary with respect to how well they realize the goals of an inclusive, wide-ranging, deep, and effective democracy.

We do know enough, however, to challenge both versions of the realist objection. Some democratic innovations, especially those in Kerala and Brazil, are redistributing both power and opportunities. Moreover, we are learning ways to improve democratic practice so that new institutions more fully approximate the ideal. The ideal is something to guide action and remedy shortcomings, not an impossible dream.[73]

The lessons learned through the hundreds of innovative democratic practices around the world also provide lessons for how to get from a thinly democratic and unjust world to a more deliberative and just world. Here Archon Fung's recent work is particularly instructive. Fung distinguishes between deliberative and non-deliberative methods for advancing the goals of deliberative democracy. And he distinguishes two very different sorts of obstacles, each of which comes in degrees, to the realization of these goals: (1) unwillingness to deliberate, and (2) inequality.

Where members of a group are more or less willing to deliberate, they often find institutional designs for improving the quality of deliberation. These devices are most successful when group members are similar and relatively equal, as was the case with Alkire's three communities. The arrangements, however, are also effective – if there is willingness to deliberate – in overcoming inequality of various sorts. For example, participants in a deliberative exercise may be randomly selected or invited from under-represented groups. Seats for women or historically discriminated-against groups are set aside in assemblies. Skilled facilitators fairly distribute chances to participate in deliberative give and take. Agreed-upon rules give women, junior members, or those who have not yet spoken the right to participate first or next. Higher-level structures "capacitate" members of lower-level groups, monitoring and improving their deliberative skills. Deliberative exercises provide information on the issues to less informed or less educated participants. These arrangements, whether employed in setting up or improving a democratic body and whether used in groups with unequal or equal members, all presuppose that group members are of good will and willing to deliberate.

To meet the realist objection more adequately, however, Fung considers cases where there is both significant unwillingness (and even hostility) to deliberate, and inequality among group members. Under these circumstances he wisely rejects two options. Deliberative democrats should not foolishly use deliberative methods when they have no chance of working, any more than a proponent of reasoned persuasion should try to reason with a crazed and knife-wielding killer. Neither should deliberative democrats go to the other extreme and indiscriminately use any and all non-deliberative methods to work for a more deliberative society. Those methods not only include the legal staples of power politics – log-rolling, lobbying, clientalism, public shaming – but also illegal methods such as "dirty tricks," vote-stealing, bribes, and worse.

The deliberative democrat seeking to advance the prospects of deliberative democracy in an unjust world may choose non-deliberative methods but only when he (1) initially acts on the rebuttable presumption that those opposing deliberation are sincere, (2) reasonably exhausts deliberative methods, and (3) limits non-deliberative or nondemocratic means by a principle of proportionality, analogous to a proportionality principle in justification of civil disobedience. The more extreme the hostility to deliberative democracy and the more entrenched the power asymmetries, the more justified are political mobilization and even coercive means, such as political pressure and public shaming. Just as the person engaging in an act of civil disobedience is willing to be arrested and tried, rather than flee the law (because he is protesting against one law or policy and not the rule of law), so the deliberative democrat in an unjust world limits how far he goes in pursuing his goal. What Fung has given deliberative democrats is not only a model of deliberative democracy that indicates how unjust and undemocratic structures can be transformed. He has also provided a compelling "political ethic that connects the ideal of deliberative democracy to action under highly hostile circumstances." As he concludes his essay:

In such a world, the distinctive moral challenge is to maintain in thought and action the commitment to higher political ideals, despite the widespread violation of those norms. Deliberative activism offers an account of how it is possible to practice deliberative democracy in the face of inequality and hostility without being a political fool.[74]

The objection to equality

I turn now to the fourth and last objection, one that differs from the first three because it challenges the egalitarian and democratic assumptions of my version of the capability approach. Let us call this version ACDD (agency-focused capability plus deliberative democracy). The counterargument goes like this: ACDD assumes without argument that equality and democracy are good things. But not everyone agrees with these assumptions. Economic libertarians value liberty rather than equality, and most Chinese believe that economic prosperity and social stability trump or altogether exclude human rights and democracy. Hence, the ACDD gives no reason for anybody but egalitarians and democrats to accept its vision and, hence, is preaching to the choir.

How should we assess this argument? First, the fact that some people do not share ACDD's egalitarian and democratic commitments, let alone the vision of deliberative participation, does not entail that the commitments are not reasonable. Flat-earth believers do not undermine the reasonable view that the earth is not flat. Second, although they ascribe somewhat different meanings to key terms, some libertarians, as I show below, *do* accept the ideal of equal agency or equal liberty. Likewise, Chinese human rights and democracy activists and scholars sometimes are committed to (and risk their well-being for) some sort of egalitarian and democratic commitments.[75] And even those who propose a normative political philosophy compatible with Asian "values" may defend an "Asian" version of democracy and human rights.[76]

A third response to the equality objection is that ACDD does not just *assume* that democracy is a good thing but *defends* an inclusive, broad, and deep conception of democracy on the basis of democracy's intrinsic, instrumental, and constructive value. One instrumentalist defense of democracy is that even minimalist democracy, as Sen and others argue, tends to be instrumentally better than autocracies in preventing and responding to natural and human catastrophes.[77] Moreover, the intrinsic value argument that I set forth for democratic rule, based on the premises that agency is a good thing and that democracy optimally manifests agency, shares some commonality with libertarianism. Philosopher Robert Nozick, perhaps the purest of recent libertarians, affirms the moral importance of agency and defends it in relation to the notion of having or striving for a meaningful life:

What is the moral importance of this . . . ability to form a picture of one's whole life (or at least significant chunks of it) and to act in terms of some overall conception of the life one wishes to lead? Why not interfere with someone else's shaping of his own life? . . . A person's shaping his life in accordance with some overall plan is his way of giving meaning to his life; only a being with the capacity to shape his life can have or strive for meaningful life.[78]

But, the anti-egalitarian might respond, although Nozick endorses agency, he rejects *equality*. That response, too, misses the mark. Sen is surely right that most thinkers – Nietzsche would be a notable exception – are egalitarians in some sense. Few escape the importance of, or fail to answer, Sen's question, "Equality of what?"[79] Nozick answers the question with "Equality of liberty" or "Equality of agency" – construed as each person's right – without interference from others – to shape his or her own life. What is right for one (not being coerced) is right for all, regardless of such things as riches, ethnicity, religion, gender, age, sexual orientation, and nationality: "Individuals have rights, and there are things no person or group may do to them (without violating their rights)."[80] Sen and I differ from Nozick not because we have a concept of equal agency that he altogether lacks, but because our concept of agency is more robust than his. Agency is linked not only to the absence of others' interference (in the shaping of one's life) but also to the presence, which others may be obligated to supply, of real and valued options. That of which we try to convince right-wing libertarians, by actual and hypothetical examples, is that it is just as bad to limit someone's agency by refusing to provide the necessary means – such as food and security – as it is to limit it by coercion, such as rape and torture.[81] We are not struck defenseless, but argue for a better account of those common premises that in turn will support better conclusions.

The inequality objector is not finished. She might concede that all individuals have equal agency (and hence moral worth) and even should be afforded equal protection of the law and from rights-violating coercion. But she might insist that neither the state nor other people have the duty to provide people with *economic* equality (equal income and wealth) or exactly the same sort and level of capabilities (for such equality would require coercive redistribution from the rich to the poor).

Here the inequality objector has misunderstood ACDD. The proposal is not that distributive justice requires strict equality of income or capabilities, but that each community should decide on its own distributive principles. Within the capability space, among those matters to be decided are the most important capabilities and the principles for their promotion and distribution. Sen's own proposal to democratic bodies is not that they put everyone on the same level of income or capability, but to ensure that everyone who so chooses (to exercise her agency) is able to get to a communally determined moral minimum. What is important is not strict equality but a certain sort of equality of opportunity or freedom. Whether she chooses to get to that level or go beyond it is (if she is not disabled) up to her. The choice, however, of a specific distributive principle or principles is up to the collective agency of the community in question – as is the question of the weight of that principle in relation to such values as economic prosperity and social stability.

The inequality objector, however, might press on. Is it not the case, she might argue, that Sen is concerned that democratic processes will reinforce inequalities of economic and political power unless citizens deliberate in conditions of strictly equal economic and political power? Is not ACDD begging the question with respect to its egalitarian "enabling conditions?" No and yes. On the one hand, only "rough" economic and social power is called for in the sense both that all citizens are able, if they so choose, to get to the threshold, and that the remaining inequalities do not permit the rich and well connected unfairly to dominate the have-nots. Moreover, given this enabling condition of rough equality, the community may exercise its agency and choose an inegalitarian distributive principle or to outweigh justice with other values. One the other hand, it is true that the notion of a fair process (including the rule of law) presupposes not just that all persons have moral worth (agency) as human beings but that *all* group members should be relatively free to participate fully in deliberating and deciding. Is it possible to convince someone that believes in rule by experts or guardians to give up this belief in favor of democratic rule by group members "roughly" equal in economic and social power? Perhaps not – especially if the objector is privileged and benefiting from inequality – and we may be at the end of the line.

The proponent of inequality might at this point take refuge in the assumption that motivation is always and only self-interested and that any appeal to the justice of rough economic and political equality would require a degree of altruism that is not psychologically possible. In response, both economists and philosophers have cast reasonable doubt on self-interest as the *only* motive. And even if self-interest were true (most of the time), a Rawlsian thought experiment along the lines of the "original position" (where the deliberators do not know whether or not they are or will be privileged or destitute) is a device to get people to affirm fair procedures and just arrangements. It is in each person's long-term self-interest to agree to an arrangement in which she can achieve at least minimally adequate well-being regardless of her fortune.

In this chapter I have set forth and defended the way in which an agency-focused capability approach coupled with deliberative democracy generates a deliberative ideal of local and participatory development. I have concluded by replying to four objections to the normative vision (Chapters 4–6 and 9) and its application to a deliberative reconstruction of citizen participation in grassroots development. To avoid dogmatism, a critical development ethics must seek out and engage serious criticisms and alternative perspectives.

NOTES

A shorter version of this chapter appeared as "Deliberative Participation in Local Development," *Journal of Human Development*, 8, 3 (2007): 431–55. The second section draws on my "Foreword" to Denis Goulet, *Development Ethics at Work: Explorations 1960–2002* (London and New York: Routledge, 2006), xxv–xxix. I first articulated these ideas in my contribution to a World Bank project, which I co-directed with Sabina Alkire, entitled "Responding to the Values of the Poor: Participation and Aspiration," February 2002–December 2003. I gave presentations based on this research at St. Joseph's University; Fundación Nueva Generación Argentina and Centro de Investigaciones Filosóficas, Argentina; Michigan State University; the University of Maryland; and the University of Groningen. I received valuable comments from Sabina Alkire, Jay Drydyk, Verna Gehring, Douglas Grob, Laura Antkowiak Hussey, Judith Lichtenberg, Christopher Morris, Joe Oppenheimer, and Henry Richardson.

1. For a helpful recent discussion, with full references, on both the theoretical and policy-oriented discussion of participation in development, see Bina Agarwal, "Participatory Exclusions, Community Forestry, and Gender: An Analysis for South Asia and a Conceptual Framework," *World Development*, 29, 10 (2001): 1623–48; and Sabina Alkire, *Valuing Freedoms: Sen's Capability Approach and Poverty Reduction* (Oxford: Oxford University Press, 2002), ch. 4.
2. See M. Rahnema, "Participation," in *The Development Dictionary: A Guide to Knowledge as Power*, ed. Wolfgang Sachs (London: Zed Books, 1992), 116–31; *Participation: The New Tyranny?*, ed. Bill Cooke and Uma Kothari (London: Zed Books, 2001); Sanjay Kumar and Stuart Corbridge, "Programmed to Fail? Development Projects and the Politics of Participation," *The Journal of Development Studies*, 39, 2 (2002): 73–103; Glyn Williams, "Evaluating Participatory Development: Tyranny, Power, and (Re)politization," *Third World Quarterly*, 25, 3 (2004): 557–78; William Easterly, *The White Man's Burden: Why the West's Efforts to Aid the Rest Have Done So Much Ill and So Little Good* (New York: Penguin Press, 2006), 144–5, 195–9.

3. Jay Drydyk, "When is Development More Democratic?," *Journal of Human Development*, 6, 2 (2005): 247–67.

4. I have adapted this section from my "Foreword" to Goulet, *Development Ethics at Work*, xxv–xxix.

5. Denis Goulet, "Participation in Development: New Avenues," *World Development*, 17:2 (1989): 165–78. This article is partially reprinted in Denis Goulet, *Development Ethics: A Guide to Theory and Practice* (New York: Apex Press, 1995), 91–101. Paulo Freire's classic is *Pedagogy of the Oppressed* (New York: Continuum, 1970).

6. Goulet, "Participation," 165.

7. Marshall Wolfe, *Participation: The View from Above* (Geneva: United Nations Research Institute for Social Development, 1983), 2. Goulet cites Wolfe in "Participation," 165.

8. Goulet, *Participation*, 175.

9. See Gianpaolo Baiocchi, "Participation, Activism, and Politics: The Porto Alegre Experiment," in *Deepening Democracy: Institutional Innovations in Empowered Participatory Governance*, ed. Archon Fung and Erik Olin Wright (London: Verso, 2003), 45–76. Goulet applauds Porto Alegre participatory budgeting process in "Global Governance, Dam Conflicts, and Participation," *Human Rights Quarterly*, 27, 3 (2005): 890–2.

10. T. M. Thomas Isaac and Patrick Heller, "Democracy and Development: Decentralized Planning in Kerala," in *Deepening Democracy*, ed. Fung and Wright, 78. For Jean Drèze and Amartya Sen's discussion of the Indian constitutional amendments that facilitated the renovation of the Panchayat system of governance, see their *India: Development and Participation*, 2nd edn. (Oxford: Oxford University Press: 2002), 349, 358. In many nations one sees recent efforts to decentralize the national government and put more power and resources under the control of state or local governments. Recent comparative studies confirm anecdotal evidence that decentralization has had a mixed record in making local (or national) democracies more deliberative. See James Manor, *The Political Economy of Democratic Decentralization* (Washington, DC: World Bank, 1999); *Decentralization, Democratic Governance, and Civil Society: Perspectives from Africa, Asia, and Latin America*, ed. Philip Oxhorn, Joseph S. Tulchin, and Andrew D. Selee (Baltimore: Johns Hopkins University Press / Woodrow Wilson Center Press, 2004); and Andrew D. Selee, "The Paradox of Local Empowerment: Decentralization and Democratic Governance in Mexico," PhD dissertation, University of Maryland, School of Public Policy, 2006. The latter study includes an exhaustive bibliography.

11. Easterly, *White Man's Burden*, 195–9, and ch. 10.

12. Goulet, "Participation," 167.

13. Agarwal, "Participatory Exclusions."

14. Ibid., 15–18.

15. See Jules N. Pretty, "Alternative Systems of Enquiry for Sustainable Agriculture," *IDS Bulletin*, 25, 2 (1995): 37–48; John Gaventa, "The Scaling Up and Institutionalizing of PRA: Lessons and Challenges," in *Who Changes?: Institutionalizing Participation in Development*, ed. James

Blackburn and Jeremy Holland (London: Intermediate Technology Publications, 1998), 157; Jay Drydyk, "When is Development More Democratic?" 259–60.

16. Petitionary participation differs from consultative participation because the activity of petitioning is more robust than merely expressing views and making proposals; in the former but not the latter, the non-elite have the right to be heard and the elite have the duty to "receive and consider" petitions. James W. Nickel briefly discusses the nature and importance of the right of citizens to petition governments and the related "duty of governments to receive and consider petitions" in "Gould on Democracy and Human Rights," *Journal of Global Ethics*, 1, 2 (2005): 211. In consultative participation, the non-elite are dependent on the favor rather than the duty of the elite to "receive and consider."

17. In "Participatory Exclusions," Agarwal calls this mode "activity-specific participation," but I believe my term better captures the idea that the elite decide on the plan and the non-elite carry it out.

18. For a defense of *bargaining* with the state, with the community, and within the family, see Agarwal, "Participatory Exclusions," 18–22. For a fairly sharp distinction between bargaining and deliberation based on the former's prudent motivation and latter's desire to justify one views to others, see Amy Gutmann and Dennis Thompson, *Democracy and Disagreement* (Cambridge, MA: Harvard University Press, 1996), 52–63, 349–50; and *Why Deliberative Democracy?* (Princeton: Princeton University Press, 2004), 113–15, 148–9. There are, of course, various models of both bargaining and negotiation, some of which include a deliberative component rather than excluding it altogether. Moreover, a group may deliberately decide to bargain, and its bargaining now may be a means to achieve eventual deliberation. In future work I intend to clarify the relations between, and assess the respective merits of, different models of bargaining, negotiating, and deliberating.

19. In his normative conception of democracy, Jay Drydyk helpfully emphasizes the concept of control understood as people's influence over decisions and the social environment, especially well-being freedoms and achievements. See Drydyk, "When is Development More Democratic?", esp. 252–57.

20. Goulet, "Participation," 172.

21. Ibid., 166. In *Development Ethics*, p. 93, Goulet uses the term "reciprocal dialogue."

22. Ibid., 168.

23. Denis Goulet, "World Interdependence: Verbal Smokescreen or New Ethic?," Development Paper 21 (Washington, DC: Overseas Development Council, 1976), 29.

24. Amartya Sen, "Democracy and Its Global Roots," *The New Republic*, 229, 4 (2003): 33.

25. Amartya Sen, *Development as Freedom* (New York: Knopf, 1999), 291.

26. In contrast to much government-to-government funding by the US Agency for International Development, for more than thirty years the US Inter-American Foundation (IAF) has emphasized grassroots development. See *Direct To The Poor: Grassroots Development In Latin America*, ed. Sheldon

Annis and Peter Hakim (Boulder, CO: Lynne Rienner Publishers, 1988); and Ramón Daubón, "A Grassoots View of Development Assistance," *Grassroots Development: The Journal of the Inter-American Foundation*, 23, 1 (2002): 1–9. For an assessment of recent efforts of USAID to promote both citizen participation in its projects and broad-based governmental democracy, see David A. Crocker and Stephen Schwenke, "The Relevance of Development Ethics for USAID," Desk Study for USAID (April 2005).

27. See Alkire's brief overview of Finnis's work in *Valuing Freedoms*, 15–18. See also John Finnis, *The Fundamentals of Ethics* (Oxford: Oxford University Press, 1983).

28. See Agarwal, "Participatory Exclusions"; and Judith Mashinya, "Participation and Devolution in Zimbabwe's CAMPFIRE Program: Findings from Mahenye and Nyaminyami," PhD dissertation, School of Public Policy, University of Maryland, 2007.

29. Alkire, *Valuing Freedoms*, 218–22.

30. Ibid., 225. An aspect of this participatory manner becomes important below. Although the outside assessors spoke Urdu, a language that many group members spoke, the assessors did not speak the group members' first language.

31. Alkire's account would be enhanced by further attention to the ethical issues that emerge when outsiders question insiders about their values. See Deepa Narayan, Robert Chambers, Meera K. Shah, and Patti Petesch, *Voices of the Poor: Crying Out for Change* (New York: Oxford University Press for the World Bank, 2000); David Ellerman, *Helping People Help Themselves: From the World Bank to an Alternative Philosophy of Development Assistance* (Ann Arbor: University of Michigan Press, 2005).

32. Robert Chambers, "All Power Deceives," *IDS Bulletin*, 25, 2 (1994): 14–26. See also Robert Chambers, *Ideas for Development* (London: Earthscan, 2005). Citing Nicolas van de Walle (*Overcoming Stagnation in Aid-Dependent Countries* [Washington, DC: Center for Global Development, 2005], 67), Easterly identifies a less inadvertent kind of ventriloquism: the World Bank and the International Monetary Fund no longer impose certain conditions on loans to poor countries, but rather listen to what the poor country plans to do with the loan. But the effect is the same: "So the poor-country governments, instead of being told what to do, are now trying to guess what the international agencies will approve their doing": Easterly, *White Man's Burden*, 146. Cf. van de Walle, *Overcoming Stagnation*, 67.

33. Richard F. Fenno, Jr., *Watching Politicians: Essays on Participant Observation* (Berkeley, CA: IGS Press, 1900); Peter Balint, "Balancing Conservation and Development: Two Cases Studies from El Salvador," PhD dissertation, School of Public Policy, University of Maryland, 2000; and Mashinya, "Participation and Devolution," 82.

34. Martha Nussbaum, "Capabilities and Human Rights," in *Global Justice and Transnational Politics*, ed. Pablo De Greiff and Ciaran Cronin (Cambridge, MA, and London: MIT Press, 2002), 128.

35. Ibid. See also Martha Nussbaum, "Women's Bodies: Violence, Security, Capabilities," *Journal of Human Development*, 6, 2 (2005): 178–9.

36. Alkire, *Valuing Freedoms*, 224.
37. Ibid., 282; see also 118.
38. Sabina Alkire, personal communication, April 6, 2003.
39. Alkire, *Valuing Freedoms*, 225.
40. John Finnis, *Natural Law and Natural* Rights (Oxford: Clarendon Press, 1980), 90. See Alkire, *Valuing Freedoms*, 224.
41. Nussbaum, *Women and Human Development: The Capabilities Approach* (Cambridge: Cambridge University Press, 2000), 77. Nussbaum also allows that a community may contest and remake items on the list, but Nussbaum's list is meant to have a prescriptive and perhaps presumptive force.
42. Alkire, *Valuing Freedoms*, 38.
43. Ibid., 221.
44. Sabina Alkire, personal communication, April 6, 2003.
45. Alkire, *Valuing Freedoms*, 225. Italics in Alkire's text.
46. Sen, *Development as Freedom*, 11.
47. Deepa Narayan and colleagues note that the investigations, which issued in the three volumes *Voices of the Poor*, often failed in their moral obligations to share the results of their studies with the people whom they investigated. See Deepa Naranyan *et al.*, *Voices of the Poor: Crying Out for Change*, 16–18.
48. Alkire, *Valuing Freedoms*, 225.
49. Alkire, personal communication, April 6, 2003.
50. For the way in which use of a local language can protect a community from fragmentation and outsider control, see Ariel Dorfman, "Into Another Jungle: The Final Journey of the Matacos?," in *Grassroots Development: Journal of the Inter-American Foundation*, 12, 2 (1988): 2–15.
51. Alkire, *Valuing Freedoms*, 289.
52. Ibid.
53. Ibid.
54. Ibid.
55. Alkire, *Valuing Freedoms*, 127–8. In ibid., 128, n. 10, Alkire refers to the work of both Richardson and Bohman on public deliberation and says that "both of whom carry forward Sen's work directly." For a similar comment, with reference to Bohman, see Alkire, "Why the Capability Approach?," *Journal of Human Development*, 6, 1 (2005): 130.
56. An important topic for further research would be the differences as well as the similarities between the global, national, and middle levels – especially governmental ones – of deliberative democracy and the sorts of grassroots development projects, whether governmentally or nongovernmentally funded, which this chapter has addressed.
57. Alkire, *Valuing Freedoms*, 129; see also 283.
58. *Deepening Democracy*, ed. Fung and Wright, 21.
59. Ibid., 22.
60. Iris Marion Young helpfully analyzes and evaluates these and other objections in *Inclusion and Democracy* (Oxford: Oxford University Press, 2000), 36–51.
61. Such is the strategy of Iris Marion Young, when she criticizes the "face-to-face" and "rationalism" arguments, and of Jane Mansbridge, when she responds to the "impartiality" objection. See Young, *Inclusion and Democracy*;

and Jane Mansbridge, "Practice-Thought-Practice," in *Deepening Democracy*, ed. Fung and Wright, 178–95.

62. See, for example, Carol C. Gould, *Globalizing Democracy and Human Rights* (Cambridge: Cambridge University Press, 2004), ch. 1, esp. 31–42.

63. Martha Nussbaum, "Women's Bodies: Violence, Security, Capabilities," *Journal of Human Development*, 6, 2 (July 2005): 179. I indicate three omitted endnotes by [*]: the first two refer, respectively, to Martha C. Nussbaum, "Capabilities as Fundamental Entitlements: Sen and Social Justice," *Feminist Economics*, 9, 2–3 (2003): 33–59; and the third to Sen, *Development as Freedom*.

64. Sen, *Development as Freedom*, 17, 285, 290–2.

65. Nussbaum repeatedly argues that since the items on her list are incommensurable (which I accept), they cannot be traded off. See, for example, Martha C. Nussbaum, *Women and Human Development*, 81; *Frontiers of Justice: Disability, Nationality, Species Membership* (Cambridge, MA: Harvard University Press, 2006), 174–6. The conclusion does not follow from the premise. Just because love of life and love of country are incommensurable, it does not follow that the Moroccan deciding whether or not to escape severe privation in his homeland cannot – when he cannot have both – decide for one good (more opportunity in Spain) rather than the other (being part of his family and country). Given insufficiency of resources, governments must choose among or prioritize various goods, such as health care and lower taxes. It is not that more of one good makes up for or compensates for less of the other, but that we often cannot have two good things at the same time and must choose between them. Citing Finnis, Deneulin states the "no trade-off" claim in an uncompromising way: "The choice of pursuing one component of human well-being should not damage another: what can be referred to as *the requirement of non-compensation*. This requirement directly follows from the plural and incommensurable nature of the human good to be pursued (each central human capability is irreducible to each other, there are no possible "trade-offs": Séverine Deneulin, "Promoting Human Freedoms under Conditions of Inequalities: A Procedural Framework," *Journal of Human Development: Alternative Economics in Action*, 6, 1 (2005): 88; her note 8, citing Finnis, is omitted.

66. The 1988 Brazilian Constitution defines health as both a right of all citizens and the responsibility of the state to provide through its Unified Health System (SUS). The SUS in turn "introduced the notion of accountability (*controle social*) and popular participation" and "stated that the health system had to be democratically governed and that the participation of civil society in policymaking was fundamental for attaining its democratization": Vera Schattan P. Coelho, Barbara Pozzoni, and Mariana Cifuentes Montoyo, "Participation and Public Policies in Brazil," in *The Deliberative Democracy Handbook: Strategies for Effective Civil Engagement in the 21st Century*, ed. John Gastil and Peter Levine (San Francisco: Jossey-Bass, 2005), 176. Within this Brazilian legal framework, health councils, in which citizens deliberate on health priorities and policies, have proliferated at federal, state, and municipal levels of government.

67. William A. Galston, *Liberal Pluralism* (Cambridge: Cambridge University Press, 2002).

68. For Sen's assessment of this argument, see *Development as Freedom*, 241–2.

69. Deneulin, "Promoting Human Freedoms," 89.

70. Ibid., 81.

71. The three most important anthologies are *Deepening Democracy*, ed. Fung and Wright; *Democratizar la democracia: Los caminos de la democracia participativa*, ed. Boaventura de Sousa Santos (Mexico: Fondo de Cultura Económica, 2004); and *The Deliberative Democracy Handbook*, ed. Gastil and Levine. For the point about theorists and other scholars benefiting from learning about concrete cases, see Peter Levine, Archon Fung, and John Gastil, "Future Directions for Public Deliberation," in *The Deliberative Democracy Handbook*, ed. Gastil and Levine, 280–1.

72. Levine, Fung, and Gastil, "Future Directions for Public Deliberation," 271–86, esp. 280–1.

73. See the case studies in the anthologies cited in n. 71.

74. Fung, "Deliberation before the Revolution: Toward an Ethics of Deliberative Democracy," *Political Theory*, 32, 2 (2005): 416.

75. Xiaorong Li, *Ethics, Human Rights and Culture: Beyond Relativism and Universalism* (New York: Palgrave Macmillan, 2006). Cf. Amartya Sen, *Development as Freedom*, chs. 6 and 10.

76. *The East Asian Challenge for Human Rights*, ed. Joanne R. Bauer and Daniel A. Bell (Cambridge: Cambridge University Press, 1999); and Daniel A. Bell, *Beyond Liberal Democracy: Political Thinking for an East Asian Context* (Princeton and Oxford: Princeton University Press, 2006).

77. Morton H. Halperin, Joseph T. Siegle, and Michael M. Weinstein, *The Democracy Advantage: How Democracies Promote Prosperity and Peace* (New York: Routledge, 2005); and Larry Diamond, *Developing Democracy: Toward Consolidation* (Baltimore and London: Johns Hopkins University Press, 1999).

78. Robert Nozick, *Anarchy, State, and Utopia* (New York: Basic Books, 1974), 50.

79. Amartya Sen, "Equality of What?," in *The Tanner Lectures on Human Values*, I, ed. Sterling M. McMurrin (Salt Lake City: University of Utah Press, 1980), 197–220; and *Inequality Reexamined* (Cambridge, MA: Harvard University Press, 1992).

80. Nozick, *Anarchy, State, and Utopia*, ix.

81. David A. Crocker, "Functioning and Capability: The Foundations of Sen's and Nussbaum's Development Ethic, Part 2," in *Women, Culture and Development: A Study of Capabilities*, ed. Martha Nussbaum and Jonathan Glover (Oxford: Clarendon Press; New York: Oxford University Press, 1995), 182–96. See also David A. Crocker, *Praxis*, 68–76, 114–28.

11   Development ethics, democracy, and globalization

Globalization and democratization – and their links – are matters of intense and often bitter worldwide debate. How should globalization be understood and assessed? Is globalization a permanent change in the world order or an "over-hyped fad of the 1990s,"[1] to be replaced by forces – such as terrorism and US unilateralism – that tear the world apart? Is globalization good or bad? Who should say and in what terms? What should we mean by global democracy? Can and should democracy be "globalized" – imposed in authoritarian countries, resuscitated in countries in which it is under attack, and installed or deepened in global institutions? Can democracy be "imposed" or "installed" without undermining its moral foundations?

This final chapter in our study makes a case that globalization is an important worldwide change that development ethicists and others should ethically assess as well as understand with respect to its causes and consequences. Moreover, the chapter argues that ethically justified globalization promotes and is promoted by the sort of robust local, national, and global democracy defended in Chapters 9 and 10. Urgently needed, increasingly argue development ethicists, are both a democratization of globalization and a globalization of (a kind of) democracy.

The present chapter draws on the conception of the nature and practice of development ethics I set forth in Chapter 2 and other chapters above, and argues that such an ethics is one resource that can and should be applied to the ethical evaluation of globalization and democratization. I first discuss leading theories of globalization. Next I consider both empirical and ethical issues in assessing globalization. In the final section I analyze and evaluate three strategies for "humanizing" and "democratizing" globalization.

Globalization and development

Development ethics faces the new and pressing task of understanding and ethically evaluating "globalization" and proposing ethically

375

appropriate institutional responses to this complex and contested phenomenon. The debate about globalization since the late 1990s reminds one of earlier controversies about development. Like the term "development" in the 1960s through the mid-1990s, "globalization" has become a cliché and buzzword that the mainstream celebrates and dissenters condemn. Moreover, like "development" earlier, "globalization" challenges ethicists to move beyond simplistic views – such as "globalization is (exceedingly) good" or 'globalization is (terribly) bad" – and to analyze leading interpretations of the nature, causes, consequences, and value of globalization. Development ethicists, committed to understanding and reducing human deprivation, will be especially concerned to assess (and to defend norms for assessing) the changing global order as well as local, national, and regional development. How should we understand globalization and evaluate its impact on individual and communal well-being? Which types of globalization are *most threatening* to ethically based development at all levels? Which kinds are *most promising*?

It is important to ask and sketch the answers to four questions about globalization:

(1) What is globalization?
(2) What are the leading interpretations of globalization? What explains globalization, and how unique is it in relation to earlier forms of global interaction and integration? Does globalization result in the demise, resurgence, or transformation of state power? Does globalization eliminate, accentuate, or transform the North/South divide?
(3) How should (different sorts of) globalization be assessed ethically? Does globalization (or do some of its variants) undermine, constrain, enable, or promote ethically defensible development?
(4) Can and should globalization be resisted, contested, modified, or transformed? If so, why? And, finally, how, if at all, should globalization be humanized and democratized, and what role does democracy play in this humanization?

What is globalization?

First, what should we mean by "globalization"? Just as it is useful, prior to assessing particular normative approaches to the ends and means of development, to demarcate development generically as "beneficial social change," so it is also helpful to have a (fairly) neutral concept of globalization. David Held, Anthony McGrew, David Goldblatt, and Jonathan Perraton have suggested an informal definition useful for this purpose: "Globalization may be thought of as the widening, deepening and speeding up of worldwide interconnectedness in all aspects of contemporary social life, from the cultural to the criminal, the financial to the spiritual."[2] More rigorously, the same authors characterize globalization as: "A process (or set of processes) which embodies a transformation in the spatial organization of social relations and transactions – assessed in terms of their extensity, intensity, velocity and impact – generating transcontinental or interregional flows and networks of activity, interaction, and the exercise of power."[3]

Three interpretations of globalization

Similar to the theories of development discussed above in Chapters 2 and 3, interpretations or theories of globalization – which all contain historical, empirical, and normative components – differ with respect to (1) the nature, number, variety, and relation of *processes* or flows, for example tokens (money, for instance remittances from Mexicans working in the USA to their kin south of the border), physical artifacts (goods), people (immigrants, tourists), symbols, and information; (2) *causation*: monocausal or reductive (economic or technological) approaches versus multi-causal or non-reductive approaches; (3) *character*: inevitability versus contingency and open-endedness; (4) *consequences*, for example the impact on state sovereignty and the division of countries into North or South; and (5) *desirability* (and criteria for assessment).

Although no one generally accepted theory of globalization has emerged, at least three general interpretations or models of globalization are on offer. Following Held *et al.*, I label these approaches (1) hyperglobalism, (2) skepticism or anti-globalism, and (3) transformationalism.[4]

Hyperglobalism, illustrated by journalist Thomas L. Friedman[5] and trade economist Jagdish Bhagwati,[6] conceives of globalization as a qualitatively unique global age of economic (capitalist) integration characterized by open trade, global financial flows, "outsourcing" of work to producers in other countries, and multinational corporations. Driven by capitalism, communications, and transportation technology, integration into one world market is increasingly eroding state power and legitimacy. The hierarchical North/South dichotomy is being rapidly – and fortunately – replaced by a "flat" global entrepreneurial order structured by a "level playing field" and new global "rules of the game," such as those of the World Trade Organization (WTO). Although hyperglobalism concedes that there are short-term losers as well as winners, it insists that the rising global tide will eventually lift all national and individual boats – except for those who perversely resist the all but inevitable progress. *Newsweek* editor and hyperglobalist Fareed Zakaria, sympathetically reviewing Thomas Friedman's bestselling book *The World is Flat*, observes:

> He (Friedman) ends up, wisely, understanding that there's no way to stop the [globalization] wave. You cannot switch off these forces except at great cost to your own economic well-being. Over the last century, those countries that tried to preserve their systems, jobs, culture or traditions by keeping the rest of the world out all stagnated. Those that opened themselves up to the world prospered.[7]

Commenting on Bhagwati, economist Richard N. Cooper exactly captures the normative dimension of hyperglobalism:

> His [Bhagwati's] main thesis is that economic globalization is an unambiguously good thing, with a few downsides that thought and effort can mitigate. His secondary thesis is that globalization does not need to be given a "human face"; it already has one . . . His conclusion: that the world, particularly its poorest regions, needs more globalization, not less.[8]

At least when development is identified with economic growth, "global integration," as Dani Rodrik observes, "has become, for all practical purposes, a substitute for a development strategy."[9] According to this view, a nation's government should focus its attention and resources on rapidly (and often painfully) removing tariffs, quotas, and other devices, especially agricultural subsidies, that block access to the globalizing world. Former British Prime Minister Tony Blair succinctly expressed the hyperglobalist faith:

> [We] have an enormous job to do to convince the sincere and well-motivated opponents of the WTO agenda that the WTO can be, indeed is, a friend of development, and that far from impoverishing the world's poorer countries, trade liberalization is the only sure route to the kind of economic growth needed to bring their prosperity closer to that of the major developed economies.[10]

Skepticism rejects hyperglobalism's view that global economic integration is (or should be) taking place and that states are (or should be) getting weaker. Skeptics argue that regional trading blocs are (or should be) getting stronger, that resurgent fundamentalisms either insulate themselves from or clash with alien cultures, including those shaped by North American consumerism, and that national governments are (or should be) getting stronger. These skeptics of hyperglobalism include Stephen Krasner,[11] Paul Hirst and Grahame Thompson,[12] and Samuel Huntington.[13] In a more explicitly normative approach, Herman Daly goes beyond empirical skepticism to anti-globalism. He concedes that globalizing trends, which hyperglobalists celebrate, exist, but argues that states should be "brought back in," should resist economic openness, and should emphasize national and local well-being.[14] Instead of extinguishing the North/South divide, skeptics and anti-globalists argue that economic integration, cross-boundary financial investment, the digital revolution, and multinational power have increased inequality between and within countries and have mired poor countries in the South in even greater poverty and autocracy. Rodrik, for example, argues:

> By focusing on international integration, governments in poor nations will divert human resources, administrative capabilities, and political capital away from more urgent development priorities such as education, public health, industrial capacity, and social cohesion. This emphasis also undermines nascent democratic institutions by removing the choice of development strategy from public debate.[15]

Marxist skeptics contend that the hyperglobalist thesis is a myth that rich and developed countries perpetrate to maintain and deepen their global dominance over poor countries. Countries – especially poor and transitional ones – must resist the sirens of economic and cultural openness; instead, they should aim for national or regional sufficiency and develop themselves by their own lights. Authoritarian skeptics endorse efforts – such as those of Fidel Castro in Cuba or Hugo Chávez in Venezuela – to centralize power, pull out of free-trade pacts, reduce the presence or power of multinationals, bring top-down improvement in living standards, and weaken civil society. Liberal skeptics emphasize that national sovereignty, with its demanding duties of justice, cannot and should not be replaced by global economic or political institutions that either lack legitimacy or threaten global tyranny. Democratic skeptics promote national and local control, target health and education, and promote public deliberation about development ends and means. In sum, the variants of skepticism conceive of globalization as something inimical to genuine development.

Transformationalism, such as that which Held and his colleagues advocate, conceives of recent globalization as an historically unprecedented and powerful set of processes (with multiple causes) that is making the world more interconnected and organizationally multi-leveled. They argue that it is too simple to say that states are being either eroded or reinforced; it is more accurate to conclude that states are (and should be) reconstituting themselves in a world order increasingly populated by global and regional economic, political (regulatory), and cultural institutions, and by social movements.

Transformationalists insist that globalization is not one thing – and certainly not merely economic – but many processes with diverse consequences. The new economic (trade, finance, transnational corporations), political, cultural, criminal, legal, and technological global processes proceed on multiple, sometimes interlinked, and often uneven tracks. Rather than being inexorable and unidirectional, globalization is more or less contingent, open, and multidirectional. Rather than uniformly integrating communities, globalization results in new global and regional exclusions as well as novel inclusions, new winners and new losers. The nation-state is (and should be) increasingly reconstituted in relation to regional, hemispheric, and global institutions; the old North/South dichotomy is being replaced by a trichotomy of elite/contented/marginalized that cuts across the old North/South polarity (and justifies development ethics in confronting poverty wherever it exists):

North and South are increasingly becoming meaningless categories: under conditions of globalization distributional patterns of power and wealth no longer accord with a simple core and periphery division of the world, as in the early twentieth century, but reflect a new geography of power and privilege which transcends political borders and regions, reconfiguring established international and transnational hierarchies of social power and wealth.[16]

Just as development ethicists have stressed that national and local development – while complex and multi-causal – is a pattern of institutionalized human activity that can and should be a matter of voluntary, humanizing, and democratic collective choice, so transformationalists emphasize that globalization can and should be civilized and democratized. Transformationalists are both less enthusiastic than hyperglobalists and less pessimistic than skeptics. Transformationalists insist that a globalizing world shows neither the uniform and unalloyed good that hyperglobalists celebrate nor the pervasive and unmitigated bad that skeptics worry about. Instead, globalization at times impedes, and at times enables, good human and communal development.

Globalization, poverty, and inequality: empirical issues

Regardless of how globalization – its character, causes, and consequences – is understood, development ethics should evaluate it ethically. Throughout its history, development ethics has emphasized ethical assessment of the goals, institutions, and strategies of national and subnational development and constructively proposed better alternatives. In a globalizing world, development ethics takes on the additional task of offering an ethical appraisal of the global order and suggesting more just ways of managing new and evolving global interconnectedness.

How is this evaluation to be done? There are empirical, conceptual, and normative aspects of inquiry, but, unfortunately, this diversity is often unheeded. Globalization's multiple, often uneven, and frequently changing influences on individuals and communities require empirical investigation, while deciding which consequences are ethically significant and which are the best future options requires the application of ethical criteria and judgments about global as well as national justice.

Even empirical investigation on the effects of globalization, however, is not disconnected from conceptual and even normative considerations. Consider, for example, the oft-repeated anti-globalist claim that the effect of globalization is that "the rich are getting richer and the poor are getting poorer." Heated debate exists about the truth of this claim and related contentions that global inequality is increasing or decreasing. World Bank economist Martin Ravallion nicely captures this debate:

On the one side, the website of a prominent nongovernmental organization (NGO) in the antiglobalization movement, the International Forum on Globalization, confidently claims "globalization policies have . . . increased inequality between and within nations." This stands in marked contrast to the claims made by those more favorable to globalization. For example, an article in the *Economist* magazine states with equal confidence that "globalization raises incomes, and the poor participate fully."[17]

Drawing on Ravallion's important article and recent work by Branko Milanovic, another World Bank economist, I analyze, explain, and recast this controversy in ways relevant to the ethical assessment of globalization. Sometimes analysts disagree with respect to whether or not inequality is increasing because they employ time-frames that range from a year to a millennium. Of especial relevance to the globalization debate is what has occurred on the world scene from 1980 to 2000 or the present, but longer or shorter time-frames may change one's judgment with respect to increasing or decreasing inequality.

Sometimes the disputants cite different data. Some conceptions of inequality take national accounts data, Gross National Product (GNP), Gross Domestic Product (GDP), or Gross National Income (GNI) and simply divide them by the country's inhabitants. Frequently, in an effort to account for price differences and differences in purchasing power across countries, international financial organizations use "purchasing power parity (PPP)." As the United Nations Development Programme (UNDP) explains it, PPP is "a rate of exchange that accounts for price differences across countries, allowing international comparisons of real output and incomes."[18] Instead of employing national accounts data, whether or not adjusted to purchasing power parity, researchers increasingly employ household surveys to identify individual or family actual expenditures or disposable income.

Differences between the two camps run deep and rest finally on conceptual and normative disagreements. Given my analysis of development theory-practices in Chapter 3 and of ethics as a way of seeing in Chapter 8, this diagnosis is not surprising. What we take as important facts (for instance, whether we take the country or the individual as our unit of analysis) is often a function of our concepts and ethical commitments. The facts matter, and I shall discuss where empirical issues (from different perspectives) stand on world poverty and inequality. Concepts and value judgments, however, also matter and are often the root of differences in factual claims. Instead of fans and critics of globalization passing each other like ships in the night, it is imperative that conceptual and normative differences, as Ravallion argues, "be brought into the open and given critical scrutiny before one can take a well-considered position in this debate."[19]

What conceptual and normative differences exist with respect to the controversy about the impact of globalization – understood, for the nonce, as economic integration – on poverty and inequality? First is the question that Sen first raised in 1979: "Inequality of what?" and "Poverty with respect to what?" In Chapters 4–6, I analyzed and defended Sen's own answer to these questions: the best "space" for understanding and measuring both poverty and inequality is not income but agency, functionings, and capability for functioning. Global inequality and poverty may be falling with respect to one metric, such as income ($1 or $2 per person per day), and rising with respect to some other, such as health, education, and agency or power.[20] In some cases, of course, the different metrics may be moving in the same direction. UNDP, for example, reports: "In human development terms the space between countries is marked by deep and, in some cases, widening inequalities in income and life chances."[21] Even if two metrics are going in the same direction, however, the gap with respect to one may be proportionately greater than that with respect to another. As Erik Thorbecke remarks in his response to Ravallion's paper, "worldwide inequality would be significantly lower if measured in terms of health or educational status than in terms of income and might reflect more accurately the actual welfare (happiness) enjoyed by different individuals in different settings."[22] If we look at poverty defined exclusively by UNDP's human development index (HDR), it is clear that poverty is worsening in at least 18 countries: "In 2003, 18 countries with a combined population of 460 million people registered lower scores on the human development index (HDI) than in 1990 – an unprecedented reversal."[23]

Second, even if we stick with the conventional metric of income, estimates of poverty differ with respect to geographical focus, and those of inequality differ according to the specific concept of inequality employed. In relation to income poverty and using the $1 a day figure for (extreme) poverty, from 1981 to 2001 the number of those living on $1 a day fell from 1.5 to 1.1 billion and "the percentage of the population of the developing world living on less than $1 day was almost halved from 40 to 21 percent."[24] However, when we subtract China's achievements in poverty reduction from this total, the number of the world's poor has remained at 850 million over this twenty-year period. If we focus exclusively on African countries, the results are significantly more discouraging.

If we employ the metric of income, is world inequality decreasing or increasing? Here answers diverge not (only) because of country or regional focus, but because analysts employ – whether unwittingly or intentionally – radically different concepts of "inequality" and "equality." Although Ravallion began to diagnose this ambiguity, it is Branko Milanovic who has recast the inequality debate by clearly and graphically distinguishing three concepts of inequality: concept 1, concept 2, and concept 3.[25]

In *concept 1* inequality, the focus is on countries, and each country's poverty is represented by the income of that country's median person.[26] This concept assumes, obviously contrary to fact, that everyone in the country receives the median income and that single figure represents the country as a whole. The analogy is with the UN General Assembly, in which each country has one vote regardless of its size (or the US Senate, in which each state, regardless of population or geographical size, has two senators). One advantage of this concept of inequality is that it emphasizes the point that the *country* in which one is born or lives makes a huge difference to one's opportunities. Another advantage is that concept 1 inequality favors smaller states in the sense that a small country, or its inhabitants, may receive greater international attention than would an area of the same size or number of inhabitants in a large country. Trinidad and Tobago, with a population of little more than one million inhabitants, had the same right to play in the 2006 World Cup as did much larger countries such as Brazil or the United States. No matter how good its soccer players, the Indian state of Kerala, with a population of about 32 million, could not qualify a team for the World Cup. The notable disadvantage of concept 1 (and concept 2) poverty is that the representing of all a nation's inhabitants by a "median" person completely ignores differences among regions, groups, and individuals within a country. For example, a country's per capita GNP may be climbing, but large groups and many individuals may be falling even further behind and more deeply into poverty.

Using concept 1, is inequality among countries growing, shrinking, or staying the same? Much depends, as mentioned above, on the time-slice one chooses. According to Milanovic, the gap between the median income of the richest and the poorest country has grown in the last 100 years from 10:1 to 60:1. In 1990 the average American had 38 times the income of the average Tanzanian, but today the gap has grown to 61 times.[27] In general, since the late 1970s or early 1980s, the rich Western countries have pulled ahead of the rest of the world, and, while poor countries are growing, their growth (with the exception of the Asian tigers) has been slower than that of the rich countries; hence, they are falling even further behind.

Milanovic designates Fourth World countries as those with less than one third of the income of Greece, the poorest Western country, and shows that the number of such countries, including most African countries, has increased three-fold between 1960 and 2000. The Gini coefficient, when used to measure concept 1 inequality between countries, is 20 percent higher (more inequality) in 2000 than it was in the mid-1970s.[28]

Given concept 1 inequality, the evidence is pretty clear that, although there are some poorer countries that have caught up with the rich countries, in general there is a reduction in the number of middle income countries and a trend toward a greater gap between the top and the bottom. Even when a poor country is growing (and some are not), their growth rate is slower than the rich countries.

It is not so easy, however, to say with confidence that globalization is *the* cause or even *one* cause of increasing inequality in the sense of concept 1. The correlation of globalization and increasing inequality (concept 1) does not entail that the former caused the latter. Milanovic identifies many alleged causes of the widening gap: the US deficit (caused by rearmament and Reagan's tax policy, which in turn caused higher interest rates); the oil crisis of 1979 (which forced poor countries to borrow but at interest rates they could not pay back and that resulted in deeper debt); and the end of the Cold War (which removed many poor countries from the radar screens of benefactor rich countries).[29] Although we can view some of these candidate causal factors as part of a capacious concept of globalization, Milanovic reasonably argues that in the 1980s, rich country trade quotas, subsidizing of agriculture, and the GATT's and WTO's expensive dispute settlement system harmed poor countries and helped rich ones.[30] Ravallion also comments that economic failure in particular poor countries was due less to global factors than to indigenous ones such as climate, paucity of resources, or endemic corruption. Hence, even if we accept that concept 1 inequality is increasing, we cannot without more argument blame globalization for (increasing) poverty.

In Milanovic's classification, *concept 2*, like concept 1, uses national accounts data and represents an entire country by per capita GNP, GDP, or GNI, but, unlike concept 1, weights the result by population. Concept 2 inequality, like concept 1, assumes that everyone in the country has the same, that is, median income, but adjusts the result in relation to the number of people in the country. In 2003, China, Lebanon, and Cape Verde had similar achievements in GDP per capita: China PPP, US\$ 5,004; Lebanon PPP, US\$ 5,074; and Cape Verde PPP, US\$ 5,214.[31] But due to China's vast population of 1.3 billion persons, compared with 3.5 million in Lebanon and 0.5 million in Cape Verde, an improvement in China's median income would decrease concept 2 inequality 371 times more that the same median improvement in Lebanon, and 260,000 times more than the same median improvement in Cape Verde. If the analogy with concept 1 equality/inequality is that of the US Senate, in which each state gets the same number of senators regardless of the states' populations, the analogy with concept 2 equality/inequality is the US House of Representatives, in which the greater a state's population, the greater the number of its congresspersons.

Given concept 2 inequality, what has happened to the gap between countries in, say, the last twenty years? Ravallion and Milanovic concur that since 1980, due to the rapid economic growth of and poverty reduction in China and India, concept 2 poverty has decreased substantially.[32] The Gini coefficient of countries weighted by population has decreased as much as 10 percent. Numbers of persons do matter. As Ravallion remarks, "The lack of policy reform and growth in a small country surely cannot be deemed to cancel out the policy reforms that helped generate so much economic growth in China over the last twenty years or so."[33] It is this concept of inequality that globalization and free market fans employ when they celebrate economic integration.

Three facts, however, cause one to be less than sanguine. First, if we subtract China and India from concept 2 inequality calculations, the decrease in inequality either "largely vanishes"[34] or is reversed.[35] Second, analysts increasingly doubt the reliability of China's official estimates of its high growth rates.[36] Finally, China's and India's accomplishments lose their luster when one retains concept 2 inequality but disaggregates the two countries into their subunits (provinces and states, respectively). The growing inter-regional inequality in both countries suggests that on a countrywide basis concept 2 inequality is not decreasing and that "as more Chinese (and Indian) provinces become rich while others stay behind, world inequality will rise."[37] Examining countries with respect to one representative and average person and weighting these countries for population makes the world look (in Thomas Friedman's term) "flat" in the sense that per capita GNPs weighted for population are converging.[38] But if we look inside the country's black box at its constituent subunits and treat these subunits as countries, converging flatness becomes more like the diverging averages as viewed from the lens of concept 1 inequality.

Why, however, should disaggregation stop with provinces and states? Ultimately development ethicists worry about the impact of globalization on individuals. *Concept 3* inequality likewise is concerned with inequality of individuals and not groups, with flesh-and-blood human beings and not with means, averages, or abstract persons representing thousands or millions. As I argued in Chapter 3 and as Ravallion clearly sees, the choice of the unit of analysis in development is an ethical decision. Are we finally concerned with what development does to individuals and what individuals can do with development? Or should our main focus be on countries (or subnational communities) and average persons?

Although Milanovic recognizes that concepts 1 and 2 have some value, his work as a whole is dedicated to proposing and improving a third concept of inequality. Just as we must look beyond national per capita income to find how much inequality exists among individuals in a particular country, so ideally, to see whether global inequality is changing, we would line up all individuals in the world from richest to poorest (however conceived) and investigate their changing (if any) relations. Rather than using national accounts, investigators like Milanvoic employ household surveys. Rather than taking national boundaries and group membership as ultimately important, individuals and their well-being are determinative.

From the lens of concept 3, global inequality is, to employ Milanovic's language, "staggering."[39] Analysts and commentators make this point in different ways. Milanovic himself shows that the household surveys reveal that both the richest 5 percent of the world's individuals and the poorest 80 percent get 1/3 of the world's total PPP-valued income. The ratio of the average PPP-valued income of the richest 5 percent of individuals to the poorest 5 percent is 165:1. For those who like their statistics a bit more concrete, this ratio means, remarks Milanovic, that the richest earn the same in 48 hours as the poorest do in a whole year.[40] UNDP makes a related point: "On the (conservative) assumption that the world's 500 richest people listed by Forbes magazine have an income equivalent to no more than 5% of their assets, their income exceeds that of the poorest 416 million people."[41]

Has this gap been changing in the last twenty years and, if so, in what direction? Here analysts disagree, although according to Milanovic these disagreements are at least partially due to differences in methodology and data sets. Xavier Sala-i-Martin and Surjit Bhalla contend that global (concept 3) inequality has declined by 3–4 Gini points. Francois Bourguignon and Christian Morrisson, and Yuri Dikhanov and Michael Ward, argue that concept 3 inequality rose about 1 Gini point. Bob Sutliffe finds no change, and Milanovic himself identifies zigzags, with inequality rising 3 Gini points from 1988 to 1993, declining by 1 Gini point from 1993 to 1998, and rising again by 1 Gini point from 1998 to 2002.[42]

To what extent, if any, is globalization causally responsible for these changes in concept 3 inequality? Not surprisingly, since analysts do not agree on whether or not there is change in these matters or – if there is – what direction it takes, they are unlikely to agree on causation in general and the role of globalization in particular. And among the reasons for differing views on the impact of globalization on inequality is that the impact in fact may differ depending on such things as (1) whether people within a nation are rich or poor; (2) whether a nation as a whole is poor or rich, big or little, and densely or sparsely populated; and (3) a nation's past history.[43]

It is reasonably clear, however, that there is one way in which globalization – as economic openness and rapid communication across national boundaries – affects individual happiness and capability poverty even if concept 3 inequality remains unchanged. Poor persons in poor (or rich) countries become aware, through travel, television, movies, or newspapers, of the contrast between their deprivation and others' affluence. Further, they frequently view their lot in life – their being left out – as undeserved and unfair. Such awareness is likely to cause unhappiness, frustration, and even anger, with the result that the person's well-being is lowered.[44] Moreover, such loss of well-being is not unusual on the part of a person who "falls behind" when she receives the same percentage or proportionate pay increase as those with higher salaries but one that increases the absolute gap between herself and those others.[45]

This debate over whether or not global inequality is growing is an important one, and development ethicists can contribute to its

resolution by assessing different ways of counting the poor and conceiving of inequality. Yet, as Sen powerfully and correctly asserts, we also
must not lose sight of the big picture – the "massive levels of inequality
and poverty":

> This debate [over whether the rich are getting richer and the poor getting poorer]
> does not have to be settled as a precondition for getting on with the central
> issue. The basic concerns relate to the massive levels of inequality and poverty –
> not whether they are also increasing at the margin. Even if the patrons of the
> contemporary economic order were right in claiming that the poor in general had
> moved a little ahead (this is, in fact, by no means uniformly so), the compelling
> need to pay immediate and overwhelming attention to appalling poverty and
> staggering inequalities in the world would not disappear.[46]

An ethical assessment of globalization

In the last section we saw that analysts may have very different concepts
of poverty and inequality, and that even when they agree they may
evaluate the same data in different ways. In employing one method
rather than another, analysts assume certain values. Or if we focus on
results, we can say, using a phrase from Charles Taylor, that different
methodologies "secrete"[47] different values. Most basically, those for and
against globalization, as economist Ravallion remarks, do "not share the
same values about what constitutes a just distribution of the gains from
globalization."[48] In a passage worth quoting in its entirety, Ravallion challenges economists and policy analysts to make their values explicit, subject
them to rational scrutiny, and engage in ethical analysis and argument:

> The empirical facts in contention do not stem solely from objective data on
> incomes, prices, and so on but also depend on value judgments made in meas-
> urement – judgments one may or may not accept. It can hardly be surprising that
> different people hold different normative views about inequality. And it is well
> understood in economics that those views affect how one defines and measures
> inequality – although it is ethics, not economics, that determines what trade-offs
> one accepts between the welfare of different people. A class of "ethical measures"
> of inequality is built on this realization. What is more notable in the present
> context is that important differences on values have become embedded in
> the methodological details underlying statements about what is happening to
> inequality in the world. These differences are rarely brought to the surface and
> argued out properly in this debate.[49]

Ravallion's point is noteworthy, because many economists and
policy analysts seek to divorce economics from ethics and back away
from engaging in ethical critique and argument with respect to what

justice requires. For example, the authors of the World Bank's *World Development Report 2006* break new ground when they argue that "equity considerations need to be brought squarely into the center of both diagnosis and policy," since "equity is central both to the investment environment and to the agenda of empowerment, working through the impact on institutions and specific policy designs."[50] Just when we think, however, that the Bank will go further, engage in moral argument, and make proposals for how analysts, policymakers, and citizens should understand national and global justice, it pulls back and makes equity either exclusively a matter of personal opinion or a causal factor in bringing about growth and reducing poverty: "Some may value equity for its own sake, others primarily for its instrumental role in reducing absolute poverty, the World Bank's mission."[51] In spite of its recognition of the importance of "equity" understood as "equal opportunity," "avoidance of absolute deprivation," and "fair processes," it retreats behind the Bank's traditional "nonpolitical" conception of its role: "It is neither the mandate nor the comparative advantage of the World Bank to engage in advice on issues of political design."[52] Moreover, although the *World Development Report 2006* argues for equity and fairness as means to "long-term prosperity," it refrains from taking a stand with respect to whether those are right who "prefer fairness"[53] or "see equal opportunities and fair processes as matters of social justice and thus as an intrinsic part of the objective of development."[54]

Absent from much of the *World Development Report 2006* and even more so from conventional investigations into globalization are precisely the efforts to clarify and defend criteria by which to identify whether and in what ways globalization is good or bad for human beings, enhances or limits valuable freedoms, protects or constrains democracy, respects or violates human rights, and fairly or unfairly distributes benefits and burdens within and between nations. It is not enough to inquire *if*, *how*, or *why* globalization affects human choice and institutional distribution. One must also have a reasoned normative view of what counts as beneficial and deleterious consequences, and how the concept of justice should be understood or decided.[55] Otherwise we will know what globalization is, how it came about, and what its future career is likely to be, but will have no basis for deciding whether to embrace it or to fight it – in whole or in part.

The most promising approach to such explicitly normative dimensions of development ethics is, I believe, the "agent-oriented" capability perspective that I have explained, defended, and applied throughout this book. Applying a conception of the human as agent and of human well-being as a plurality of capabilities and functionings that humans have good reason to value, the capability development ethicist can inquire into the effects different kinds of globalization have on *everyone's* agency and capability for living lives that are – among other things – long, healthy, secure, socially engaged, and politically participatory. Because agency and these valuable capabilities (or functionings) are the basis for human rights, social justice, and both individual and collective duties, a development ethic will also examine how a globalized world is a help or a hindrance as individuals and institutions fulfill their moral obligations to respect rights. The long-term goal of good and just development – whether national or global – must be to secure an adequate level of agency and morally basic capabilities for everyone in the world – regardless of nationality, ethnicity, religion, age, gender, or sexual preference.

Some kinds of globalization – for instance, such global phenomena as money-laundering, illegal drug distribution, weapons-smuggling, sex tourism, trade in human organs and endangered species, forced migrations, epidemics, and HIV-AIDS[56] – are bad and there is a duty to resist them. Other kinds of global interconnectedness are good and should be promoted. These include commercial linkages that result in more affordable food, medicine, and travel, and fuller exchange of ideas (e.g., through the internet). Good globalization also includes the global dispersion of democratic norms, and the ideal of global citizenship. Most kinds of globalization, such as open trade, financial liberalization, foreign direct investments, outsourcing of work, migration, labor mobility, development of international law, and multinationals, are a mixed blessing. For example, reduction of trade barriers may increase commercial opportunities for some producers and decrease them for others. What international legal theorist Kim Lane Scheppele calls "the first wave of public law globalization" emphasized international human rights and universal jurisdiction and had a progressive impact on national constitutions. A second wave globalizes an "international security law," promotes constitutional changes in favor of national security, and both strengthens executive power and attenuates civil liberties.[57] The extent to which these sorts of globalization either undermine and reduce or, alternatively, enhance, secure, or restore agency, human capabilities, and justice will depend on context and especially on a reform of global institutions and how national politics integrate and shape global forces.

The agency-focused capability approach judges both hyperglobalism and skepticism as empirically one-sided and normatively deficient. Nation-states are not obsolete entities of the past, nor do they possess a monopoly on global agency. A globalizing world weakens some states and strengthens others, and all states find themselves interconnected in various ways. Our approach challenges global institutions as well as national and subnational communities to protect, promote, and restore human capabilities, among them the capabilities for political participation. Our approach also challenges both territorial and non-territorial political communities in two related ways. First, territorial political communities and transnational agencies – such as the EU, the UN, the WTO, the World Bank, Amnesty International, Human Rights Watch, and the International Criminal Court – are responsible for setting policies that improve – rather than reduce – the chances of all persons to live decent lives. Second, these overlapping political communities, for reasons I advanced in Chapters 9 and 10, should themselves be "civilized and democratized."[58] These communities must be venues in which people exercise their agency and have substantive freedoms, including some kind of effective political participation, such as democratic deliberation. They should also be imaginatively restructured so as to achieve greater democratic accountability. As Held and his associates put it:

National boundaries have traditionally demarcated the basis on which individuals are included and excluded from participation in decisions affecting their lives; but if many socio-economic processes, and the outcomes of decisions about them, stretch beyond national frontiers, then the implications of this are serious, not only for the categories of consent and legitimacy but for all the key ideas of democracy. At issue is the nature of a political community – how should the proper boundaries of a political community be drawn in a more regional and global order? In addition, questions can be raised about the meaning of representation (who should represent whom and on what basis?) and about the proper form and scope of political participation (who should participate and in what way?).[59]

As Held and his colleagues go on to insist, the new normative challenge is "how to combine a system of territorially rooted [and, I would argue, *deepened*] democratic governance with the transnational and global organization of social and economic life."[60] Part of this challenge is that of deciding each governance level's responsibilities, whether unique or shared. The Spanish parliament struggles, sometimes through deliberation, to define the relative distribution of powers, rights, and duties between the central government and the seventeen constituent subnational units. Likewise, in regional organizations, such as the European Union and the Andean Pact nations, and in global institutions, such as the WTO and the UN, national entities negotiate and deliberate about the best balance between national and supernational responsibilities.

Is this articulation and defense of a normative vision of good and just development and globalization incompatible with my emphasis throughout this volume on individuals and groups taking charge and deciding their own development ends and means? One reason why the authors of the *World Development Report 2006* do not take a stand on questions of equity and justice is that they believe that such judgments usurp a society's *own* prerogative:

> Whatever such tradeoffs [between components of equity as well as between equity and efficiency] exist – which is most of the time – no textbook policy prescription can be provided. Each society must decide the relative weights it ascribes to each of the principles of equity and to the efficient expansion of total production (or other aggregate). The report will not prescribe what is equitable for any society. That is a prerogative of its members to be undertaken through decision-making processes they regard as fair.[61]

In this passage the *World Development Report 2006* rightly challenges societies to be self-directing agents and resists the temptation to prescribe from above and outside specific institutional designs. But the report abdicates its own responsibility to articulate a vision of the ethically justified ends, means, and responsibilities of development in a globalized world – a vision not to be uncritically, mechanically, or slavishly applied but one to be democratically debated, criticized, adapted, and improved. To take a stand on national and global justice is not to impose the moral truth from on high but to stimulate and contribute to morally informed policy debate on local, national, and global levels. I turn now from the importance of moral assessment of globalization to three proposals for making it more humane, ethically defensible, and democratic.

Humanizing and democratizing globalization: three projects

Development ethicists have identified three proposals or projects that respond to the normative challenges presented by globalization. If development ethics has the task of "keeping hope alive," one way to do so is to identify best practices and promising projects for globalization with a human and democratic face.

Liberal internationalism

One project – which, for example, the Commission on Global Governance's *Our Global Neighbourhood* expresses – aims at incremental reform of the existing international system of sovereign nation-states, and international organizations and regimes.[62] Popular governance takes place in nation-states in which democracy is either initiated or made more robust. In addition, argues philosopher Thomas Nagel, sovereign governments have unique duties to protect not only the civil and bodily rights of their citizens but also their socioeconomic rights.[63] In the face of cross-border threats of various kinds, nation-states can and should cooperate in regional and global trade, and in financial, military, legal, environmental, and cultural institutions. To protect national self-interest and sovereignty, national governments try to negotiate favorable loans and loan forgiveness with international financial institutions. The International Criminal Court (ICC) came into being in early 2002, when over sixty national governments ratified a treaty, which national delegates signed in Rome in 1998. The ICC has jurisdiction over war crimes and other violations of internationally recognized human rights, but only when a nation-state is unwilling or unable to try its own citizens for war crimes or crimes against humanity. It is anticipated that, with the existence of the ICC, the UN will increasingly represent the will of the majority of participating states and not (so much) the members of the Security Council. Although human individuals have rights and responsibilities, and international bodies have responsibilities, the rights and duties of (legitimate) *nation-states* are the most fundamental.

Radical republicanism

Expressed systematically by Richard Falk's *On Humane Governance: Toward a New Global Politics* and fervently by many anti-globalizers, radical republicanism or localism seeks to weaken – if not dismantle – existing nation-states and international institutions in favor of self-governing alternatives and largely local communities committed to the public good and harmony with the natural environment.[64] The current global order, argues this project's proponents, is inherently unjust, for it systematically favors affluent nations and corporations and is stacked against poor nations, peoples, and individuals. Giving priority to the empowerment of grassroots and indigenous communities that resist and struggle against the many forms of globalization, this bottom-up approach (ironically enough) utilizes communications technology to enable grassroots groups to become a global civil society of concern and action. Advocates of this perspective contend that institutions such as the World Bank will or should become obsolete or decentralized. An elite-dominated ICC or a UN-promoted transnational security law at odds with national and local judicial processes would do more harm than good. Indigenous communities, whether or not located within only one nation-state, should govern themselves according to their own rules and traditions. The right of communal self-determination will support enhanced subnational autonomy and, in extreme cases, secession. Democracy, largely direct and local, must operate on the basis of consensus.

Cosmopolitan democracy

Proponents of this third approach to humanizing globalization seek to "reconstitute" rather than reform (liberal internationalism), or abolish(radical republicanism) the current system of global governance. This reconstitution, to be guided by an evolving "cosmopolitan democratic law," consists in a "double democratization."[65] First, nation-states should either initiate or deepen and widen both direct and representative democratic rule. Such internal democratization will include some devolution of power to constituent territorial units and civil society. Rather than merely holding periodic voting, democracy should – as I argued above in Chapters 9 and 10 – include public debate and democratic deliberation from top to bottom. Elected representatives would regularly deliberate with – and be held accountable by – their constituents as well as their parliamentary colleagues. Second, one can anticipate that nation-states would come to share sovereignty with transnational bodies of various sorts (regional, intercontinental, and global), and these bodies themselves would be brought under democratic control. For instance, given the atrocious global inequalities viewed through the lens of Milanovic's concept 3 inequality, one would anticipate some sort of global system of progressive redistribution in which richer individuals would be taxed and poorer individuals would benefit.[66] Although the details would vary with the organization, this cosmopolitan democratizing will institutionalize popular and deliberative participation in global institutions – such as the UN, the WTO, the ICC, the World Bank, and the proposed global taxing authority – and in regional institutions – such as the Inter-American Development Bank, NAFTA, and the Organization of American States.[67] Among the possibilities for "democratic cosmopolitanism" is a form of world government compatible with "soft nationalism."[68]

Contributory to this institutional democratization, as well as one of the latter's results, will be new and complex individual moral identities and new ideals of "interculturalism" (*interculturalidad*)[69] and multiple citizenship.[70] People would and should no longer view themselves as nothing more than members of a particular local, ethnic, religious, or national group, but rather as human beings with the freedom to be responsible for all people. And one can anticipate, as Held and his colleagues argue, that citizenship will become multi-layered and complex – from neighborhood citizenship, through national citizenship (often in more than one nation-state), to regional and world or "cosmopolitan" citizenship":

Citizenship in a democratic polity of the future . . . is likely to involve a growing mediating role: a role which encompasses dialogue with the traditions and discourses of others with the aim of expanding the horizons of one's own framework of meaning and increasing the scope of mutual understanding. Political agents who can "reason from the point of view of others" will be better equipped to resolve, and resolve fairly, the new and challenging trans-boundary issues and processes that create overlapping communities of fate.[71]

Regardless of scope, citizenship is neither trivial nor absolute. Each kind of citizenship is partially constituted by a commitment to human rights, including the right of democratic participation, and the duty to promote human development at every level of human organization:

Democracy for the new millennium must allow cosmopolitan citizens to gain access to, mediate between and render accountable the social, economic and political processes and flows that cut across and transform their traditional community boundaries. The core of this project involves reconceiving legitimate political authority in a manner which disconnects it from its traditional anchor in fixed borders and delimited territories and, instead, articulates it as an attribute of basic democratic arrangements or basic democratic law which can, in principle, be entrenched and drawn on in diverse self-regulating associations – from cities and sub-national regions, to nation-states, regions and wider global networks.[72]

In the same spirit, Milanovic anticipates and implicitly endorses the increasing importance of new global institutions, especially in relation to tackling the challenge of global poverty and concept 3 global inequality:

We are bound to move toward global community and global democracy, and once we do, many of the functions of today's national governments – including dealing with extreme cases of inequality and poverty – will be taken over by new global institutions. The road to that goal will be long and arduous . . . Yet, if we consider the path that has been traversed in the past two centuries – from a consortium of powers ruling the world without bothering to consult anyone else and bent on the sheer exploitation of the weak, to today's host of international institutions and the willingness, however begrudgingly, to share wealth – and if we project these developments into the future, there is, I think, little doubt that further inclusion of all peoples and globalization of decision-making awaits us there.[73]

How should we assess these three political projects for humanely responding to globalization and what might be the relations among them? Each of the three projects has different emphases and normative commitments. One task of development ethicists and others is to weigh the advantages and disadvantages of each approach and to examine whether the three projects must be mutually exclusive or may be combined in some way. Although better ways of combining may come to light, one way would be to say something like the following. Liberal internationalism has current institutional salience and should become a starting point and platform for (as well as a constraint on) the more substantive changes that local and cosmopolitan democracy requires. Radical republicans rightly insist on the importance of local and deep democracy. Cosmopolitan democrats share many democratic and participatory values with radical republicans, but the former judge the latter as too utopian about grassroots reform that is not accompanied by "double democratization," and too pessimistic about the democratic potential of transnational institutions. On the agenda for development ethicists and others is the pressing question of whether national governments – in contrast to both subnational and global institutions – have distinctive duties of justice with respect to protecting the socioeconomic rights of their citizens.

Insofar as the globalization processes are neither inexorable nor fixed, development ethics must consider, then, the kinds of globalization most likely to benefit human beings as well as the best ways to humanize and democratize them. Such an inquiry, we have seen, requires that one have criteria for normative appraisal as well as a basis for assigning duties to the various agents of development and globalization. The challenges of globalization expand – rather than narrow – the agenda of development ethics. Interdisciplinary and cross-cultural dialogue and forums of democratic deliberation enable development ethicists to contribute to the understanding and securing of genuinely human development at all levels of political community and in all kinds of regional and global institutions. As Sen remarks in concluding "How to Judge Globalism":

The central issue of contention is not globalization itself, nor is it the use of the market as an institution, but the inequity in the overall balance of institutional arrangements – which produces very unequal sharing of the benefits of globalization. The question is not just whether the poor, too, gain something from globalization, but whether they get a fair share and a fair opportunity. There is an urgent need for reforming institutional arrangements – in addition to national ones – to overcome both the errors of omission and those of commission that tend to give the poor across the world such limited opportunities. Globalization deserves a reasoned defense, but it also needs reform.[74]

Concluding remarks

If humankind is to confront and reduce global poverty, inequality, and the violence that they breed, global development – like local, national, and regional development – merits both a "reasoned defense" and significant reform. In this volume I have argued that development ethicists, both philosophers and non-philosophers, have an important role in meeting this challenge. Articulating and applying a vision of ethically appropriate social change, development ethicists both assess present institutional arrangements and argue for improved local, national, and global policies. My own path has led from moral reflection on the development challenges facing Colorado mountain towns and Costa Rican fishing villages to reasoned scrutiny of the ends and means of national development in a globalizing world. Beginning in and returning to their own local and national communities, development ethicists become part of global efforts to build institutions in which all human beings, regardless of where they are born, have a say in policies that affect them and fair opportunities to achieve a life they have reason to value.

NOTES

I adapted the first and fourth sections from "Development Ethics, Democracy, and Globalization," in *Democracy in a Global World: Human Rights and Political Participation in the 21st Century*, ed. Deen Chatterjee (Lanham, MD: Rowman & Littlefield, 2008), earlier versions of which appeared as "Development Ethics and Globalization," *Philosophical Topics*, 30, 2 (2002): 9–28; "Globalization and Human Development: Ethical Approaches," in *Proceedings of the Seventh Plenary Session of the Pontifical Academy of Social Sciences*, ed. Edmond Malinvaud and Louis Sabourin, the Vatican, April 25–8, 2001 (Vatican City: Pontifical Academy of the Social Sciences, 2001), 45–65; "Globalización y desarrollo humano: Aproximaciones éticas," in *¿Republicanismo y educación cívica: Más allá del liberalismo?*, ed. Jesús Conill and David A. Crocker (Granada: Editorial Comares, 2003), 75–98; and "Development Ethics and Globalization," in *The Ethical Dimensions of Global Development*, ed. Verna V. Gehring (Lanham, MD: Rowman & Littlefield, 2007), 59–72. The second and third sections have not previously been published. For helpful comments, I thank Deen Chatterjee, David P. Crocker, Edna D. Crocker, Nigel Dower, Jay Drydyk, Arthur Evenchik, Des Gasper, Verna Gehring, Denis Goulet, Xiaorong Li, Toby Linden, Nasim Moalem, Jerome M. Segal, and Roxanne Walters.

1. Moisés Naím, *Surprises of Globalization* (Washington, DC: Carnegie Endowment for International Peace, 2003), 3.
2. David Held, Anthony McGrew, David Goldblatt, and Jonathan Perraton, *Global Transformations* (Stanford: Stanford University Press, 1999), 2.
3. Held *et al.*, *Global Transformations*, 16.

4. Ibid., 2–16.
5. Thomas L. Friedman, *The Lexis and the Olive Tree: Understanding Globalization* (New York: Farrar, Straus & Giroux, 1999); *The World is Flat: A Brief History of the 21st Century* (New York: Farrar, Straus & Giroux, 2005).
6. Jagdish N. Bhagwati, *Free Trade Today* (Princeton, NJ: Princeton University Press, 2002); *In Defense of Globalization* (New York: Oxford University Press, 2004).
7. Fareed Zakaria, "The Wealth of Yet More Nations," *New York Times Book Review* (May 1, 2005), 11.
8. Richard N. Cooper, "A False Alarm: Overcoming Globalization's Discontents," *Foreign Affairs*, 83, 1 (January/February 2004): 152–3.
9. Dani Rodrik, "Trading in Illusions," *Foreign Policy* (March/April 2001): 55.
10. Quoted in Ibid., 57.
11. Stephen Krasner, *Sovereignty: Organized Hypocrisy* (Princeton, NJ: Princeton University Press, 1999).
12. Paul Hirst and Grahame Thompson, *Globalization in Question: The International Economy and the Possibilities of Governance* (Cambridge: Polity Press, 1996).
13. Samuel P. Huntington, *The Clash of Civilizations and the Remaking of the World Order* (New York: Simon & Schuster, 1996).
14. Herman E. Daly, "Globalization and Its Discontents," *Philosophy and Public Policy Quarterly*, 21, 2/3 (2001): 17–21. See also Herman E. Daly, "Globalization's Major Inconsistencies," *Philosophy and Public Policy Quarterly*, 23, 4 (2003): 22–7. Both essays are reprinted in *The Ethical Dimensions of Global Development*, ed. Gehring, 73–80, 81–8.
15. Rodrik, "Trading in Illusions," 55.
16. Held *et al.*, *Global Transformations*, 429.
17. Martin Ravallion, "Competing Concepts of Inequality in the Globalization Debate," *Brookings Trade Forum 2004: Gobalization, Poverty, and Inequality*, ed. Susan M. Collins and Carol Graham (Washington, DC: Brookings Institution 2004), 1. Ravallion draws the first quotation from <www.ifg.org/store.htm> and the second from *The Economist* (May 27, 2000), 94.
18. United Nations Development Programme, *Human Development Report 2005: International Development at a Crossroads: Aid, Trade and Security in an Unequal World* (New York: Oxford University Press and United Nations Development Programme, 2005), 359. Cf. the World Bank's definition of "PPP gross national income" in World Bank, *World Development Report 2006* (New York: World Bank and Oxford University Press, 2005), 302. For a searching criticism of PPP, see Thomas Pogge and Sanjay G. Reddy, "Unknown: The Extent, Distribution, and Trend of Global Income Poverty"; and Sanjay G. Reddy and Thomas Pogge, "How *Not* to Count the Poor": both papers were accessed on June 14, 2006, and are available at <www.socialanalysis.org>.
19. Ravallion, "Competing Concepts," 22.
20. Mainstream economists, including those at the World Bank, have used income metrics for both poverty and inequality. In contrast, the United

Nations Development Programme, influenced by Sen and others, has supplemented income measures with those of longevity, health, education, and agency or power measures. In its *World Development Report 2006*, the World Bank decisively breaks with an exclusively income metric and also measures "equity" and poverty in relation to opportunity, health and educational status, and agency or power. See United Nations Development Programme, *Human Development Report 2005: International Cooperation at a Crossroads: Aid, Trade, and Security in all Unequal World* (New York: Oxford University Press, 2005), esp. chs. 1–2; World Bank, *World Development Report 2006*, esp. chs. 1–3. Reddy and Pogge criticize the widely used $1 per day measure of extreme poverty and the $2 per day measure of poverty in "How *Not* to Count the Poor."

21. UNDP, *Human Development Report 2005*, 3.
22. Erik Thorbecke, "Comments and Discussion," *Brookings Trade Forum 2004*, 22.
23. UNDP, *Human Development Report 2005*, 3.
24. Ravallion, "Competing Concepts," 5.
25. Branko Milanovic, *Worlds Apart: Measuring International and Global Inequality* (Princeton: Princeton University Press, 2005); "Global Income Inequality: What It is and Why It Matters," World Bank Development Research Group, February 2006. In *World Development Report 2006*, Box 3.1, p. 57 and elsewhere, the World Bank draws on Milanovic's and Ravallion's work and dubs Milanovic's three concepts intercountry inequality (concept 1), international inequality (concept 2), and global inequality (concept 3). I find the *World Development Report's* account of these concepts confusing, and prefer to adopt both Milanovic's nomenclature and his definitions, not least because of the ambiguities of "intercountry," "international," and "global."
26. See Milanovic, *Worlds Apart*, Parts I and II.
27. UNDP, *Human Development Report 2005*, 36–7.
28. Milanovic, *Worlds Apart*, 40. According to UNDP, the Gini index "measures the extent to which the distribution of income (or consumption) among individuals or households within a country deviates from a perfectly equal distribution" (*Human Development Report 2005*, 356). The higher is a country's Gini score or coefficient, the greater is its inequality. Similarly, using the HDI as the measure for median country scores, UNDP finds that convergence of countries is slowing and in at least eighteen countries going in the other direction.
29. Milanovic, *Worlds Apart*, 79.
30. Ibid., 81.
31. UNDP, *Human Development Report 2005*, 267.
32. Ravallion, "Competing Concepts," 8–12; Milanovic, *Worlds Apart*, ch. 8.
33. Ravallion, "Competing Concepts," 10.
34. Ibid., 11.
35. Milanovic, *Worlds Apart*, ch. 8.
36. Ravallion, "Competing Concepts," 11–12; Milanovic, *Worlds Apart*, 93–6.
37. Milanovic, *Worlds Apart*, 100.
38. Friedman, *The World is Flat*.

39. Milanovic, *Worlds Apart*, dustcover. Sen also describes the current global economic order as one with "staggering inequalities" as well as "appalling poverty": Sen, "10 Theses on Globalization," *Global Viewpoint* (July 12, 2001) (available at <www.digitalnpq.org/global_services/global%20view point/07-12-01>).

40. Milanovic, "Global Income Inequality," 16.

41. UNDP, *Human Development Report 2005*, 38.

42. See Milanovic, *Worlds Apart*, ch. 9; "Global Income Inequality: What It is and Why It Matters," World Bank, Development Research Group Working Paper, 24–5. See Xavier Sala-i-Martin, "The Disturbing 'Rise' of World Income Inequality," NBER (National Bureau of Economic Research) Working Paper No. 8904 (April, 2002) (available at www.nber.org); "The World Distribution of Income," NBER Working Paper No. 8905 (May, 2002) (available at www.nber.org); Surjit Bhalla, *Imagine There Is No Country* (Washington, DC: Institute for International Economics, 2002); François Bourguignon and Christian Morrisson, "The Size Distribution of Income among World Citizens, 1820–1990," *American Economic Review* (September, 2000): 727–44; Yuri Dikhanov and Michael Ward, "Evolution of the Global Distribution of Income, 1970–99," August, 2001, draft; Bob Sutcliffe, "World Inequality and Globalization," *Oxford Review of Economic Policy*, 20, 1 (2003): 15–37.

43. Milanovic, "Global Income Inequality," 21–3.

44. See Milanovic, *Worlds Apart*, 155–6; and Carol Graham and Stefano Pettinato, *Happiness and Hardship: Opportunity and Insecurity in New Market Economies* (Washington, DC: Brookings Institution Press, 2002).

45. See Ravallion, "Competing Concepts," 18.

46. Amartya Sen, "10 Theses on Globalization." See also "Globalization and Poverty," transcript of a lecture given at Santa Clara University, October 29, 2002 (available at <www.scu.edu/globalization/speakers/senlecture>).

47. Charles Taylor, "Neutrality in Political Science," in *Philosophy, Politics and Society*, 3rd series, ed. Peter Laslett and W. G. Runciman (New York: Barnes and Noble, 1967), 40.

48. Ravallion, "Competing Concepts," 2. In *World Development Report 2006*, 57, the World Bank authors quote Ravallion's phrase verbatim.

49. Ravallion, "Competing Concepts," 2.

50. World Bank, *World Development Report 2006*, 3–4.

51. Ibid., 4.

52. Ibid., 10.

53. Ibid., 80.

54. Ibid., 75. Cf. ibid., 206.

55. Philosophers take up these issues in *Democracy in a Global World*, ed. Deen Chatterjee. See *Making Globalization Good: The Moral Challenges of Global Capitalism*, ed. John H. Dunning (Oxford: Oxford University Press, 2003) for a recent interdisciplinary volume – with essays by religious leaders, politicians, businesspeople, and scholars (but no philosophers). For an important consideration of a human rights approach to the moral founda-tions for international law and global institutions, see Allen Buchanan,

Justice, Legitimacy, and Self-Determination: Moral Foundations for International Law (Oxford: Oxford University Press, 2004).

56. Moisés Naím, *Illicit: How Smugglers, Traffickers, and Copycats are Hijacking the Global Economy* (New York: Doubleday, 2005).

57. Scheppele argues that as part of the global war on terrorism, transnational institutions, such as the United Nations Security Council, are developing and promoting new transnational security laws that national executives use as a cover to undermine domestic constitutions. Among the provisions that enshrine "a state of emergency" are new surveillance policies, weakened data protection, vaguely defined crimes, retroactively applied laws, new exercises and defenses of executive power, elimination of habeas corpus, truncated immigration procedures, increased banking regulations, and increased preventative detention. See Kim Lane Scheppele, "The Migration of Anti-Constitutional Ideas: The Post-9/11 Globalization of Public Law and the International State of Emergency," in *The Migration of Constitutional Ideas*, ed. Sujit Choudhry (Cambridge: Cambridge University Press, 2007); and "The International State of Emergency: Challenges to Constitutionalism after September 11," paper presented to CP4 seminar, University of Maryland, February 9, 2007.

58. Held *et al.*, *Global Transformations*, 444.

59. Ibid., 446–7.

60. Ibid., 431. See also Amartya Sen, "Justice across Borders," in *Global Justice and Transnational Politics*, ed. Pablo De Greiff and Ciaran Cronin (Cambridge, MA: MIT Press, 2002), 37–55. For the notion of global as well as national civil society, see David A. Crocker, "Truth Commissions, Transitional Justice, and Civil Society," in *Truth v. Justice: The Morality of Truth Commissions*, ed. Robert I. Rotberg and Dennis Thompson (Princeton, NJ: Princeton University Press, 2000), 99–121.

61. *World Development Report 2006*, 20.

62. Commission on Global Governance, *Our Global Neighbourhood* (Oxford: Oxford University Press, 1995).

63. Thomas Nagel, "The Problem of Global Justice," *Philosophy and Public Affairs*, 33, 2 (2005): 113–47.

64. Richard Falk, *On Humane Governance: Toward a New Global Politics* (Cambridge: Polity Press, 1995).

65. Held *et al.*, *Global Transformations*, 450. See also *Democratizar la Democracia: Los caminos de la democracia participativa*, ed. Boaventura de Sousa Santos (Mexico: Fondo de Cultura Económico, 2004).

66. As a step in this direction, Milanovic endorses the suggestion of François Bourguignon, among others, for the creation of an international income tax on financial flows, plane tickets, CO_2 emissions, or weapons exports. See Milanovic, *Worlds Apart*, 160, and an interview with François Bourguignon, cited by Milanovic, in *La Tribune* (November 13, 2003).

67. *The Political Economy of Globalization*, ed. Ngaire Woods (New York: Palgrave Macmillan, 2000), 202–23; David Held, *Models of Democracy*, 3rd edn. (Stanford: Stanford University Press, 2006); *Democracy and the Global Order: From the Modern State to Cosmopolitan Governance* (Stanford:

Stanford University Press, 1995); James Bohman, "International Regimes and Democratic Governance," *International Affairs*, 75 (1999): 499–514; "Citizenship and Norms of Publicity: Wide Public Reason in Cosmopolitan Societies," *Political Theory*, 27 (1999): 176–202; *Democracy across Borders: From Dêmos to Dêmos* (Cambridge, MA, and London: MIT Press, 2007). See also *Democratizar la democracia*, ed. de Sousa Santos and Buchanan, *Justice, Legitimacy, and Self-determination*.

68. See Louis P. Pojman, *Terrorism, Human Rights, and the Case for World Government* (Lanham, MD: Rowman & Littlefield, 2006).

69. See Adela Cortina, *Ciudadanos del mundo* (Madrid: Alianza, 1997); "Ciudadanía intercultural," in *Glosario para una sociedad intercultural*, ed. Jesús Conill (Valencia: Bancaja, 2002), 35–42; Joaquín García Roca, "Integración," in *Glosario*, ed. Conill, 203–11.

70. For the idea of open and flexible personal identity, see Amartya Sen, "Reason Before Identity," Romanes Lecture, given in Oxford, November 17, 1998; "Beyond Identity: Other People," *The New Republic*, 223/5 (December 18, 2000): 23–30; and *Identity and Violence: The Illusion of Destiny* (New York and London: W. W. Norton, 2006). For the ideal of global citizenship, see Nigel Dower, *An Introduction to Global Citizenship* (Edinburgh: Edinburgh University Press, 2003).

71. Held *et al.*, *Global Transformations*, 449.

72. Ibid., 450.

73. Milanovic, *Worlds Apart*, 162. Instead of dismissing the idea of world government as impossibly utopian or dangerously authoritarian, Louis Pojman courageously takes the idea of institutionalizing democracy further: "Globalism makes world government possible and a recognition of universal human rights makes it desirable: The synthesis makes it actual": Pojman, *Terrorism, Human Rights, and the Case for World Government*, 69.

74. Amartya Sen, "How to Judge Globalism," *The American Prospect*, 13, 2 (January, 2002): 14. See also Sen, "10 Theses on Globalization," and "Globalization and Poverty."

Index of names

Index of subjects

adaptive preferences 128
achievement
  agency achievement (success), realized
    and instrumental 153–4
  and freedom 112–13, 150–3, 269
addictive and habitual behavior 226–8
advantage, personal or rational 116, 119,
  151, 163, 178, 181, 269; see also
  well-being
aid, foreign 54 n. 54
agencies 56
alienation 43
agency 12, 13, 24, 38, 45–6, 47, 48–9,
  68, 79, 87, 94, 126–7, 146, 180 n. 25,
  245, 287, 300–2, 323, 339, 344,
  360–2, 366
  and well-being 18, 112–13, 127,
    137, 150–3, 221–2, 298, 304,
    357–8
  as meta-capability 223
  basic need approach and 137–8
  citizen 13
  collective 77, 87, 90, 158–9, 321–8
  Cortina and Conill on 217–48
  direct and indirect 153, 154–6,
    180 n. 19, 313
  economists concept of 158
  Marx on 17
  Nussbaum on 19, 127, 150, 159–63,
    188, 190
  Sen on 14, 17, 19, 20, 21, 112–13, 137,
    146 n. 94, 150–3, 152–9, 156–9, 162,
    178, 180 n. 20, 181, 202, 203,
    217–48, 272–4, 298, 300–2, 344, 360–2
  See also equality, threshold view of;
    freedom, and determinism
"Agency and Well-being: The
  Development Agenda" (Sen) 150
Amnesty International 391
Andean Pact 391
anti-corruption strategies 38, 60
anti-development 4, 7

anti-materialism 219
anti-perfectionism
  Cortina on 220, 226
  Rawls on 116–18, 121–3
  See also justice, political conception of
applied ethics, see philosophy, practical
Arabsolangi rose cultivation initiative
  7, 345
Arctic National Wildlife Refuge 69, 70
Argentina 81
*The Argumentative Indian: Writings on
  Indian History, Culture, and Identity*
  (Sen) 297
Aristotelianism 17, 46, 123, 162, 190
Aristotelian/Marxist tradition, 16
Asian values 365
Asociación Talamanqueña para
  Ecoturismo y Conservación
  (ATEC) 13
autonomy 157, 249–50 n. 12
  autonomy criticism of deliberative
    democracy 360–2
  Cortina on 14, 218, 219–20, 232, 236,
    249 n. 12
  moral (Kant) 20, 46, 127, 190,
    249 n. 12, 250
  personal autonomy 249 n. 12

basic capabilities
  Nussbaum on 177
  Sen on 135–6, 305–6
basic needs 14, 38, 68, 148 n. 123
  basic and nonbasic needs, relationship
    between 134
  Nussbaum on 138–40
basic needs approach (BNA) 129–40
  capability approach and 129, 131,
    132–3, 134, 136, 137–9, 140,
    148 n. 120
  economic growth and 129–40
  Sen on 68, 129–40, 148 n. 120
Bengal Relief Fund 7

407

CPSIA information can be obtained at www.ICGtesting.com
Printed in the USA
LVOW051625270712

291846LV00002B/5/P